M000238637

# Vanguard of the Imam

# Vanguard of the Imam

*Religion, Politics, and Iran's Revolutionary Guards*

AFSHON OSTOVAR

OXFORD
UNIVERSITY PRESS

# OXFORD

UNIVERSITY PRESS

Oxford University Press is a department of the University of Oxford. It furthers
the University's objective of excellence in research, scholarship, and education
by publishing worldwide. Oxford is a registered trade mark of Oxford University
Press in the UK and certain other countries.

Published in the United States of America by Oxford University Press
198 Madison Avenue, New York, NY 10016, United States of America.

© Oxford University Press 2016

First issued as an Oxford University Press paperback, 2018

All rights reserved. No part of this publication may be reproduced, stored in
a retrieval system, or transmitted, in any form or by any means, without the
prior permission in writing of Oxford University Press, or as expressly permitted
by law, by license, or under terms agreed with the appropriate reproduction
rights organization. Inquiries concerning reproduction outside the scope of the
above should be sent to the Rights Department, Oxford University Press, at the
address above.

You must not circulate this work in any other form
and you must impose this same condition on any acquirer.

Library of Congress Cataloging-in-Publication Data
Names: Ostovar, Afshon, author.
Title: Vanguard of the Imam : religion, politics, and Iran's revolutionary guards / Afshon Ostovar.
Description: New York, NY : Oxford University Press, [2016] |
Identifiers: LCCN 2015049055 (print) | LCCN 2016002422 (ebook) |
ISBN 9780199387892 (hardback) | ISBN 9780190491703 (E-book) |
ISBN 9780190491710 (E-book) | ISBN 9780190491727 ( Online Component) |
ISBN 978-0-19-088289-1 (paperback)
Subjects: LCSH: Sipāh-i Pāsdārān-i Inqilāb-i Islāmī (Iran) |
Iran—History, Military. | Civil-military relations—Iran. |
Iran—Politics and government—1997– |
BISAC: POLITICAL SCIENCE / International Relations / Arms Control. |
POLITICAL SCIENCE / Political Freedom & Security / International Security.
Classification: LCC UA853.I7 O84 2016 (print) | LCC UA853.I7 (ebook) |
DDC 355.3—dc23
LC record available at http://lccn.loc.gov/2015049055

*For Michele and Ladan*
*For their love, patience, and for keeping me humble.*
*Very, very humble.*

*So turns the world; her favors are soon passed,*
*All whom she nourishes must die at last.*
*One she will raise from earth to heights unknown,*
*One she will cast down from a royal throne;*
*But there's no cause to triumph or complain,*
*Such is the way she turns, and turns again:*
*Where are those heroes now, those champions, where?*
*Drive out such mortal thoughts, that bring despair.*
                    —Abol-Qasem Ferdowsi, *Shahnameh*

# CONTENTS

# ACKNOWLEDGMENTS

Many people contributed to this endeavor, both directly and indirectly. I am grateful to the three anonymous reviewers who took the time to read and respond to my manuscript. Their criticism and suggestions were invaluable. The editorial and production staff at Oxford University Press have been exceptional. David McBride's calm stewardship has made this experience nearly painless. Kathleen Weaver was instrumental in getting this book through production and gently prodded me along the way. Deepti Agarwal was likewise patient and professional throughout the production process.

Juan Cole, Kathryn Babayan, Sussan Babaie, and Farina Mir commented extensively on this study when it was still in dissertation form. Their critical feedback has stayed with me and informs the present text. Ryan Evans read and commented on chapters of the book. Ryan identified weak points and encouraged me to strengthen certain arguments. Will McCants was a trusted sounding board, as well as a cheerleader when I needed it the most. Abbas Milani offered pithy, keen guidance at the outset of this effort. Daniel Byman, William Rosenau, Carter Malkasian, and Ryan Gingeras all provided excellent advice at various stages. My colleagues at CNA, especially Mike Connell, Eric Thompson, Ken Gause, and Ralph Espach, have contributed to my thinking on security issues and political organizations. Connie Custer provided generous support while at CNA. I am also indebted to Michael Markowitz for producing the maps in this book.

I am appreciative of the community of analysts, researchers, and academics working on religious and political affairs of the Middle East. I have benefited immensely from their work, as well as from our conversations and debates. This is particularly true for the relatively small community of researchers who write on the IRGC. Although I find myself at times in disagreement, their critical perspectives have been vital to the development of my own. The journalists covering Iran and the Middle East are the unsung heroes of this study. Contemporary history cannot be engaged effectively without their reporting. Reporters such as Jason Rezaian, who, as of writing, has remained in Tehran's Evin Prison, in solitary confinement, for over a five hundred days—despite penning dispatches that showcased a softer, more humane side of Iran—are essential to our understanding of the world, especially its ugly side, and often take risks in doing so.

I am forever thankful for the support and love of my family. Even if they did not always understand what I was writing about or why, the encouragement of my dear mother and my father, as well as my sister, aunts and uncles, never ceased. Michele and Ladan endured my preoccupation with grace and humor. They made it easy for me to write, tolerated the music that came from my office, and provided the best excuse to stop typing. Michele also created the design concept for the book's cover and helped in the preparation of the images used in this study, for which I am deeply grateful. Finally, I am thankful for my record player. I could not have finished this book without it.

# NOTE ON TRANSLITERATION

For the transliteration of Persian and Arabic words, I generally follow a modi-
fied version of prevailing academic systems. I avoid using all diacritical marks,
and with the exception of certain instances, I also avoid using marks for the
letter 'ayn and hamza glottal stop. Such marks are superfluous to specialists
for ordinary words, and are needlessly (if unintentionally) exoticizing to general readers. I tend to use the most common spellings for proper nouns that
appear frequently in English. A notable exception is the Islamic Revolutionary
Guards Corps, which is often referred to as a "Guard." The organization's name
in Persian (*sepah-e pasdaran-e enqelab-e eslami*) literally translates to Corps of
the Guardians of the Islamic Revolution. It is not a "guard" in the sense of the
National Guard, but rather an army of sentinels. I refer to the organization in
many ways (IRGC, Revolutionary Guards, Guards Corps, the Guards) throughout the book, but always retain the plural meaning of "Guards" (*pasdaran*).

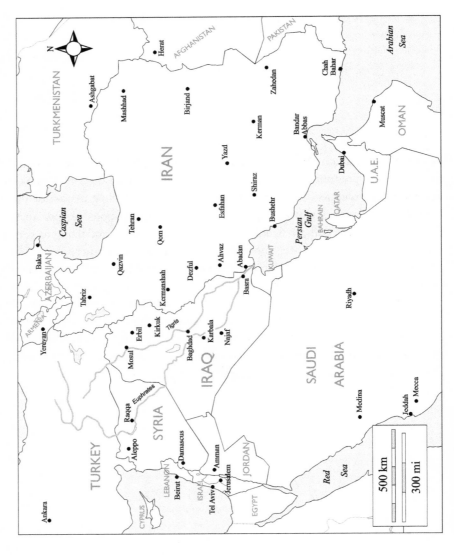

Map 1 The Middle East

# Introduction

The crowd seethed. Thousands of university students had amassed outside the gates of the British Embassy on November 29, 2011. They shouted slogans and held signs to express their fury. With police and security forces standing on the sidelines, the students pressed forward and meticulously broke through the massive iron gate that separated the embassy—and sovereign British soil—from the streets of central Tehran.[1]

About fifty protestors pushed into the embassy compound. They smashed windows, broke doors, and set fires. Iranian state television cameras recorded some of the mayhem. Students pillaged the embassy and looted associated buildings of works of art, valuables, and odd decorative items such as a *Pulp Fiction* movie poster. A portrait of Queen Elizabeth II was brought into the courtyard and provocatively smashed and set alight. A few miles away, hundreds of students broke into the walled Qolhak Garden complex—an area that housed much of the British staff and their families. There, protestors pillaged homes, harassed residents, and at one point, encircled a group of British staff members who were let go only after police intervened. Fires glowed through the dense trees of the once serene compound.

The students were furious at the United Kingdom's policies toward Iran and demanded that its ambassador be deported. They were more broadly protesting foreign pressure on Iran. Britain had recently agreed to join the United States in sanctioning Iran's access to international banking systems—essentially cutting off the Islamic Republic from most forms of transactions with foreign entities. This was in addition to the already harsh sanctions that the United States and the United Nations Security Council had imposed on Iran in response to its nuclear enrichment program.

Sanctions were unpopular in Iran, but this was no popular protest. The students belonged to a government-funded militia: the Basij. Most came from the militia's local university chapters, but some—including clerics, commanders, and older associates—were not students at all.[2] The protestors represented the various political, ideological, and religious perspectives of the Basij and its parent organization, the Islamic Revolutionary Guards Corps (IRGC). Indeed, the semiotics of the event (i.e., the students' actions and the symbols they used to express their furor) reveal much about the IRGC, its worldview, and its place within Iran's theocratic system.

Religion, for instance, was at the forefront of the demonstration. Among the countless signs hoisted aloft by protestors were large, black-and-red banners invoking Imam Husayn, the third leader (*imam*) of the Shiite religion and its most revered martyr-hero. Numerous demonstrators wore headbands or held placards expressing similar Shiite invocations. Their protest calls were punctuated with chants of "God is Great!" (*allahu akbar*). Once inside the courtyard a cleric led students in ritual group prayer. Impromptu prayer broke out inside the Qolhak Garden compound as well. With these elements, the protest became as much about the fervent expression of faith as the critique of a foreign power. Shiism is both a medium of expression for the politics championed by the country's hardliners—particularly the IRGC and Basij—and a lens of interpretation through which politics writ large are understood. It is a symbol of national identity and a cudgel used against Iran's enemies—a chauvinistic assertion that only Iran's faithful and their allies are on the right side of God. It is, above all, what gives the students—and the organizations they represent—legitimacy.

Embedded within these expressions of faith were those of loyalty to Iran's Supreme Leader, Ali Khamenei. Posters bearing the leader's image or quotes from his sermons were ubiquitous. The protestors were announcing their devotion to the leader—a devotion imbued with the same religious connotations as reserved for the Shiite Imams—and claiming to act in his name. Such ardent devotion resides at the core of the IRGC's identity. The organization is mandated to defend the place and function of the supreme leader in Iran's revolutionary system. Its top command serve at the leader's behest and its members serve to safeguard his exalted station. The leader's symbolic presence in this demonstration is therefore emblematic of the powerful symbiosis between him and his followers in the IRGC and Basij.

These broad religious sentiments add an aura of sacredness to what is otherwise a condemnation of foreign policy. The thrust of the protest was to denounce Britain's support for sanctions against Iran. Chants against British prime minister David Cameron and the catch-all cries of "Death to Britain!" underscored the main target of the students' derision. But Britain was not alone. Similar vitriol was directed at the United States and Israel. In addition to the calls of "Death to America!" and "Death to Israel!" demonstrators burned American and Israeli flags next to the Union Jack. Through such acts the crowd made their enemies known. The threat was not simply Britain; rather it was a cabal of foreign powers that sought to destroy Iran and its Islamic system.

The students were similarly successful at identifying their allies. Palestinian flags and those of Lebanese Hezbollah were prominently displayed. Iranian media photographed demonstrators flaunting these flags next to Shiite banners from atop the British Embassy's outer wall. Many of the protestors wore checkered *keffiyehs* around their necks in a manner popular among members of the IRGC and Basij to symbolize solidarity with the Palestinian cause. As they had done with their enemies, the students were announcing their allies, the network of causes and organizations that stood in resistance against those foreign powers that were hostile to their Islamic movement.

The students saw their act as part of a much larger conflict. Posters celebrating martyred heroes epitomized the transgressions of Iran's enemies and the sacrifices of those that faithfully served the Islamic Republic. One sign in the crowd read: "Israel will vanish from the pages of time"—a quote from Ayatollah Khomeini that, for the students, is both prophecy and promise of Israel's eventual demise. Beneath that quote were images of Iran's supreme leaders and martyrs associated with the IRGC or that symbolized its grievance against Israel. The martyrs included IRGC personalities such as Mostafa Chamran, a founding member of the Guards killed in 1981 on the frontlines of the Iran-Iraq war, who had devoted much of his career to the social upliftment of the Shia of southern Lebanon. Next to Chamran was his mentor, the cleric Musa al-Sadr, a spiritual and community leader for southern Lebanese Shia who disappeared mysteriously on a trip to Libya in 1978. Imad Mughniyeh, Hezbollah's terrorism chief and a close associate of the IRGC, who was assassinated in Damascus in 2008, was also included. Other prominent signs memorialized Majid Shahriari, a nuclear engineer who was assassinated in Tehran exactly one year earlier. IRGC scientist Fereydoon Abbasi Davani was targeted in a similar attack that same day but survived. These incidents were part of a string of assassinations of Iranian nuclear scientists and seen as egregious crimes in the West's campaign against Iran's nuclear program.

Also significant were placards in honor of Qassem Soleimani—the architect of the IRGC's foreign operations. Soleimani earned the reputation as a savvy strategist during the US occupation of post-Saddam Iraq, during which he organized an effective counterweight to American influence through the development of a Shiite militant clientage. This work made Soleimani—often referred to with the honorific "Hajj"—a revered figure within IRGC ranks.[3] He was considered the one most directly responding to Iran's grievances by confronting its enemies on the battlefield. The supreme leader even referred to Soleimani as a "living martyr" for his efforts—placing him within the pantheon of Shiite-Iranian heroes. As one sign proclaimed, "We are all Hajj Qassem!"

Taken together, these symbolic elements elucidate some of the core characteristics of the IRGC's identity and politics. Perhaps nothing better exemplifies the organization's place within contemporary Iran than the protest itself. Political demonstrations by the Basij and other groups aligned with hardliner interests are not uncommon in Iran. They are regularly deployed in response to perceived foreign insults or to mark important events such as the anniversary of the revolution. They are a normal fixture of Iranian political theater. But this protest was different. This was a provocative act that severely impacted Iran's relations with a foreign power. It transgressed norms of Iranian politics and international conventions. It also evoked the takeover of the US embassy in 1980—an act that ended Iran's relations with the United States and created its most costly foreignpolicy challenge.

Since the popular unrest that followed the 2009 disputed presidential election, Iran's security forces have refined the art of counter-protest operations. Protests do not happen on this scale without a serious and violent response by law enforcement. Rumors of this protest had been circulating on hardline blogs and websites for days. Yet, it proceeded without interference from Iranian authorities. Embassy security stayed out of the fray and Iranian police did not attempt to break up the demonstration until hours after it had begun. In the end, only a dozen protestors were arrested. The students stormed the British Embassy and a highly secure foreign diplomatic compound with impunity. They could do this only because of their association with the IRGC. Their act was a manifestation of the IRGC's stature in the Iranian regime. The student mob not only had a purpose, it had a sponsor that was one of the most powerful institutions in the country.

What is the IRGC and what makes it such a domineering force in Iran and such an influential player in the Middle East? This book explores those questions through an examination of the organization's history. Its chapters investigate the themes described above through discussions of the organization's religious and ideological foundations; its development during the Iran-Iraq war; the distillation of its culture and politics in the 1990s; the impact of post-9/11 American foreign policy on the organization; and its interventions in Syria and Iraq following the Arab Spring. To piece together this narrative I draw primarily from the IRGC's own statements and publications, reporting on the organization's activities outside of Iran, and secondary scholarly literature. Interviews conducted for a study on the Basij also inform the book.[4] What follows is a short overview of the IRGC in its contemporary form, a brief literature review, a discussion of the concepts and theoretical issues that underpin this book, a quick introduction to each chapter, and the issues that will be addressed in the conclusion.

# Brief Overview of the IRGC

The IRGC is a multifaceted organization with reach into many different areas. It is a security service, an intelligence organization, a social and cultural force, and a complex industrial and economic conglomerate. It is foremost a military organization. Iran has two militaries: the regular military (*artesh*) and the IRGC. What separates the IRGC from the regular military is its distinct raison d'être. The regular military's primary responsibility is the defense of Iran's territorial integrity. The IRGC, however, is tasked with both the defense of Iran and the much more amorphous safeguarding of Iran's theocratic system. It has been the latter mandate that has facilitated the IRGC's rise as a pillar of the Islamic Republic. Pursuing that broad mission has allowed the IRGC to expand beyond the military sphere and become influential in the political, economic, strategic, and sociocultural arenas.

The IRGC and regular military have parallel ground, maritime, and air forces. The regular military has an estimated 350,000 troops, whereas the IRGC has around 125,000. These forces are designed to work together during times of war but mostly operate within separately designated areas during peacetime. The IRGC's navy and the regular navy, for instance, are both involved in the defense of Iran's coastline but in different maritime zones. The IRGC is in charge of naval operations in the Persian Gulf, while the regular navy oversees the southern and Caspian coasts. Respective capabilities also differ. The regular navy controls Iran's larger, more traditional blue-water naval vessels, whereas the IRGC owns the majority of smaller watercraft, including a fleet of thousands of lightly armed speedboats. Likewise, the regular air force is larger and controls more aircraft than the IRGC's aerospace division. However, the IRGC's aerospace division oversees Iran's ballistic missile program, which is the foundation of the country's strategic defenses.

The IRGC has additional oversight of two powerful entities: the Basij and the Quds Force. The Basij is a massive organization encompassing millions of members. Iranian officials claim that the Basij has over fifteen million members, but a more realistic figure is probably closer to four million.[5] It pervades all levels of Iranian society through local chapters affiliated with schools (primary schools through universities), factories, government offices, and mosques. Iran's regime has encouraged the development of the militia as a means of creating an ideologically and religiously orthodox citizenry devoted to the leader and Iran's theocratic system. Ayatollah Khomeini spoke of establishing a twenty-million-person popular army after the revolution and Iran's leaders consider the Basij as the institution to achieve that objective.

The Basij functions primarily as a sociocultural organization. It provides instruction and sponsors religiously oriented events meant to cultivate affection for Iran's Islamic system, its social mores, and the supreme leader. It also acts as a security force involved in activities such as morals policing and counter-protest operations. More advanced levels of the organization are involved in armed operations, including as part of the IRGC. Aside from its broad spectrum of activities, the Basij is set apart from other Iranian security forces by its refusal to take conscripts. It is an organization made up entirely of volunteers, the vast majority of whom do not earn a salary. Members are vetted along political and ideological lines before they can join.[6] Because of its ideological standards, the Basij is highly trusted by regime officials and has been used as a pressure group to squash political dissent, such as in the suppression of pro-democracy protests following the contested 2009 re-election of Mahmoud Ahmadinejad.

Though many of its members begin their careers as youth in the Basij, the Quds Force is a far more selective organization. As its name implies, the Quds Force—Quds means Jerusalem in Persian and Arabic—was originally conceived as a division that would lead the IRGC's efforts against Israel. However, its mandate has grown over the years to encompass all of the IRGC's foreign covert and military operations. Its members are some of the best trained in the IRGC, having received advanced instruction in areas such as explosives, espionage, trade craft, and foreign languages. There is no accurate reporting of the Quds Force's size, but estimates generally peg its membership between five thousand and twenty thousand individuals. The primary function of Quds is to develop and assist allied armed groups outside of Iran. It helps train, equip, and fund a variety of organizations across the greater Middle East. This work has brought it into close partnerships with groups such as Hezbollah in Lebanon, Hamas in Gaza, the National Defense Forces in Syria, the Badr Organization in Iraq, and Ansar Allah (also known as the Houthis) in Yemen.

Through its work with these clients, Quds has emerged as Iran's primary mechanism of coercive influence outside its borders and a pillar of its defense strategy. In Iraq, for example, Quds chief Qassem Soleimani was able to subvert the influence of the United States by building up a network of pro-Iranian, anti-American Shiite militant groups. These groups fought American and allied troops, and secured powerful positions in Iraq after US combat forces withdrew in 2011. They remain one of the most powerful constituencies in Iraq and have made Iran a dominant player in that country. Quds has similarly helped expand Iranian influence in Syria, Lebanon, and Yemen. Although this form of influence by proxy has given Iran leverage in some important regional matters, it has also caused a considerable amount of animosity from Iran's critics. They see Iran's activities as meddling in the affairs of sovereign states and a principal source of regional destabilization.

In addition to these areas, the IRGC controls an economic empire driven in part by lucrative no-bid contracts awarded by the Iranian government. The

IRGC's Khatam al-Anbia Organization and its subsidiaries are Iran's largest recipient of state contracts. They oversee large industrial projects such as dams, railroads, and industrial complexes. The IRGC controls various other companies that have investments in the petroleum and gas industries, shipping, and telecommunications. They have also helped fund the IRGC's media empire, which includes numerous news-oriented websites and publications. Some of these—such as Sepah News, Basij News, and Sobh-e Sadegh—are run directly by the organization. Other prominent sites—such as Fars News and Tasnim—are closely associated with the organization and run by current and former IRGC members. These media organs allow the IRGC to control news and political commentary to suit its interests.

Despite the IRGC's prominence in the post-revolution period, only a small handful of studies have engaged the subject directly.[7] The bulk of these are studies on Iran's military capabilities written from a strategic studies perspective.[8] Although most provide useful analyses of the structure and capabilities of Iran's armed forces, they are generally limited by their narrow focus, their intended audience (mostly American policy makers and defense analysts), and their concentration on secondary English-language sources. As such they tend to embody several assumptions regarding the underlying cultural, religious, ideological, and social factors that have shaped Iranian society and its military organizations. Also problematic is the politicized nature of some of this literature. Political bias does not invalidate these works, but does detract from their utility.

There are a few works on the IRGC worth mentioning further. Sepehr Zabih's *The Iranian Military in Revolution and War*, for instance, offers a brief but valuable early history of the IRGC.[9] Published in 1988, Zabih marshals a variety of Persian sources and includes sections on the IRGC and Basij as part of a larger study on Iran's armed forces. The only real limitation of Zabih's study is its temporal and thematic scope. A similar study by Nikola Schahgaldian and Gina Barkhordarian, *The Iranian Military under the Islamic Republic*, was published by the nonpartisan Rand Corporation in 1987. It is similar to Zabih's work in both subject matter and in the period covered. While the authors' treatment of ideological and religious factors is likewise limited, they provide an informative analysis of the early structure of the IRGC.[10]

Kenneth Katzman's *Warriors of Islam* was the first and, up until now, only serious scholarly monograph devoted to the IRGC. Published in 1993, Katzman uses Samuel Huntington's theory of institutionalization to examine the internal makeup and development of the Revolutionary Guards. He concludes that although the IRGC had taken on the airs and some of the institutional characteristics of a professional military organization, its dedication to radical ideology and involvement in politics had prevented it from becoming a professional armed force. Katzman's study is restricted by the absence of non-English sources and the limits imposed by the theoretical construct of his inquiry—which, as a theory developed to understand Western-oriented political institutions, is perhaps ill-fitted to explain the development of an unconventional, clerically sponsored, and religiously minded armed force in Iran.[11] Even so, Katzman provides astute observations on the IRGC's structure and political development, and offers a valuable analysis of IRGC factionalism through the early 1990s.

More recently, a couple of publications have added to our understanding of the IRGC. The Rand Corporation released a useful study in 2009, which offers a broad overview of the IRGC's domestic activities and the organization's politics. Its authors (led by Frederic Wehrey) offer a few interesting chapters, including a survey of the IRGC's economic and financial interests, which provides a solid introduction to the subject. The study is a useful primer on the organization, despite its constricted conceptual and temporal focus. The second, *Iran Unveiled*, is a collection of essays by Ali Alfoneh and published by the American Enterprise Institute—a conservative think tank based in Washington, DC. Alfoneh has the interests of a historian and engages Persian-language IRGC literature for his research. Although the essays have a historical focus, Alfoneh's primary intention is to influence policy debates in Washington. The author puts forward essays on the IRGC's formation, the role of the supreme leader's representative in the organization, and its economic involvement as a means to make a provocative claim: the Islamic Republic is transforming into a military dictatorship under the IRGC. Alfoneh's evidence for this claim is lacking. But his view is representative of a growing anxiety over the IRGC's power in Iran—an anxiety that was particularly prevalent during Mahmoud Ahmadinejad's presidency (2005–2013) when Alfoneh's essays were written. The sensationalized thesis of his text unfortunately dilutes what is otherwise a useful contribution.

There are three major limitations in this body of literature: First, no study to date has offered a comprehensive history of the IRGC. Second, no study has adequately contextualized the IRGC and its maturation as an organization within the Islamic Republic's own development. Third, the processes that have shaped the organization's worldview, the cultural and religious dimensions of that worldview, and the relationship between these factors and the organization's place and work within and outside of Iran have not been sufficiently explored. The present study addresses these shortcomings. It considers the various dynamics and pressures that have shaped the IRGC over its career and influenced its impact on the Islamic Republic. To that end the book is both a history of the organization and a thematic history of the Islamic Republic. To further broaden our understanding of the IRGC, I also consider larger conceptual and theoretical issues. Because it is important to me that this book be open to a spectrum of readers, I limit the discussion of these concepts to the following section and some brief comments in the book's conclusion. Theory can bog down studies and reduce accessibility beyond the confines of academia. So by limiting its discussion, it is hoped that the body of the book will be accessible to non-specialists while still useful for scholars.

## Conceptualizing the IRGC

The IRGC has been viewed primarily as an ideological military. This perception is not incorrect, but it fails to adequately describe the organization. To form a better understanding of the organization, we need to re-conceptualize it by better identifying the forces that have shaped its development. I consider the IRGC to be the product of three intersecting impulses and experiences: (1) pro-clerical coercive activism; (2) devotion to the leader; and (3) the impact of conflict on organizational development and state formation. The first is firmly grounded in the Shiite religion, particularly as it has developed in Iran and in the shrine cities of Iraq (*'atabat*). The second is similarly grounded in Shiism and Islamic history. I suggest that it also shares parallels with historical models of leader-loyalist relationships in Eurasian history. The third is an artifact of the IRGC's reality as an armed force and political organization in the making of the Islamic Republic. I will briefly discuss the first two. I will discuss the third at more length because there is a mature body of literature devoted to the subject that requires a bit more consideration. These concepts underpin this study. They are threaded through the narrative of each chapter and the dynamics I view as most vital for understanding the IRGC.

## Pro-clerical Activism

The centrality of the clergy (*ulama*) in Shiite Islam has given this class a unique political role in Shiite society. One function that clergy have held is as local community leaders. Clerics did not exercise political authority in Iran until the revolution; however, this did not mean that they did not exercise political influence. Clergy in both Iran and in the Shiite centers of Iraq have held powerful social and political positions due to their religious authority. At the local level, prominent clergy formed a symbiotic relationship with their community of supporters, including with local strongmen and gangs. These pressure groups could advocate for their cleric, his rulings, help collect his taxes, or even act in his honor. They did this primarily through acts of intimidation and coercion. A gang's interests did not always mirror those of their local clergy, but when they did they could be used as an effective tool to pressure rivals or in political protest.[12]

The cleric-supporter nexus has been a feature of Shia society for centuries. Through the nineteenth and twentieth centuries, it became an increasingly important feature of political contestation. For example, pro-clerical gangs in Karbala, Iraq helped lead rebellions against Ottoman rule in the first half of the nineteenth century.[13] The Tobacco Revolt of 1890 likewise saw the most prominent cleric of the day, Mirza Hassan Shirazi, inspire droves of followers and sympathizers to revolt against the proposed sale of Iran's tobacco industry to Britain. By the mid-twentieth century, a pro-clerical group, the Fada'iyan-e Islam, turned to terrorism and assassinations to protest against the secularization of Iran. Local toughs in Tehran associated with Ayatollah Abol-Qassem Kashani helped bring down the rule of Iranian prime minister Mohammad Mossadegh. These gangs, led by the infamous strongman, Shaban "the Brainless" Jafari, terrorized Mossadegh supporters and effectively served as the ground soldiers for what was later revealed to be an operation funded by US and British intelligence.[14] In each of these cases, cleric-aligned gangs and followers used acts of protest—including physical violence and intimidation—as methods of coercion to influence politics at the local and national levels.

The Iranian revolution is the best example of such activism. Revolutionary activism was not the sole domain of pro-clerical supporters. Numerous groups as well as everyday, non-affiliated Iranians took part in the protests that brought down the Pahlavi throne. But pro-clerical militants were the most effective at using violence and coercion toward political ends. These militants were not initially united. Most held Ayatollah Khomeini in high esteem, but for some that political relationship was complicated by stronger ties to other, generally more local, clergy. Clerics both in line with Khomeini and not—such as Mahmoud Taleqani, Hosayn-Ali and Mohammad Montazeri, Hadi Ghaffari, and Mohammad Kazem Shariatmadari—had networks of militant activists that were primarily loyal to them and acted on their behalf.

For Khomeini and his cadre to succeed in the post-revolution, they needed to bring together a critical mass of these militants under a single banner and organize them into a united force. This was achieved through the formation of the IRGC. The IRGC became the superstructure by which the impulse of pro-clerical activism was harnessed. It legitimated this social and political function by aligning it with the state and giving it a mandate that transcended parochial activism. The IRGC's formation did not end the tradition of cleric-oriented gangs—indeed, they can still be found in Iran and Iraq (and other countries) today—but it helped institutionalize it. Within the IRGC, the Basij militia functions closest to pre-revolution pro-cleric gangs. Its units retain affiliations with local clergy and neighborhood mosques, and are similarly deployed to intimidate foes through violence and coercion. The main difference between the IRGC and Basij and their pre-revolution antecedents is in terms of organization (centralized and national versus decentralized and local) and relationship with the state. The inclination to support clergy and religious politics through violence remains a part of contemporary Iranian society; however, it is now almost entirely channeled through the IRGC and its associates.

## Primacy of the Leader

The IRGC's proximity to Iran's clerical leader has given it immense power. This has led some scholars to view the organization through the lens of praetorianism.[15] The Praetorians were military guardians of Roman emperors from the late third century BCE through Constantine I in the fourth century. Their loyalty to the emperor afforded them power and influence. Eventually the Praetorians got so powerful and corrupt that they began to displace the authority of the emperors, collaborating with the Senate to appoint rulers favorable to them. In modern scholarship, the term *praetorianism* is used to describe regimes with militaries that overstep their traditional role, regularly intervene in politics, and come to dominate all civilian institutions of the state. Praetorianism often leads to military coups and can describe countries such as Iraq, Pakistan, Turkey, Egypt, Burma, and much of Latin American at various points in modern history.[16] The term accurately describes some features of the IRGC, particularly its involvement in politics. However, it undervalues the importance of the supreme leader's authority to the organization. Praetorianism is found where civilian institutions lack power and legitimacy—neither of which is the case in Iran. The supreme leader's office continues to be the most powerful entity in Iran, and the civilian government retains arguably more legitimacy than any other state institution. Viewing the IRGC as a praetorian military further assumes that it could or would displace the leader as the ultimate authority—either by playing puppet master to a future leader or by ruling outright. Some would argue that the IRGC has already done that.[17] I disagree. I consider the leader—and the leader's ability to exercise authority—to be essential to the IRGC's enterprise. For the IRGC to displace the power of the leader, the organization would have to undergo a fundamental transformation, and put at risk the basis of its legitimacy in Iran's Islamic system.

What differentiates the IRGC from its contemporaries is its special devotion to Iran's supreme leader. Leader devotion is not unique to Iran—North Korea is another example—but how it functions in Iran is unique. For the IRGC, devotion to the leader stems from the organization's raison d'être of safeguarding the revolution. Iran's revolution is defined by one thing above all others: the Islamic system of clerical rule (*velayat-e faqih*). The heart of this system is the leader (*vali-ye faqih, rahbar*), who functions as both a political authority and a spiritual guide. He is a symbol of the revolution, the primacy of Shiite Islam, and the divine.

The IRGC's vow to defend the leader and the Islamic system (*nezam*) he oversees has made it an inseparable agent of his rule. If the supreme leader represents the power of the pen, the IRGC is his sword. It is the mechanism that translates the leader's authority into organized armed force and coercion. In order to retain its loyalty, the leader is incentivized to keep the organization and its top commanders content. This dynamic creates a symbiotic relationship: The IRGC serves at the leader's behest and remains obedient to his will. In return, the leader rewards it with certain privileges, political influence, and an unparalleled status. It has been this mutually beneficial relationship that has secured the place of both the leader and the IRGC in the post-revolution.

Praetorianism does not adequately describe the symbiosis between the leader and the IRGC in revolutionary Iran. As an alternative, I suggest considering another historical model: the *comitatus*. The comitatus was a common mode of political organization in Central Eurasia from the ancient Scythians through the early modern period.[18] It was a simple political structure composed of a lord and his personal guard corps. The members of this guard swore absolute loyalty to their leader. They served him with complete submission, and in extreme instances committed suicide and were buried with the leader after he died. In order to sustain their loyalty, the lord rewarded his guards with riches and lavish gifts. As Christopher Beckwith argues, the need to reward the comitatus was a fundamental aspect of the Eurasian economy, so much so that it was in part what drove commerce across the Silk Road.[19] When Islam entered the scene, the nature of the comitatus slowly changed. Ritual suicide no longer was a part of the tradition, but Muslim rulers maintained the need for a personal retinue of warriors. A new form of comitatus arose, wherein the ruler's devoted guardian warriors were slaves (*ghulams, mamluks*) who were raised from an early age to serve their lord. These slave-warriors held immense power and were often the most trusted confidants of their sovereign. This system flourished in early modern Iran under the kings of the Safavid dynasty.[20] Here the relationship was underpinned by Perso-Shiite conceptions of divinity, wherein the king was more than a human, he was "the Shadow of God on earth."[21]

What makes the comitatus a useful conceptual model for the IRGC is the inextricable place of the leader within its structure. Prior to Islam, the members of a comitatus could not exist after their lord's passing. The leader was fundamental to their position in society and without him their position ceased to be. In post-revolution Iran, what we have is of course different. But I suggest that while the IRGC can exist in absence of a particular leader, it cannot exist as it is currently structured in absence of the institution of the leader. The place of the leader in Iran's Islamic system is the life force of the IRGC, and without it the organization would not have the legitimacy, status, or the pretensions of spiritual orthodoxy that it does today. The primacy of the leader in Iran's theocratic system is something that the IRGC must maintain in order to protect its own place and function. I am not arguing that the IRGC represents a reincarnation of the pre-modern comitatus, nor am I attempting to establish a teleological line between it and those historical institutions. Rather, what I am suggesting is that the comitatus as a cultural and political precedent—particularly in Iran and Central Eurasia more broadly—is useful in helping us understand the nature and purpose of the IRGC in post-revolution Iran. It is, above all, a model in which the leader cannot be simply bypassed or transcended by his guardian retinue.

## Conflict and State Formation

Viewing the IRGC through the lenses of pro-clerical activism in the Shiite tradition and leader devotion are helpful in demystifying some of the organization's inclinations. The organization's reality as a military institution and the role that conflict has had in shaping the organization and its impact on the Islamic Republic are factors that must also be considered. Over the last few decades, numerous studies in history, sociology, and political science have examined the war-making/state-making nexus. Macro-comparative investigations by scholars such as Charles Tilly and Michael Mann (both rooted in the ideas of Max Weber) have produced useful theoretical models that place war and militaries at the center of state formation.[22] These frameworks are helpful for understanding the place of military power in the state formation of modern Europe; however their European bias limits the utility of their application elsewhere. That is, the European model of state formation through warfare is, as has been noted by some scholars, more exception than rule. For instance, in a study on the significance of war to the creation of states and national armed forces in Latin America, Miguel Centeno questions the viability of Tilly's model of state formation and military development for non-European states.[23] Centeno brings to the fore another weakness in the literature on armed forces and politics: the focus on conventional militaries. Conventional militaries are generally conceived as centralized national institutions that are subordinate to the state. These militaries include hierarchical command structures, rigid institutional cultures, and an officer corps comprised of the social elite. Further, and perhaps most significantly, these armed forces are designed to concentrate on external threats, particularly those posed by neighboring states, and have only a limited sub-national role. The focus on conventional forces thus includes a number of assumptions regarding the place of military power in national politics.

Studies on conventional militaries and their role in political development created an impressive body of literature during the Cold War. Foundational studies in this genre generally referred to as civil-military relations include works
by Samuel Huntington, Alfred Vagts, Alain Rouquie, and Karen Remmer.[24]
Collectively these works explore the ways in which militaries have either promoted or prohibited transitions to democracy. Instead of being concerned with
state formation per se, these studies present different takes on modernization
theory, particularly on the idea that the subjugation of military power to civilian leadership is essential to establishing a democratic regime. The framework
they present focuses on the relationship between regime type (e.g., democratic,
totalitarian, or authoritarian) and military power. Democracies in this typology are defined as regimes wherein civilian control over the military has been
achieved and where the military is subordinate to the interests of the state and
as such has a limited political role. Authoritarian regimes are defined as those
wherein the military plays a more significant role in political and governmental
matters, shares some authority with the state, and can be used to partly suppress
civil society. In totalitarian regimes, the military dominates the state and uses its
power to crush internal dissent and curb political freedom in all areas of society.[25]

These definitions have helped shape how politics and military power have
been conceived by scholars and policy makers since the Cold War. However,
a consequence of this static typology has been the perpetuation of certain
assumptions regarding the relationship between regime type, military power,
and politics, particularly in the post–Cold War era. In their important edited
volume *Irregular Armed Forces and Their Role in Politics and State Formation*
(2003), Diane Davis and Anthony Pereira tackle many of these assumptions as
well as some of those inherent in the state-formation models of Tilly and others.
They argue that the existing literature has neglected the roles of unconventional,
"alternative," or irregular armed forces in national politics. Their central thesis is
that armed forces "do much more than make war."[26] As Davis argues:

> [S]cholars rarely examine the wide variety of diverse social and politi-
> cal and even economic institutions in which military personnel or
> other "armed forces" play a part. These include intelligence agencies,
> militia, paramilitary forces, police, and even veterans associations; and
> they entail an understanding of the ways that these forces contribute to
> the development of [state] policies.[27]

Davis and Pereira present a novel approach to the study of politics and military power, one that focuses on alternative types of armed force, coercion, and
conflict. Their work is an important intervention and a departure from the
available models of political development. It offers a starting point for new

studies on irregular and nontraditional armed forces in society. It is also useful for understanding the larger political impact of the IRGC in Iran and in the Middle East more broadly. The IRGC is neither a regular nor irregular military force. It embodies elements of both. Its formalized structure, relationship to government bodies, and some of its military capabilities, such as its aerospace division, all resemble qualities of a regular state military. However, the IRGC retains an identity, internal culture, and practices rooted in its beginnings as an irregular militia. It sees itself as an unconventional and revolutionary force, and has developed tactics and operational strategies to match. This is best exemplified in the military doctrine of its ground and maritime forces, which emphasize "asymmetrical," guerilla-like tactics; the cultural and political role of the Basij; and the IRGC's close camaraderie with like-minded irregular armed forces outside of Iran. These qualities, combined with the unique political structure of the Islamic Republic's theocratic system, make the IRGC a military organization without an obvious parallel in the modern period.

But because the IRGC does not resemble the armed forces considered in Davis and Pereira's volume, it can help reveal some gaps in their contribution. First, although Davis and Pereira emphasize the utility of their work to understanding contemporary and even future forms of warfare, coercion, military power, and political development, most of their case studies focus on long-term state formation from the seventeenth through mid-twentieth centuries and only three of the thirteen studies touch upon or focus on the post–Cold War period. Second, while Davis and Pereira cast a wide net by considering the role of irregular forces around the globe, they neglect the Middle East entirely and only present one piece (a comparative study on Western African states) that briefly considers armed forces in Muslim societies.[28] Third, while they rightly address the assumptions of past literature, they follow those earlier works in ignoring the significance of culture, religion, and, to a lesser extent, ideology. That is, like their predecessors, Davis and Pereira retain a bias for the secular state and do not take possible exceptions into account.[29] They do not examine the impact of culture on conflict and politics, nor do they investigate connections between religion and military power.[30]

These omissions present an opportunity for scholars of the Middle East and Islam to contribute to the discussion. It is in the Middle East and Muslim societies more broadly where irregular armed forces have had the most significant impact in the contemporary era. A vivid example is ISIS (the Islamic State in Iraq and al-Sham, more simply known as the Islamic State), which has erased modern boundaries in its attempt to establish a contiguous political entity under the leadership of its self-declared caliph, Abu Bakr al-Baghdadi. Hezbollah in Lebanon, Hamas in Gaza, the Taliban in Afghanistan, Al Shabab in Somalia, Shiite militias in Iraq, and the competing armed groups in post-Qaddafi Libya are further examples. Similar to the IRGC, these groups have been viewed as many things (e.g., terrorist organizations, extremist movements, and insurgencies) but generally not appreciated as state-builders.[31] This is perhaps unsurprising given that they are considered sub-state or non-state actors; however with the increasing importance of these groups locally, regionally, and internationally, a reconceptualization is warranted. This is not to minimize the severe violence generated by these organizations or their appetites for destruction; rather it is in recognition of what conflict—in all its forms—achieves for them politically. Thus, in order to better understand the trajectories of such groups and their potential impact on state formation we must first expand how we conceive of them.

What I am suggesting then, and what will be—along with pro-clerical activism and the centrality of the leader—the subtext of this study, is that irregular armed forces and conflict continue to be important to the political development of states in the contemporary period. By viewing militant organizations and movements through frameworks of conflict, military power, and politics, while also considering the role of other driving forces such as culture and religion, we can attain a more coherent and historical perspective about how militancy operates within society and why its prevalence continues in the Middle East today. My focus, however, is specific: the IRGC in revolutionary Iran. And though this study does not explore comparisons between the IRGC and the groups mentioned above, I nonetheless hope that the present work will encourage a reassessment of armed groups in the contemporary Middle East and of religion-oriented armed groups more broadly.

## Chapters and Questions

This book examines the IRGC and the religious, ideological, cultural, and political factors that have contributed to its development. It follows the organization from its birth in the midst of the 1979 revolution through the succeeding decades of the Islamic Republic's maturation. Over this period the IRGC has transformed from a poorly funded, poorly organized militia into the most formidable entity in Iran next to the supreme leader. To ground the study, the book begins with a brief overview of Shiite Islam and the Islamic movement in Iran. Shiism is a central facet of the IRGC. It animates its identity, legitimizes its beliefs, and facilitates many of its relationships outside of Iran. In order to understand the place and function of religion in the organization, it is important to first be familiar with some of the foundational moments in Shiite history and how the tradition developed in Iran through the 1979 revolution. The second chapter begins by tracing some of the central events in Shiism's early history. These events, such as the succession to the Prophet or the martyrdom of the Imam Husayn, play a vital role in Shiite culture and animate Shiite political ideologies. The second part of the chapter looks at the rise of clerical authority in Iran and the politicization of the clergy in the late nineteenth and twentieth centuries.

The third chapter, "Vanguard of the Imam," is the first part of the book that focuses on the Revolutionary Guards. The early history of the IRGC has been poorly understood, so this chapter provides a detailed narrative of the organization's formation and first several months of operation. Compared to the chapters that follow, this chapter covers a short period of time, from the collapse of the Pahlavi regime in February 1979 to the ratification of the Islamic Republic's constitution in December of that year. This crucial period witnessed the first major test for the revolution as various factions and organizations struggled for control of the post-Pahlavi state. As an armed force organized by clerics loyal to Ayatollah Khomeini, the Revolutionary Guards served as the leading coercive apparatus of the pro-Khomeini faction and helped this faction consolidate power in the post-revolution.

The next four chapters focus on the 1980s. Chapter four, "The Imposed War," looks at the first two years of the Iran-Iraq war, from Saddam Hussein's invasion of Iran in September 1980 to Iran's counter-offensives in 1982. Chapter five, "The Long War," discusses the period from Iran's counter-invasion of Iraq in 1982 to the conflict's conclusion six years later. Both chapters explore the IRGC's experience in the war and development during that period.

In chapter six, "Exporting the Revolution," we look at the roots of Iran's desire to export its revolution beyond its borders and the IRGC's role in that effort. The question of how to spread Iran's revolutionary ideals became increasingly divisive as the war with Iraq went on. Proponents of a radical interventionist approach saw exporting the revolution as a fundamental responsibility of Iran's government. Opponents of interventionism felt it was contrary to Iran's national interests to become intertwined in outside conflicts and contended that the war with Iraq should take priority. These two positions highlighted a deep divide between conservative and radical factions in the Khomeinist movement and within the IRGC.

The seventh chapter, "Warriors of Karbala," explores the formation of IRGC identity. It looks at the religious and ideological perspectives that defined the organization at its founding and how the organization's self-conception evolved during the war. The heart of the discussion focuses on the IRGC's own culture work, especially the visuality it produced to articulate its identity.

The ramifications of IRGC identity are central to the cultural positions and political activism of war veterans in the postwar period. I take up this theme in chapter eight, "When Johnny Comes Marching Home," which explores the expansion of the IRGC, its subordinate forces, and war veterans groups into various extra-military state sectors. A key transformation during this period was the decision by Iranian president Akbar Hashemi Rafsanjani to avoid total demobilization by instead expanding the purviews of the IRGC and its popular militia, the Basij, to include domestic security and state-funded industrial construction. Although Rafsanjani hoped that such moves would help curry favor among these institutions for his political project, they had the opposite effect. Consequently, the expansion of these organizations gave the IRGC a greater stake in the regime and more power to influence policy. The permeation of military power into extra-military sectors paralleled the war veterans' movement and helped assist that movement's impact on domestic politics.

Whereas chapter eight explores the rise of the IRGC, chapter nine, "The War on Terror," explores the blossoming of the organization's influence. The chapter examines the impact of post-9/11 American foreign policy on Iran. Here I argue that Iran was not only the main beneficiary of the Bush administration's wars in the Middle East, but that the Bush administration's broader approach to containing the Iranian threat legitimized the further expansion of the IRGC's role in domestic politics and facilitated its influence in regional conflicts.

The Arab Spring fundamentally altered the landscape of the Middle East. It also coincided with increased pressure against Iran and its nuclear program, including sanctions, sabotage, and the assassination of Iranian scientists. Chapter ten, "Big Bang, Big Crunch," explores how these factors affected Iran's contested 2009 presidential election, Iranian regional policies, and sparked an aggressive, forward-leaning posture for the IRGC. Chapter eleven, "In Defense of the Family of the Prophet," builds on this theme and examines in more depth the IRGC's expanding influence and activities in Syria's civil war and the conflict against ISIS in Iraq. It further looks at the problem of sectarianism and the sharpening of Shiite identity in the IRGC and their regional allies. These issues are continued in the book's epilogue.

In the concluding chapter, I return to the concepts presented above and consider some of the overarching themes of the book. I discuss the IRGC's impact on the Islamic Republic, how conflict helped shape its development, the role of religion in its domestic and foreign involvement, and the major challenges it faces. A brief exploration of these issues will draw out the larger implications of the IRGC's career and provide a view of what is to come.

# 2

# From Ali to Khomeini

We have two paths ahead of us: the first is martyrdom and departing for
heaven, the second is victory over the enemies of Islam and establishing a government of Islamic justice. Therefore, we are not afraid of anything. We are not afraid of the army of America, nor are we afraid of the
Soviet military. We are not afraid of any power. Because we have faith
in the next life, faith in Day of Judgment, faith in meeting with God
(*liqa allah*), and because we have faith that after death we will associate with the saints, the prophets, and the devoted, we are not afraid of
death and we will make our country the graveyard of foreign soldiers.[1]
—Abu Sharif, IRGC Operations Commander

The Shiite religion radiates through every pore of Iran's Islamic system. It is
the moral, historical, and spiritual touchstone of the Islamic Republic. It offers
a lexicon, a system of poetics through which and by which Iran's leaders both
understand the world around them and communicate that understanding. To
comprehend—or at least appreciate—the role that religion plays in Iran's system, one must be first familiar with the story of Shiite Islam and its development
in Iran. It is particularly important to understand the religion's foundational episodes from the perspective of its adherents. Early moments in Islamic history,
such as the succession to the Prophet Muhammad and the martyrdom of his
grandson, Imam Husayn, are foundational to the Shiite tradition. They created
the political dynamics and the cultural context for the spiritual evolution of the
faith. The development of Shiism coincided with the gradual rise and expansion
of clerical authority in the Shiite community. As the stewards of their religious
community, the influence of the clergy on modern Shiism has been pronounced.

The Islamic world's experience with Western imperialism triggered a number
of religiously inspired responses. In Iran, those responses were led by both the
clergy, who largely drew from Shiite traditionalism, and intellectuals who incor-
porated aspects of secular ideology (such as Marxism) to advocate for politics
of resistance and reform. The politicized, ideological renderings of Islam that
grew out of this period gave rise to the revolutionary movement in Iran, which

culminated in the 1979 revolution. After the revolution, the ideological thought
of Ayatollah Ruhollah Khomeini came to dominate political life and pervade all
levels of society. Ideology remains vital to the Islamic Republic and the IRGC.
It underpins policies, shapes culture, and is the heart of identity. It is also central
to expressions of political violence. The religious framework of Islamic activism
allows violence to be seen as a justifiable if not righteous response to perceived
injustice and threats to Islam. That framework has helped legitimize the violence
of Iran's Islamic system, and of that exercised by the IRGC, both inside and outside of Iran—themes that carry forward through this book.

## The Formation of Shiite Islam

The Prophet Muhammad brought a divine revelation to the Arab people. These
teachings, which were communicated to the Prophet by the Angel Gabriel and
collected in the Quran, helped Muhammad unite numerous Arab tribes under a
new monotheistic order. By the end of his life, the nascent Muslim community
had conquered important parts of Arabia and had grown in number and wealth.
After the Prophet's death in 632 CE, there was a disagreement regarding who
would succeed him. A lot was at stake. The fundamental tenet of Islam—unity
of all believers—quickly gave way to greed and ambition. This issue split the
Muslim community into two main factions: those who supported Abu Bakr and
his successors Umar and Uthman, and those who supported Ali ibn Abi Talib—
the Prophet's cousin, son-in-law, and most trusted confidant. Those who supported Ali and later supported his descendants came to be known as the *shi'at
'Ali* or the "partisans of Ali." Although this was a political distinction, it was from
Ali's supporters that the Shiite religion gradually emerged as a separate and distinct variant of Islam. As the dispute over the succession to Muhammad is at
the root of Shiism, it is important to understand how the Shia understand this
dispute and how it has influenced their religion and culture.[2]

Numerous traditions (*hadith*)—which are second only to the Quran in their
importance to Islamic theology—recognized by both Sunnis and Shiites, attest
to Muhammad's favoring of Ali and the latter's unparalleled valor and morality.[3]
For Sunnis, these traditions simply reinforce the notion that Ali was a central
figure in early Islam and should be revered as such. Shiites, however, point to
these traditions as evidence that the Prophet had intended for Ali, and later
Ali's sons, to succeed him in leading the Muslim community. Perhaps the most
important tradition supporting the Shiites' claim is an account from the last
year of the Prophet's life. This account, recorded in a Sunni collection of traditions, states:

We [the Prophet's companions] were with the Apostle of God [Muhammad] in his journey and we stopped at Ghadir Khumm. We performed the obligatory prayer together and a place was swept for the Apostle under two trees and he performed the mid-day prayer. And then he took 'Ali by the hand and said to the people: "Do you acknowledge that I have a greater claim on each of the believers than they have on themselves?" And they replied: "Yes!" And he took 'Ali's hand and said: "Of whomsoever I am Lord [*mawla*], then 'Ali is also Lord. O God! Be Thou the supporter of whoever supports 'Ali and the enemy of whoever opposes him." And 'Umar met him ['Ali] after this and said to him: "Congratulations, O son of Abu Talib! Now morning and evening [i.e., forever] you are the master of every believing man and woman."[4]

To Shiites the implication of this tradition is evident. It shows that Muhammad appointed Ali as his successor and indicates that Umar (the future second caliph) understood and acknowledged this fact. This is important to note because, to Shiites, it suggests that Umar's later nomination of Abu Bakr as caliph and the first successor to the Prophet not only betrayed the Prophet's wishes but also went against Umar's understanding of those wishes.

Another significant episode involving the Prophet and Umar, known as the Episode of Pen and Paper, casts further doubt in the eyes of Shiites on Umar's faithfulness and on his role in usurping Ali's rightful successorship. This tradition, which is recognized but understood differently by both Sunnis and Shiites, recounts a conversation between the Prophet and his followers as he lay bed-ridden during the last days of his life. The tradition states:

When the Prophet's illness became serious, he said: "Bring me writing materials that I may write for you something, after which you will not be led into error." 'Umar said: "The illness has overwhelmed the Prophet. We have the Book of God [the Qur'an] and that is enough for us." Then the people differed about this and spoke many words. And he [the Prophet] said: "Leave me! There ought not to be quarrelling in my presence." And Ibn 'Abbas [the Prophet's cousin] went out saying: "The greatest of calamities is what intervened between the Apostle and his writing."[5]

Shiites understand this episode as Muhammad's attempt to write a will and testament that would have confirmed Ali's role as successor. Umar's interference in this matter is yet another reason why Shiites came to consider him a chief conspirator against Ali.

Without a will, Muslims were forced to choose a leader themselves. Soon after the Prophet's death, Umar met with a group of Muslim notables in Medina to discuss matters of succession. It was during this meeting that Umar nominated and pledged his allegiance to Abu Bakr who was in turn elected by those present as the Prophet's successor and the caliph (*khalifa*) of the Muslims. This election, however, had taken place in the absence of Ali, who—along with his wife Fatima (the Prophet's daughter) and much of Muhammad's family—was preparing the Prophet's body for burial. Although angered at the nomination of Abu Bakr, Shiites believe that Ali held back formal protest for the sake of Muslim unity.[6]

Although Ali continued to have his own avid supporters, there were two more successors (Umar and Uthman) to the role of caliph before he held that office. Ali's ascension to the caliphate came on the heels of the controversial reign and murder of the third caliph, Uthman, in 656 CE. Uthman's rule had brought the formidable Banu Umayyad clan to power. Under Uthman, the Umayyads, a native Meccan clan, had become entrenched in leadership roles throughout Muslim territory, including important governorships. This gave the Umayyad clan a privileged and powerful position in the Muslim community, but also caused resentment among many Muslim tribes, which eventually led to Uthman's murder. After Uthman's death, Ali's supporters urged him to accept the caliphate. Although reluctant, Ali ultimately accepted the role and became the fourth and last "rightly guided" caliph—according to Sunnis. For Shiites, on the other hand, this was the first and only time in the history of Islam that the Muslim community was led by a faithful and true successor to the Prophet.[7]

The tumultuous political climate that led to Uthman's murder continued after Ali came to power. The Umayyad clan and their supporters disputed Ali's election to the caliphate and blamed his followers for Uthman's murder. Many from the Umayyad clan relocated to Damascus to support their own candidate for caliph, Muawiya Ibn Abi Sufyan, the military governor of Syria. After Muawiya refused to swear allegiance to Ali, a conflict erupted between the armies of the two Muslim leaders. A court of arbitration was called to settle the conflict diplomatically, though little progress was made. Instead, some of Ali's supporters, who thought his agreeing to arbitration compromised his claim to the caliphate, turned against him. This group, known as the Kharajites (*khawarij*), argued that Ali's choice of arbitration was against God's will, and, for having gone against God, Ali was no longer a faithful Muslim. This act of declaring Ali a non-Muslim, known as *takfir*, was the philosophical basis for the Kharajites' rebellion against Ali and their murder of him in 661.

The murder of Ali ended the only period in Muslim history where a Shiite imam led the Islamic community. After Ali's death, the Umayyads extended their control over Muslim lands and Muawiya was declared caliph. Support for Ali and his descendents continued, though most of his followers were isolated to the frontiers of Muslim territory, including in the garrison town of Kufa in modern-day southern Iraq. Many of these supporters turned to Ali's sons, Hasan and Husayn, to continue their father's rightful struggle for leadership of the Muslim community. However, shortly after his father's murder, Hasan—the elder of the two and the second imam in the Shiite tradition—renounced his claim to the caliphate in order to avoid more bloodshed and disharmony among Muslims. Shiites believe that, eight years after his abdication, Hasan was poisoned to death by his wife on Muawiya's behalf.

It was not until the death of Muawiya and the ascension of his son Yazid to the caliphate in 680 that Husayn—Ali's second son and the third Shiite imam—would press his claim to the leadership of the Muslim community. Yazid's reputation as a morally lax drunkard made his ascension infuriating to many Muslims. Urged by his supporters in Kufa, Husayn decided to make a bid for his rightful claim to the caliphate. He led a small group of companions and family members toward the Umayyad-ruled town of Kufa, where he planned to join up with a few thousand of his supporters and lead a campaign against Yazid in Damascus. When the Umayyad governor of Iraq, Ubaydallah Ibn Ziyad, discovered news of this plot, he executed some of Husayn's leading supporters in Kufa and dispatched an army to block the Imam's access to that city. Despite being informed of this turn of events, Husayn continued toward Kufa only to be forced north of the city by Umayyad troops. Ibn Ziyad's army surrounded Husayn and his companions, making them decamp in the barren desert plains of Karbala. For the next several days the Umayyads tried to coerce Husayn into renouncing his claim of leadership by cutting off the supply of fresh water to his camp. Finally, on the tenth day of the Muslim month of Muharram 680 CE, after failed negotiations and Husayn's refusal to pay tribute to Yazid, nearly four thousand Umayyad troops stormed Husayn's camp and slaughtered his companions.

The Shiite recollections of this event—known as Ashura (literally the "tenth")—are tragic and brutal. Husayn and about seventy of his supporters were killed. His eldest son, Ali al-Akbar, died a valiant death fighting the Umayyad forces. Husayn's half brother, Abbas, was killed after both his arms were cut off as he attempted to deliver drinking water to the women and children of the camp. Husayn's nephew, Qasim, was killed on what was to be his wedding day, in front of his bride. There is also the story of Husayn's infant son Ali al-Asghar, who was killed in his father's arms when an Umayyad archer shot the small child in the throat.[8] In one popular Shiite oral tradition, Husayn is imagined to have lamented the deaths of his family and the tragedy that was to befall him:

> The infidels [i.e., the Umayyads] are one side, and my sorrowful self on the other. The rose has fallen in one direction, and the thorns in the other. O friends, in one quarter Akbar fell by treachery, a martyr . . .

Kasim [Qasim] the disappointed, has been killed on one spot, and on the other I myself experience the cruel oppression of the spheres. In one corner the mother of 'Ali Akbar is smiting her head, while the sorrowful bride of Kasim is moaning in another. . . . I am sore distressed at the unkind treatment received at the hands of the cruel heavens. Pitiful tyranny is exercised towards me by a cruel, unbelieving army! All the sorrows and troubles of this world have overwhelmed me! I am become a butt for the arrow of affliction and trouble. I am a holy bird stripped of its quills and feathers by the hand of the archer of tyranny, and am become, O friends, utterly disabled, and unable to fly to my sacred nest. They are going to kill me mercilessly, for no other crime or guilt except that I happen to be a prophet's grandson.[9]

Ultimately Husayn was killed and decapitated by the Umayyad assailants. A few women and children—among them Husayn's son Ali Zayn al-Abidin (the fourth Shiite imam) and his sister Zaynab—were spared, and along with Husayn's severed head, taken to Yazid in Damascus. (A mosque built near Damascus in memory of Zaynab remains an important site of Shiite pilgrimage to this day.) After the slaughter, the camp was put to fire.

The tragedy of Karbala is the single most important event in the early formation of the Shiite religion.[10] Before the martyrdom of Husayn, the supporters of Ali and his sons practiced the same form of Islam as their non-Shia rivals. Heinz Helm, a German scholar of Islamic history, argues that the tragedy of Karbala "marked the 'big bang' that created the cosmos of Shiism and brought it into motion."[11] It was through the mournful commemoration of Ashura that the Shia began to develop a separate religious identity.[12] The Kufan Shia began the tradition of commemorating Ashura soon after the events at Karbala. Members of this community were burdened with an intense shame due to their failure to aid Husayn and his companions against Umayyad aggression. Instead, out of fear of the Umayyad authorities, the Kufan Shia—who had encouraged Husayn to come to Kufa with the promise of joining his struggle—did not rebel, and were left with a guilt that for many was worse than death.[13] In remorse, they began commemorating Ashura in informal gatherings during which they would pray for Husayn and his companions and beseech God for forgiveness. A subset of this community, led by Sulayman Ibn Surad, looked for a more emphatic solution to their suffering. This group, known as the Penitents (*tawwabun*), wanted to die as Husayn had died in an attempt to absolve their sins for failing to come to the Imam's aid. Eventually they decided to lead a campaign against Umayyad forces, which they intended to lose. In early 685 they engaged a much larger Umayyad military contingent, and most—as they had hoped—were killed.

Halm has argued that the movement of the Kufan Penitents marked the true beginning of the Shiite religion, as it "expressed all the essential elements and concepts of Shiʻi piety. The willingness for self-sacrifice is the most outstanding feature, and it has remained unchanged to the present day."[14] Such thinking often links the campaign of the Penitents and their religious quest for martyrdom to the modern self-sacrifice or "suicide" operations undertaken by Shiite militants, such as by Iranian soldiers in the Iran-Iraq war or by Lebanon's Hezbollah, but I would not suggest such a direct correlation. Religion has a place in militancy, as this book argues, but, to appreciate the true spiritual potency of the Pentitents' sacrifice, one needs to view their story and that of Ashura independent from contemporary political concerns. The events associated with the martyrdom of Imam Husayn are at the heart of Shiite spirituality and religious culture. Indeed, as the Kufan practice of commemorating the events of Karbala began to spread across the wider Shiite community, so too did the Shiite community begin to form an identity and system of belief that differed from the ruling Sunni majority. With the popularization of the Ashura ritual, what had begun as a localized redemptive act particular to the Kufan supporters of Husayn slowly emerged as the central tradition of Shiite Islam.

# Rise of the Clergy

Following the events of Karbala, Shiite communities turned inward and practiced a quietist form of their religion for several centuries.[15] Husayn's defeat ended the period of imam-led military revolts and ushered in a period wherein the imams—all male descendants of the Prophet through his grandson Husayn—lived in virtual house arrest under Sunni rulers. This contributed to the depoliticization of the role of the imams in the Shiite community and to their marginalization in the political sphere of the Muslim world.[16]

Although understanding the lives of the eight imams subsequent to Husayn is important, providing adequate discussion of their careers is beyond the scope of this chapter. However, a few brief points should be made. Each of these eight imams lived under some sort of house arrest and none were able to exercise complete political control over the Shia community. They lived as political prisoners to the Sunni regimes that ruled the Islamic world during this period. Although these imams remained the center of the Shiite community, they had limited political influence. Shiites believe that, in order to keep the Shia marginalized and oppressed, all of the Imams (except for the Twelfth and final imam) were killed by Sunni rulers, with most (like Hasan, the second imam) murdered by way of poisoning.

The case of the Twelfth Imam is more complicated. Shiites believe that the Twelfth Imam, Muhammad al-Mahdi, never died, but rather passed into a spiritual occultation. Shiites believe this imam will one day return and lead the Shia in an apocalyptic battle against the forces of evil, purify Islam, and restore justice to the world. A tenth-century Shiite text serves as an example of how Shiites have imagined the return of the "Hidden" Imam:

> [A] cry (will come) from the sky (in such a way) that all the people will hear it in their own languages; a face and a chest will appear in the sky before the people in the centre of the sun; the dead will arise from their graves so that they will return to the world and they will recognize one another and visit one another; that will come to an end with twenty-four continuous rain storms and the land will be revived by them after being dead and it will recognize its blessings; after that every disease will be taken away from those of the Shi'a of the Mahdi, peace be upon him, who believe in the truth; at that time they will know of his appearance in Mecca and they will go to him to support him. . . . In his [the Mahdi's] time, injustice will be removed and the roads will be safe. The earth will produce its benefits and every due will be restored to its proper person. No people of any other religions will remain without being shown Islam and confessing faith in it. . . . At that time, men will not find any place to give alms nor be generous because wealth will encompass all the believers.[17]

The disappearance or occultation (*ghayba*) of the Imam Mahdi ("the rightly guided one") and the messianic expectations surrounding his return (*raj'a*) are significant elements of the Shiite religion. The absence of the Twelfth Imam ended the line of Shiite imams that began with Ali and led to a crisis within Shiism. The Shia believed that only an imam could rightfully lead the Muslim community. Also, the imam was the only one who had the authority to lead Friday prayers and declare an offensive jihad (i.e., a military campaign to spread the Islamic faith and expand its geographical domains). Without a living, infallible imam interacting with Muslim society, Shiites were forced to question the very legitimacy of temporal Muslim rule. This quandary led to the rise of the Shiite *ulama*, or clergy, as the de facto leaders of the Shiite community in the absence of the imam.[18]

The Shiite clergy were the first to grapple with the complexities of temporal rule without an imam.[19] These scholars, trained in the religious sciences and Islamic jurisprudence, slowly emerged as the religious authorities within the Shiite community. Over the next few centuries, Shiite clergy established a similar legal system to that of their Sunni counterparts.[20] Although these scholars developed a strong intellectual tradition during this period, which focused on rationalist arguments and textual evidence, popular Shiite piety continued to be centered on the oral narratives of the Imam Husayn and similar Shiite lore. By the sixteenth century, it was the power of these stories and the rituals surrounding their commemoration that continued to serve as the basis for popular Shiite identity and activism. Clerical influence remained marginal and mostly confined to important Shiite urban centers in Iran and Iraq.[21]

A major turning point for Shiism came in 1501 when Ismail Safavi, the spiritual leader of a Shiite Sufi brotherhood, led a tribal military conquest of Iran and established that country's first Shiite dynasty. Ismail declared himself *shah* (king) and decreed that Shiism would be the state religion of Iran. Although Ismail had originally claimed to be the Mahdi (or return of the Hidden Imam), this fact was initially minimized and later ignored by his successors, who instead claimed to rule on *behalf* of the Hidden Imam. Through that distinction, Safavid shahs, who were known as the representatives of the Hidden Imam on earth, found a unique solution to the question of temporal rule: they ruled at the pleasure of the Hidden Imam but still awaited his return.[22]

Iran was mostly Sunni at this time, with only a small Shiite minority. This made the spread of Shiism within Safavid domains a difficult task for Shah Ismail and his successors. To help them in their effort, the Safavid shahs turned to Shiite scholars from the Arab world and offered them state patronage to relocate to Iran.[23] The introduction of Shiite scholars to the political scene helped the Safavid state routinize Shiite practice, law, and tradition within their territories. As the head of this campaign, Shiite clergy were granted a level of political influence they had not previously enjoyed.[24] This created a sort of power-sharing arrangement between the Shiite clerical class and the Safavid shahs, which granted the former jurisdiction over the religious affairs of the Safavid state while the latter claimed to rule at the behest of the Hidden Imam.

Under Safavid rule (1501–1722), Shiism gradually emerged as the religion of Iran's majority. The process of converting Iran was slow and gradual, and ultimately owed more to the growing influence of Shiite popular culture—especially the spread of narratives about the imams Ali and Husayn—than to the empowerment of the Shiite clergy.[25] The clergy, however, gained unparalleled influence over their Shiite constituents during this time, which made them among the most powerful political actors in Iran.

By the nineteenth century, debates within the clerical ranks began to consider a way that would help centralize clerical control over the Shiite community. Up until this time, religious authority was dispersed among numerous clerics, who held generally limited and localized authority. The leading Shiite clergy wanted to establish a system of authority wherein the top-ranking cleric would be the central authority for all Shiites in the world. These debates gave birth to the institution of the *marja al-taqlid* or the "point of emulation"—an office to be held by the most senior Shiite cleric. This cleric, or *marja*, would be the person whom all lay Shiites had to "emulate" or imitate in matters concerning religious life. In theory, there would be only one marja for the entire Shia world and all Shiites would have to follow his decrees.[26] However, the institution of the *marja al-taqlid* only lasted in this form through the tenures of the first two marjas. Afterward, and through most of the twentieth century, several of the day's top-ranking clergy could hold the rank of marja simultaneously. Their influence, instead of being universal, became more regional in nature.[27]

The creation of the institution of the *marja al-taqlid* was an important turning point in Shiite clerical authority, as it expanded both the social and political influence of the clergy over Shiite society. An example of this came during Iran's Tobacco Revolt of 1890–1891—an episode that occurred in response to growing Western intervention and imperialism in the Muslim world. The British were especially active in this era, establishing imperial control over the Indian subcontinent and initiating exploitative commercial ventures across the Middle East. In one such scheme, a British businessman was granted a monopoly over the production, export, and sale of Iranian tobacco by the Qajar Shah of Iran.[28] In March 1890, news of this concession was leaked to the public by anti-imperialist factions within the Qajar regime, causing popular protests across Iran. As noted historian, Nikki Keddie, explains,

> The tobacco concession elicited far more protest than any other because it dealt not with areas that were unexploited, or almost so, by Iranian businessmen, but rather with a product widely grown in Iran, and profiting many landholders, shopkeepers, and exporters.[29]

The tobacco concession affected nearly every strata of Iranian society. In December 1891, a *fatwa* (religious edict) attributed to the Shiite *marja al-taqlid* of the time, Mirza Hasan Shirazi, was issued calling for a nationwide boycott of tobacco. With the religious authority and legitimacy of the *marja al-taqlid* behind the order, Shiites from every class and standing (reportedly even including the Shah's own wives) staged a boycott and massive protests that forced the Shah to cancel the concession. Although significant in and of itself, this event also marked the first time the Shiite populace was encouraged into political protest by a ruling *marja*, and signaled the emergence of the Shiite clergy as a leading force against Western imperialism.[30]

# The Islamic Movement

The long twentieth century saw the disintegration of empires, the rise of nation-states, the emergence of two superpowers, and the fall of one. This ebb and flow of global political power drastically affected the Middle East. Britain and France reinvigorated their imperialistic hold on the Middle East in the first half of the century only to see these adventures collapse in the second. Later, during the Cold War, Middle Eastern states were used as pawns in the global chess match between the United States and the Soviet Union. By the end of the century, the legacy of Western imperialism left much of the Middle East embroiled in political and social instability.

The political impotence of Middle Eastern states and their leaders in resisting foreign domination caused unrest throughout the region. The influence of Western secularism drew the ire of religious traditionalists, while the political oppression of Western-backed dictators inspired the activism of progressive elements. Dissent was fueled by the introduction of numerous political ideologies such as communism, socialism, and nationalism, which gained particular popularity among secularists and certain ethnic and religious minorities. The spread of these ideologies also caused a backlash by the religious sector, which considered secularism in all its forms to be a major threat to Islam. In order to counteract the influence of these ideologies and Western secularism, Muslim intellectuals and religious leaders began to develop their own political ideologies, which put an emphasis on the superiority of Islam over all other political systems. Commonly referred to as Islamism or political Islam, these ideologies gave motivation and religious legitimacy to political organizations throughout the region. These ideologies have had a significant influence on both Sunni and Shiite societies. Their impact on Iran was especially pronounced.[31]

Muslim activism against the spread of Western culture and the adoption of Western forms of government was a powerful force in Iran during the first half of the twentieth century. During Iran's Constitutional Revolution of 1905–1911— a popular movement that established a constitution and democratically elected parliament (*majles*) under Iran's Qajar regime—Muslim leaders denounced the idea of a parliamentary government as a secular threat to Islam.[32] Shaykh Fazlollah Nuri, a senior Shiite cleric, was the chief organizer of clerical opposition to the Iranian parliament. Nuri articulated his faction's objections to parliamentary government in a series of published letters distributed throughout Iran and the Shiite centers of Iraq. Many of his objections concerned provisions in Iran's constitution which expanded the rights of women, allowed for freedom of the press, and gave equal rights to nationalities and religions. These innovations, Nuri argued, were against the sacred law of Islam and undermined the traditional authority of the clergy. Further, Nuri was troubled by the European trappings of the Iranian parliament and constitution which seemed to devalue the divinity of Islam. As Nuri wrote: "Fireworks, receptions of the ambassadors, those foreign habits, the crying of hurrah, all those inscriptions of Long Live, Long Live! Long Live Equality, Fraternity. Why not . . . Long Live the Sacred Law, Long Live the Qur'an, Long Live Islam?"[33]

Nuri wanted to secure the centrality of traditional Islamic law (*sharia*) in Iran, which he felt was being weakened and replaced by Western-inspired civil law. To ensure the integrity of Islamic law in Iran, Nuri's camp pressed for changes to the constitution which made all parliamentary legislation subject to ratification by a committee of five top-ranking clerics. In doing so, Nuri proved the power of the clergy in organizing resistance to any threat to Islamic law and traditional clerical authority in Iran. Although his faction ultimately crumbled—and Nuri later killed by constitutionalist supporters—he set a precedent within Iranian Shiism by giving the traditionally apolitical clergy a significant political role in state government—a precedent that laid the foundation for the Islamic Republic's theocratic system.[34]

Nuri's movement dwindled in the following years. With leading Shiite clergy returned to their traditional political quietism, Iran underwent a military coup d'état that toppled the Qajar dynasty and brought Reza Shah Pahlavi to power. Reza Shah instituted several modernizing and westernizing reforms inspired by the secular nationalism of Turkey's Mustafa Kemal Ataturk. The new reforms took aim at traditional religion in Iranian society. Veiling for women was banned and other religious garb was restricted. Turbans were to be replaced by Western hats and traditional robes for the Western suit. Reza Shah was forced to abdicate his throne in 1941 by the Allied powers.[35] His son and successor, Mohammad Reza Pahlavi, continued much of his father's westernizing reforms and suffered the fallout of those policies.[36]

A young Ruhollah Khomeini was a vocal opponent to the Pahlavi reforms.[37] Like Nuri before him, Khomeini's main early concern was the perceived dilution of Islamic law and the clergy's traditional role in society. Khomeini not only considered clerical authority under attack by the Pahlavi regime, but also threatened by intellectuals and Muslim reformists. The latter were of particular concern to Khomeini because they framed their modernist critiques within the frame of religion. Prominent Iranian historian Ahmad Kasravi, for example, was accused by Khomeini of espousing anti-clerical ideas. Khomeini saw the anti-clericalism of modernist intellectuals such as Kasravi as an insidious threat to Shiism. He likened their critiques to the virulent anti-Shiite sectarianism advocated by the fourteenth century Sunni theologian Ibn Taymiyya and the puritanical, Wahhabist form of Sunnism patronized by Saudi Arabia's ruling family. Or, as Khomeini put it, intellectuals were parroting "Ibn Taymiyya and the savages of Najd" and "the camel-herders of Riyadh."[38] Khomeini further argued:

You [secular intellectuals and Muslim reformists] want to reduce the power of the clergy and to eliminate its honour among the people, you are committing the greatest treason to the country. The undermining of clerical influence produces defects in the country one hundredth of which hundreds of Ministers of Justice and Police Departments cannot repair.[39]

Khomeini also took the Pahlavi regime to task for its reforms concerning dress, writing: "They have put chamber-pot-shaped hats over your heads and gladdened your hearts with naked [i.e., unveiled] women in the middle of the streets and swimming pools."[40] These statements exemplify Khomeini's rhetorical approach to defending Shiite traditionalism and clerical authority from the onslaught of secularism. In this regard, his political project can be seen as an extension of Nuri's during the Constitutional Revolution. This period of Khomeini's activism marked the young cleric's entrance into the political sphere; an arena he would come to dominate later in his career.[41]

World War II brought increased foreign intervention to Iran. Both the British and the Soviets had strategic interests in Iran and used their political might to undermine the Pahlavi regime's autonomy. The British and Soviet militaries respectively occupied southern and northern Iran during the war, and continued to have troops on the ground for years to come. The Soviets used their supremacy in the north to instigate uprisings among the Azeri Turkish (1945) and Kurdish (1946) minorities of Iran's northwest.[42] The United States also had a small presence in Iran during this time, sending advisors such as Colonel Norman Schwarzkopf—father of US Army General H. Norman Scharzkopf Jr.—to help develop Iran's gendarmerie and internal security force along the American model.

Despite the political interests of the Soviets, their paramount concern centered on Iran's oil.[43] However, while the Soviets and Americans were blocked from gaining oil concessions by Iran's Majles, the British had already established a monopoly over Iran's vast oil reserves in the south through the Anglo-Iranian Oil Company (AIOC).[44] Anglo-Iranian's control over Iran's southern oil fields was granted in a concession by the Qajar Shah in 1909. Resentment against this concession had been steadily growing throughout Iran since before the war, and by the late 1940s it had become the number one issue among Iran's opposition factions. Iranian discontentment focused on two key issues: (1) the exploitative financial arrangement between the Iranian government and AIOC, which saw Iran receiving less that 25 percent of AIOC's annual profits; (2) the appalling working and living conditions of laborers at the AIOC refinery in Abadan in southwestern Iran. The director of Iran's petroleum institute during this period comments on the predicament of Iranian AIOC workers:

Wages were fifty cents a day. There was no vacation pay, no sick leave, no disability compensation. The workers lived in a shantytown called Kaghazabad, or Paper City, without running water or electricity, let alone such luxuries as iceboxes or fans. In winter the earth flooded and became a flat, perspiring lake. The mud in town was knee-deep. . . . When the rains subsided, clouds of nipping, small-winged flies rose from the stagnant waters to fill the nostrils, collecting in black mounds . . . and jamming the fans at the refinery. . . . Summer was worse. . . . The heat was horrid, the worst I've ever known—sticky and unrelenting— while the wind and sandstorms whipped off the desert hot as a blower. The dwellings in Kaghazabad, cobbled from rusted oil drums hammered flat, turned into sweltering ovens. . . . In every crevice hung the foul, sulfurous stench of burning oil—a pungent reminder that every day twenty thousand barrels, or one million tons a year, were being consumed indiscriminately for the functioning of the refinery, and AIOC never paid the [Iranian] government a cent for it.[45]

These comments echo the sentiments felt by Iranian activists during this period. While the nationalist faction led by lawyer and Majles member Mohammad Mossadeq spearheaded the campaign against the AIOC, activists connected to senior Shiite clergy took the most drastic steps.[46] The Fada'iyan-e Islam, a small group of young radicals associated with the prominent Shiite cleric Ayatollah Abol-Qasem Kashani, gained considerable notoriety for a series of high-profile assassinations during the 1940s and 1950s.[47] Formed in 1945 by Sayyed Mojtaba Navvab-Safavi, a young seminarian and former AIOC employee, the Fada'iyan-e Islam was the first Shiite Islamist organization to employ terrorism as a primary method of political activism. Similar to Khomeini, Navvab-Safavi first came to public attention in 1945 for his outspoken public lectures in Abadan castigating the "evil" anti-clericalism promoted in Ahmad Kasravi's writings. A year later, Navvab-Safavi and two of his followers (with the blessings of Shiite religious leaders) assassinated Kasravi and the writer's secretary. The assassination of Kasravi was hailed by some Shiite clergy as a righteous act.[48] The Fada'iyan later articulated the motivation for Kasravi's murder in their newspaper, *Manshur-e Baradari* (The Brotherhood Circular):

For the first time in 1324 [1946], the sparkling fire of these manly youth burned the life and existence of Ahmad Kasravi, who was the greatest tool of the British imperialists and who was the agent assigned to create division among Muslims and to prepare the grounds for exploitative domination. . . . The bullet that struck his brain forced the British to retreat for a few years.[49]

Over the next few years, the Fada'iyan continued to assassinate prominent political figures. Their most notorious killing was that of Iran's prime minister Ali Razmara. Razmara had been in charge of negotiating a new oil agreement with the AIOC, but the agreement he proposed to the Majles went against popular sentiment of the period, which favored nationalization of the oil industry. Blamed as the main impediment to oil nationalization, Razmara was killed in 1951 by the Fada'iyan. Navvab-Safavi later took credit for the assassination in 1954 during a speech to the Muslim Brotherhood in Egypt, reportedly telling the crowd of fellow Muslim activists: "I killed Razmara."[50]

After Razmara's murder, Ayatollah Kashani broke off support for the Fada'iyan. He had entered into the National Front coalition of Mohammad Mossadeq, and once the latter had been installed as prime minister in April 1951, Kashani could no longer be an advocate for the Fada'iyan's antigovernmental violence. This split signaled a growing divide between the more quietist senior clergy and the growing militancy of a younger generation. Even though the Fada'iyan saw their project as a continuation of Fazlollah Nuri's pro-clerical struggle, their militancy and use of terrorism marked their movement as the beginning of something new. In the organization's manifesto, the Fada'iyan proclaim their readiness to restore Islamic purity to Iran and violently purge all signs of Western imperialistic influence from Muslim society. The Fada'iyan warned Iran's leaders:

> If you do not follow our instructions immediately or are slipshod in carrying them out, with the help of God, we shall destroy you and take revenge for the disrespect and crimes that you have committed against Islam and Muslims. We shall establish the just and rightful Islamic government and carry out all the rules of Islam. We shall put an end to the long-lived miseries of the Muslim Iranian nation with the help of God.[51]

With the Fada'iyan, a new ideological strand of Shiite Islam began to emerge: an ideology that promoted both pro-clerical and anti-imperialist positions through direct activism and political violence.

Mohammad Mossadeq came to power on an anti-imperialist platform that advocated the nationalization of Iran's oil. With a broad coalition that included secularist, communist, and religious parties, Mossadeq began his short-lived tenure as prime minister by signing a bill that nationalized Iran's oil industry. This move infuriated the British, who not only considered Iranian oil to be their rightful domain but also feared that reverberations of Iran's nationalization would undermine their interests in other parts of the Third World. The British set plans to retake Iran's oil fields by force; however, American president Harry Truman intervened and called a halt to British aggression. Truman, who was sympathetic to the demands of the Iranians, tried to solve the dispute diplomatically. The intransigence of both the British and Mossadeq hindered Truman's efforts. The British and their allies organized a blockade against Iran's oil exports. This had a crippling effect on the Iranian economy and weakened Mossadeq's position at home. When President Dwight Eisenhower took office in 1953, his administration quickly turned against Mossadeq due to the later unfounded fear that the increasingly alienated Mossadeq would turn to the Soviets for support. Through a conspiracy between the CIA, MI6, and anti-Mossadeq elements in Iran that included the supporters of leading clergy such as Ayatollah Kashani, the CIA orchestrated a coup d'état that toppled Mossadeq and reinstalled Mohammad Reza Shah on August 19, 1953. This coup, code-named "Operation Ajax," marked an end to Mossadeq's popular anti-imperialist campaign and introduced the United States as the dominant foreign power in Iran.[52]

## Revolutionary Ideology

After the 1953 coup, the clergy—who had largely turned against Mossadeq near the end of his tenure—briefly aligned themselves with the Shah's regime and were allowed a limited degree of political freedom.[53] Without prominent clerical support, antigovernmental activism met with little success. A failed assassination attempt on the new prime minister in 1955 by a Fada'iyan member led to the arrests of several Fada'iyan activists and the execution of its top four leaders (including Navvab-Safavi) in 1956.[54] Such stiff government action forced most anti-imperialist and religious activists to remain underground for the next several years. During this time, the Third World was experiencing great upheaval. Egypt's nationalization of the Suez Canal (1956), the Cuban Revolution (1959), and the Algerian war for independence (1954–1962) were but a few monumental episodes that signified the power of anti-imperialist movements and the successes they could achieve. Combined with the Shah's repressive policies and the increasing political influence of the United States, the spread of revolutionary thought helped fuel anti-imperialist and antigovernmental dissent in Iran. By the early 1960s, Iranian intellectuals and religious leaders began to develop their own revolutionary ideas—ideas both inspired by and formed in response to the ideologies of Third World resistance. Iranian religious ideologies used Shiite culture and symbolism as mediums through which new forms of radical political thinking could be expressed.[55]

Revolutionary literature influenced some of Iran's leading intellectuals. One of these, Ali Shariati, became familiar with revolutionary politics while pursuing a doctorate in sociology at the University of Paris.[56] By 1962, Shariati had become convinced that only a revolutionary movement could topple the Pahlavi regime and liberate Iran from Western imperialism. In Paris, Shariati became familiar with the anti-colonialist works of Jean-Paul Sartre and Frantz Fanon. Fanon's writings had a particular effect on Shariati, so much so that Shariati translated Fanon's *Wretched of the Earth* (1961) into Persian, entitling the Persian edition *Oppressed (mostaz'afin) of the Earth*. In this book, Fanon addresses "natives" of the Third World, encouraging them to rise up against Western colonialism and create new societies, which instead of merely imitating the West would find their own path. Drawing on his experiences fighting for the Front de Libération Nationale (FLN) during the Algerian war against France, Fanon argued that foreign dominion over Third World societies was inherently violent, and, as such, required greater violence to overcome:

> The exploited man sees that his liberation implies the use of all means, and that of force first and foremost. . . . [C]olonialism only loosens its hold when the knife is at its throat . . . [it] is not a thinking machine, nor a body endowed with reasoning faculties. It is violence in its natural state, and it will only yield when confronted with greater violence.[57]

Inspired by Fanon, Shariati developed an entirely new interpretation of Shiism, reformulating the religion into a revolutionary ideology. Shariati argued that God had created Islam as a dynamic ideology to lead the Muslim community (*ummat*) to a classless utopia. In this schema, Islamic terms such as *towhid* (monotheism) and *jihad* were recast as "social solidarity" and "liberation struggle." The imams Ali and Husayn became revolutionary heroes, with the latter likened to a premodern Che Guevara.[58] Husayn's battle at Karbala became the ultimate metaphor for revolutionary struggle of the oppressed versus the oppressors. For Shariati, Shiism was a complete ideology superior to all other political systems, including capitalism and Marxism—the latter having gained wide currency in Third World resistance movements. In his words:

> Shiites do not accept the path chosen by history. They negate the leadership which ruled over history and deceived the majority of the people [i.e., Sunnism] through its succession to the Prophet. . . . Shiites turn their backs on the opulent mosques and magnificent palaces of the caliphs of Islam and turn to the lonely, mud house of Fatima. Shiites, who represent the oppressed, justice-seeking class in the caliphate system, find, in this house, whatever and whoever they have been seeking [to overthrow the existing order].[59]

Shariati considered the clergy and their centuries-old hold over Islam to be one of the main impediments to the progression of Muslim society. He argued that there were two versions of Shiism: "red" Shiism, the true essence of revolutionary Islam, and "black" Shiism, the stagnant tradition of the clergy or what Shiism had become.[60] In order to restore true, "red" Shiism, Shariati argued, it was incumbent upon intellectuals (*rowshanfekran*) to "rediscover and revitalize the original meaning of revolutionary Islam."[61] Shariati considered both his writing and teaching to be laying the groundwork for the revitalization of Shiite Islam and revolution in Iran.

Shariati's message inspired scores of activists during the 1960s and 1970s. He was considered by some leaders of the Iranian revolution of 1979 to be *the* ideologue of the revolution. His mix of Marxist ideology, Third Worldist anti-imperialism, Shiite symbolism, and Iranian nationalism proved to be a powerful combination. Young Muslim activists who found the traditionalism of the clergy lacking in political sophistication and vigor were inspired by Shariati's leftist radicalism and its strong Islamic foundation.[62] Most clergy, however, considered Shariati dangerous to Islam and a Marxist in disguise. His pro-intellectual and anti-clerical stance enraged the religious leaders who accused him of "Wahhabist" (i.e., anti-clerical) tendencies. Mohsen Makhmalbaf, noted contemporary filmmaker and a teenage activist during this period, relates how he was inspired by a local mosque preacher to confront and perhaps assassinate Shariati:

> And so, it was around this time that Shari'ati was coming to be known. We were already beginning to think more seriously about armed resistance, and so when this person Shari'ati came along and was starting to undermine Shiite causes, it seemed crucial to find him. I went with some of the other guys to investigate whether or not to kill Shari'ati. . . . I went [to his school] and listened to him speak, to hear what he was saying—I was thinking who is this person they [the clergy] say is attacking Imam Ali? He spoke for four hours, and I never returned to that mosque. I became a devotee of Shari'ati. . . . The next day I began distributing Shari'ati's books, and they barred me from the mosque, from the library, people from the neighborhood began to avoid me, and I was treated like an infidel. But I kept on buying Shari'ati's books and giving them to my friends. . . . I read all of his books from beginning to end, twice over. I became a new person.[63]

Shariati was particularly popular on university campuses where his radical reinterpretation of Shiism resonated with young middle-class Muslim students. Some of these students were inspired by Shariati's call to take up armed resistance against the Pahlavi regime. The most important group to emerge at this time was the Mojahedin-e Khalq Organization (MKO).[64] The MKO, or People's Mojahedin, began in 1965 as a revolutionary guerilla movement committed to the Islamic ideology of Shariati and inspired by the liberation movements of the Third World. They wanted to end foreign control over Iran and sever America's support from the Pahlavi regime. After the 1953 coup, the United States had an increasingly visible presence in Iran. As America was the main patron of the Pahlavi regime, many Iranian activists considered it complicit in the Shah's repressive policies. Thus, in order to undermine the Shah, the MKO decided to target American interests and personnel in Iran. Like the Fada'iyan-e Islam before them, the MKO used assassinations and terrorism as their method of political activism, murdering several American servicemen and civilian contractors in the 1970s. However, unlike the Fada'iyan, the MKO were disconnected from the clergy and advocated against traditional Shiite authority. By the mid-1970s, the Shah had imprisoned and executed most MKO activists, though a small cell under the leadership of Masud Rajavi survived and expanded its ranks in prison, later emerging as a significant force after the 1979 revolution.[65]

Revolutionary ideas were also gaining steam within clerical circles during this period. The brief rapprochement between the clergy and the Pahlavi regime had fallen apart by the early 1960s as the clergy renewed its vocal criticism of the Shah's social reforms.[66] The Shah responded with a crackdown on clerical activists, culminating in the violent sacking of Qom's main theological college, Fayziyyeh, in March 1963. This event further radicalized a number of leading clerics and seminary students, and provoked public outcry against the Pahlavi regime. At the head of the dissent was Ayatollah Khomeini, who had become the leading clerical opponent to the Shah. Khomeini considered the Shah's crackdown on the clergy an attempt to destroy Islam in Iran. In June of that year, during the Shiite commemoration of Ashura, Khomeini delivered a speech which likened the Shah's oppression of the clergy to the violent oppression of the early imams by the Umayyads. Just as the Umayyads had tried to destroy the family of Muhammad, Khomeini argued, the Shah's actions proved the regime was "fundamentally opposed to Islam itself and the existence of the religious class." Khomeini also played on anti-imperialist themes, evoking the memory of the British and Soviet occupations during World War II, and suggested Israel had influenced the Shah's attack.[67]

By 1964, intense clashes between pro-clerical elements and government forces resulted in Khomeini's exile. Traveling first to Turkey and then settling in the Shiite center of Najaf, Iraq, for thirteen years, Khomeini continued to criticize the Pahlavi regime and call for its overthrow. It was during this period that Khomeini articulated his solution to the dilemmas facing Muslim nations as the establishment of Islamic governments.[68] Khomeini argued that following the usurpation of Ali's rule by Muawiya, Islamic society had been governed by monarchies that separated temporal authority from religious authority. It was this division—akin to the separation of church and state—that was the root of

Islam's problems. For Islam to truly reach its potential, Khomeini contended, Muslim states must be led by the clergy. Khomeini termed this form of Islamic government the *velayat-e faqih* or the "guardianship of the jurist." In Khomeini's estimation, a true Islamic government must be headed by a senior cleric (*marja al-taqlid*) or by a committee of similarly high-ranking clergy (*fuqaha*). This role would give the ruling jurist (*vali-ye faqih*) the same temporal function—but not status—as the imams. The jurist would be in charge of "the administration of the country, and the implementation of the sacred laws of the *shari'a*."[69] Khomeini argued that establishing the government of the jurist would "deliver Islamic countries from the clutches of imperialism" and restore justice to Islamic society.[70]

Although Khomeini's concept of *velayat-e faqih* was unpopular among the leading clergy of the early 1970s because it went against the clergy's traditional aversion to government involvement, his influence over the revolutionary movement in Iran continued to grow. Through the distribution of works and sermons, Khomeini's popularity became widespread. Khomeini used vague catchphrases—such as "Islam is for equality and social justice," "Islam will eliminate class differences," and "The duty of the clergy is to liberate the hungry from the clutches of the rich"—which played to populist sentiments to inspire the Shiite masses.[71] One of these—the oft-cited "Every day is Ashura, every land is Karbala"—evoked the memory of Imam Husayn and equated current socio-political upheavals with Imam Husayn's righteous struggle against injustice and oppression. By the revolutionary period of 1978–1979, Khomeini had positioned himself as both a staunch anti-imperialist and a champion of Islam. The main elements of Khomeini's political thought, what I will call Khomeinism— radical anti-imperialism, economically conscious Shiite populism, and Islamic government under clerical rule—garnered him wide support among Islamist segments of the guerilla movement, activist clergy, and other revolutionary leaders. Such support and that of the hopeful masses enabled Khomeini and his supporters to seize control of post-revolutionary Iran and establish an Islamic Republic under the rule of the guardian jurist (*vali-ye faqih*).

# 3

# Vanguard of the Imam

I have said time and time again that to build a society on the basis of the principles of Islam is an ideological choice, not just a religious one. Islam in fact is an ideology, in which religion represents one aspect. In our view of the world, it is the people who interpret divine will and therefore the Islamic Republic can only be based on the peoples' will, in other words, universal suffrage.[1]

Our nation gave its blood to create an Islamic Republic, not a democratic republic.[2]

—Ruhollah Khomeini, 1979

Revolutionary fervor erupted across Iran in 1978. Pressure against Iran's ruling monarch, Mohammad Reza Shah, was widespread and intense. Civil disobedience on a massive scale—general strikes, popular demonstrations, and urban violence—was gradually eroding the foundations of the Pahlavi throne. Numerous groups championing a host of conflicting ideologies were involved in the tumult. Major political organizations active at this time included the relatively pragmatic, pro-democratic Liberation Movement of Iran, headed by Mehdi Bazargan; the National Front, a nationalist party of Mossadegh loyalists; the Islamist-Marxist Mojahedin-e Khalq; the communist (pro-Soviet) Tudeh Party; and the Marxist People's Fadai. Islamists loyal to Ayatollah Khomeini and other clerics were another significant faction in the activism. Various smaller groups and unaligned members of the intelligentsia and traditional (bazaari) merchant class also played vital roles. What held these elements together was shared antipathy for the Shah and a fierce desire for Iran to be free from foreign political influence and from the United States in particular.

Political groups were important, but the real force on the ground was that of the people. Everyday Iranians—students, teachers, bazaari merchants, workers, seminarians, local mosque congregants—were the front line activists whose efforts brought the Pahlavi regime to the brink of collapse. Indecisive and insecure, the Shah and his reactive policies did little to slow the cascading revolution.

The monarch was hesitant to crack down too hard, worried that stiff repression would escalate the situation. To appease the opposition, the monarch incrementally ceded more ground to them, including certain liberalizing reforms and the release of thousands of political prisoners. The concessions did not work. Instead they emboldened the revolutionary movement, confirming to the opposition that the pressure they were imposing on the Shah was weakening his hold on power.[3] Riots across Iranian cities became increasingly destructive and acts of rebellion became more violent. An especially bloody incident occurred on August 19—the thirty-fifth anniversary of the 1953 coup—when Islamist activists killed 480 civilians after they set fire to a popular cinema in the southern city of Abadan to protest Western influence. The government responded to the intensifying disorder by declaring martial law on September 8. That evening government troops fired on demonstrators who had gathered at Tehran's Jaleh Square, killing at least dozens.[4] The event became known as Black Friday and was one of the events that galvanized Iranians against the Pahlavi regime.

The revolution was aided by Ayatollah Khomeini's expulsion from Iraq and subsequent relocation to the Paris suburb of Neauphle-le-Château in October. Now in France, Khomeini and Iran's revolutionary movement were thrust into the spotlight. Foreign media met with the septuagenarian senior cleric almost daily, taking with them quotes and testaments that helped fuel activism in Iran. He spoke to the issues that unified Iran's opposition while deftly avoiding his own objectives which would later prove divisive and exclusionary. Opposition leaders traveled to Neauphle-le-Château for audiences with Khomeini, seeking to associate themselves with his project and confirm their place in the movement against the Shah. These acts codified Khomeini as the leader of Iran's revolution. The attention he received from the international media further solidified that perception both internationally and in Iran. Non-Islamist opposition figures did not necessarily agree with Khomeini's religion-based ideas, but they were willing to see in him an authentic national savior. He was a senior Shiite cleric whose religious authority added legitimacy to their aspirations for political freedom and a genuine Iranian alternative to the Westernism of the Shah.

By mid-January 1979, the pressure against the Shah had increased to such an extent that the monarch fled the country with his family. What remained was a civilian government with limited authority and no popular recognition. Iran's generals were neutered by their own indecision and Washington's insistence that they give the new civilian government time before contemplating a coup d'état.[5] When Khomeini returned to Iran on February 1, 1979, the revolution was nearly complete. A popular slogan declared, "Shah raft, Imam amad," or "The Shah has gone, the Imam has come!" Khomeini was the Imam, the leader of Iran's revolution. He was the "idol-smasher," a title that, similar to "imam," adorned his political leadership with a sense of divinity. These terms resonated with Iranian activists across the political spectrum, but they held far deeper meaning with Khomeini's devotees, who saw in him an unparalleled religious authority and political leader.

Among his most ardent supporters was the Islamic Revolutionary Guards Corps, or IRGC. The organization had been erected as Khomeini's vanguard and the self-proclaimed defender of his revolution. As the strong arm of Khomeini's political project, the IRGC's impact on the post-revolution was pronounced. In the first year of the revolution, the Guards transformed from a poorly funded, loose coalition of Islamist guerilla factions into a formidable armed force with a national reach. With the backing of Khomeini and his clerical cadre, the IRGC was able to act with impunity. It suppressed rival organizations through intimidation and violence, and helped commute the diverse 1979 revolution into a distinctly Khomeinist enterprise. In the IRGC, Khomeini's ideological and religious authority was fused with the effective organization of armed force and coercion. This, perhaps more than any other factor, enabled Khomeini to dominate his opponents and establish a regime in his image.

## Enter the Vanguard

Ayatollah Khomeini's return to Iran after fifteen years of exile symbolized the end of monarchical rule in Iran. Arriving on the heels of the mass strikes and demonstrations that had crippled the Pahlavi regime and led to the flight of the Shah on January 16, 1979, Khomeini's return amplified an already nearly complete revolution. For the next several days, armed revolutionaries clashed with the remaining state entities loyal to the Pahalvi regime. The most significant confrontation occurred between the revolutionaries and the military. Although numerous military defections had already occurred in the buildup to the "three glorious days" of February 9 to 11,[6] the military remained the last bulwark against the revolutionary movement.[7] The turning point came on February 9 when a group of eight hundred air force technicians and mechanics, known as the Homafaran, defected en masse and joined the revolutionary struggle. After watching a replay of Khomeini's return on state television, Homafaran stationed at Dowshan Tappeh airbase in Tehran demonstrated in support of the senior cleric, provoking a violent reaction by loyalist Imperial Guards. The confrontation soon turned into an armed conflict between the Imperial Guards and the rebelling Homafaran, who were later joined by militants from major revolutionary groups—the Marxist-Leninist People's Fadai and the Islamist-Marxist Mojahedin-e Khalq Organization (MKO)—in an effort to overtake the airbase. Fighting continued through the following morning when the fighters finally succeeded in overtaking the airbase's barracks and looted the armory. The weapons from the armory were sent to mosques and other community centers to be distributed among revolutionary elements.[8]

The repercussions of the Dowshan Tappeh takeover were massive. Revolutionary organizations, especially the People's Fadai, used the event to bring their members and supporters together in a centralized manner, instilling a sense of group solidarity that helped in the effective coordination of further attacks.[9] Revolutionary elements began attacking police stations throughout the city, leading to the capturing of additional armories and weapons stores, which provided the militants with a flush of arms. The once proud military began to collapse from within. Mass defections of all ranks took place, including the top commanders of the Imperial Guards, Generals Neshat and Biglari, who ordered the complete surrender of their units.[10] By the morning of February 11, the Supreme Council of the Armed Forces convened a meeting during which a declaration of neutrality was drafted. The announcement of this declaration on state radio that afternoon sealed the fate of the Pahlavi regime and signaled victory for the revolutionary movement.

The revolution ushered in a period of transition and consolidation. Although Khomeini was the clear charismatic authority and acknowledged leader of the revolution, political power in the post-revolutionary regime was divided into two main camps: (1) the Provisional Government under Prime Minister Mehdi Bazargan, which was appointed by Khomeini but composed of members from the non-clerical middle class; and (2) the Revolutionary Council, led by Khomeini and dominated by anonymous members of the clergy.[11] The Provisional Government took charge of the fractured institutions of the police, gendarmerie, and military, and held responsibility for general administration. It played a subordinate role to the Revolutionary Council, however, which had influence over the vast network of revolutionary committees (komitehs), mosque-oriented gangs (hezbollahis), the revolutionary courts, and the Revolutionary Guards. Beyond these official centers of power, the post-revolutionary regime also had to contend with the numerous guerilla organizations, political parties, independent clergy, and localized militias that did not fall under the control of either the Provisional Government or the Revolutionary Council.[12]

Although the government controlled the police and military, both of these institutions were near-paralyzed by the damage they incurred during the revolution.[13] Both also suffered from an association with the previous regime, which gained them little favor in revolutionary circles. The vacuum created by the absence of these security forces at the local level was quickly filled by the numerous armed militias and neighborhood gangs that thrived in the resulting anarchy. Law and order took a back seat to vigilante justice and the settling of vendettas. The entire infrastructure of Iranian society, from basic governmental services to the rule of law, had been crippled by the revolution. In response, the Khomeinist-aligned militias became increasingly active in all aspects of society across the country, partially filling the void left by the shattered security forces.

It was in this context that that the Revolutionary Guards first appeared. Elements operating under the banner of the "Guardians of the Islamic Revolution" (*pasdaran-e enqelab-e eslami*) had been active throughout Iranian cities within days of Khomeini's return on February 1, 1979. The first communiqué released by an organization calling itself the "Islamic Revolutionary Guards Corps" (*sepah-e pasdaran-e enqelab-e eslami*) was on February 21, 1979. The IRGC considers this the organization's first official message, but in truth the organization had not fully coalesced yet.[14] Initially, the Guards were associated with the command staff (*setad*) of the Khomeini-appointed revolutionary committees and worked in conjunction with them and other Khomeinist militias.[15] The Guards functioned similarly to other militias in that they were primarily involved in fighting loyalist elements and were utilized to help secure important positions and telecommunications centers.[16] At times their areas of responsibility also included more mundane matters, such as directing traffic and trash removal.[17] What separated the Guards from other militias, however, was the suggestion that they served in an official capacity under the post-revolutionary regime. This was partly due to Khomeini's inclusion of the Guards in some of his early messages concerning Iran's military. For instance, on February 14, Khomeini released a message to the "struggling soldiers" who had defected from the military in solidarity with the Islamic revolution. In this message, Khomeini commands these soldiers to "return to their relevant garrisons and units at the earliest opportunity and continue their sacred military service as the struggling soldiers of Islam." He adds, "It is necessary that the soldiers in service—the *guardians of the revolution* and the fighting sons of Islam—report to their relevant garrisons as soon as this message reaches them."[18] In this way, Khomeini hinted at a more official role for the Guards, which, unlike the committees and unofficial militias, placed them in the arena of Iran's national armed forces.

The Provisional Government's first official statement on the Revolutionary Guards implied something similar. During a February 21 press interview with the deputy prime minister, Amir Entezam, the government announced that the Revolutionary Guards "Corps" would be formed and that the rules and regulations of its formation had already been established. Entezam suggested that the "decision" to establish the Guards Corps was made by the government, insinuating that the new Guards Corps was to be an organ of the Provisional Government.[19] This interview is the first time that the government referred to the Revolutionary Guards as a "Corps" (*sepah*).[20] This distinction elevated the

Guards—at least in name—from a disparate band of militants into a lawful armed force associated with the government. This was an important transition for the Revolutionary Guards that publicly strengthened their organizational legitimacy.

Despite this announcement, however, neither the government nor its prime minister, Mehdi Bazargan, seemed to have much confidence in the IRGC as an effective military institution. In his February 28 address, Bazargan highlighted the immense damage that the Iranian military had suffered as a result of the revolution. While he stressed the need for the public's cooperation in achieving stability, he also lambasted the revolutionary militias that called for the complete disbandment of the "imperialist" army and its replacement by a people's army composed of the revolutionary militias themselves. On this point, Bazargan asked:

> Could the safeguarding of the realm and the defense of its borders—and at that a realm as vast as ours on which eyes are focused from the four corners of the world—be possible without an army? Could a people's army or revolution guards be able so soon to take the place of regular, well-equipped armies, which possess aircraft, tanks, armored cars, and thousands of technical and military items? Could the training of such a cadre, which has been prepared after spending billions of dollars, be achieved so easily? Is there any country in the world, whether leftist, rightist, old or new, which could protect itself without an army?[21]

Bazargan's speech highlighted a tension between the radical revolutionary camp and the government. Like Khomeini, Bazargan stressed the importance of the military to Iran's national sovereignty, an idea criticized by the left and much of the Islamist bloc (including IRGC leadership) which considered the military a bastion of Pahlavi influence and a tool of Western imperialism.[22] Khomeini and the government argued that the revolutionary militias (including the Guards) lacked the training, expertise, and discipline needed to effectively protect the vulnerable post-revolutionary regime from outside forces.[23] Both Khomeini and the government seemed to question the loyalty of the major leftist militias—the Fadai, MKO, and Tudeh—and, while both the Revolutionary Council and the government appeared to be backing the Revolutionary Guards, neither seemed ready to trust them with the military's arsenal.

The government, however, continued to stress the IRGC as a "national army" that would, in time, "operate as an army alongside" the country's other armed forces.[24] The government suggested that, before the organization could reach the stage of a martial institution complementary to Iran's other national forces, a national recruitment effort would have to begin and the new (and existing) troops would need professional military training.[25] Such public statements by the government portrayed the IRGC as an institution that was in the initial stages of formation and had yet to begin its official duties.[26] The reality, however, was that militants operating under the name of the Revolutionary Guards had been already active throughout the country. By late March, Guards had been involved in security details, arrests, arms collection, and armed conflict throughout Iran, most notably in the cities of Tehran, Shiraz, Abadan, Qom, Mashhad, Sari, Tabriz, and Gonbad-e Kavus.

In each location, IRGC units seemed to operate independently and in different capacities.[27] The Guards of Mashhad, for example, underwent military training with advisors from the Palestinian Liberation Organization,[28] and Guards in Abadan established a "naval unit" to patrol the area waterways and prevent political dissidents from leaving the country.[29] In Gonbad-e Kavus, a contingent of Guards clashed with demonstrating Turkmen residents, setting a precedent for the IRGC in the suppression of similar ethnic uprisings that began to erupt around Iran's periphery. The Guards in Tehran were involved in numerous operations aimed at securing key positions and combating dissent, while the Guards in Qom and Sari were largely involved in security details and weapons collection. Although its units were highly localized, the Corps also developed a more national, centralized presence in the form of a Command Headquarters (*setad-e farmandehi*), which released its first public announcement on March 24.[30]

The highly individual character of local IRGC units and the relative autonomy with which they operated led to numerous reports of abuse. Most of the incidents arose as a result of the Guards' broad effort of disarming the populace and its arrests and detentions of suspected counterrevolutionaries as an arm of the shadowy revolutionary courts—areas in which the committees were also involved. These abuses gained national and international attention after the press reported that two sons and a "non-Iranian" daughter-in-law of Iran's second most popular cleric, Ayatollah Mahmud Taleqani, had been arrested, beaten, and detained for sixteen hours by elements of the IRGC.[31] The main target of the arrest was Mojtaba Taleqani, a member of the Marxist-Leninist Paykar Organization,[32] who was suspected of illegally possessing firearms.[33] As a sign of protest, Ayatollah Taleqani went into hiding, causing public outcry against the arrests and similar maltreatment linked to the Guards and committees.[34] Taleqani's widespread support among democratic and leftist organizations, as well as his allies in the Provisional Government (such as his protégé Mehdi Bazargan), led to numerous demonstrations calling for his return. These protests, especially those organized by the MKO and Fadai, exposed a growing rift between the parties and organizations that looked toward Taleqani for moral legitimacy and those forces loyal to Ayatollah Khomieni.[35] Faced with building public pressure and mounting discontentment, both the government and Revolutionary Council were forced to address the incident.

Through its own investigation, the Revolutionary Council concluded that neither the "official committees of the Imam [nor] the leadership of the corps of the Revolutionary Guards" were involved in the incident. However, they conceded that "not all the branches of the corps of the Revolutionary Guards" had "been brought completely under the control of the Revolutionary Council," thereby suggesting some complicity on the part of the local Guards.[36] Khomeini met with Taleqani in Qom to help resolve the issue, which led to some assurances by the former that the committees would be purged of "seditious elements." Taleqani, for his part, blamed neither the committees nor the Guards directly, but rather suggested that the abuses of power had come from "irresponsible people" who had "penetrated the committees and made trouble in the name of revolutionary guards," but who were not themselves "the real revolutionary guards."[37]

Khomeini soon altered his pledge in a meeting with the heads of Tehran's fourteen revolutionary committees. Instead of "purging" or "abolishing" the committees, Khomeini suggested the committees should be "reformed" and "seditious" members removed. He blamed the abuses on agents of foreign powers—"most likely Americans"—and argued that they emboldened the opposition. Khomeini assured the committees that they would "remain in force until the authority of the Government is established," which would be manifested by the "achievement of disarming." Likewise, he added: "[w]e shall not remove the guardians, so that the way will not be free for our enemies. We shall strengthen the guardians and the committees until the day when the Government will be able to maintain a firm conduct of affairs."[38]

The government's response was also mixed, but appeared more critical of the IRGC. The Chief Public Prosecutor's office curtailed the authority of the committees and the Guards by invalidating all official warrants for the "detention of persons or property, or for the search of houses" previously issued to both groups, thereby suspending them from such activity.[39] In a press conference, Amir Entezam denied that either Khomeini's committees or the revolutionary courts had been involved in the matter. "Rather," he asserted, it was "the guardians [who] had arbitrarily got themselves involved in the incident."[40] A few days later, Prime Minister Bazargan partially contradicted his deputy by placing indirect blame on elements of both the committees and the Guards.[41] Although he maintained the abuses were committed by rogue elements, he argued that vigilante tactics associated with these groups were undermining the goals of the revolution. Citing the Taleqani incident and numerous accounts of similar abuse, Bazargan continued:

The Iranian nation has now acquired a state of instability. Everyone is asking about and is fearful that if the committees, the guards and those individuals who are acting in the names of the committees, guards and—most shamelessly and in a most cowardly way—in the name of the Imam—and have arms in their possession—continue to act in a similar vein, and should the current state of affairs continue as it is, what would ultimately happen to this realm, nation, people and our republic? When guilty and innocent people continue to be arrested for reasons of personal enmity and personal motives, life itself can no longer exist let alone progress.[42]

The IRGC publically addressed the issue. Concurrent with the announcements on their establishment and areas of responsibility, the Guards released an additional statement blaming "opportunistic elements" for the recent abuses. They acknowledged that "for some time now a number of people, in the guise of members of the committees and officials of the Islamic Revolutionary Guards Corps, have been looting the people's property and households by threat and intimidation, entering houses in Tehran and the provinces." They "condemned" these "ugly actions" and reminded the public that "no official has the right to enter houses on the authority of the Islamic Public Prosecutor without presenting his identity card and written orders from the Revolutionary Guards and the committee." Finally, the Guards asked for the public's help in identifying and turning in these rogue elements.[43] In this way, the IRGC confirmed what had already been suggested by the post-revolutionary regime and blamed not its own cadre, but rather those who operated inappropriately in the guise of the organization. This admission could not have been very reassuring to the public.

## Roots and Radicals

The Taleqani incident illustrated a growing division between the Khomeinist camp on the one hand, and the government, democratic organizations, and leftist groups on the other. It was a harbinger of things to come and an outgrowth of the Khomeinist camp's push for power. However, it also demonstrated the confusion surrounding the IRGC. Who exactly were the "Revolutionary Guards" and how were they distinct from the other Khomeinist committees and militias? Neither the government nor the Revolutionary Council appeared to have a firm grasp of the organization and the dynamics of its membership. Part of the problem undermining the Corps, its functionality, and its position in the post-revolutionary regime was the fluidity of its membership and lack of effective centralized control. Since its inception, the ranks of the IRGC had been occupied by activists generally operating within more than one organization—such as the Mojahedin of the Islamic Revolution, hezbollahi groups, committees, or even local gangs—simultaneously.[44] The abundance of willing participants was as much a blessing as it was a detriment to the Guards. The lack of structure allowed individual units to act with impunity, sometimes in the interest of other parties, while the multiple responsibilities of the Corps were too many and too broadly defined to be successful in the short term.[45] Lack of funding was also a problem. In the six months following its establishment, the IRGC received little support from the government despite its official mandate and was forced to rely on individual benefactors and confiscated property, arms, and vehicles to run its operations.[46] These issues highlighted the fact that the IRGC was still a new, struggling institution, which acted more like the hodgepodge collection of individual militias that it was and less like the government organ it was portrayed to be. On May 5, the IRGC boldly announced its legitimate standing:

> By the command of the illustrious leader of the Islamic Revolution, the Imam Khomeyni, the Islamic Revolutionary Guards Corps has been established under the auspices of the Revolutionary Council. The Corps Command Council has been approved and sanctioned by the Revolutionary Council. It is hoped that the chosen responsible officials and the competent persons involved, with the support of Almighty God and in accordance with the approved rules, will strive to fulfill the momentous task of the Islamic revolution and will be successful in carrying out the duties entrusted to them. [47]

Although it had attained a place in the post-revolutionary state, it was still a poorly funded, loosely bound militia, whose identity and politics were derived as much from the interests of its individual members as from Khomeini and the revolutionary regime.

Many of the challenges facing the IRGC were rooted in the provenance of the organization. According to a founding member of the Guards, Mohsen Rafiqdust, the concept behind the establishment of a post-revolution armed force composed of Islamist militants was first introduced by Hojjat al-Islam Mohammad Montazeri. In a meeting held during the buildup to the February revolution, Montazeri—an influential guerilla leader and the son of senior cleric Ayatollah Hosayn-Ali Montazeri—is said to have opined "Now that the revolution will be victorious, an armed force must be formed to safeguard the revolution."[48] Although no steps were taken at the time to create such a force, Montazeri suggested the idea to Khomeini. Shortly after the February victory, Montazeri approached Rafiqdust with the news that Khomeini had ordered the establishment of the Revolutionary Guards.[49]

Overseeing the formation of the Guards, which was initially to be under the jurisdiction of the Provisional Government, were Montazeri himself and senior cleric Ayatollah Beheshti, leader of the clerically dominated Islamic Republic Party (IRP). A mid-level cleric, Hojjat al-Islam Hasan Lahuti, was appointed Khomeini's representative to the organization, and the task of organizing the Guards' leadership was given to Rafiqdust.[50] Through meetings with the clerical leaders of the IRP (including Beheshti, Ali-Akbar Hashemi-Rafsanjani, and Ali Khamenei) and the representatives of several militant organizations, Rafiqdust and his associates established the IRGC, chose its official name, and appointed its first commanders. Ali Danesh Monfared became the first commander of the Corps; Gholam-Ali Afruz headed personnel; Engineer Zarami became the head of training; a Mr. Mahmudzadeh led additional units; and Rafiqdust was charged with logistics. Shortly afterward, these individuals formed the Central Office (*daftar-e markazi*) of the IRGC, which held its meetings in a former SAVAK headquarters.[51]

Although Rafiqdust had consulted various revolutionary leaders before establishing the IRGC, all were reticent to assimilate their forces into this burgeoning enterprise.[52] Their main objection, typified by the position held by Montazeri, was the Guards' lack of autonomy.[53] These revolutionaries had built a career on resisting state control, and, even though their revolution had been victorious, the new regime was still too young to inspire much trust. Further, militants such as Montazeri and Abbas Aqa-Zamani (more commonly known by his nom de guerre "Abu Sharif") were internationalists who were as—if not more, in Montazeri's case—committed to assisting liberation movements outside Iran as they were to creating a new society within it. Losing the independence and freedom they had fought so long for in order to join a state-controlled, national army may not have been very appealing.

Despite a refusal to absorb their forces into the IRGC, Montazeri and Abu Sharif (who also had strong ties to hezbollahi groups) were closely aligned with the organization from its inception.[54] They represented two of the four factions that made up the heart of the early IRGC.[55] The leaders of these factions— which also included Mohammad Borujerdi (representing the Mojahedin of the Islamic Revolution organization) and Rafiqdust and his associates Monfared and Zarami—formed the core of the Revolutionary Guards and elected the organization's first Central Council (*shura-ye markazi*) from among their ranks. Further elections created the Command Council, which included members of each faction: Javad Mansuri and Mohsen Kolahduz from Pasa became the chief IRGC commander and head of training, respectively; Abu Sharif was charged with operations; Yusef Forutan of MIR headed public relations; and Rafiqdust remained the head of logistics.[56] The establishment of these leadership councils and the involvement of each major faction paved the way for additional members from these factions and other groups to participate in the IRGC.[57]

Although each faction influenced the makeup and direction of the IRGC, the individuals who had perhaps the greatest impact on the organization came from the Mojahedin of the Islamic Revolution (MIR).[58] Much of MIR's success in post-revolutionary politics was due to the patronage they received from Khomeini and other revolutionary leaders. With Khomeini's support, MIR activists were placed into high-ranking positions throughout the regime, including key leadership posts in the IRGC and the committees.[59] Although MIR activists made up only a small fraction of the overall IRGC ranks, they were entrusted with many of the organization's top leadership positions.[60] Some of these initial appointments included Borujerdi, who helped in the establishment of the IRGC and later became its western regional commander, and Mohsen Rezai—a founding member of MIR and part of its central committee—who served as MIR's second representative to the Guards. Other senior MIR members, such as the aforementioned Yusef Forutan and Morteza Alviri, also became influential in the organization. Alviri, who was appointed to the Command Council, also served on the central council of the revolutionary committees.[61]

The involvement of MIR members in the new regime made its status as an independent organization unclear. The confusion surrounding MIR permeated the highest levels of the government, which at one point erroneously stated the organization had been absorbed into the IRGC.[62] Any official relationship between the two was denied by MIR, however, which declared that the organization was "in no way connected with any Government organ."[63] Although MIR remained independent, its influence on post-revolutionary institutions, particularly the IRGC, was pronounced. The MIR faction eventually became the dominant faction in the IRGC leading to the appointment of Mohsen Rezai as the organization's chief commander in 1981—a post he held until 1997.

Despite its importance in post-revolutionary politics, MIR was itself a fledgling organization. It was established in the wake of the February 1979 revolution as an umbrella organization for seven regional revolutionary groups: *Mansuran* (the Victorious, led by Mohsen Rezai), *Movahhedin* (the Monotheists), *Towhidi Saf* (the Monotheistic group, led by Mohammad Borujerdi), *Fallah* (the Peasant group, led by Alviri), *Towhidi Badr* (the Monotheistic Badr group),[64] *Falaq* (the Dawn group), and *Ommat-e Vahedeh* (Unified Nation, led by Behzad Nabavi). Some of these groups (such as Towhidi Saf and Mansuran) had been in existence prior to the revolutionary upheaval of 1978–1979; however, others (such as Ommat-e Vahedeh) were established in the midst of it. The key commonalities shared by each of these groups were their involvement in anti-shah activism and their disillusionment with the revolutionary left.

MIR's disdain for the left stemmed as much from its members' specific religious leanings as it did from their collective experience with leftist organizations, particularly the Islamist-Marxist Mojahedin-e Khalq Organization (MKO), of which many MIR leaders had once been a part.[65] The split between Islamists and the MKO took place on a number of fronts, but its epicenter was Evin prison in Tehran. The prison experience during the 1970s, as described by numerous accounts of former political prisoners, was a combative arena of ideological contestation.[66] Every group struggled to spread its politics among the inmates and increase adherents to its cause. The clash of ideas resulted in a divide between the secular left and the Islamist-minded prisoners. However, the Islamist-minded sector also eventually split, as more and more individuals became disenchanted with the Marxist tenets and autocratic culture of the MKO (then the largest of the Islamist-minded organizations).[67] This split reflected a more general deterioration of support for the MKO—and the Islamic left in general—outside of prison, particularly within the clergy, throughout the 1970s.[68] Within the prison system, the MKO utilized rumors and accusations to undermine their opponents and cast suspicion on dissenters. Mohsen Makhmalbaf, noted contemporary filmmaker and early MIR member, recalls: "they [the MKO] . . . began spreading [false] rumors . . . any person who wasn't a part of their organization was automatically considered to be associated with SAVAK."[69] The fallout of this experience split the Islamists into two opposing factions: those who supported the MKO and those who did not.[70] This emergent Islamist camp was motivated not only by its opposition to the Pahlavi regime, but increasingly by its opposition to the leftists and the MKO, which they considered equally dangerous.

It was within this charged, divisive atmosphere that the components of MIR began to take shape. For instance, one of the seven founding organizations of MIR, Ommat-e Vahedeh (the Unified Nation group), was established in 1978 by newly released political prisoners opposed to the MKO. Makhmalbaf, an original member of Ommat-e Vahedeh, discusses the impetus behind that group's establishment and MIR's initial raison d'être:

[I]n 1977 I separated myself from the [MKO]. Earlier, I had a very close relationship with them, but I didn't say anything for fear of SAVAK's taking advantage of the situation. But they themselves began spreading rumors about me, so I was forced to speak out against them. . . . And when I decided to break with the organization, at first I tried to simply remain silent, but that became impossible. And when I began speaking out against them, of the fifty-six people who were in our section, about twenty-eight broke off from them in sympathy with me . . . [and] they just made their own group. A group which was solely in opposition to the [MKO]. This group later evolved into Ommat-e Vahedeh. . . .[71] So when I was released, I was worried about the oppression I had experienced from the [MKO] in prison would be unleashed on the entire populace should they come to power. You might not believe it, but even with the worst conditions that I've observed under the ruling clerics, I'd still prefer their rule a thousand times to that of the Mojahedin. They're Stalinists! The Mojahedin are a catastrophe waiting to happen. . . . When I left prison, I joined [MIR]. You see, to prevent the leftists and the [MKO] from imposing their program upon the people, in order to oppose them, all of us grassroots groups began to build organizations that would stand up against them.[72]

Makhmalbaf's recounting of his falling out with and subsequent rivalry to the MKO is illustrative of the experiences of other top MIR and IRGC activists such as Behzad Nabavi (leader of Ommat-e Vahedeh), Morteza Alviri, and Mohsen Rezai.[73] Other prominent members of the post-revolutionary regime, including IRGC commander Monfared, Abbas Duzduzani (who attended early IRGC leadership meetings), Mohammad Montazeri, and the future prime minister and president of the Islamic Republic, Mohammad Ali Rajai, were also former MKO members who had turned against the left.[74] In all, most MIR members had some prior relationship with the MKO.[75] Those who moved away from the MKO tended to turn toward the clergy in general and Khomeini in particular for guidance. The split pitted the largely anti-clerical MKO against the more pro-clerical Islamists and created a divide along political, ideological, and religious lines.

In an effort to undermine the left and prevent it from gaining influence in post-revolutionary Iran, MIR self-consciously formed an ideology and identity that were in direct opposition to the MKO. MIR constructed a veneer that appeared more authentically Islamic than the Islamist-Marxist MKO, but retained fixtures—such as the term "Mojahedin"—to challenge the latter's near trademark association with that term.[76] This type of outward or symbolic challenge to the MKO is perhaps best represented in MIR's official emblem. MIR's emblem can be seen as a visualization of its ideological and political bases. It simultaneously affirms the organization's motivating principles while denouncing those held by the MKO. From the images below (figs. 3.1 and 3.2), we can see the emblems of both the MKO and MIR, respectively. Both share graphic similarities. Each includes a quote from the Quran, a clenched fist holding a rifle, a geographical reference, the name of the organization, and the year of its founding. The MKO's emblem, however, includes additional Marxist symbols—the five-pointed star, the anvil (representing the working class), and the sickle (representing the peasantry); an outline of Iran (representing the group's nationalistic agenda); leaves (suggesting a desire for world peace); and a graphical representation of the globe (symbolizing the internationalist struggle).[77]

Most of these symbols are excised from MIR's emblem and are replaced with more explicit Islamic motifs. At the center of the design sits a prominent

Figure 3.1  Official emblem of the Mojahedin-e Khalq

Figure 3.2  Official emblem of the
Mojahedin of the Islamic Revolution

representation of the Arabic negative article *"la,"* out of which grows a clenched fist holding a rifle.[78] The Arabic *"la"* stands for the Muslim proclamation of faith *"la ilaha ilallah . . ."* ("There is no God but God . . ."), which is also written on the banner in the upper right hand of the emblem. These elements, combined with the Quranic verse at the bottom right hand of the design, are overt testaments to the religiosity of the organization and are employed to counter the MKO's Marxist imagery.[79] Likewise, MIR replaces an image of Iran with an image of the globe as a way of distancing itself from the nationalistic sentiments of the left, while retaining a similar commitment to internationalism. In a sense, MIR's emblem stripped away what its members found objectionable in the MKO to reveal the religious core of a new brand of Islamic revolutionism. This visual turn not only symbolizes the shifting ideological and religious sentiments of the Islamist revolutionary bloc, but it also forms the graphic template adopted by the IRGC (and later by Lebanese Hezbollah).[80] MIR's emblem, then, can be seen as the branding of an emergent anti-leftist, pro-Khomeini faction, which helped form the foundational ideology and religiosity of the IRGC and shape post-revolutionary politics.

Through their rivalry with the MKO and general enmity of the left, MIR members in the IRGC, committees, and elsewhere in the post-revolutionary regime increasingly used their positions to subvert their rivals. The campaign against the left took different forms and operated under various auspicious. Anti-left propaganda accused the left of being a front for Western powers, fomenting counterrevolutionary sentiment among ethnic minorities, and of undermining the position of the clergy. The left's vocal support for ethnic minorities and their embrace of "foreign" ideologies provoked much of this sentiment, but it was their advocacy of secularism, or in the case of the MKO, a Shariati-style anti-clerical Islam, that most directly threatened the clerical establishment. Khomeini continuously attacked the left on this point, even though many of the leftist organizations had publicly voiced their support for him and other senior clerics.

# Khomeini Über Alles

Khomeini's move against the left gained momentum after a shadowy terrorist organization began assassinating rumored members of the Revolutionary Council.[81] The group, known as Forqan, came to the fore after they claimed responsibility for the assassination of Major General Mohammad Qarani on

April 20.[82] Their next assassination, that of prominent Shiite cleric Ayatollah Morteza Motahhari, exposed the group's strident anti-clericalism and gained them lasting infamy. Forqan took credit for the May 1 murder in an anonymous phone call to an Iranian media organization. In that call, the group claimed that they had killed Motahhari for being the "head of the Revolutionary Council" and as part of the group's greater "struggle against mullahism."[83]

Ayatollah Motahhari was a leading ideologue of the revolution. A close ally of Khomeini, and an ardent critic of the left, his writings articulated Islam as a political worldview opposed to capitalist materialism and socialist atheism. In one essay published before the revolution, Motahhari wrote:

> Today there is no longer any room for doubt that a teaching, an ideology, is among society's most pressing needs. . . . Ideology calls for faith. An appropriate ideology should, on the one hand, rest on the kind of worldview that can convince the reason and nourish the mind, and on the other hand, logically deduce attractive goals from its worldview. . . . Islam, in being founded in such a world view, is a comprehensive and realistic teaching. It considers every aspect of human needs, whether this worldly or otherworldly, physical or spiritual, intellectual or emotional and affectual, individual or social.[84]

Through such arguments, Motahhari brought an intellectual sophistication to Khomeini's movement. He offered pro-clerical Islamists an alternative ideological path to Marxism and Shariati-style Islam, one that was authentic and conservative but also modern. His writings and commitment to the revolution endeared him to Khomeini's followers. He was revered by the IRGC, and his ideas had a lasting impact on the organization.

Perhaps unsurprisingly, Motahhari's death was seized upon by Khomeini as an opportunity to move against his rivals. The senior ayatollah publicly lambasted the left, took aim at the critics of his clerical camp, and called the Iranian press "traitors" to the revolution.[85] His outspoken criticism of the press, which had already caused the closing of one major Iranian newspaper,[86] compelled another major newspaper (*Kayhan*) to purge its staff of suspected anti-Khomeinists and leftist sympathizers.[87]

Less than a month later, Forqan struck again. It claimed responsibility for the shooting of Hojjat al-Islam Akbar Hashemi Rafsanjani, a mid-level cleric and one of Khomeini's closest lieutenants. Rafsanjani survived the attack despite two bullet wounds to the torso. The incident added further vitriol to Khomeini's push against his rivals. The left was again accused of conspiring with the revolution's enemies and working to undermine the clergy. As Khomeini charged, "from among the webs of these terrors one [can] see the footsteps of superpowers and international criminals. . . . America and the other superpowers must know that they cannot assassinate our revolution."[88] In another statement, he warned: "[n]o individual and no group is allowed to insult the clergy, and if it happens the offenders should be prosecuted and punished by the local revolutionary court."[89] The subtext of the message could not have been lost on Khomeini's supporters. It was a condemnation of the left and a sanctioning of anti-leftist activism.[90]

The Forqan assassinations lent credence to Khomeini's campaign against the left. It gave his forces the sympathy and top-cover needed to engage in the overt suppression of leftist and democratic organizations. The IRGC, committees, and other hezbollahi groups led the ground war against these organizations, operating more openly and more aggressively than before. Some of the pressure exerted on leftist organizations seemed to have its desired effect. Although both the MKO and People's Fadai had earlier acknowledged Khomeini's position of authority, the latter announced that it had gone so far as to propose changes to its constitution to bring it in line with Khomeini and his faction.[91] These changes, most of which contradicted the group's Marxist-Leninist ideological foundation, included articles that claimed: the Fadai would act according to "divine Islamic law, the Koran, and the exalted commandments of Islam"; the Fadai would support the establishment of an Islamic Republic; the Fadai would "perform its mission according to the instructions and orders of Imam Khomeyni and his policy"; the Fadai would "conduct its activities publically and openly and avoid any kind of clandestine actions"; and the Fadai would "recognize and not dispute the orders of the Guardians of the Islamic Revolution."[92] These were dramatic (if politically motivated and superficial) concessions on the part of the Fadai. They are not only evidence of Khomeini's political authority, but also speak to the growing influence and status of the Revolutionary Guards as an official arm of that authority.

The growing conflict with the left brought the IRGC to the ethnic minority (i.e., non-Persian) regions of Iran. The People's Fadai and other Marxist groups had long expressed solidarity with Iran's Kurdish, Turkmen, Arab, Azeri, and Baluch minority communities. After the revolution, they helped spread Marxist politics and organize local councils in minority areas. They might have also funneled weapons to strengthen ethnic armed insurgencies.[93] In early May, the IRGC responded by establishing units in regions such as Khuzestan and Kermanshah to fight against armed dissident groups. The IRGC quickly became engaged in armed clashes, and its heavy-handed tactics sparked protests from local communities. [94] A leader of the local Arab community in Khuzestan, for example, blamed the Guards for inciting violence with local activists.[95]

The fighting in Khuzestan mirrored the ethnic unrest that had already erupted between the IRGC, regime forces, and the ethnic Turkmen, Baluch, and

Kurdish populations in the northeast, southeast, and western regions of Iran, respectively. Local populations in these areas accused the Guards and other Khomeinist elements for initiating the violence. Revolutionary leaders in Tehran blamed foreign influence and "counterrevolutionaries" for stirring up ethnic and religious tensions that did not previously exist.[96] The Provisional Government charged the left, and the People's Fadai in particular, for fueling the violence. Prime Minister Bazargan, in a speech to the IRGC, denounced the Fadai for its "treachery" against the revolution and for having a "hand" in all of the incidents of ethnic unrest throughout the country.[97]

The IRGC had the support of both Khomeini and the government in its crackdown on leftist organizations. It pursued that effort under the official auspices of disarming the public and unsanctioned militias.[98] As the head of the disarmament campaign, the IRGC continually clashed with groups that refused to give up their weapons. This included the Mojahedin-e Khalq, whose leadership, in a June 4 interview, proclaimed that so long as "the imperialist interests have not been touched, we will not give up our arms."[99] The dispute between the MKO and the post-revolutionary regime over arms led to direct conflict with the IRGC. In early July, the Guards training facility in Qom was attacked by armed assailants. The attackers were not initially known, but the MKO was accused and its local headquarters was raided by the IRGC.[100] The Revolutionary Guards legitimated this raid by claiming they had seized a large stash of weapons belonging to the Mojahedin. Although the MKO protested the actual number of weapons confiscated—suggesting the IRGC had inflated the number for political purposes—it argued that its members "only carry weapons to protect [themselves] against plots of imperialism and SAVAK."[101] The MKO also called for talks with the government to discuss the issue of disarmament, suggesting they would abide by Khomeini's decision on the matter.[102]

The seizure of arms from the MKO emboldened the disarmament efforts of the IRGC. The incident led to a declaration against armed groups by the regional prosecutor's office, which charged the Revolutionary Guards to "use all of their ability and Islamic decisiveness to disarm, arrest, and detain any person or persons found carrying arms." The order continued, "[t]he formation of armed groups, except with respect to the aforementioned officials [IRGC, security officials, and the military], is forbidden anywhere and those contravening this order will be regarded as enemies of the revolution and plotters against the Islamic Republic."[103]

The illegalization of arms gave the IRGC and other official security organizations the legal mandate to pursue the armed militias that were antagonistic or not sufficiently obedient to Khomeini. Effectively, this meant that the major leftist militias, including the MKO, People's Fadai, and Tudeh, had become legal targets of the post-revolutionary regime. The government added to the anti-leftist climate by publicly denouncing that camp as "anti-Islamic" and questioning the true intentions of its associated organizations. In his August 1 message to the nation, Prime Minister Mehdi Bazargan stated:

> Those familiar anti-national and anti-Islamic groups who claim to defend freedom, democracy and support the interests of the masses and security, let us assume that they have good intentions, and they really do support freedom and democracy at the same time as being socialist or Marxist, and that they are not the mercenaries and agents trained and under the command of the foreign enemies of Iran. They too, with the disturbances, problems and anxieties they create and the confusion, sabotage and subversion which takes place, if it were anything like the opposition demonstrated by the Leftist parties or the opposition party against the government of the time in democratic countries, with publicity campaigns, presentation of candidates towards their coming to power, it would be acceptable. They could come and take over the government and if they enjoyed the support of the majority of the people they could act on their plans which would inevitably follow their own principles. But they are not doing that here; they are committing acts of sabotage and subversion, here they are trying to create confusion and shake the foundations of the Government.[104]

Through such public denunciations, the movement against dissent gained increasing public support. The embattled leftist organizations, while still popular among students and the intelligentsia, were losing the ground war to Khomeini. The flowing tide of anti-leftist sentiment and support for Khomeini's campaign became evident in the wake of a crackdown on the press. A new law passed by the government enabled the shutting down of newspapers critical of the post-revolutionary regime. Soon the offices of Iran's leading newspaper, *Ayandegan*, were occupied by the IRGC and its operations shut down. Foreign correspondents, notably Americans from the *New York Times*, the *Los Angeles Times*, and NBC, were also ordered to leave the country.[105] In response, major leftist and democratic organizations (with the exception of the MKO, which did not participate) organized mass protests in Tehran, calling for an end to "censorship." [106] The protests, which swelled to an estimated one hundred thousand, were met by smaller, but more violent, counter-protests led by the pro-Khomeini Mojahedin of the Islamic Revolution and overseen by the IRGC.[107] The following day, the official offices of the MKO and the People's Fadai were attacked by armed Khomeinist gangs chanting "Communism is destroyed! Islam is victorious!"[108]

Although the left and democratic opposition were able to display the immense size and passion of their support base, the Khomeinist faction was able to enunciate its superior political power through intimidation and violence.

## One System to Rule Them All

Eruptions of dissent were an outgrowth of the revolution's inherent disunity. Major political forces were engaged in a competition for Iran's future, one that would in part be determined by the the drafting of a constitution. Beyond the street activism of the Khomeinist militias, committees, and IRGC, the clerically-dominated Islamic Republic Party (IRP)—the chief proponent of Khomeini's doctrine of the "guardianship of the jurisprudent"—was another front in the power struggle. As the Khomeinist faction gained strength, the IRP succeeded in pressuring Prime Minister Bazargan to include its members in his cabinet. In late July, Bazargan invited four leading IRP members into his administration: Ayatollah Mahdavi-Kani as Interior Minister, Akbar Hashemi Rafsanjani as Deputy Interior Minister, Ali Khamenei as Defense Minister, and Mohammad Javad Bahonar as Minister of Education. With those appointments, Khomeinist clergy now held powerful positions in both the Revolutionary Council and the Provisional Government. This gave Khomeini greater political leverage over his opponents, and strengthened the IRP's ability to pursue its pro-Khomeini agenda. The IRP also dominated the August 11 election of the Assembly of Experts—a publically elected clerical council that would oversee the drafting of the Islamic Republic's constitution. This ensured that Khomeinists would have the strongest voice in the ensuing constitutional debates.

With the death of Ayatollah Taleqani in early September, the democratic and leftist opposition lost its leading clerical supporter and chief bulwark to Khomeinist aspirations. Taleqani's absence emboldened Khomeini's political project. Khomeini appointed his trusted ally Ayatollah Montazeri as the new Friday congregational prayer leader for Tehran—an influential position previously held by Taleqani—and charged the IRGC with the security detail for these massive ceremonies.[109] Montazeri used the pulpit to articulate both the Khomeinist line and his own revolutionary agenda. Montazeri, like his son Mohammad, represented the radical-internationalist current of the Khomeinist camp. His focus was as much about external affairs as it was about Iranian politics. Through words and deed, the senior Montazeri strove to bring Iran's revolution to other parts of the Muslim world to combat "global Zionism" and Western imperialism. In an October interview, Montazeri mentions using his new position as prayer leader to promote those ideas, and argues: "[W]e, as Muslims, must be interested in each other's affairs and support one another whenever we can. This is the duty of every Muslim. I would like to assert that we in the Muslim revolution [in Iran] cannot remain calm or sleep on silk while the rest of the Muslim peoples and countries are encountering danger, injustice and oppression—oppression by dictatorships and imperialism."[110]

The notion of combating imperialism, in all its forms, was central to the operations of the IRGC. For instance, the local IRGC unit of Abadan declared a day of fasting in solidarity with a hunger strike undertaken by Palestinian prisoners in Israel. In their message to the Palestinians, the Abadan Guards promised the destruction of the "illegitimate offspring of world imperialism-zionism [sic]" and the "liberation" of the Palestinians.[111] Fighting imperialist and Zionist "plots" was at the heart of the IRGC's campaign against leftist organizations and other suspected "counterrevolutionaries." Such rhetoric was used to describe the ongoing conflict between the government's forces (led by the IRGC) and the forces associated with mainly two Kurdish organizations: the leftist Kurdish Democratic Party (KDP) and the Marxist-Leninist Komala. The language used by Iran's leaders to describe the ethnic unrest in Iran's western Kurdish region made the terms "imperialist" and "counterrevolutionary" nearly synonymous. The regular military described its role in the fighting as "cleansing" the "cities in the west of the country . . . from alien elements and the stooges of imperialism."[112] The IRGC similarly announced its readiness "to eradicate all the counterrevolutionary elements . . . in the country—or even outside the country."[113]

The influence of Khomeinist radicals was on the ascent. They viewed Western imperialism (and everything associated with it) to be the main threat to Islam and Iran's Islamic revolution. When a photograph of Prime Minister Bazargan shaking hands with US National Security Advisor Zbigniew Brzezinski in Algiers became public, Khomeinist radicals and their leftist rivals shared a brief confluence of fury. Both sides condemned the November 1 meeting as a prelude to the return of American influence in Iran. While both sides sponsored protests, only the Khomeinists managed to take full advantage of the situation. Ownership of the anti-imperialism issue, which had been championed by the left, was emphatically seized by the Khomeinists through the storming of the US embassy on November 4. The IRGC had been protecting the US embassy and had resisted previous attacks; however, this time its members did not intervene and probably helped facilitate it.[114] The pro-Khomeini group "Students in the Line of the Imam," which had planned the attack and succeeded in capturing US embassy employees, likely had contacts with the IRGC through its radical MIR and Montazeri factions.[115]

The sacking of the U.S. embassy and taking of American hostages began what sociologist Said Arjomand has called, "Khomeini's phantasmagorical struggle with the imperialist Satan." It made fear of a US-led counterrevolution an animating facet of Khomeinist political discourse, and cemented the place of antagonism to the United States in Iran's Islamic system.[116] It was also the death knell for the Provisional Government. Humiliated and defeated, Bazargan resigned in protest on November 6 when Khomeini refused to move against the student protesters. The government fell with him. This left the regime in the hands of the clerically-dominated Revolutionary Council. With the political tide rising in their favor, the Khomeinist faction in the Assembly of Experts succeeded in including the "guardianship of the jurist" in the draft constitution (article 105) and was able to pass the most controversial articles (107–110) associated with that office.[117] The new constitution, which was ratified in a popular referendum on December 2–3, gave the ruling jurist (now Khomeini) "absolute power without the slightest responsibility."[118] It also made Khomeini the commander-in-chief of the regular military and IRGC, and gave him the authority to appoint and dismiss the head commanders of each. The democratic opposition looked to senior cleric Ayatollah Kazem Shariatmadari, who had been a leading critic of the constitution and the principle of the "guardianship," to articulate its discontent.[119] The Islamic People's Republican Party, which was allied with Shariatmadari, led an uprising in his home province of Azerbaijan that was quickly put down by the IRGC and associated pro-Khomeini militants. The opposition proved once again to be too weak to challenge Khomeini's will. [120]

The events of November and December 1979 have been referred to as the "second Islamic revolution" and a "clerical coup d'état."[121] By utilizing the issue of imperialism and the fear of an American-sponsored counterrevolution, Khomeinists became the dominant political force in the post-revolution. Through their dominance of the Assembly of Experts, the exploitation of the anti-imperialist climate following the US embassy takeover, the fall of the Provisional Government, and the passing of the theocratic constitution, the Khomeinist clergy were now in the position to rewrite the revolution in their own name. If clerics were the leaders of the new state, the Revolutionary Guards were their enforcers. The IRGC led the violent campaigns against dissenting forces, and through official patronage by the state made Khomeini's will the law of the land. The IRGC laid the groundwork for the clerical enterprise of the Islamic Republic. It entered the scene as the Imam's vanguard and was now in position to truly defend his Islamic system (*nezam*)—a system whose essence was derived from primacy of the supreme jurist. Fulfilling that task is what would drive the organization's development and politics from this point on.

# 4

# The Imposed War

What counts in war is not numbers, but experience, morale and resilience—attributes which [the believers] in the dawn of Islam possessed and used in routing big armies. Thank God, although we are few in number in our country and although our enemies are among the big powers, our people are facing up to the test. They can, through unity and faith in God Almighty, inflict defeat on the big and multitudinous armies. Therefore, what must be available is the strength which individuals derive from [faith]. Thank God, this strength is currently available. It exists in the army, the [IRGC] and the other forces. When facing death, each one of them derives strength from shouting God is Great and charging on.[1]

—Ruhollah Khomeini

Just as revolutionary regimes are taken to have produced new and progressive societal forms, so too the armies associated with the new order are assumed to possess the moral essence of the revolution and thereby become successful. Citizen-soldiers, embodying revolutionary sociopolitical principles, evolve innovative tactics and through their commitment to the cause carry all before them. The foundation of a new socio-political order, in short, lies behind the foundation of a new and progressive military order.[2]

—S.P. Mackenzie, *Revolutionary Armies in the Modern Era*

As factional infighting continued in the months after Khomeini's constitutional success, the revolution's greatest threat emerged from the west. Instead of the United States, it was Iraq under its new president, Saddam Hussein, that sought to gain from Iran's morass. Saddam's military invasion was a dramatic disruption to Iran's already shaky post-revolution political climate. Not only did this "imposed war" thrust Iran into a long and bloody conflict with its neighbor, it did so at tremendous cost to Iran's social fabric and international standing.

Prospects were dire for Iran. According to then president Abolhassan Bani-Sadr, Khomeini and other senior leaders thought Iran would be defeated.[3] Outwardly, Khomeini expressed confidence. In a message to the Iranian and Iraqi people on September 26, 1980, Khomeini framed the conflict as a contest between the forces of God and those of an apostate. He juxtaposed Iran's armed forces with those of Iraq, claiming that while the latter fought for the sake of only "one person," Iran's troops were "fighting for a [divine] cause." Iran's regular military and Revolutionary Guards were "equipped with divine power," Khomeini announced, whose weapon would be the Islamic invocation "God is Great!" "There is no sharper weapon on earth," the supreme leader assured his forces.[4]

If Khomeini's implicit promise that God was on the side of the Iranians was meant to convey strength, his appeals to Iraqis in the same message hinted at a more deep-seated uncertainty. Khomeini urged the Iraqi soldiers to "return to Islam before it is too late" and not "follow an unbeliever and an apostate." In the hopes of sewing turmoil in Iraq's ranks, Khomeini encouraged Iraqis to rebel against their Baathist leaders:

> Follow God's Prophet, not Saddam. Dissociate yourselves from these men because if you do, they would be worth nothing. Abandon them and, if you can, kill them. Aim your guns at them and kill them. If you cannot reach them, abandon them. Come to Iran. You are most welcome here. This Muslim country will protect you. We welcome you here and are ready to serve you. . . . The Iraqi people must rise. Rise against Saddam. You will triumph, as we have triumphed by depending on God. Let us hold hands to crush this man and his party. Let us do away with the evil of these men. . . . Let each of us establish an Islamic government. . . . Let Iran have its own government and Iraq its own government, but united under the banner of Islam.[5]

Khomeini's passionate plea did little to treat the many self-inflicted wounds that plagued Iran at the outset of the war. The purges of Iran's regular military had decimated its officer corps and sunk morale within its ranks. The enduring hostage crisis, which Khomeini had adopted as his own, had led to a severing of ties between the United States and Iran. It also prevented Iran from receiving crucial, previously purchased military hardware from Washington (Iran's chief military supplier) and made the purchase of additional materiel and spare parts nearly impossible. Without replacement parts, large swaths of Iran's military (from tanks and artillery to aircraft and helicopters) became intermittently inoperable. Additionally, a leadership crisis in Iran, which pitted President Bani-Sadr against the clerical leaders of the Islamic Revolution Party (IRP), severely undermined war planning and decision-making. As a result, Iran's early war effort was muddled, disjointed, and at times disastrous.

The war, however, also opened the door for the IRGC to expand its purview into military matters. The organization entered the war as an urban militia with no real military knowledge. Outside of brief operational experience fighting Kurdish insurgents in western Iran, the IRGC was a military institution in name only. Within two years, the IRGC emerged as a pillar of the war effort. Its aggressiveness, tactics, and influence within leadership circles helped the organization gain a foothold in the war-planning process and enabled it to become a leading force on the battlefield.

## Invasion

Iraq's military invasion of Iran began on September 22, 1980, through four major thrusts across a 450-mile front. The main advance aimed at capturing land on Iran's side of the Shatt al-Arab—a waterway, known as the Arvand River in Persian, that marks the border between Iran and Iraq from near the city of Khorramshahr to the Persian Gulf—and parts of Iran's oil-rich southwest province of Khuzestan. Iraqi aircraft bombed nine Iranian airfields in an unsuccessful attempt to disable Iran's air force. Although Iranian forces had been on alert since border clashes had increased in recent weeks, and had called up reservists, the sheer scale of the Iraqi advance surprised Iran and quickly overwhelmed its ill-prepared forces. The majority of Iran's troops remained stationed along the Iranian-Soviet border (a carryover from the Cold War policies of the Shah), which delayed the arrival of reinforcements to the western front by weeks.

There were a few bright spots for Iran, however. First was the poor planning of the Iraqi military, which, after initial successes, found it difficult to provide logistical support and reinforcements to the frontlines and quickly became bogged down in the face of stiff Iranian resistance. Second was Iran's air force, which had numerous successes against Iraq in the early stages of the war. Faced with potentially steep losses, Saddam Hussein relocated much of his combat aircraft to neighboring Arab countries in order to protect them from Iranian bombing raids.[6] Third was the patriotism of the Iranian people, who began to volunteer for the war effort in droves, and the staunch bravery of the revolutionary and regular forces, who engaged the Iraqis on the front lines despite the inefficacy of their political leadership.

The IRGC had a salient role in this period. When the conflict began, Iranian president Mohammad-Ali Rajai put forward the idea that if the regular army were defeated, the Guards should step in and wage a guerrilla-style war.[7] This is precisely what the IRGC began to do. With the regular forces overwhelmed and overstretched, guardsmen were deployed to the southern front to help stem the tide. Neither trained nor experienced, local units learned to fight on the job, experimenting from operation to operation, utilizing their superior mobility, knowledge of local terrain, and daring to strike at the enemy in unconventional ways. In the border province of Khuzestan, where Iraqi forces had begun to lay siege to the cities of Khorramshahr, Abadan, and Dezful, IRGC units struck at the Iraqis through various forms of irregular combat. The IRGC's early operations included night raids, small kamikaze-style attacks, and larger ambushes against fixed Iraqi positions. These operations were a testing ground wherein the IRGC developed a style of fighting that matched its values and its limited resources. As the organization later explained:

> Scattered, tactical guerrilla attacks and harassing operations opened a new phase in the war which not only forced Iraq to halt its advance, but enabled us to obtain precious experience at the cost of the lives of our martyrs, in spite of all negative propaganda, the significance of IRGC men as well as the value and importance of the popular forces began to dawn upon the world.[8]

By the end of October, the IRGC announced that it would wage a long term, guerilla-style war against the Iraqis, focusing on limited attacks to harass and demoralize the enemy.[9] The organization regularly publicized its operations.[10] The IRGC regularly released communiqués to claim credit for certain attacks and as a form of psychological warfare aimed at the Iraqis. For that reason, the IRGC's public statements often exaggerated successes and minimized losses. That practice was not unique to the IRGC. All Iranian and Iraqi forces approached wartime propaganda in that way. Despite their exaggerations, descriptions of operational successes, particularly those in the beginning of the war, are still useful in that they provide a view of the IRGC's approach in the early war effort. For instance, the IRGC describes its "first night raid" as a bold but haphazard operation. The attack was designed to prevent Iraqis from taking a stretch of highway that would have cut off Iranian access to the city of Ahvaz. The operation was disorganized, and relied on the bravery of volunteers who had limited firepower and ammunition.

> On that night [a] number of volunteers for martyrdom, under the leadership of Ghayur Asli, were picked out. It was decided that only those who sought martyrdom should join the group and that [they] should not think of returning. The only [significant] weapon available was the RGP7; and the group armed mostly with guns and rifle-grenades, started the operation. Prior to the assault, [Iraqi] personnel carriers were patrolling the road, reconnoitering for the moves of the next day. At 1:00 a.m. with the first of nine RGP7s [firing] on the enemy's tanks and personnel carrier, the night raid was started and the enemy taken

by surprise was utterly overrun and destroyed. The operation was not
organized and several times their ammunition ran out but the raiders
returned for supplies and went back again to the scene of battle.[11]

The IRGC emphasizes the bravery of its fighters, who all "sought martyrdom,"
and the paucity of their resources. These were themes the IRGC expressed consistently throughout the war. They speak to what the organization considered its
real strength: the devotion and selflessness of its fighters. For the IRGC, it was
above all faith in God, the revolution, and Khomeini that underwrote their success in the war.

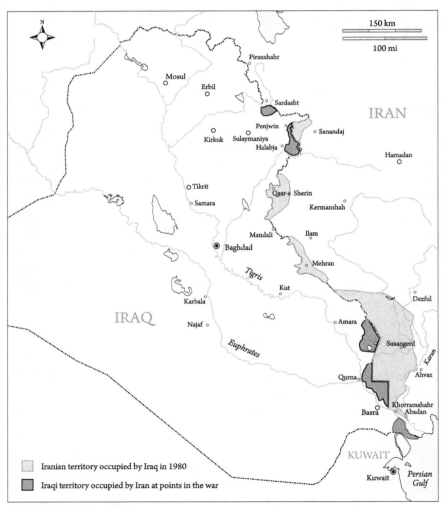

*Map 4.1* Territorial advances in the Iran-Iraq War

But even as it boasted of its victories, IRGC commanders decried what they considered the government's lack of support for the organization, which left it barely armed, undermanned, and its volunteers poorly trained. That frustration inspired a damning October 25 missive from Ali Shamkhani, then the IRGC commander for the Khuzestan theater. Addressed to Iran's leaders, Shamkhani passionately describes the dire situation of his men and their paucity of resources. In a challenge to the government, which he blames for favoring the regular military, Shamkhani vividly describes the IRGC's situation in a call for aid. "Why must I say this?" he writes:

> I say this because of the 150 guardsmen in Khorramshahr only 30 remain. I say this because with 30 mortar pieces we'd be able to protect the Bloodied City [Khorramshahr] for 30 months. Today we don't even have 30 rifles. This is why those illegitimate organizations with abundant resources [i.e., the Iraqi military] are repelling us and will continue to repel us. The reality is this: our military of today cannot [win this fight] without the Guards Corps, and on the contrary, would only be able to make the slightest movement. . . . God knows that we [the IRGC] have felt the enemy's tanks. We've heard their shrieking shouts during their night assaults. . . . Hear *our* call. We are in need of arms and resources. We live in the path of God. . . . Guardsmen are crying out because of the lack of resources, which has constricted our efforts. . . . If you intercede and arm us with the iron of God, we will continue to smite their necks until Iraq's Baathist government and other oppressive and thuggish regimes fall. Otherwise, until that time, we will carry on fulfilling our religious duty and fight till martyrdom.[12]

The lot of IRGC units at the front was indeed grim. They generally operated outside of military bases, in ramshackle camps, or in makeshift control centers in urban areas. Guardsmen who were deployed to the besieged city of Khorramshahr—often referred to as *khuninshahr*, or the "Bloodied City," by Iranians because of the massive violence done to it and its citizens by the Iraqi military—led much of the urban resistance against the Iraqis out of a mosque in the city.[13] The guardsmen in Khorramshahr faced Iraqi tanks and artillery with little more than rifles and other makeshift weapons. With no heavy weaponry and inadequate support from the regular military, the IRGC's situation in the city was so precarious that one guardsman told a foreign journalist, "If you're tired of life," come to Khorramshahr.[14] Unsurprisingly, the Iraqis overran the port city in late October and held it for the next nineteen months.

Although the Iraqis were able to take Khorramshahr, stiff Iranian resistance prevented them from taking Abadan, Ahvaz, and Dezful—other strategically important cities in oil-rich Khuzestan that were besieged by Iraqi forces. Much of the fighting done by the IRGC in Khuzestan involved units that had been sent there from Iran's Kurdestan region. These units had been involved in fighting the Kurdish insurgency, and were the most experienced the IRGC had at the time. They brought with them a basic knowledge of combat and operational planning. They also possessed a more developed command-and-control structure than their local IRGC counterparts, most of which were bogged down in the cities.

One of the guardsmen transferred from Kurdestan was Yahya Rahim Safavi, an early IRGC member from Esfahan and later one of the commanders of southern operations in the Khuzestan theater. (He was eventually appointed IRGC chief in 1997, replacing Mohsen Rezai.) Safavi arrived in the area near the end of October and was initially stationed near the village of Darkhovin, where he and his troops were part of the effort to break the Iraqi siege of Abadan.[15] As Safavi explains, life at the front was Spartan and difficult:

> I was deployed to the Darkhovin region along with other fellow fighters who had been in Kurdestan. . . . It was initially difficult to set up defenses for the forces in this axis, which were in date palm groves and [defended by] boys (bacheh) in trenches. The boys did not even have a good place to rest, and from night to morning swarms of mosquitoes and other insects made sleeping unbearable. Feeding the troops was even worse. It was difficult managing to supply [each man] just two rations of food a day. . . . We had further problems with hygiene, bathing, and in supplying clothing to the forces. I explained [to my superiors] that there was no way to overtake the front in the first days and months of the war because logistical support for the troops was extremely weak. When our clothes got soiled we would sit in the creeks that flowed through the palm groves. This meant we either had to wear our drenched clothing or wrap ourselves in a sheet until our clothes dried. But even though we did not have a spare set of clothes, and were faced with all of these difficulties and hardships, the youth never showed weakness.[16]

Safavi was in charge of a contingent of young Basij militia volunteers (the "boys" mentioned above) that had been sent to the front from Esfahan. Although the volunteers were eager and brave, Safavi makes several references to their lack of training and unfamiliarity with weaponry and warfare. The training they received at the front was not much better, consisting of "two or three days" of instruction on how to use various machine guns, RPGs, mortars, and how to neutralize land mines. Civilian volunteers also came to the front, including a group of Loristani tribesman, who, as Safavi recounts, exited their bus dressed in traditional tribal clothing, armed with a variety of single-shot hunting rifles, and enthusiastically proclaimed: "We have come to expel the Iraqis from Khuzestan."[17]

## A Stymied War Effort

The war worsened an already deteriorating leadership crisis within Iran. The government was split between the Khomeinist bloc and President Bani-Sadr. Khomeini had appointed Bani-Sadr commander-in-chief of the armed forces and as head of the newly established Supreme Defense Council (SDC), a seven-member body tasked with decision-making for the war.[18] As the chief architect of the war effort, Bani-Sadr became a lightning rod for critics who questioned the ineffectiveness of Iran's early operations, particularly those of the regular military. The most glaring failure, aside from Iraq's initial advances, was the fall of Khorramshahr on October 24—a defeat that magnified the regular military's ineffectiveness and escalated pressure on Bani-Sadr. When Iran went on the offensive, the regular military's performance was mixed, but at times also disastrous. This included inopportune attacks in early January 1980, which took place in the midst of the rainy season when Khuzestan's vast desert plains became thick, untraversable mud. Iran's forces made limited gains in the operation, but also lost over two armored divisions and countless vehicles, which were either destroyed by the Iraqis or abandoned in the mud by their drivers in a humiliating display of poor planning and execution.[19] The failed attack was considered a "great victory" by Iraqi commanders, whose troops gained confidence and improved morale as a result.[20]

Such failures became fodder for the commander-in-chief's most vocal detractors. Among them was Ayatollah Hosayn-Ali Montazeri, the presumed successor to Khomeini and a vocal proponent of the IRGC. Montazeri blamed Bani-Sadr for a failing war plan and warned that a sinister "anti-clerical propaganda campaign" had been recently "initiated within the army" under the president's watch.[21] This charge, of spreading anti-clerical dissent in the military and in society more broadly, was commonly thrown at Bani-Sadr and his supporters. It sprung from the relative secularism of Bani-Sadr, who was labeled a "liberal" by his enemies. Accusations of liberalism and anti-clericalism became pillars of the IRP's crusade against him and against those who dissented from the Khomeinist line. As one local IRGC commander warned: "any efforts to weaken or denigrate the clergy . . . and any counter-revolutionary actions [will] be resisted [by the IRGC]."[22]

Lacking a constituency of his own, Bani-Sadr attempted to cultivate a close relationship with the military, a link aided by his role as commander-in-chief. This provoked the ire of Khomeinists, who distrusted the military and worried that an alliance with Bani-Sadr would be to the detriment of the clergy. The clerics considered this relationship a direct challenge to their power, as did the IRGC, which worried that Bani-Sadr sought to dissolve the organization or merge it with the regular military.[23]

After the fall of Khorramshahr, major Iraqi advances ceased and the front stabilized. Perceived inaction by the regular military led Montazeri and other IRP officials to decry the lack of Iranian aggression in the war. In a provocative December 31 public message, Montazeri lauded the IRGC and regular military for their bravery and sacrifice, but questioned "why [the armed forces] refrain from going on the offensive to attack the treacherous enemy, which has occupied our country." He continued:

> I do not know whether or not the Supreme Defense Council has clearly informed the leader of the revolution of current events on battlefronts, which as a whole could be overlooked easily. The Supreme Defense Council is aware of the fact that the policy of killing time and giving respite to the tyrannical regime of Iraq to reinforce its units will cost us the blood of hundreds of Muslim youths and will encourage America to continue its satanic conspiracies.[24]

Though he did not mention Bani-Sadr by name, the target of his charge was clear. The president issued a quick response, dismissing Montazeri as an ignorant bystander and suggesting the senior cleric "should visit the front himself before making judgment." Montazeri countered by accusing the commander-in-chief of being out of touch with his armed forces:

> I think your judgment would have been different and you would not have recommended my renewed visit to the front in meeting with the commanders if you were in my place and were in contact with . . . the militant and devoted youths, the soldiers, noncommissioned officers and revolutionary guards who come to me every day to report and with painful hearts complain of the negligence and ask to do their religious duty.[25]

This exchange echoed the severe and acrimonious divisions within Iran's leadership. There was no unity among Iran's war planners and an equally problematic split between Iran's armed forces. Though thrust into action together by the invasion, there was extreme mistrust between the IRGC and the regular forces. Suspicions of the military's political sympathies remained rife within the IRGC, and senior military planners viewed the IRGC as an upstart that knew little about fighting a war. Discord was also fueled by the reported use of guardsmen as minders during battle, tasked with shooting any soldiers that retreated—an aspect of the war that faded over time.[26]

At the ground level, the IRGC and regular forces generally did not form mixed units, and often coordinated poorly in operations.[27] The two forces were mostly split into separate roles. The regular military oversaw supportive functions (such as transportation, communications, and logistics), the operation of complex machinery (such as tanks, helicopters, and aircraft), and operational planning. The IRGC was primarily frontline infantry, and placed in defensive positions in cities and villages. In the southern front of Khuzestan, Bani-Sadr had ensured that the military maintained control over the battlefield. This required IRGC units to obtain permission from military commanders for all operations, including basic patrols, leaving it little autonomy or influence in war planning.[28] The IRGC and its supporters in the IRP considered this division of labor unfair. A common argument at the time was that guardsmen were doing all the fighting and dying while the military was sitting back out of harm's way. Although this was an unfair assessment, and regulars fought and died alongside IRGC units across the front, it had a ring of truth.[29]

Khomeinists fumed at the unequal status of the IRGC and blamed Bani-Sadr for marginalizing the Guards in the fight. IRP leaders championed the IRGC in Tehran and sought to gain it a greater role in the war. They eventually succeeded in getting the organization access to heavier weapons and to conscripts, which had previously been the sole purview of the regular military. IRGC chief, Mohsen Rezai, was given a full-member seat on the SDC, thereby giving the Guards a direct role in war planning and decision-making.[30] Clerics also spearheaded the recruitment drive for the Basij, whose mostly teenage volunteers became a critical source of manpower for the IRGC. Indeed, through the first twenty months of the war, Basij volunteers reportedly made up 75 percent of the forces at the front.[31]

# Death of the Opposition

As fighting continued along the front, another conflict was taking place in Tehran and other cities across the country. Armed clashes between leftists and Khomeinists had continued sporadically since the revolution. Attacks on IRP-associated entities gradually escalated. Offices of the IRGC and the committees were bombed, and IRP officials were targets of assassination. This included a bombing attack on Ali Khamenei in June 1981, which left him severely wounded and paralyzed his right arm.[32] Clerics denounced the violence and intensified a widespread crackdown on all leftist organizations and on suspected Bani-Sadr supporters. The IRGC had a leading role in the campaign, which included storming the offices and safe houses of opposition groups, confiscating weapons, arresting individuals, and engaging in armed street battles. These activities led to numerous accusations of violence and abuse by the Guards, committees, and others. While mostly unsympathetic to the opposition's grievances, Khomeini condemned the abuse of authority, and, in an April 1981 message, ordered the IRGC to stop "interfering in matters which are up to the courts or other institutions," and called on its commanders to purge and arrest guardsmen who misused their power.[33] In response, the public relations office of the IRGC released a statement to the Iranian people, assuring them that its members always "wear a uniform with a special mark and [carry] an identity card, and in cases of carrying out an order hold a warrant," and reminded guardsmen to not overstep their bounds. Such tepid statements, which were intended to distance the organization from what it claimed were the actions of mostly unaffiliated individuals and a smattering of rogue members, were common. The organization often announced the purging of wayward guardsmen and at times shut down entire local units to investigate transgressions.[34] But such actions did little to stem the violence or charges of overreach.[35]

With pressure mounting against them, Bani-Sadr encouraged his supporters, which included leftists such as the MKO, People's Fadai (minority faction), and Paykar, as well as nationalist and liberal groups, to take to the streets and protest against the ruling IRP clergy. Street clashes erupted in cities throughout Iran between the opposition's supporters and pro-Khomeini hezbollahi gangs, which were often backed by IRGC and committee units. In a major show of support, the MKO organized a demonstration on April 27 that brought an estimated 150,000 people to the streets of Tehran, parading in solidarity with Bani-Sadr and in condemnation of the IRP. The sight so terrified the IRP, that Iran's chief justice instituted a ban on street demonstrations the next day, thus outlawing the freedom of assembly which had been one of the hallmark achievements of the revolution.[36]

Clashes between opposition and IRP-aligned forces continued to escalate through the summer of 1981, ultimately leading to Bani-Sadr's downfall. With every violent encounter, anger and determination grew on both sides. Although Bani-Sadr had tried desperately to overwhelm the IRP through mass demonstrations of popular support, and had mustered a broad swath of organizations and individuals to his side—including leftists, liberals, nationalists, students, and a handful of senior clergy—he and his mostly middle-class supporters were outmatched. The Khomeinist network controlled all significant elements of coercive state power. They held much of the government, controlled the courts, had the support of the revolutionary organizations (especially the IRGC and committees), maintained allegiances with a large proportion of mosques and clergy throughout Iran, and retained the support of the urban and rural poor, who were the bulk of the manpower in the IRGC, Basij, and hezbollahi gangs. Finally, they had the backing of Khomeini, who had tried to maintain a balance between Bani-Sadr and the IRP, but ultimately (through the persuasive efforts of Ayatollah Mohammad Beheshti, Ayatollah Montazeri, Ali Akbar Hashemi Rafsanjani, and other IRP leaders) turned against the president.[37]

The end for Bani-Sadr and the opposition was swift. Khomeini stripped the president of his powers as commander-in-chief on June 12, and he was impeached by a Majles vote nine days later. Bani-Sadr went into hiding and fled to Paris with MKO head Massud Rajavi. The president's fall paralleled a period of open resistance to the Khomeinist government by leftist organizations. The IRGC promised to tackle the opposition's armed resistance "against Islam and the Quran" head-on, vowing to "punish these enemies of the people for their anti-Islamic and anti-religious acts."[38] The fighting between the IRP-aligned forces led by the IRGC and the oppositionists resulted in the deaths of thousands of Iranians, many of whom were jailed, subjected to torture, and executed by court order. The clergy-led terror not only decimated the ranks of opposition groups and their student supporters; it also targeted innocent, non-political civilians, such as members of the Baha'i religious minority, and others deemed problematic by the IRP.[39]

As opposition forces suffered severe losses in the fighting, the MKO initiated a series of suicide bombings and assassinations aimed at the clerical leadership—a vigorous campaign that continued through 1982.[40] The MKO, which had suffered the greatest losses of any opposition group, was accused of bombing the IRP headquarters on June 28, which resulted in seventy-three dead, including party secretary Ayatollah Beheshti and Mohammad Montazeri, the son of Ayatollah Montazeri. Less than two months later, another bombing killed IRP leaders Mohammad-Ali Rajai and Hojjat al-Islam Javad Bahonar— then the acting president and prime minister of the Islamic Republic, respectively. These were the last major gasps of the leftist opposition to Khomeini. The vicious eradication of their presence in Iran continued for several months, and was made virtually complete by the destruction of the communist Tudeh party in 1983.[41]

The MKO, however, gained new life in exile and continued to conduct limited terrorist attacks in Iran for years. By 1983, Massud Rajavi had come to side with Saddam Hussein in the war in exchange for financial support. Later, in June 1986, Rajavi relocated his forces to military camps inside Iraq after he was expelled by France.[42] Calling its forces the "National Liberation Army," the

MKO in Iraq acted as an adjunct of Saddam, taking part in operations against Iranian forces and Iraqi Kurds, mostly in the central sector. Unsurprisingly, the decision to fight alongside Saddam was viewed as traitorous by the vast majority of Iranians and destroyed the MKO's standing in its homeland.

## The Islamic Republic Strikes Back

With the impeachment of Bani-Sadr and the destruction of the opposition, the IRP's push to monopolize power was complete. Led by Majles Speaker Akbar Hashemi Rafsanjani and President Ali Khamenei, the IRP now dominated the government, the Guardian Council, and held significant influence in the SDC and in the revolutionary organs (IRGC, committees, Basij, Reconstruction Crusade, and the wealthy Foundation for the Oppressed). Although it came at tremendous social cost, the end of the leadership crisis improved Iran's war effort. Now less divided, Iran's military and civilian leaders turned their attention to establishing a more coherent approach to the war. The resulting strategy, which focused on ground warfare, was developed by Lieutenant General Ali Sayyad Shirazi, then the regular ground forces commander, and the IRGC. Code named "Karbala," after the Shia holy city in Iraq that houses the shrine of Imam Husayn, the plan aimed to maximize pressure on the Iraqis through a series of aggressive assaults, while ensuring any gains could be held by a relatively small force.[43] The Guards inclusion in the planning process was a direct result of the IRP's victory over Bani-Sadr. No longer marginalized, the IRGC was incrementally gaining more say in the war, and a more significant role on the battlefield.

The reconfigured war effort resulted in four major offenses that lasted from September 1981 through May 1982. The first offensive was designed to break the siege of Abadan, a strategically important city that contained Iran's largest oil refinery. Sometimes referred to as Abadan Island because it is flanked by the Shatt al-Arab to the west and the Bahmanshir River to the east, Abadan had been home to around three hundred thousand civilians before the war. But violence committed by the besieging Iraqi forces, which regularly barraged the city with artillery fire, had driven out nearly 90 percent of its population and severely damaged its industrial infrastructure. Abadan's lifeline came through its southernmost end, which Iran still controlled and used to supply the ten thousand regular and 4,500 IRGC troops defending the city and its remaining inhabitants.[44]

Strikes against Iraqi forces surrounding Abadan began in early September. In a series of maneuvers, combined regular and IRGC forces gradually broke through Iraqi lines, retook Iranian territory, and in a final thrust pushed the Iraqis out of the city. By September 29, the siege of Abadan had ended, and the critical Ahvaz to Abadan road (a transportation route that allowed reinforcements and supplies to travel to critical battle points further west) reopened. Iraqi troops were forced into a hasty retreat, abandoning scores of tanks and armored vehicles as they withdrew north into the occupied city of Khorramshahr. About three thousand Iranian troops were killed in the September fighting. Iraqi losses were fewer, estimated at around 600 to 1,500 dead and 2,500 captured.[45] Foreign journalists who visited Iranian forward positions for the first time noted high morale among the Iranians and better integration between the IRGC and the military.[46] Their victory had been decisive, and appeared to be a testament to Iran's more unified approach to the war, improved coordination between IRGC and regular forces, and an invigorated esprit de corps.

This was a period of important tactical innovation for the IRGC, which began using mass infantry assaults, or "human wave" attacks, to overwhelm Iraqi defensive positions. The first occurred in late November as part of Operation Tariq al-Quds (the "Path to Jerusalem"), which targeted Iraqi positions around the occupied village of Bostan. Led by a regular military commander, it involved around thirteen thousand troops, more than half of which were IRGC. After thirty-six hours of fighting, the Iranians were able to retake Bostan and push the Iraqis several miles to the west. The assault succeeded in large part because IRGC troops, in an apparent disregard for the battle plan, charged forward en masse into enemy fire.[47] The kamikaze-style assault was able to break Iraqi lines through relentless persistence. The success of this style of attack opened up new possibilities for the IRGC in the war. As it later assessed, Tariq al-Quds "marked the beginning of the organization of popular forces within the framework of the IRGC and Basij. We knew that if we organized the great power of the people who were willing to volunteer for the war, we could launch [even greater] offensives."[48] In other words, the IRGC realized that its main advantage over the Iraqis was superior numbers, and the willingness of its fighters (especially those in the Basij) to charge into enemy lines toward certain death. This line of thinking formed the basis of mass infantry assaults, a tactic the IRGC championed until the end of the war.

Improved coordination, high morale, and the introduction of human wave attacks turned the war in Iran's favor. In late March 1982, under the command of Lieutenant General Shirazi, Iranian forces pushed north of Bostan toward the towns of Shush and Dezful, in what was to that point the largest Iranian offensive of the war. Code named Fath al-Mubin ("Clear Victory"), the operation involved around one hundred thousand troops, 70 percent of which were IRGC and Basij. These forces again utilized mass infantry assaults against hardened Iraqi defenses. Organized into brigades of one thousand men, lightly armed IRGC and Basij troops advanced into enemy fire in successive waves separated by around a half mile. The aim was to overwhelm the enemy through a seemingly endless series of zombie-like advances that exhausted the ammunition and resolve of the Iraqi defenders. An Iraqi officer present at the battle recalled: "They came at us like a crowd coming out of a Mosque on a Friday. Soon we were firing into dead men, some draped over the barbed wire fences, and others in piles on the ground, having stepped in mines."[49] The advancing troops were rallied on by clerics, who encouraged the fighters, reminded them of the divine nature of their battle, that they were the warriors of Islam, and that heavenly paradise awaited those who achieved martyrdom. IRGC commander Ali Shamkhani noted the clergy's role in the fight: "The brother clergy, devout and pious, with a pen in one hand and a rifle on their shoulder, provided [spiritual] illuminations with their speech. They had an important role in this victory. No trench, group prayer, or forward line was devoid of their presence, participation, or calls."[50]

After eight days of combat, Fath al-Mubin was a success. Iran regained 850 square miles of territory and captured thousands of Iraqi troops and large stores of military equipment. The victory firmly shifted momentum to the Iranians, who now turned their eyes toward Khorramshahr. Iran wanted to quickly build on its victory. Reinforcements, most with minimal training, were sent to the southern front from across the country. There they amassed in bases and garrisons with the more seasoned troops of the Khuzestan theater. All were aware that a decisive battle against the Iraqis would soon be launched. Reporters for the IRGC's biweekly journal *Payam-e Enqelab* (*Message of the Revolution*), described the scene of a Basij battalion that was about to leave the Jerusalem base near the village of Hamidieh:

> A bit after we arrived, a group of Basij brothers got ready to be deployed to the frontlines. We got on one of the buses that was taking these brothers. Of all the brothers on the bus, most were youth from Sistan-Balochestan province. The task of this battalion was to provide and protect munitions. Many of the brothers sitting in the back of the bus were so small that they practically got lost in their seats. . . . I asked one of the boys, who couldn't have been more than 14 years old, why they were headed to the front. He replied "Because Islam is in danger." The buses gradually got underway. The caravan of youth was en route to serve on the front lines. . . . They left to offer up their little, pure hearts for the sake of Islam and the Imam.[51]

The ensuing operation was code named Bayt al-Muqaddas ("The Sacred House," another name for Jerusalem). It entailed a series of offensives in two major stages, separated by a two-week pause in fighting. The battle lasted over three weeks, from April 30 to May 23, and involved around sixty-five thousand Iranian troops, with the IRGC and Basij being in the majority. It began on the morning of April 30 with a rousing call from IRGC commander Mohsen Rezai broadcast to all bases and front line positions: "In the Name of God, He who Smites the Necks of the Cruel (*qasim al-jabarin*)! O Ali bin Abi Talib! O Ali bin Abi Talib!"[52]

The ensuing Iranian assaults included a diversionary thrust near the village of Shush toward the Iraqi border intended to draw Iraqi forces away from Khorramshahr. Other Iranian troops moved across the Karun River and set up a beachhead in the direction of Khorramshahr. IRGC forces advanced through cascading mass infantry movements similar to those used in Fath al-Mubin, but faced stiffer Iraqi resistance and sustained heavier losses. Describing the fight for the Ahvaz-to-Abadan road, a critical artery that when taken would sever Iraq's forces in Khorramshahr from reinforcements and supplies, a guardsman said: "The conditions were so unbearable under the enemy pressure that our boys would [have] readily [gone] under the ground if the earth had [opened] its mouth, but no one was thinking of retreating."[53] Iranian forces pressed forward and made progress across their offensive lines. As positions were gained on the southwestern side of the Karun, Iranian forces began to harden their positions by erecting earthen barriers, digging trenches, and establishing other battlements.

By May 10, Saddam ordered a hasty retreat of his forces around the Hamidieh village area, leaving dozens of tanks, armored vehicles, stockpiles of ammunition, and other materiel behind. These forces moved to strengthen the defensive perimeter of Khorramshahr, which extended up to about twelve miles from the city's edge.[54] A two-week pause followed, which gave the Iranians time to resupply and prepare for the next major offensive. IRGC journalists visiting trenches along the frontlines described the scene:

> The call to prayer reminded us it was noon. One brother had hung a picture of the Imam on the wall of his trench. He was standing. The call to prayer was chanted, "Hasten toward the best of deeds! Hasten toward the best of deeds! (*hayya 'ala khayr il-'amal*)"[55] The desert was hot. The warm wind blew causing everyone's face to dry out. Warm air, parched earth, with green flags flying above the trenches. It is here where the prayer of "the best of deeds" took place and where Husayn's Karbala was remembered. Indeed, this *was* Karbala. The front. Husayn's front. Each frontline trench was the locus of purity and faithfulness. The soldiers' weapons were devotion and fidelity. Their bullets, the ambassadors of monotheism and God's message (*resalat*).[56]

Here Shiite symbols are used to transmute the harsh realities of war into a markedly spiritual experience. The line from the call to prayer recalled by the author is one distinct to Shiism. The hot, parched desert setting, replete with waving green flags, clearly evokes the memory of Imam Husayn's stand at

Karbala. The parallel to Karbala is made explicit by the author, who suggests that this landscape is not only reminiscent of Karbala, it is, in its own way, the same thing. The guardsmen in the trenches are not simply soldiers, they are Muslims, *Shia* Muslims. Their war is not unlike that of their religion's foremost heroes and saints. It is spiritually significant and fundamentally about safeguarding the sanctity of their faith. The war thus becomes an exercise of devotion, a reliving of tradition, an opportunity to fight and die for something infinitely more meaningful than the politics of power. This scene, as it is imagined, gets at how the IRGC understood the conflict and how it wanted its soldiers to conceive of their role within it. Like this IRGC journalist, clerics at the front used such metaphors, mixed with a variety of Quranic verses, Islamic traditions, and political propaganda to motivate the troops. It was their contention, and perhaps sincere belief, that even something as horrific and ugly as the war could be spiritually beautiful. It was a theater of religious expression, and contained a vast depth of meaning for its faithful participants.

Iraqi forces used the break in fighting to heavily fortify their defenses in Khorramshahr. The city and its environs were turned into a minefield, with extensive barbed-wire entanglements, booby traps, earthen barriers, trenches, and other defensive structures. Lieutenant General Shirazi ordered Iran's next advance on May 21. Through successions of human wave attacks, IRGC troops with some mixed regulars pushed toward the city, eventually encircling Iraqi defenders. Iraqi defensive lines began to disintegrate. Taking heavy losses, Iranians managed to break through enemy lines and enter the city by the 23rd. From the IRGC's perspective, the willingness of its forces to press forward in the face of escalating carnage "horrified and disillusioned [the] enemy" to such an extent that the Iraqis "finally came to the conclusion that [they] could no longer withstand the crushing waves of attacks by troops who actually mocked" the volleys of incoming fire and artillery barrages.[57] Once inside the city, Iranian forces fought the Iraqis street to street. Overwhelmed and unable to receive reinforcements, Iraqis retreated to positions across the Karun River, many drowning as they tried to swim to the opposite bank. Some twelve thousand Iraqi troops remained inside the city and were captured. After three weeks of battle, Iranian forces succeeded in uprooting the last major Iraqi foothold in their country.

After Khorramshahr, Iran's top military commanders left little doubt about what they thought should come next. Mohsen Rezai announced that "so long as Saddam exists, the war will continue."[58] Lieutenant General Shirazi similarly proclaimed two weeks later that the war would not end until Saddam was overthrown and Iranian forces could pray in the shrine of Imam Husayn in Karbala.[59] "The road to Jerusalem runs through Karbala," had already become a popular slogan used by Iran's regime. Liberating Karbala from atheist Baathist hands became both a literal goal for Iran's forces and a symbol for the grander project they hoped to achieve: the eventual restoration of Muslim control over Jerusalem. Iran's leaders considered Saddam Hussein to be a barrier to the Islamic revolution imposed by the United States and Israel. As long as he remained, the spiritually and politically liberating forces that the revolution had unleashed could not fully penetrate other Muslim lands or reach their fullest potential. The goal was not simply the toppling of a belligerent neighbor but the full maturation of the Islamic revolution, which they believed would restore dignity to the Islamic world and purge Western influence from the Middle East.

# The Long War

In the marshlands, he was inundated with death and destruction. The
air was stifling, the maddening heat stagnant. Everything seemed futile
and in vain.[1]

— Davud Ghaffarzadegan, *Fortune Told in Blood*

The success of the spring 1982 offenses gave Iran the upper hand. Ayatollah
Khomeini had a decision to make: sue for peace from a position of strength or
continue the fight. There was considerable debate on which direction to choose.
Top military commanders made it clear that they wanted to push on into Iraq.
Khomeini was among others who reportedly worried that invading Iraq would
erode any sympathy Iran had in the international sphere and possibly turn popular Iraqi sentiments against it.[2] Those in favor of continuing the war, particularly IRGC chief Rezai, ground forces commander Shirazi, and Majles speaker
Rafsanjani, argued that there could be no victory without toppling Saddam
and that that could be realized only through invading Iraq.[3] They further contended that Iran's advantages in manpower and the revolutionary zeal of its
forces—factors that had helped them expel the Iraqis from much of Iran's southwest—would be enough to overwhelm the technological and defensive advantages of their adversary. These arguments, and the assurances of his commanders
that victory could be achieved, swayed Khomeini's decision to take the fight into
Iraq.

Iran's invasion put the conflict on a new course—one that would have no
decisive end. What resulted was a bloody and fruitless war of attrition that
lasted nearly six more years. This period saw the IRGC develop as a military
institution and gradually come to displace the regular military as Iran's leading
operational voice in the conflict. The IRGC had demonstrated that its nontraditional approach to combat could be effectively deployed against the Iraqis. The
human wave attacks that had been decisive in pushing Iraqi forces back across
the border remained the foundation of the IRGC's strategy. Yet, what had sty-
mied Iraq's efforts in Iran—poor logistics, inadequate supply lines, underesti-
mating the patriotic response of the local population, and the overall inability

to hold territory—also impeded Iran's advances. As the war dragged on, the intractable reliance on human wave attacks in the face of repeated failure, and the insistence on overthrowing Saddam, drove mounting Iranian losses. The IRGC's central role in wartime decision-making afforded it a high degree of influence over how the conflict was fought. It also made it more responsible for the war's outcomes.

## The International Dimension

Iran's counter-invasion shifted already imbalanced international opinion heavily toward Iraq. The Arab sheikhdoms of the Persian Gulf strongly supported Saddam Hussein. They helped Iraq sustain its war effort and continually outpace Iran in military procurement and expenditures. Having already established the Gulf Cooperation Council (GCC) in 1981 as a unified security front to counter the spread of the Islamic revolution, Iran's Arab neighbors (Kuwait, Bahrain, United Arab Emirates, Qatar, Oman, and Saudi Arabia) believed that Iran's stated desire to "export" the Islamic revolution (a concept explored in the next chapter) had taken on an overt military dimension with the counter-invasion of Iraq. Saddam became viewed as a bulwark between the GCC's monarchies and Iran's anti-monarchical ascendency. Saudi Arabia led this effort and along with Kuwait provided Iraq somewhere between $25 to $50 billion in financial loans and grants during the war. Egypt and Jordan also supported Iraq and provided military supplies and weapons at crucial points in the war.[4]

Similar anxieties about Iran's political intentions tilted the balance of international support toward Iraq. The Soviet Union and France were the primary military suppliers to Saddam Hussein. Moscow was initially neutral in the war, and had robust sales to both countries, but its sales to Iran were severely reduced after 1983 in protest over Iran's harsh crackdown on the pro-Soviet Tudeh Party. Moscow turned to favor Saddam, and sold approximately $11.5 billion in military supplies to Iraq between 1984 and 1987. In comparison, sales to Iran totaled around $5 million during this period.[5]

France was Saddam's second largest military supplier, and was repeatedly condemned by Tehran for its partiality. The IRGC considered France a pillar of the Western "imperialist front," which was using Iraq as a proxy force to crush the Islamic revolution and prevent its message from spreading beyond Iran's borders.[6] Although France's military sales to Iraq were about a third of what the USSR provided Saddam—approximately $4.5 billion between 1982 and 1986—they included some of Iraq's most sophisticated weaponry, including the Mirage F-1 and Super Étendard combat fighter aircraft, Super Frelon helicopters, and Exocet AM39 air-to-surface missiles.[7] France helped subsidize some of these purchases through $5 billion in loans to Iraq.[8] France's sales to Iran were a fraction of that during this period, totaling around $40 million.

By focusing its procurement on a few main sources, Iraq was able to continually rearm, refurbish, and deploy integrated weapon systems. In contrast, Iran was forced to seek poorer-quality supplies from a number of different sources. Iran's bellicose rhetoric, hostility toward the United States and Israel, and inability to form a pragmatic foreign policy during the war alienated it from much of the international community. Washington pressured its Western allies not to do business with Iran, and with the loss of the Soviet Union as a major supplier, Iran was limited to seeking deals from sympathetic countries such as Syria, Libya, Algeria, North Korea, Eastern European Soviet Bloc states, and China. These piecemeal purchases provided materiel that matched poorly with Iran's mostly American-made military stock. Although Iran was able to secure some critical shipments of American spare parts via Israel through a convoluted, covert operation that later became known as the Iran-Contra scandal, Iran's ability to secure essential military supplies and advanced weaponry during the war was significantly restricted. Iran managed under $12 billion in foreign military purchases between 1980 and 1987, whereas Iraq's purchases were closer to $44 billion.[9] This imbalance gave Iraq a distinct advantage in the latter years of the war, when its ability to replenish sophisticated weaponry proved to be decisive.[10]

Iraq's superior foreign backing, and Iran's comparative lack of international support, was a major factor during the war and one that was continually utilized by Iraq toward strategic ends. Iraq not only benefited from financial aid and access to more sophisticated weaponry, but also from the diplomatic cover and intelligence provided to it by its wartime allies, especially the United States, who is believed to have provided Baghdad with satellite imagery of Iranian formations at critical junctures in the war. These tools gave Iraq the wherewithal to fight a war of attrition and the political cover to engage in war crimes without fear of repercussions. Indeed, although Iran accused Iraq of using chemical weapons at points in the war—and provided evidence to international observers verifying that use—Washington's favoring of Saddam shielded him from international criticism and pressure.[11] The totality of foreign assistance factored heavily in Iraq's ability to survive Iran's onslaught and enabled it to gain strength throughout the war. It also created an imbalance in military power that in part led Iran to rely on high cost, massive infantry offensives to take the fight to Iraq.

## Running into Walls

Iran's decision to invade Iraq came on the heels of its successful campaigns in Khuzestan and the liberation of Khorramshahr. Several factors contributed to the successes of operations Fath al-Mubin, Bayt al-Muqaddas, and Tariq al-Quds, but it was the tactic of human wave assaults that proved to be the most decisive element. This tactic became the focal point of the majority of campaigns thrust into Iraq. It also placed the IRGC—as the chief proponent of and participant (along with the Basij volunteers, and a smaller proportion of regular infantry) in mass infantry assaults—at the center of the war-planning process. The immense sacrifices of its troops combined with the victories in Khuzestan to give the IRGC an enhanced degree of legitimacy within Iran's leadership. Through the support of key leaders and Khomeini, the IRGC was able to continue deploying a strategy of human wave assaults despite early signs of its ineffectiveness. The endorsement of the human wave approach by civilian leaders did not mitigate tensions between the IRGC and the regular military. The regular military commanders largely disapproved of mass infantry assaults, seeing them as unsustainable and a waste of human resources. Such philosophical differences caused a growing rift between the regular military and IRGC commanders as the war progressed.

Although human wave attacks proved decisive against Iraqi positions within Iran, they quickly proved to be ineffective against hardened defenses inside Iraq. Now defending their home territory, the Iraqis held numerous advantages over the invading Iranians. Superior knowledge of the terrain, the patriotic response of the Iraqi people, and effective logistics networks, which enabled supplies, reinforcements, and better battlefield intelligence to reach front line positions, all aided Iraq's defensive effort. Iraqi military planners also learned to adapt to human wave attacks, and developed tactics to counter those assaults (such as by strategically retreating, drawing the invaders in, and then corralling them into a "killing zone"), which exacted steep death tolls on the Iranians. In the southern front, several operations between 1982 through 1985 deployed mass infantry assaults to little effect. While Iran was able to regain some territory and take small patches of land inside of Iraq's border, the overall failure of these operations (e.g., Operations Ramadan al-Mubarak in 1982, Wal-Fajr 1 in 1983, and Khaybar in 1984) emboldened the morale of Saddam's forces. In Operation Ramadan al-Mubarak, which was Iran's first attempt to take the Iraqi city of Basra, Iran's military planners hoped their operation would be aided by a popular uprising among Basra's Shia majority—something that never materialized. The ground assault featured mostly IRGC and Basij troops advancing through marshland headlong into hardened Iraqi defenses. Bogged down and unable to seriously challenge Iraqi defenses, Iranian forces took heavy casualties and managed to seize only a small strip of Iraqi territory.[12] Iran had even less success with this tactic in the middle and northern fronts, which occurred in the mountainous border regions of Iranian Kurdistan. Mountainous terrain, with its narrow valleys and strategic peaks, was topographically ill-suited to mass infantry assaults, in that it forced advancing troops into narrow formations that could more easily be defended from positions situated at higher ground.

The viability of human wave attacks became the subject of vigorous debate in Tehran. IRGC chief Mohsen Rezai was the leading advocate for mass infantry assaults. He found support from Majles speaker Rafsanjani, and among other influential clergy. Top officers of the regular military, particularly Lieutenant General Qassem Ali Zahirnejad (the Chief of Joint Staff from 1982 to 1984) and Lieutenant General Ali Sayyad Shirazi (ground forces commander from 1981 to 1986), considered such tactics unsustainable and encouraged a more conservative approach. The regular military at times found sympathy with some civilian leaders, such as President Khamenei and Prime Minister Mir Husayn Musavi, but Rafsajani's support for the IRGC's human wave-centric strategy was enough to sway Khomeini and earn his endorsement at crucial points in the war. As the war dragged on and the death toll mounted, Rafsanjani's backing of the IRGC waned. However, by that point, Mohsen Rezai had a more entrenched, influential position with Khomeini, who, despite attempts at neutrality between the forces, more often than not endorsed the IRGC's strategy or let it proceed without interference. Failed offensives such as Operation Khaybar in 1984 exacerbated the divide between the regular military and the IRGC on the effectiveness of mass infantry assaults.[13] Tensions culminated in July 1986, when Mohsen Rezai and Lieutenant General Ali Sayyad Shirazi clashed (perhaps physically) over the direction of the war. Khomeini interceded and stressed the importance of unity and equality between the forces, but within weeks, removed Shirazi from his command. Shirazi outwardly transitioned into a senior advisory role to Khomeini, and became one of the leader's representatives on the Supreme Defense Council, but was in effect cast out of the war-planning process.[14] Khomeini had again, in his own way, sided with the IRGC.

Disagreements on war planning went deeper than tactics and strategy. At their root was a competition for influence. Although the regular military was politically marginalized after the revolution, it retained the trust of Iran's leaders to lead the fight against Saddam. The IRGC was still a fledgling organization when the war began, and even its staunchest backers such as Ayatollah Montazeri, Rafsanjani, and Khomeini did not believe it could replace the military, much less lead the war. It was not until the introduction of mass infantry assaults that the IRGC's role in the war began to expand. The effectiveness of these attacks in the Khuzestan theater was a boon to the IRGC's status in the war. The successes in Khorramshahr and elsewhere earned legitimacy for the organization and gave its leadership, particularly Mohsen Rezai, an influential place in wartime decision-making. In many ways, the IRGC owed its leading position in the war-planning process to the collective willingness of its troops to engage in kamikaze infantry operations and die by the thousands. The Guards had proved capable in small, guerilla-style attacks early in the war, but such operations no longer had much of a place in the massive, total war Iran was engaged in. For the IRGC to maintain its place in war planning, both to ensure its voice was heard and to defend its interests, it needed human wave assaults to remain a central fixture of Iranian strategy. If war planners had abandoned that tactic after the counter-invasion of Iraq, the IRGC's development as a military organization would have remained constrained.

The IRGC's central role in the war helped it expand its political influence and military capabilities. By late 1982, through lobbying efforts and those of its clerical advocates, the IRGC succeeded in establishing its own government ministry separate from the Ministry of Defense. Mohsen Rafiqdust, part of the original coalition that brought the IRGC into existence, headed the new IRGC ministry and became the organization's main intermediary with the government in Tehran.[15] The creation of the IRGC ministry reinforced the notion that the Guards were not simply another branch of Iran's armed forces, but their own entity, with greater political capital than the regular forces. The Guards also succeeded in establishing their own air and naval forces—parallel to those of the regular military—made possible through decree by Khomeini on September 17, 1985. Even as he effectively weakened the regular military through this redundancy, Khomeini's decree emphasized the need for the IRGC to improve coordination with the regular forces.[16] The establishment of parallel IRGC naval and air forces was a clear indication of Khomeini's favoritism and led to speculation of a deepening rift between the Guards and their regular counterparts.[17] This move was more symbolic than immediately transformative. The IRGC lacked the funds to adequately develop their ground forces, and managed to develop only limited air and naval capabilities by the end of the war. However, it enabled the expansion of the IRGC into realms that had been dominated by the regular military. It was a meaningful evolution for the IRGC, and ensured that the organization's position within the military sphere would not be temporary or confined to the war.

## In the Path of the Divine

In pursuing a high-cost, infantry-based strategy, Iran's forces required a continual massive supply of conscripted and volunteer soldiers. The bulk of this manpower was funneled into the IRGC and the Basij. Both organizations grew rapidly through the war. The ranks of the IRGC swelled from around 25,000 in 1980 to an estimated 350,000 by 1986.[18] Iranian leaders claimed that the Basij had grown to include three million volunteers by 1986, with around 600,000 deployed to the front.[19] While the IRGC accepted both conscripts and volunteers, the Basij was a volunteer organization that drew the majority of its members from those too young and, to a lesser degree, too old to serve in the IRGC or regular forces. The Basij was notorious for its use of child soldiers, generally boys between the ages of twelve and sixteen. Iran received international condemnation for this practice, but its leaders rejected such criticism and did little to hide the role of the young in the war.[20]

Young Basij members played a supporting role in the first stage of the war, but increasingly became used as front-line forces in human wave attacks and other large-scale infantry movements. In these operations, the Basij were cannon fodder, asked to charge headlong into enemy fire, often with limited or no weapons of their own. Iranian clergy, working as wartime propagandists, led the IRGC and Basij recruitment efforts. They blended evocations of Shia tradition with stories of Saddam's atrocities to ignite the religious consciousness and national pride of Iranian youth. The boys were assured that heavenly paradise awaited those who achieved martyrdom on the battlefield in defense of Khomeini and Islamic Iran. Headbands with prayerful invocations, along with plastic "keys to heaven" worn as necklaces, were distributed to basijis to symbolize the connection between them, their activity on the front lines, and the divine rewards awaiting them. This approach, backed by state resources, endorsed by Iran's leaders, and fueled by social pressure to participate in the war, brought hundreds of thousands of Iranian youth to recruitment centers and eventually to the front lines.

Examples of how this process was interpreted by those who joined the Basij can be found in the interviews Ian Brown conducted with Iranian prisoners of war. Brown served as an educator assigned to a unit of Iranian child POWs in Iraq's Camp 7 prison in Ramadi from 1987 to 1989. The perspectives of his interview subjects reveal a spectrum of attitudes and sensibilities, and provide glimpses into the lives of the often nameless Basij soldier. Brown found an attitudinal difference between those POWs who were older in age and had joined earlier in the war, and those who were younger and had joined later. Ahmad, who volunteered when he was fourteen, is representative of the latter group. He recalls being inspired by the liberation of Khorramshahr, and the desire to fight for his country.[21] In his words:

> It's true that martyrdom is important to Shiites—we all learn about the Imams and how they died—but I didn't go to war to die for Islam. I went to defend Iran and I think most of my friends went for the same reason. . . . In my case, my father and mother never wanted me to go to the front. Neither did my teacher. But I was determined to do so. I've never heard any stories of mothers forcing their sons to join the basij. It

was the opposite case with all my friends. . . . I was so determined to go to war that I ran away from home. The first time I was sent back home because the officer said I was too young—I was thirteen at the time. The second time I tried was a year later when I was fourteen. I went to the local HQ of the basij. The officer told me that I had to be fifteen to join up, so I told him I was. He wanted to see my identity card, so I gave it to him, and he saw I was only fourteen. Then he asked what my parents had said, because he needed their permission if I joined before I was fifteen. I said they agreed and he allowed me to join up. There were hundreds of young boys pushing to get into the office that morning. All were very young, so the officer had no choice but to let us all in.[22]

A similarly conflicted perspective was shared by Samir:

It was a game for us. On the television, they would show a young boy dressed as a soldier, carrying a gun and wearing the red headband of the basij. He would say how wonderful it was to be a soldier for Islam, fighting for freedom against the Iraqis. Then he would curse the Iraqis and all Arabs, saying they were not good Muslims. Next he would tell us to join him and come to war. We didn't understand the words "patriotism" or "martyrdom," or at least I didn't. It was just an exciting game and a chance to prove to your friends that you'd grown up and were no longer a child. . . . The mullahs said it was an honour to go and fight for Islam and to be martyred for Islam, just like Imam Hussein. I didn't want to die for anyone, but wanted to stay in school. . . . I should have stayed, but all my friends were leaving, too, and I was excited about going. I'd already done some training in the camp and I knew how to use a gun and throw hand grenades.[23]

Hashemy had a different experience and expressed a less ambiguous sense of purpose.

All Iranians came to war to defend their country from the Iraqi invasion. That is a normal thing to do. I think British people did the same in the Second World War against Germany. . . . We are Shiite Muslims, not Sunni. Only a small proportion of Muslims are Shiite, but ours is the true faith. Since the beginning of Islam, we have been fighting and dying for our rights. Imam Ali became the leader of the Muslims, but was martyred while reading the Qur'an. Imam Hussein was decapitated at Karbala, trying to defend our religion. We are not afraid to be

martyred for Islam. On the contrary, we are proud to do so, because we
are following our Imams and doing our duty for the whole Shiite community. It is something more than patriotism we feel when we fight. We
want to die for Islam, not Iran, like Imam Hussein. . . . We had propaganda to inform the people of what the Iraqis were doing to our towns
and our people. You know the story of Khorramshahr, I think, when
Iraqi soldiers raped Iranian women? This shocked many people and
made them come and fight. And the religious men [i.e., clergy] talked
to people in mosques and schools about Islam, the revolution and the
war, but no one was forced to do anything. In fact, mothers, fathers and
teachers often tried to persuade young boys not to go, myself included.
So we had to run away from home to join up with the [Basij].[24]

Brown claims Hashemy's perspective was less common and held by a minority of prisoners. But he also suggests that such attitudes tended to be stronger
among the older prisoners who were more religious and held on to Shia traditions (such as prayer and fasting) more firmly than the younger captives.[25]

A unifying element in these anecdotes is the central place religion and spirituality had in the propaganda and recruitment efforts that targeted youth. Appeals
to Shia identity, and its inherent connection to Iran's national consciousness,
were the mechanisms through which nearly all aspects of the war were communicated. Iran's leaders made the connection between the war and Shiism explicit
at the outset. But as the conflict continued, and the death toll snowballed, religion became less a metaphor for the war than war became a part of the Iranian
national religion. Through the war, Iranians symbolically relived the formative
events in Shia history while simultaneously inventing new national narratives.
The IRGC was at the heart of this interweaving of religion and culture. It was
both a megaphone for the religious messages that sought to define the war, and a
recipient of the promises and spiritual assurances of Iran's clerical leaders.

As the war moved into its fifth year, the morale of Iranian forces had reached
one of its lowest points. The war had expanded and was taking a mounting economic and psychological toll on Iran. Iraq had expanded its military campaign to
include targeting Iran's economic infrastructure and population centers. Saddam
sought to destroy Iran's economy by attacking oil refineries and Iranian-flagged
oil vessels in the Persian Gulf—a stage of the conflict known as the tanker war.[26]
In a "war of the cities," Iraq used ballistic missiles, bombing raids, and artillery
to strike Iranian cities and towns. According to official Iranian sources, those
attacks killed nearly seven thousand and injured over twenty-five thousand civilians between 1984 and 1986.[27] Iran responded in kind and targeted both Iraqi
civilian centers and shipping, but Iraq was able to better weather the economic
toll of the conflict through superior access to foreign aid.

Iran's land operations in the southern theater continued to be ineffective despite the tens of thousands of lives cost. Operation Khaybar, which aimed at taking the strategic Basra-to-Baghdad highway, was one Iran's largest and boldest in the war. In one part of the operation, which lasted from February to March 1984, tens of thousands of basijis, backed by IRGC battalions, launched successive human wave attacks across Iraq's Hawizeh marshes. Iraq deployed artillery, tanks, helicopter gunships, and chemical weapons against them, crushing the advance. Although Iran managed to occupy an abandoned Iraqi oil complex known as Majnun Island, the operation was considered a massive failure. An estimated 250,000 troops were involved in the operation, with up to 20,000 mostly Basij and IRGC killed, another 20,000 to 30,000 wounded, and an unknown number captured or missing.[28] A year later, Iran launched Operation Badr, a smaller but still major offensive with a similar goal. Although Iranian forces had learned lessons from the failures of Khaybar and were better prepared, so were the Iraqis. Badr was equally unsuccessful, leaving up to twelve thousand mostly Basij and IRGC killed, with little to show for it.[29]

By this time the IRGC had deemphasized coverage of wartime operations in its primary publication—the biweekly journal *Payam-e Enqelab* (*Message of the Revolution*)—and expanded reporting on religious topics. Reports from the battlefield still occurred, but in the absence of major victories, more attention was given to the religious aspects of war and Shia identity, such as essays on the spiritual culture of the front, extended series on the meaning of war in the Quran and the Karbala narrative, retellings of Shia history, interviews with prominent clergy, and pages devoted to remembering the organization's countless war martyrs. Short biographies and will and testaments of the IRGC's war dead were routinely published, which highlighted the spiritual devotion of martyrs and celebrated their sacrifice.[30] The tonal shift in *Payam*'s pages over time exemplifies one way the IRGC sought to deal with the morass and uncertainty of the war. With victory no longer on the horizon, and with losses mounting, the war had morphed from a political mission to a spiritual enterprise, one that perhaps no longer needed a definitive conclusion—or even victorious battles—to have meaning.

Stuck in this mire, with the idea of a successful war fading, Iran's leaders did their best to rally their forces through appeals to religion. In a speech to guardsmen in January 1985, Majles speaker Rafsanjani enumerated the manifold challenges Iran was facing in the war and the profound injustice of it all. He contrasted the enemies of Iran, who had every means at their disposal, with the relative poverty of the Guards. He reminded his audience that what they lacked in material wealth and sophisticated military technology was nothing in comparison to the power that faith in God had given them, saying:

Those who have entered the [IRGC] have all taken this path in order
to serve god and in order to carry out Islamic and humanitarian duties.
. . . The living conditions of a corpsman today [are] comparable to that
of a simple labourer. He does not have housing or other employment
benefits and steps. There is no financial reward for them and only their
daily needs are satisfied. . . . Today we need the great spirit and faith of
the members of the corps. Our enemies have been planning for centuries and have prepared themselves in every aspect. However, we face
them with purity, faith and reliance on the Lord. . . . Our enemy uses
every means to deal blows against us. Its supporters are even lower and
more criminal than the enemy. Opposing this enemy and its supporters, who are armed with the most sophisticated weapons, is not possible with only materials or materialistic intentions. It is your faith and
purity which has crippled them.[31]

Similar themes were explored by Khomeini in his sermons to the IRGC faithful. In one talk marking the sixth anniversary of the revolution, the supreme
leader enumerated the place of faith in the war, reimagining victory and recast-
ing it in spiritual terms. Addressing the guardsmen he said:

The beloved ones, who in the defence of Islam and the Islamic homeland are fighting with devotion in the fronts—and the depth of their
spiritual and mystical qualities and the great value of their efforts
could not be estimated by anyone except God Almighty. . . . My dear
ones, you are victorious and successful—whether you achieve visible
success in the path of Almighty God, or whether you are martyred,
wounded or imprisoned. God Almighty is with you, and the powerful arms of the Remnant of God [the Hidden Imam], which is God's
arm, is behind you. Whoever rises up for the sake of God, the glory
of Islam and the salvation of the deprived people, will harbour no
fear concerning the events of the world. You are the followers of the
prophet of God who endured unbearable pains in the course of God's
religion, who accepted great hardships in Mecca when he was the
object of so much pressure, slanders and insults; and in Medina when
he was subjected to so many crushing wars and defensive actions.
Nevertheless, His Holiness and his faithful followers remained stead-
fast like a mountain and served Islam and the Muslims. You are the
shi'is [the followers] of the Commander of the Faithful [Imam Ali]
and his children who welcomed any pain and calamity in the path
of God.[32]

While Iran's leaders desperately wanted to win the war, the messages they sent to the troops, and those the IRGC communicated to its rank and file, sought to adjust what victory meant and what expectations for victory should be. Sacrifice, suffering, selflessness, devotion, and martyrdom became not just spiritual acts that would be rewarded, but rewards themselves. As Khomeini argued, victory was in the act of worship. And to worship during the war was to fight with faith, like the early Imams, who failed politically but succeeded spiritually.

## A Fleeting Taste of Victory

Despite the malaise that had consumed Iran through 1985, its war effort remained ambitious. On February 10, 1986, Iran launched another major offensive in the southern sector. The timing of this operation (which took place during the rainy season) was strategic; however, it was also symbolic, coinciding with the annual commemoration of the martyrdom of Fatimah—the Prophet Mohammad's eldest child, the wife of Imam Ali, and the matriarch of the eleven imams whose holy lineage ran through her—which had occurred just days before the operation began. For the IRGC, the spiritual significance of this time endowed the operation with a special potency. The organization saw parallels between their mission and Fatimah's heroic steadfastness, and used such metaphors to frame the operation and the outcomes it produced. The IRGC described its soldiers in the operation as the "warriors of Islam, [the] travelers of Hosayn's Karbala," who, in the spirit of Fatimah, were entering into an epic battle with an infidel enemy.[33] As the assault began, late into the night and during heavy rain, IRGC soldiers were said to have prayerfully beseeched Fatimah, quietly chanting "Ya Zahrah, Ya Zahrah"—or O Resplendent One, a title of reverence reserved for Fatimah—invoking her protection and fortitude as they anxiously anticipated the violence to come.[34]

The operation, code named Wal-Fajr 8, had two main thrusts aimed across the Shatt al-Arab waterway. Both the northern thrust (near Umm Rasas Island) and the southern crossing (near the Siba oil field) sought to establish bridgeheads on the western bank of the Shatt al-Arab from which Iranian forces could move toward the Basra-Faw road. Two diversionary thrusts were organized further north to draw Iraqi defenses away from the main advances. Although Iran took heavy losses, they succeeded in getting Iraq to overcommit its forces and firepower in defending against the diversionary assaults.[35] This allowed the southern movements to successfully establish bridgeheads along the western bank of the Shatt al-Arab and prepare for an advance to the Basra-Faw road. Iran was aided by the poor weather conditions it had

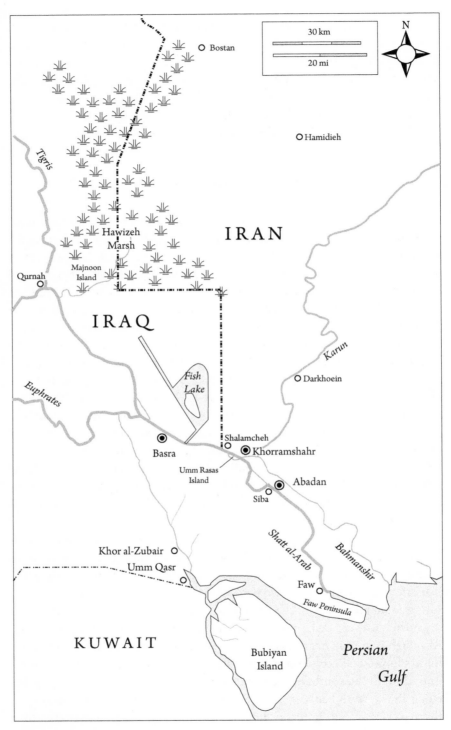

Map 5.1 The southern front

counted on, with driving rain and reduced visibility rendering Iraq's vaunted air capabilities ineffective. Despite the rain and rough waters, Iran was surprisingly successful at ferrying men, vehicles, and equipment across a roughly 300-yard-wide portion of the river.[36] Both advances reached the Basra-Faw road, at which point the northern thrust proceeded northward into stiff Iraqi resistance, and the other thrust advanced south toward Faw. By February 14, after days of heavy fighting, IRGC and mixed regular infantry were able to drive out the remaining Iraqis and take the strategic Faw Peninsula. By seizing Faw, Iranian forces were in the position to potentially cut off Iraq's access to the Persian Gulf, attack Basra to the north, and target Iraqi communications lines to Kuwait.[37]

Faw was a stunning victory for the Iranians. Given their string of ineffective offensives in the southern theater, the success of Wal-Fajr 8, with its many logistic and geographic obstacles, stunned Iraq and aroused trepidation among its supporters in the Persian Gulf.[38] The planning and execution of the operation displayed a number of areas of tactical innovation for the Iranians. The effectiveness of the initial amphibious assaults (undertaken by frogmen units), the establishment of pontoon bridges, the utilization of poor weather, and the boldness of targeting Faw (something the Iraqis did not anticipate nor think possible), and reaching striking distance of Kuwait and Basra, were all impressive developments for Iranian forces. The operation also showcased Iran's Reconstruction Jihad (*jehad-e sazandegi*) organization, which operated as the IRGC's corps of engineers during the war and was responsible for altering Iraqi terrain, forming bridge networks, and establishing defensive embankments for Iranian forces, which were all critical in the Faw campaign.[39]

Beyond these tactical and strategic victories, the IRGC considered the capturing of Faw to be a spiritual achievement for its forces, and an enlivening expression of their faith. Mohsen Rezai remarked on how "a great spirituality was brought forth into the battlefields" in the operation.[40] Ali Fazali, an IRGC brigade commander, expanded on this notion and claimed that while the spirituality displayed during Wal-Fajr 8 was similar to past operations (he specifically mentions the great victories of Fath al-Mubin and Bayt al-Muqaddas), it was also unique. He gives the example of prayer, and says that while it was always present at the front, this operation was different; this time his soldiers "prayed an *extreme* amount."[41] Fazali relates an anecdote from the battle that for him encapsulated both the spirituality of the war and the true nature of what IRGC soldiers were endeavoring to achieve. He recalls that during one of the battles he and some of his men had noticed a person slowly approaching from the distance.

We didn't know if he was one of our forces or the enemy. We waited until he got closer and we could get a look at him. When he got near us we saw that he was one of the dear basijis, around 15 to 16 years old. We embraced him. We noticed that his leg had been severed below the shin. . . . His boots were removed and draped across his neck so that he could crawl. He had crawled a great distance. We quickly went to help him. We spoke to him a lot over there but he said one sentence that [is worthy of] much commentary and is very profound. . . . Those words of his were these: "Going to Karbala is an experience that is beyond comprehension (*bas majara darad*)."[42]

The scene for Fazali is striking. Here was a boy, severely wounded, exhausted from having crawled a great distance through an open battlefield, who seemed to be overwhelmed not by the harm that had befallen him, but by an undefinable mystical experience. The boy had not simply fought in a violent clash and suffered a devastating injury; he had been on a spiritual journey. Karbala is more than a metaphor for the basiji and Fazali; it describes a state of being, a glimpse of the divine. As Fazali explains, "the reality is that going to Karbala is not simple. We cannot just say to go to Karbala in slogans." In other words, Karbala *can* be an empty metaphor, but, for this boy and others, it was not. It was real. Profound. Something that could only be lived and experienced firsthand through faithful action and sacrifice.

The victory gave Iran a strategic foothold in southern Iraq. Iran quickly worked to capitalize on its gains by funneling troops and equipment into the peninsula, amassing an estimated force of twenty-five thousand mostly IRGC with mixed regulars in Faw, along with assorted materiel and military equipment.[43] Mohsen Rafiqdust, the head of the IRGC Ministry, boasted: "We have placed so many men and so much materiel in Faw today . . . we have more than 10 bridges over the Arvand River for transporting men and materiel."[44] Rafiqdust saw this as a testament to Iran's resolve to finish the war, adding: "We did not go to Faw to capture it and then retreat in haste. We have come to stay until we have liberated Iraq. We are here to stay."[45] From Faw, Iran was in position to threaten Basra from the south and to further restrict Iraqi access (including oil shipments) through the Shatt al-Arab if not sever its access to the Persian Gulf entirely. Iran was also now in close proximity to Kuwait—one of Saddam's chief supporters—and could potentially use the presence of its forces to compel Kuwait to reduce its aid to Baghdad. Mohsen Rezai emphasized these points:

Statesmen of the world also know that Faw is on the way to Umm al-Qasr and on the way to Basra, and in addition to this, it is possibly on the way to Saddam's defenders in the region. This is terrifying for them. They're witnessing our dominance over the Persian Gulf, which has been one of the most important outcomes of this operation.[46]

A corresponding boost in morale benefited Iran's forces the most. They were reenergized, rejuvenated, and the hope of a potential victory was restored. Rezai spoke at length about the successes of the operation, ranking it "among the unparalleled, most magnificent operations in the history of warfare in the world" and saw it as a galvanizing moment for Iran:

> Operation Wal-Fajr 8 marked the beginning of an evolution in our country. Many of our internal and external issues were solved . . . solidarity at home became even more than before; the command of war was taken more seriously, and the uncertainties regarding the war in our country were resolved.[47]

This was a moment Rezai wanted to seize. The capture of Faw had been Iran's biggest success since the liberation of Khorramshahr, and for the first time Iran had a strategic foothold in Iraqi territory. For Rezai, the time was right for a massive expansion of the war effort, including a more dramatic utilization of popular forces and a complete devotion of Iran's national resources to the fight. He began to advocate a new war plan that would "completely transform [the conflict] into a people's war." All schools, factories, and industrial centers would begin to do the work of "hundreds of factories" by manufacturing ammunition and materiel at several times the then-current rate. A vast expansion in the volunteer forces was even more crucial. As Rezai contended, "the only path" for Iran was to transform the conflict into a "full-scale people's war."[48] He added:

> If up to yesterday we were fighting in Faw with 150,000 men, today Islam's forces should be vastly increased on the battlefields and we should plan a full-scale people's war. At a time when, with 150,000 men we could create this great epic of Faw and cross Iraq's borders, how could we fail to carry out other attacks when armed with several times the power used in Faw. . . . And if we were to succeed in organising the people at a level several times the military might of Faw and bring the country's capabilities into the war, the problem of the war would be solved easily and rapidly.[49]

Rezai's plan was an implicit challenge to Iran's leadership, which had been divided on war strategy, and whose support he called for to make this drastic expansion of the war become reality. Yet, Rezai's vision did not take into consideration the manifold challenges Iran still faced in the war—challenges that could not be escaped or transcended by force of will.

## The Bitter End

Iran began 1987 with an ambitious attempt to take Basra and hopefully end the war. The offensive, code named Karbala 5, was launched on January 9 from the Shalamcheh border area and lasted through February 25. It involved an estimated one hundred thousand IRGC and Basij forces, with thirty-five thousand leading the advance and the remaining troops acting as reinforcements. Drawing from the success of the amphibious operations of the Faw offensive, Karbala 5 focused its advance on a strategic sixteen-mile-wide water barrier known as Fish Lake. The lake lay just inside Iraqi territory between the Iranian border to the west and the Shatt al-Arab to the east, and was built as a defensive bulwark to protect Basra from just such an advance. IRGC troops moved through Fish Lake along a several-mile-wide front, wading through water booby-trapped with barbed wire snags, mines, and electrodes. Although IRGC troops were able to seize a small portion of Iraqi ground east of the lake, and bring artillery forward that could target Basra, they took massive casualties, with an estimated twenty thousand Iranian troops killed. Iran claimed victory, but the operation did little to advance its stake in the war and came at steep cost.

In response to the operation and to Iranian artillery fire on Basra, Saddam Hussein renewed attacks on Iranian cities. From mid-January through February, Iraqi aircraft and SCUD-B missiles struck thirty-five Iranian cities, with Qom and Tehran hit multiple times. An estimated three thousand Iranian civilians were killed and nine thousand more were injured. Iraq also relentlessly pursued its campaign against Iran's oil industry and shipping, and succeeded in widening the conflict to include GCC supporters and the United States. Iran did its best to retaliate against Iraq in the Persian Gulf. Iranian aircraft and IRGC small boats targeted Iraqi vessels, and intermittently struck Kuwaiti ships in retribution for its support of Saddam. To help protect Kuwaiti shipping, the United States agreed in March to re-flag Kuwaiti vessels with US flags and provide them a US naval escort. The United States moved additional ships into the Persian Gulf and became an active participant in the tanker war. The US Navy engaged in limited combat with Iranian vessels, and shared intelligence on Iranian ship locations with Iraq.[50] IRGC small boats and logistics ships accompanied Iranian-flagged ships to protect them from hostile forces, and often drew fire from attackers.[51] IRGC commanders viewed the US naval protection of Kuwaiti vessels as an expansion of the US involvement in the war and preparation for a possible US invasion of Iran.[52] After a couple IRGC ships were destroyed by the US Navy in September, Mohsen Rezai announced that the "aggression" had marked the beginning of a "direct war and involvement by America against our people."[53]

In late July, a separate event reiterated to the Iranians that the war front had expanded. During the annual Muslim pilgrimage (*hajj*) in Saudi Arabia, an Iranian delegation led by Hojjat al-Islam Mehdi Karrubi began a protest march in Mecca against Israel and the United States. The Iranian march was stopped by Saudi security officials and sparked a clash. In the violence and chaos that followed, 402 Iranian pilgrims were killed and many more injured. Saudi authorities claimed that the majority of those killed had been trampled by the retreating crowd. Iranian authorities claimed that a number had died of gunshot wounds, and blamed the Saudi police of using live ammunition and "choking" gas (*gaz-e khafeh konandeh*) to push back what had been a peaceful protest. Rafsanjani linked the massacre to the war against Iran, claiming that the United States must have ordered it. Speaking to a massive demonstration in Tehran, Rafsanjani said: "[we] have no doubts that this incident, this tragedy, could not have taken place unless under the orders and by special demand of the superpower, the [United States]. [America], as a master ordering the servant, has made [the Saudis] carry out this crime."[54]

Over this period, Iraq's forces had become re-energized. In a series of offenses that began in the spring of 1988, Iraq used a combination of factors, including knowledge of Iranian forward positions gained from satellite imagery supplied by US intelligence, to take the fight to the Iranians. In mid-March, Iran—with the support peshmerga forces from Iraq's Patriotic Union of Kurdistan (PUK)—had made some limited gains in Iraq's Kurdistan region, including the town of Halabja. Saddam attacked the town the next day with chemical weapons, killing four thousand mostly Iraqi Kurds.[55] Iraq also stepped up its bombing and missile attacks against Iranian cities, making Iran's leaders fear that Saddam could use chemical weapons against Iranian population centers.[56] In mid-April, Iraqi forces employed chemical weapons in a successful campaign that expelled the mostly IRGC troops from the Faw peninsula and drove them back across the Shatt al-Arab. In late May, Iraqi forces attacked Iranian positions east of Basra near Fish Lake. Through a mix of innovative tactics, new cluster munitions, and chemical weapons, Iraq succeeded in pushing Iranian forces back across the border. This was another defeat for the IRGC, whose troops largely manned the positions in these areas. The next month, Iraqi forces used similar means and the deployment of paratroopers for the first time in the war to defeat the Iranians and retake the

Majnun Island complex.[57] Thus, in three months, Iraq was able to reverse three years of Iranian achievement in the southern sector.

The war was going poorly for Iran. The involvement of other countries in support of Iraq was eroding the confidence of Iran's leaders. Foreign support had enabled Saddam to refurbish his military, and get away with the regular and increasingly bold use of chemical weapons. The totality of the war, and Iraq's campaign against Iranian oil, were having a severe economic impact. Iran's coffers were thin and could not finance the fight indefinitely.[58] By summer, Iran was no longer in the position to push forward into Iraq and had lost its few strategic gains. Pressure was building domestically to turn the page on the conflict. Khomeini looked to Rafsanjani to find a way forward.[59] In early June 1988, Khomeini appointed Rafsanjani as the commander-in-chief of Iran's armed forces. In his decree, Khomeini asked the Majles speaker to streamline and restructure Iran's war effort. This was to include, among other steps, the establishment of a general command headquarters to pave the way for "complete unity" of the armed forces, and the "consolidation" of some departments and roles of the armed forces to better facilitate their "full coordination."[60] Khomeini ended the decree with this message:

> I call on the dear people of Iran and the armed forces and security forces to stand steadfast, with revolutionary patience and endurance and with strength and resistance, in the face of the plots of global arrogance, and to be certain that victory belongs to those who are patient. Today's world is saturated with injustice and treachery and you, the true followers of Islam are at the height of purity and honor. I pray for you all. May God be the companion and protector of those that are resisting along his path. I beseech God to grant you success. May God's peace and mercy be upon you all.[61]

Rafsanjani had been a leading advocate for continuing the war over the years. Like Khomeini, Rafsanjani did not outwardly back away from his uncompromising position on the war.[62] Behind the scenes, he worked to form a consensus among Iran's leaders and military commanders to end the conflict.[63] In July 1987, the United Nations Security Council unanimously passed Resolution 598, which called for an immediate ceasefire between Iran and Iraq, and a mutual retreat from occupied territory to their respective borders. Rafsanjani's mission was in part to bring Iran's leadership around to accepting the resolution. In the process, he asked the top military commanders for their assessments of what Iran needed to continue the war. Along with forthright responses from IRGC Navy commander Ali Shamkhani, and IRGC commander Ahmad

Kazemi, he also received a bleak report from Mohsen Rezai. Rezai stated that Iranian forces would not be in the position for another victory for at least five years. He then listed several areas of procurement and military development that they would need in order to defeat Iraq. The list included the need for hundreds of new tanks, aircraft, and artillery pieces, and 350 new infantry battalions. In addition, Rezai called for the development of laser and nuclear weapons, which he deemed as necessities in modern warfare, and declared that the "United States must be driven out of the Persian Gulf." The subtext of Rezai's letter was clear: Iran could not win the war as is. However, he added: "the war must continue." The call to carry on with the war, which could have been reflexive for Rezai at this point, conflicted with his assessment, which could be taken only as an admission of Iran's inability to persist. Khomeini included excerpts from Rezai's report in his letter which set the conditions for accepting resolution 598. In that letter, Khomeini criticized Rezai's call to continue as "mere sloganeering."[64]

As the future of the war was being deliberated in Tehran, Iran's leaders were once again reminded of the obstacles in front of them. On July 3, the USS *Vincennes*, a *Ticonderoga*-class Aegis guided missile cruiser on patrol in the Strait of Hormuz, mistook a civilian airliner for an Iranian F-14 and shot it down. Iran Air Flight 655 was en route from Bandar Abbas to Dubai on a routine, previously scheduled flight. The mistake killed all 290 civilians (including sixty-six children) on board. While momentum toward ending the war was already building in Tehran, this incident drove home the notion, possessed by many Iranian leaders by this time, that the United States would not let Iran win the war.[65] Over the next two weeks, Rafsanjani conferred with Iran's leadership—the Majles, Guardian Council, prominent clergy, and military commanders—and got them all to accept UNSC Resolution 598 unconditionally. With Khomeini's approval, Iran's letter accepting the resolution was delivered to the UN secretary general at midnight on July 17.

The agreement was a blow to Iran's leaders and to the IRGC. More than any other force, the IRGC personified Iran's unrelenting quest for victory. The many slogans that gave voice to Iran's aspirations—"War, War till Victory!" "The Road to Jerusalem Runs through Karbala!"—were more than propaganda for the organization; they were the building blocks of identity, vows of a religious faithful, the promised rewards for unimaginable sacrifice. It was the IRGC's commanders who, along with Rafsanjani, sought to continue the war into Iraq and continually called for more massive offensives in the southern theater to uproot Saddam. And it was the IRGC—including the Basij—who gave more lives to the conflict than any other. In accepting the ceasefire, the IRGC was accepting defeat. It had not brought about the victory it so vigorously pursued. It could not liberate

Karbala. It could not continue to Jerusalem. Mohsen Rezai expressed support for the decision to end the war, but indicated that the decision came from above him. Addressing his soldiers and the Iranian people, Rezai stated:

> I have deemed it necessary to inform the martyr-nurturing ummah about the views and viewpoints of myself and the dear brothers of the [IRGC]. Now that the esteemed political officials of . . . our country have [made a decision that] has been approved by the esteemed leader, we seriously support this decision which has been taken in order to safeguard the interests of the revolution, society and the country. . . .
>
>    With the religious obligation that we have from all the brothers . . . we are certain that in this period we shall remain faithful and steadfast just as we were before. We have fought up to now for the sake of [our] faith; for the sake of monotheism, justice, independence and liberation of Islam, the Koran and our country. We have fought for these things. We were not thinking of capturing territory. We were thinking of the liberation of spirits belonging to humankind; consciences who were thirsty to receive the ideology of divine inspiration and of the Holy Koran. Now that the great leader of the revolution, who set down the foundations and principles of the revolution and our political system, which must be built on these foundations thanks to God, this reshaping has been in progress for several years now and since it is among the special duties of the leader to determine and decide on the phases of the war, and since this decision has been taken by the leader, we abide by this decision; we consider it as having been the prerogative of the leadership.[66]

Cross-border fighting did not halt immediately. Iranian forces pushed back Iraqi incursions all across the front lines, including a large-scale attempt to advance into Khuzestan. In the central sector, Saddam dispatched a brigade of around seven thousand members of the Mojahedin-e Khalq Organization across the Iranian border near Kermanshah. The MKO had joined up with Saddam in 1986 and had taken part in some operations against Iraqi Kurdish forces. With their advance into Iran they announced that they were marching toward Tehran to retake the revolution. The MKO forces, which included a large percentage of female fighters, received limited Iraqi air support at the outset of the operation but were soon abandoned by Saddam.[67] Left unaided, the poorly trained Mojahedin were outmatched and summarily slaughtered by Iranian troops. The fighting was at once an exercise in bloodlust and a moment of catharsis for Iranian forces. The IRGC celebrated its victory over the "hypocrites" in the pages of *Payam-Enqelab*, providing details and narratives of the operation and highlighting photographs of its aftermath.[68] The images glorified the merciless destruction of their foe—burning wreckages of tanks and armored vehicles, grease-stained roads strewn with charred and rotting corpses. The MKO had intended to challenge Khomeini directly with a military advance. What it achieved was little more than a conciliation prize for its enemies. By August 8, UN Resolution 598 went into effect. After eight of the bloodiest years in the modern Middle East, the war between Iran and Iraq was officially over and cross-border hostilities gradually fizzled out.

# Exporting the Revolution

We will export our revolution throughout the world. As our revolution
is Islamic, the struggle will continue until the call of 'There is no God
but God . . .' echoes around the globe.[1]

—IRGC, *Payam-e Enqelab*

The war forced the IRGC to develop quickly as a military organization. But
war fighting was only one facet of the organization's original raison d'être. In its
foundational charter the IRGC saw itself as far more than a military organization. It was above all the guardian of the Islamic revolution. It was a *revolutionary* organization. That distinction carried with it a certain ideological view of
international relations which stressed resistance to imperialism and solidarity
with other liberation movements, particularly those in Muslim societies. For
the IRGC, solidarity was more than a political position; it was a commitment to
safeguard the world's "liberation movements and the rights of the oppressed."[2]
That pledge was motivated as much by self-interest as by ideology:

> Imperialism and global Zionism, with the help of governments and
> their henchmen, are everyday involved in plots against the spread
> and penetration of the Islamic revolution among the hearts of the
> people of Iran and the world. . . . Therefore we can and must [rely]
> upon our foundational doctrinal, political, security, and economic
> perspectives and shoulder the global message of Islam. We have
> no recourse except the mobilization of all the faithful forces of the
> Islamic revolution and must, with the mobilization of forces in
> every region, strike fear in the heart of our enemies so that the idea
> of invasion and the destruction of our Islamic revolution will exit
> [their minds]. If our revolution does not have an internationalist
> and aggressive approach the enemies of Islam will again enslave us
> culturally and politically.[3]

To protect the revolution, the IRGC believed it needed to spread its revolutionary ideals beyond Iran's borders and work with Muslim allies in foreign states to further its own anti-imperialist, pro-Islamic goals. In other words, the best defense is a good offense.

Although a similar form of internationalism was embraced by the Marxist strains of the Iranian revolution, for the IRGC the enterprise was seen as primarily Islamic. It was not only about igniting revolution elsewhere, it was about helping other Muslims take back their societies and governments from foreign secular influence. It was a moral position as much as a political one. The organization believed so firmly in this matter that it became one of its foundational missions:

> The faithful mojahedin of Islam must be the protector and guardian of God's frontiers. . . . The spreading of the Islamic revolution and the dissemination of its message to the people of the divine domains involves combating against the commanders, leaders, and the roots of heresy, colonialism, exploitation, and polytheism within divine Muslim territories. . . . If the mojahedin of Islam abandon their global and humane calling . . .they would be hollow like the police and gendarmerie and not true guardians of the Islamic revolution.[4]

This was an ambitious and potentially hazardous policy to adopt. It was also something not uncommon for revolutionaries to embrace. What the IRGC began to call "exporting the revolution" can best be understood as a form of revolutionary or radical internationalism, which, unlike other forms of internationalism (such as liberal or imperialist), sees international relations through the lens of conflict.[5] A common characteristic of this type of internationalism is political or armed intervention, usually expressed through a revolutionary state's collaboration with like-minded armed groups as a means of influencing the internal political dynamics of foreign states. Because revolutionary governments often believe that their political systems are vulnerable to the antagonisms of foreign enemies, intervention is seen as a way of preserving a revolution, if not expanding it. Intervention can be a dangerous game. Most revolutionary states are eventually compelled to concede that point and find a way to pursue their foreign interests without inviting unmanageable blowback. As Fred Holliday has argued,

> It is not that a revolution is nothing if it is not international, but it is certainly bound to be a lot less than the makers of the revolution intended. Revolutionaries are therefore forced to be internationalist as well as cautious because of the external pressures that post-revolutionary transformation invites.[6]

Thus, while revolutionary states might be animated by an interventionist spirit, their ultimate need for international cooperation and support leads to the tempering of interventionist ambition.[7]

For the IRGC, the responsibility of exporting the revolution provided the ideological and moral bases for Iranian involvement in foreign countries— particularly in Lebanon. However, the experiences of the war with Iraq gradually changed how this concept was understood, and by the end of the war internationalist rhetoric no longer placed primacy on armed intervention. Spreading the revolution's values beyond Iran's borders—as well as maintaining relations with established allies like Lebanon's Hezbollah—were still considered important, but the war had changed how exporting the revolution would be understood. This shift in thinking coincided with the growing fractionalization of the Khomeinist movement. Although internal divisions stemmed from a number of issues, including disagreements over economic and social policy, the issue of foreign intervention played an important role in dividing Iran's leadership. Within the IRGC, the issue of supporting armed political activism abroad became increasingly problematic and created a divide between the organization's top commanders and its leading advocates of radical interventionism. This paralleled a political shift in the IRGC, with the top commanders moving closer to Iran's conservative leadership (e.g., Rafsanjani and Khamenei) and further away from the organization's radical base.

As the IRGC was the main instrument for both promoting and conducting interventionist policies, the disinclination of its head commanders toward armed interventionism limited—but did not eliminate—foreign involvement. The war hardened the IRGC's position within Iranian conservatism and accelerated its break with the Khomeinist left. IRGC leaders supported the Islamic Republic's crackdown on radicals near the end of the war and helped undermine this faction by supporting the regime's moves against prominent radical activists and by purging their supporters from IRGC ranks. By the end of the war, the conservatism of the IRGC's top command and the consequent marginalization of its more radical membership led to the organization's close association with the politics and policies of the regime's conservative and later hardline factions.

## Revolutionary Internationalism

The 1979 revolution radically altered Iran's approach to foreign relations. What had once been a pro-American, anti-Soviet Iran was now a revolutionary regime divided on how to put its ideological views into action. Outside of groups such as the Mojahedin-e Khalq and People's Fadai, which shared a strong commitment to Marxist internationalism, left-leaning elements within Iran's Khomeinist

movement were perhaps the most vocal proponents of revolutionary internationalism.[8] Much of this sentiment focused on the plight of the Palestinians,
whether in the Occupied Territories or in Lebanon, and that of Muslim movements elsewhere (such as Afghanistan, Eritrea, or the Philippines). Even though
revolutionary Iran's initial provisional government led by Mehdi Bazargan
rejected the idea of foreign intervention, many Iranian leaders issued calls to
export the revolution. [9] Abol-Hasan Bani-Sadr, after taking office as president,
proclaimed: "Our revolution will not win if it is not exported. . . . We are going
to create a new order in which deprived people will not always be deprived and
oppressors will not always be oppressors."[10] More specific calls for foreign intervention generally followed the particular political agendas of the individuals
making them. For instance, Ayatollah Sadeq Rohani, who was close to Bahrain's
Shiite resistance, called for Iran to annex Bahrain if the ruling Sunni Al-Khalifa
family did not become an Islamic republic or if the Shiite majority could not topple the regime.[11] Rohani's comments elicited harsh rebukes from both Iranian
government officials and leading radicals such as Mohammad Montazeri, who
told the Kuwaiti state press that Rohani did not represent the regime and was
actually a CIA agent.[12]

The reasons for Montazeri's outward rejection of Rohani's politics were
partially rooted in the former's own pet project: mobilizing support for the
Palestinians in Lebanon. Montazeri covertly supported Shiite radicals in
Bahrain, but the Palestinian issue took front and center.[13] Like many notables of the Islamic revolution, Montazeri (one of the original architects of the
IRGC) had spent considerable time in Lebanon working with the Palestinian
Liberation Organization (PLO) and Lebanese Shiite groups before the revolution.[14] Montazeri had established a strong network in Lebanon and actively lobbied for Iran to take a leading role in the Palestinian-Israeli conflict. Montazeri's
disagreement with Rohani had more to do with the placement of priorities than
ideology, and was connected to the former's efforts in marshalling support for
the Palestinian resistance among key Arab regimes—regimes such as Kuwait
that were alarmed by Rohani's expansionist rhetoric. Like Rohani, however,
Montazeri's activism brought him into conflict with Iranian officials. At one
point, Montazeri and several hundred supporters occupied Tehran's airport for
fifteen days and eventually staged a sit-in at the Foreign Ministry building in protest over the government's refusal to let them fly to Lebanon to fight alongside
the Palestinians.[15]

Though Montazeri ultimately succeeded in transporting some of these volunteers to Lebanon, his approach to foreign intervention was considered extreme
and uncompromising by revolutionary officials.[16] Montazeri's father, Ayatollah
Hosayn-Ali Montazeri, famously apologized for his son in a public letter blaming
the latter's actions on a psychological disorder he developed due to the torture

he had endured in prison under the Pahlavi regime.[17] The ayatollah's apology
and criticism of his "extremely revolutionary-minded" son (*khayli enqelabi fekr
mi-kard*) was seen as significant due to the elder's own outspoken support for
exporting the revolution.[18] Indeed, along with his son, Ayatollah Montazeri was
a leading proponent of revolutionary internationalism within the Khomeinist
faction. Unlike other activists, Ayatollah Montazeri's statements also carried the
weight of a senior religious authority and later as Khomeini's designated successor. His status and credentials enabled the ayatollah to become the chief ideologue for exporting the revolution in the Islamic Republic.

Ayatollah Montazeri's views on intervention were rooted in his conception
of fundamental Muslim ethics. For Montazeri, Muslims above all had a duty
to help one another. He argued that, just as Islam was imbued with a political nature, the responsibility Muslims have for one another's welfare likewise
extended into the arena of global politics.[19] It was here that Montazeri located
Iran's duty to assist foreign Muslims. Speaking at a Jerusalem Day celebration
in Tehran—an annual holiday established after the revolution to mark Iran's
solidarity with the Palestinian cause—Montazeri outlined his conception of
foreign assistance:

> Assistance is not only verbal. One day at the orders of our great leader
> (Khomeini) we declared a day as Jerusalem Day. It meant that all
> Muslims should stand up with their thoughts directed at Jerusalem.
> But it is not sufficient that we merely come out with some slogans on
> that particular day in favor of Jerusalem. Words are the prerequisites of
> deeds. Do you know what is happening to the Muslims in the south of
> Lebanon? Do you know what is happening to the Palestinian refugees?
> Do you know what problems are being faced by your Muslim brothers
> in Afghanistan? Are you aware of the condition of 6 million Muslims
> in the Philippines? Are we going to their assistance? Or are we going
> to jeopardize their interests instead of assisting them? These are our
> duties. Jerusalem Day is only a slogan. It must be followed by deeds.[20]

Statements such as this did little to distinguish Ayatollah Montazeri's form
of internationalism from the interventionist activism of his son or Ayatollah
Rohani. Further, government officials, and later Ayatollah Khomeini, made
clear that Iran's calls for "exporting the revolution" did not suggest any intentions of physical or martial intervention in foreign countries.[21] Montazeri was
thus compelled to further elaborate on his thoughts. An example of this is found
in an exchange between Montazeri and an Arab journalist. When asked by the
journalist how support for foreign liberation movements was possible "without

constituting interference in the affairs of other states," Montazeri replied that support for liberation movements was an "Islamic task" and "the duty of all Muslims," adding:

> Take our brother Muslim Lebanese and Palestinian peoples, for example; we must support them with everything we have and not be content with mere slogans. The funds and weapons we have must be made available to our sons and brothers there. . . . I would like to reassert that we in the Muslim revolution cannot remain calm or sleep on silk while the rest of the Muslim peoples and countries are encouraging danger, injustice, and oppression . . . by dictatorships and imperialism. What we seek to do does not constitute interference in other countries' internal affairs. We are acting in accordance with the Koranic verse: "The believers, men and women, are protectors of one another; they enjoin what is just and forbid what is evil." Geography does not exist here, as you can see. You Muslims should not ask us to read the verse thus: "The believers, men and women, in *Iran*."[22]

Montazeri counters the accusation that he was calling for intervention in foreign states by redefining global political geography. For Montazeri, there were no independent states in Islam. There was only the global Islamic community which was spiritually undivided and unified. International norms and borders were meaningless in the face of what Montazeri saw as the ultimate truth of the word of God. Montazeri did not call for outright military involvement in foreign countries—at least not to the effect of either his son or Rohani—but his conception of exporting the revolution certainly envisioned an interventionist role for Iran. While Montazeri's stated views changed near the end of the Iraq war, his support for intervention drove the internationalist efforts of the IRGC and Iran's Foreign Ministry through much of the 1980s.

## A Conservative Turn

The Iraq conflict caused an internal struggle within the Khomeinist movement. While the war engendered a sense of patriotism in Iranian society that lent support to the regime and its clerical leaders, differing political values within the broad ruling coalition began to surface. Such diverging trends had an impact on the IRGC, whose leadership began to forge a firm relationship with the Islamic Republic Party (IRP) and more explicitly identified their organization with clerical rule.[23] A political alliance with the clergy and a more conservative approach toward policy were largely behind IRGC chief Mohsen Rezai's resignation from the Mojahedin of the Islamic Revolution organization (of which he was a founding member) in 1981. Although MIR members continued to hold prominent roles in government, some MIR leaders began to distance themselves from the growing conservatism of the IRP and its clerical cadre. MIR and other more radical factions, including those aligned with Ayatollah Montazeri, continued to advocate revolutionary ideals in the areas of social, economic, and foreign policy; however, the IRP (especially under the guidance of President Khamenei and Majles Speaker Rafsanjani) had begun moving away from these areas of revolutionary change in order to focus on Iran's immediate domestic concerns and the war with Iraq.[24]

The factors that contributed to Rezai's departure from MIR are detailed in a September 1981 letter of resignation.[25] Although Rezai claims that his responsibilities as IRGC commander and his role in the war effort are partly behind his resignation, he also expresses dissatisfaction with MIR's leadership and politics. Rezai considers MIR's political independence to be contrary to the needs of the regime. "Government organs" (such as the IRGC, committees, or Reconstruction Jihad), Rezai argued, were committed to serving the needs of the regime, whereas "independent" groups (such as MIR) were guided by self-interest. Rezai accused MIR of promoting its own interests over those of the government and blamed its political activism for causing "discord in the line of the Imam." Rezai also questioned MIR's commitment to religious leadership, suggesting that its politics and "organizational zeal" (ta'assob-e sazmani) were tantamount to a disregard for the will of the clergy. This, he emphasized, was the organization's major failing, insisting: "leadership of the revolution must be in the hands of the clergy [rohaniyyat] and religious authorities [marja'iyyat]."[26]

In order to bring MIR back in line, Rezai offered a number of suggestions. First, MIR should "discontinue its political activities and distribute its members among governmental organs." It should "promptly form a united Islamic front with the Islamic Republic Party" and resolve any ideological contradiction with the clergy. MIR should also provide a "greater role for the Imam's representative" to the organization and allow the clergy (through its representative) to "determine the political line of the organization." Finally, MIR should recognize the "proper stance toward . . . the clergy" and strengthen the "political and social role" of these religious leaders.[27]

Through his resignation letter, Rezai was advocating Khomeinist unity for the sake of domestic stability in a time of war and was arguing against any political activism that ran contrary to the policies laid down by Khomeini and the IRP. As the leader of the Revolutionary Guards, Rezai was most concerned with fighting the war against Iraq, and viewed that conflict—and not domestic or unrelated foreign issues—as the nation's paramount concern. He saw independent political action and the promotion of policies that ran counter to the conservative positions of the IRP clergy to be a threat to the regime's existence. In this way, Rezai signaled a clear break between the IRGC and MIR along political lines and on the role of clerical political authority. His letter represents the growing conservatism of Iran's leadership and its revolutionary institutions. That conservatism sought to dampen revolutionary zeal (*ta'assob*) within the Khomeinist movement—a zeal that called for social justice and an uncompromising, radical foreign policy—in order to focus national resources toward combating Iraqi aggression.[28]

## Onward to Jerusalem

The success of the spring 1982 offensives filled Iran's leaders with confidence. The victories served to simultaneously justify the moral superiority of the Islamic revolution, the strength of its ideologically committed forces, and the innovative tactics of the Revolutionary Guards. The self-assurance that drove Iran's war policy in Iraq also inspired extraterritorial ambitions. Iran's leaders framed the Iraq war as part of the Islamic world's greater struggle against imperialist and Zionist influence. The Israeli invasion of Lebanon on June 6, 1982—and the ongoing Soviet conflict in Afghanistan—supported this line of thinking. Although it had long been part of Khomeinist rhetoric, support for the Palestinian cause became a central theme in the wartime rhetoric of the IRGC. Before Iran's counter-invasion in 1982, the Guards called for the establishment of a multinational Muslim force to liberate the holy city. The idea of the "Jerusalem Army" (*sepah-e qods*) arose from a meeting of foreign Islamic organizations in Iran in 1981.[29] As the IRGC announced,

> Now the Iranian nation eagerly awaits the establishment of the Jerusalem Army. The authorities of the revolution and especially the Foreign Ministry desire that this problem will be placed at the front of our problems so that, as Ayatollah Montazeri once said, we are going to dear Jerusalem and from there we will liberate the countryside from the arrogant criminals. And if the Islamic Republic through radio and television propagates the establishment of the Jerusalem Army throughout the Islamic world—in spite of Zionist plots—millions of Muslims will be ready to liberate Jerusalem.[30]

Referencing Ayatollah Montazeri's calls for exporting the revolution, the IRGC claimed that the liberation of Jerusalem was its "task before all tasks." However, the IRGC's "assault" on the Zionist forces occupying that holy city had been blocked by the Iraqi invasion. The IRGC argued that the "greater victory" of delivering Jerusalem from Israeli occupation could be achieved only after the "lesser victory" of defeating Saddam Hussein.[31] Iraq became seen as both the literal and figurative gateway to Jerusalem and the first step toward the ultimate emancipation of Muslim societies. The IRGC employed the idea of liberating Jerusalem in an effort to inspire (and perhaps appease) its rank-and-file, who embraced interventionist ambitions more wholeheartedly than the organization's conservative top command. The underlying conservatism of Mohsen Rezai and Iran's Supreme Defense Council is evident in the priority given to the Iraq war in the "greater" quest for Jerusalem. For, only after the war with Iraq was won could Iran advance on to Israel. The longer the war went on, however, the more distant the prospect of liberating Jerusalem grew and the more vapid the cheering of such slogans became.

The Israeli invasion of Lebanon incensed Iran's leaders. It struck at their close ties with Palestinian militants in Lebanon and was seen as another instance of US-Zionist aggression against the Muslim world. The IRGC was torn on how to respond. There was pressure from elements within the organization to shift major resources from the war against Saddam to Lebanon and take the Israelis head on. With support from Iran's top leadership, the IRGC did send troops to Lebanon, which began what was to become one of Iran's most significant foreign investments since the revolution. But the outlay of resources was constrained by the war against Iraq and was far less than Iran's radical internationalists would have preferred. In the view of IRGC's leadership, by retaining focus on the Iraq war and limiting its support to the Palestinians, it had avoided a trap set by Iran's enemies. On this decision, the organization explained:

> Of course, for a period, we also were on the verge of falling into the triangular U.S.-Israel-Iraqi trap, and we were about to relegate the war into the position of a secondary concern all because the Lebanese diversion almost distracted us. However, Imam Khomeini's warning pierced the wall of illusion, which was enveloping our minds. Then we realized that there was no other choice but to destroy the Iraqi regime and replace it with an Islamic and popular one in order to free the region from the grip of the U.S. Even if we had done all in our power to aid the people there, ultimately we would have come to the conclusion that all our efforts and resources could not have effected any considerable change in regional conditions.[32]

The war made it impossible for the IRGC to shift gears even if it had wanted to. But it also gave the organization something else to aspire to: exporting the revolution to Iraq. As the IRGC saw it, the successful 1982 offensives were "a proclamation by the Islamic revolution" that it would continue "growing and gaining fresh vigor, despite all impediments, set up on its path, by world oppressors."[33] Iran began to organize Iraqi Shiite refugees into a political movement that could take the revolution into Iraq after the anticipated fall of Saddam Hussein. Many of these ex-patriots were already associated with political Shiite organizations—especially the Dawa Party—in Iraq and fled that country after Saddam began to crackdown on those groups in the wake of the Iranian revolution. This resulted in the November 1982 establishment of the Supreme Council for the Islamic Revolution in Iraq (SCIRI). As the name implies, SCIRI had committed itself to bringing Khomeinism to Iraq. Its leader, the cleric Muhammad Baqir al-Hakim, embraced the concept of clerical rule (*velayat-e faqih*) and embraced Khomeini as the group's supreme authority (*vali-e faqih*). Al-Hakim argued that SCIRI's enterprise was different from Iran's, even if it maintained a broadly-Khomeinist line. As he explained,

> It is true that we agree with the Islamic Revolution [in Iran] . . . but we differ from the Islamic revolution in our methods and organization. . . . In many areas there are many other differences between Iran and Iraq, especially the nature of the regime in Iraq which is more repressive compared to that of the Shah.[34]

Even so, the successful imprinting of Khomeini's revolutionary ideology on an Iraqi organization was an important step for Iran. Its Iraqi clients were seen as a seed that given the right nurturing could grow into strong allies in a post-Saddam Iraq—something Iran's leaders felt was only a matter of time.

To help SCIRI put its ideological positions into action, the IRGC organized an armed wing for the organization known as the Badr Corps (*sepah-e badr* in Persian, or *faylaq badr* in Arabic). Established in 1983, Badr brought together Iraqi militants into a brigade the fell under the overall command of the IRGC. This included some Iraqi Shiites who had already been serving within Iranian ranks since the beginning of the war. Badr members were mostly enlisted from the community of Shiite activists deported to Iran by Saddam Hussein and Iraqi prisoners of war. Prisoners of war that wanted to join the group first had to receive a pardon from Baqir al-Hakim or another senior cleric. Unlike SCIRI, which operated autonomously, Badr functioned as part of the IRGC during the war. Badr units participated in a host of battles and offensives. It was deployed to the Haj Omran area of the northern theater, where its fighters secured parts of Iraqi territory seized by Iran in 1983. In addition, Badr and other SCIRI-linked groups took part in terrorist operations against the Baathist regime in Iraq, including bombings and assassination attempts on Saddam and other Baath Party officials. The group grew from a few hundred to perhaps a few thousand by the end of the war.[35] Although

Badr's role in the war was marginal, it was a significant innovation for the IRGC. Through Badr, the IRGC was able to forge strong and lasting relationships with an armed, trained, and like-minded Iraqi exile organization. The payoff for the IRGC and Iran was not immediate. It would come much later after the fall of Saddam Hussein in 2003, when SCIRI, Badr, and other Iraqi exiles gradually became the power brokers of a new Iraqi state.

## The Revolution Comes to Lebanon

Despite the IRGC's Iraq-first policy, a faction within the organization was heavily involved in the political push to expand the revolution abroad. Since its inception, the IRGC had been a vocal proponent of revolutionary internationalism. The organization initially conceived its role as defending foreign "liberation movements and the pursuit of the rights of the oppressed," and held this charge as one its official responsibilities (*vazayef*) contained in its organizational charter.[36] At the heart of the Guards' foreign efforts was Ayatollah Montazeri, whose religious authority afforded legitimacy to those who supported a radical foreign policy. Montazeri had a strong support base within the IRGC and helped foster clerical oversight and collaboration in the organization.[37] His patronage led to the creation of the IRGC's Office of Liberation Movements (OLM), which was to translate the ayatollah's vision into support for Muslim movements outside of Iran. To this end, OLM—initially led by Mohammad Montazeri until his death in June 1981 and then by Mehdi Hashemi, a relative of the Montazeri clan through marriage—announced that its primary mission was to develop contacts between the Guards and outside Muslim organizations that were "fighting for freedom from the servitude and fetters of Western and Eastern imperialism and global Zionism."[38] The office's scope of operations was conceptually wide; however, the majority of its efforts were devoted to expanding Iranian influence in Lebanon, and to a lesser extent, Afghanistan.[39]

The establishment of OLM made foreign operations an actual and not simply rhetorical part of the IRGC's mandate. More so than any other conflict, the ongoing civil war in Lebanon and the post-1982 Israeli occupation of that country provided the IRGC with an opportunity to directly work toward its strategic and moral goal of liberating Jerusalem. Israel's aggression motivated the radical internationalist cadre into action, and temporarily spurred support for foreign intervention from Iran's more conservative civilian and military leaders. A day after the Israeli invasion, the IRGC and the regular military issued a joint statement promising that Iran would send soldiers to Lebanon to "engage in [a] face-to-face battle against Israel, the primary enemy of Islam and of the Muslims." The statement added:

The self-sacrificing members of the [IRGC and Basij] and the brave fighters of the armed forces of the Islamic Republic of Iran who are engaged in unceasing battle against the criminal Ba'thist regime, will, by expanding these fronts, fight against that regime's collaborator, the primary enemy of the Muslims, thereby engaging in unceasing face-to-face battle with world imperialism.[40]

Soon after, Iranian president Ali Khamenei announced that the IRGC had begun to train fighters to send to Lebanon, arguing:

To us, there is no difference between the fronts in the south of Iran and in south Lebanon. . . . We are prepared to put our facilities and necessary training at the disposal of all the Muslims who are prepared to fight against the Zionist regime. We believe that victory will belong to the Muslims, and to those who are on the side of truth.[41]

By the end of June, over one thousand guardsmen were reported to have landed in Syria for operations in Lebanon.[42]

Iranian activists had had a long relationship with their Palestinian and Shiite counterparts in Lebanon.[43] There were two main Iranian political networks in Lebanon.[44] The first centered on Mustafa Chamran and the Amal militia he helped establish among the followers of the Iranian cleric Musa al-Sadr in southern Lebanon.[45] Chamran retained close ties with Amal leaders after the revolution, and as an early associate of the IRGC and later as Iran's Defense Minister, he had short-lived success in bringing the interests of that organization in line with the Islamic Republic. Chamran's efforts—such as the inclusion of roughly six hundred Lebanese Amal volunteers into Iranian military ranks early in the war—were temporary and dissipated after his death on the warfront in June 1981.[46]

The other major Iran-Lebanon network, which is the foundation of Iran's lasting involvement in Lebanon, was composed of Iranian activists who largely opposed Musa al-Sadr, Chamran, and Amal due to their insufficient support for the Palestinian resistance.[47] This faction, headed in part by Mohammad Montazeri, Ali Akbar Mohtashami, and Jalal al-Din Farsi, had established strong ties with Shiite clerical activists in Beirut and the Bekaa valley. Mohtashami, for instance, had taken several trips to Lebanon beginning in 1970 and helped establish strong relationships with Lebanese clerics in the Bekaa region. From his first visit to the area, Mohtashami had grown especially fond of the Shiites of the Bekaa. He found them more religious than their counterparts in Beirut, brave, and particularly "disposed toward the clergy" (*beh rohaniyyat 'alaqehmand hastand*).[48]

Montazeri, Mohtashami, and others, such as IRGC commander Abu Sharif, also established strong ties with the PLO and were part of a loose transnational network in the 1970s that helped bring anti-shah activists to Lebanon for guerrilla warfare training in Palestinian camps. The IRGC's Yahya Rahim Safavi was one of the young Iranian activists that trained and fought with the Palestinians during this time.[49] Safavi traveled to Damascus in order to evade arrest in Iran for anti-shah activism. Through the help of Mohammad Montazeri and Ali Jannati (the son of prominent Shiite jurist Ayatollah Ahmad Jannati), Safavi was sent to a camp run by Yasser Arafat's Fatah organization in Beirut. The Palestinians trained Safavi in small arms and explosives, and he eventually served as a scout and night guard for Fatah in southern Lebanon. Although Safavi vigorously supported the Palestinian resistance, he was disappointed by the lack of piety within Fatah's ranks. As he describes,

> None of the members of Fatah said their obligatory prayers [namaz]. When I asked them "Why don't you say your prayers?" They replied: "God willing, in Jerusalem." In other words, "When we liberate Jerusalem we'll say our prayers."[50]

Commenting on the Palestinians' ignorance of Islamic law, Safavi expresses bewilderment when a Fatah member tells him that not all dogs are ritually impure (najes), but rather: "black dogs are impure and white dogs are pure." Safavi was also troubled by the perceived loose sexual morality of Fatah members, particularly that the outward display of physical affection between men and women was tolerated and that genders were not segregated in instances of travel or military deployments.[51]

Due in part to this ideological and cultural divide, the ties developed between Iranian activists and secular Palestinian resistance organizations proved less durable than those forged between clerics such as Mohtashami and Shiites in the Bekaa.[52] (This is particularly true concerning Yasser Arafat, who fell out of favor with Khomeini and ultimately sided with Saddam Hussein in the Iran-Iraq war.) Mohtashami was able to bring substantial state support to his Shiite network in Lebanon through his office as Iranian ambassador to Syria. In this capacity, Mohtashami was instrumental in bringing together a collection of like-minded militants and low-level clergy in the establishment of a pro-Khomeini Lebanese Shiite resistance—a movement that eventually coalesced into the Hezbollah organization.[53] Hezbollah was unique in that it was among the first (and ultimately one of the few) non-Iranian entities to adopt the central Khomeinist tenet of the "guardianship of the jurist." The organization's leaders fully embraced this concept and turned to Khomeini as their supreme political and religious authority.[54] This gave Khomeini and

*Figure 6.1*  Official emblem of Lebanese Hezbollah

*Figure 6.2*  Official emblem of the IRGC

his intermediaries (such as Mohtashami and the IRGC) tremendous influence within Hezbollah and, by extension, Lebanese politics. Apart from the adoption of Khomeinist ideology, Hezbollah's name (which was suggested by Khomeini) and its official emblem—which is based on the IRGC's emblem (discussed in the next chapter), see figures 6.1 and 6.2 above—serve as indelible marks of Iran's foundational influence.[55]

From the beginning of its introduction to Lebanon, the IRGC helped organize and train the Shiite resistance.[56] It served as a conduit for Iranian support and helped bring military expertise to Hezbollah. Guardsmen worked hand in hand with Lebanese militants. That close collaboration linked the IRGC to the political violence of the Shiite resistance, particularly the major terrorist attacks and kidnappings associated with Hezbollah during the 1980s. The IRGC's role in these activities remains unclear, but it is believed to have played an important part in the planning, coordination, and funding of various operations against Israeli and western targets, including the simultaneous bombings of the US and French barracks in 1983, the bombing of the US embassy in 1984, and a number of killings and kidnappings from 1985 to 1988.[57] The embassy and barracks bombings killed hundreds and were the bloodiest terrorist attacks against the United States before 11 September 2001. The embassy bombing alone killed 63 civilians, including six CIA officers. The intelligence agency's country chief, deputy, and the deputy's wife were among the dead. The attack helped launch the infamous career of Imad Mughniyeh, a Lebanese Shiite who became a pillar of Hezbollah and a close partner of the IRGC. His role in the kidnappings and terrorist attacks of this period helped advance Iran's anti-American, anti-Israeli agenda, and further Hezbollah's domestic goals in Lebanon's civil war.[58] Until his assassination in Damascus in 2008, the result of a reported joint CIA-Mossad operation, Mughniyeh headed Hezbollah's terrorism and foreign operations while in close contact with IRGC officials.[59] For almost three decades he was the IRGC's most important asset outside of Iran.

The counter-invasion of Iraq and the IRGC's connection to terrorism were seen as evidence of the Islamic Republic's desire to export the revolution through war and political violence. Mohsen Rezai publically downplayed the Guards' presence in Lebanon, and rejected the idea that it was part of a broader war against "anti-Islamic conspiracies."[60] However, the organization did consider its involvement in Lebanon as exporting the revolution. Overall, the IRGC divided its work in Lebanon into four different categories. The first, which is the only category explicitly identified as "exporting the revolution" (sodur-e enqelab-e eslami), concerns "cultural activism" and the propagation (tabligh) of religious, cultural, and ideological thought. The IRGC describes the bulk of that effort as distributing revolutionary literature (including the speeches of Khomeini and Montazeri), and bringing in religious scholars from Iran to promote religious instruction and spread revolutionary values in Lebanese towns and villages.[61] The second category of assistance was the martial and ideological training of the Shiite resistance. Military training, which the IRGC says compromised 60 percent of this effort, was provided by guardsmen, while ideological instruction was overseen by Iranian clergy. The third and fourth categories were respectively described as the funding of and recruitment for the Lebanese resistance.[62]

The IRGC saw its work as an extension of the Islamic Republic's campaign to spread its ideology and religious fervor outside of Iran. To Brother Mosleh, commander of IRGC forces in Lebanon, Iran's influence in Lebanon was inculcating Khomeinist ideas in Lebanon's Shia community.

> The Muslims of Lebanon, especially the Shiites of Lebanese Hezbollah, consider themselves the offspring of the Islamic revolution and therefore know that they have a duty to imitate [taba'iyyat kardan] the Islamic revolution.[63]

To Mosleh, Iran's positive impact in Lebanon was evinced by the proliferation of images of Khomeini throughout the country and by the popularity of Iranian flags (which were sold together with Lebanese flags in Shiite areas). To illustrate this point, Mosleh shares an anecdote of an IRGC patrol unit in the Bekaa:

> One day [as we were driving through a village] a little girl approached our vehicle and said: "Brother, I would like a picture of the Imam [Khomeini]." At the time I said that we didn't have any pictures of the Imam in the car, but then I noticed we had one in the windshield. I gave this picture to the little girl. She took the picture and kissed it. This is evidence of the people's love for the Imam.[64]

From Mosleh's perspective, the impact of Iran's presence in Lebanon was nothing short of the transformation of the Shiite laity into a revolutionary population and increased goodwill toward the Islamic Republic. It was those results— i.e., the expansion of Iran's ideological and political influence abroad—that the IRGC identified as the primary goal of exporting the revolution to Lebanon. The militarization of Shiite activism and the direct confrontation with Israeli forces in that country were expressed as secondary.

## Fall of the Radicals

The vast majority of the IRGC forces deployed to Lebanon in 1982 began to return home in 1985. The issue of foreign involvement became a charged subject in domestic Iranian politics, and the war with Iraq had taken precedence.[65] This shift in policy was a consequence of the growing international condemnation of Iran's connection to terrorism in Lebanon and a simmering political divergence within Iran's leadership. By 1984, President Khamenei and Majles Speaker Rafsanjani acknowledged that there was an internal ideological dispute between conservatives and radicals within the Khomeinist bloc. Although this split had been apparent years before (e.g., as evinced by Mohsen Rezai's resignation from MIR in 1982), the intensification of the Iraq war and its impact on Iranian society brought factionalism to the political fore. Each faction included prominent members of the regime, including Khamenei and Rafsanjani for the conservatives (who Khomeini tended to support on foreign policy), and Mohtashami, Behzad Nabavi (the leader of MIR), Prime Minister Mir-Hosayn Musavi, and Ayatollah Montazeri for the more radical-minded left.[66] This ideological conflict and related political infighting permeated major political parties. It led to the dissolutions of MIR in 1986 and the IRP in1987, and had thereby undone the alliances that had laid the foundation for Khomeinist dominance in the post-revolution.

Diverging views on social and economic policy contributed to the factionalism. Disagreements on foreign policy, and the issue of foreign involvement, were also fundamental to the political divide.[67] More conservative elements led by Rafsanjani regarded foreign involvement a waste of resources, harmful to Iran's international standing, and a distraction from the conflict with Iraq.[68] On the latter issue, Rafsanjani was supported by Khomeini and the leading architects of the Iraq war, including Mohsen Rezai, who wanted to concentrate Iran's military resources toward victory in Iraq. To bolster Iran's lagging war effort, Rafsanjani opened up unofficial contacts with the United States and Israel to explore arms purchases.[69] Although Iran had been secretly purchasing American arms through Israel with Khomeini's assent since the beginning of the war, a need to replenish its stockpiles pushed Rafsanjani to seek a direct covert deal with Washington.[70] Through intermediaries in his cabinet and abroad, Rafsanjani sought shipments of anti-tank TOW missiles in return for a cessation of Iran-sponsored terrorism in Lebanon, a promise to release four American hostages held captive by Hezbollah, and a suggestion of an eventual rapprochement between the two countries. To help seal the deal with the Americans, Rafsanjani invited an US and Israeli delegation to Tehran to discuss the plan. While the secret meeting failed to produce an agreement, a commitment was made between the US delegation (headed by Robert McFarlane, National Security Advisor to President Ronald Regan) and Rafsanjani's representatives to keep back channels open for future discussions.[71]

The radical faction associated with Ayatollah Montazeri, Mehdi Hashemi (former member of the IRGC Central Council and head of OLM), and Ali Akbar Mohtashami, largely opposed Rafsanjani's overtures.[72] Montazeri, for instance, criticized Rafsanjani for the secret meeting in Tehran.[73] For this faction, which had broad support within IRGC ranks, it was Iran's moral and political responsibility to assist Muslim resistance movements. Combating imperialism and liberating Jerusalem remained at the forefront of their agenda, and they rejected any pragmatic interaction with the United States and Israel. They saw Lebanon as a successful example of what exporting the revolution could achieve and as a crucial front in the war against imperialism and Zionism. That effort required more support, not less.[74] Negotiations with the Americans, and any capitulation on the IRGC's activities in Lebanon, were redlines for the radicals.

The conservatives were the more formidable coalition. While negotiating with the Americans, Rafsanjani sought to weaken his rival Ayatollah Montazeri by undermining the influence of the latter's radical base. With the crucial support of Khomeini, Rafsanjani removed the Office of Liberation Movements from the IRGC and merged it with the Foreign Ministry. That brought OLM's operations under the direct control of the government and curtailed its semi-autonomy. This was a blow to radical interventionists. Mehdi Hashemi and his supporters, however, were able to continue some of their operations for a short time with the financial and political support of Montazeri. The beginning of the end for Hashemi's faction came after he was arrested by Saudi Arabian security agents for attempting to smuggle explosives for a purported attack during the annual Hajj in Mecca.[75] Hashemi returned to Iran where he was detained and an investigation into his activities commenced. Montazeri vigorously protested the arrest in letters to Khomeini, but to no avail.[76] In protest, some of Hashemi's associates leaked information to a Lebanese newspaper exposing the covert negotiations and attempted arms purchases between Rafsanjani, the United States, and Israel, setting off what came to be known as the Iran-Contra affair.[77]

The attempt to undermine Rafsanjani backfired. Despite political pressure from the radical faction, Khomeini intervened on Rafsanjani's behalf and blocked attempts for an official investigation into the matter. With Khomeini's backing, Rafsanjani led a crackdown on radical activists resulting in the mass arrests of Hashemi's and Montazeri's supporters, including "hundreds" from the ranks of the Revolutionary Guards.[78] By 1987, the radical faction, which had become tainted by its association with Hashemi (who was forced to publically confess to crimes against the Islamic revolution and subsequently executed that year), had lost much of its influence within both the IRGC and the government.[79] In 1988, Rafsanjani further constrained this faction by removing Ali Akbar Mohtashami from the Lebanon desk at the Foreign Ministry and replacing him with the former's own brother. Rafsanjani ensured that radicals would no longer hold sway in Iran's foreign policy. The end of the war in August 1988 marked the political decline of the radical faction. The faction's main patron, Ayatollah Montazeri, was compelled to resign from his position as Khomeini's successor in March 1989. Montazeri had sharply criticized the regime's violent suppression of political dissidents which caused an irreparable fallout with Khomeini.[80] Although the Islamic Republic and the IRGC would continue limited foreign involvement after the war, especially in support of Hezbollah in Lebanon, the style of interventionism promoted by Montazeri, Mohtashami, and Hashemi—i.e., the moralistic promotion of political violence in support of foreign Muslim movements above Iran's own self-interest—was no longer part of the political mainstream. Indeed, in the months leading up to his resignation, Montazeri himself had begun to move away from that position. His emergent attitude, which he began to articulate around this time, encapsulates the Islamic Republic's general postwar view on exporting the revolution:

> The question of exporting revolution . . . is not a matter of armed intervention. The aim was, rather, by building our country on the basis of Islam's command and making the customs of the Prophet and the immaculate Imams our model; by implementing the aims, ideas and values which have been stressed and cherished by Islam, to have our country and our revolution become a model for other deprived countries and countries oppressed by and subject to cruelty from the superpowers. They would [then] choose our way to liberate themselves from the yoke of arrogance.[81]

# Warriors of Karbala

I am a Revolutionary Guard. A seeker on the path of the heroic men of
Ashura. I have raised my head to shield the sapling revolution. I am the
gardener of its cinquefoils and a staff of support for its wayfarers. With
no gratitude and no expectations, I am a Guard.[1]

—IRGC, *Payam-e Enqelab*

In establishing the IRGC, its founders were attempting to create an ideal Islamic
military force. Achieving that, they believed, would require the organization's
soldiers to posses the faith-driven fervor of Islam's earliest heroes and an ideological commitment to the revolution. To that end, the IRGC set religious
requirements for its members and policed its ranks for ideological and political dissent—leading, for example, to the purge of leftists, Bani-Sadr supporters,
and allies of Mehdi Hashemi at different points in the 1980s.[2] The organization
presented itself as Khomeini's vanguard and the most faithful of his adherents.

Constructing an Islamic identity was also the work of imagination. When
debating the color of its uniforms, the IRGC's Central Council decided upon
plain green—the color of the Prophet.[3] The birthday of Imam Husayn became
an annual celebration in recognition of the IRGC called "Guard's Day." This not
only aligned the organization with its religious tradition, it symbolized the belief
that the IRGC was a continuation of Imam Husayn's epic struggle against injustice. By donning the color of the Prophet and marking its establishment on the
birthday of Shiism's greatest hero, the IRGC inserted itself into the pantheon
of Shiite history as the standard-bearer of a new form of Islamic military. The
Guards became, in effect, the new warriors of Karbala.

Seemingly as important as the orthodoxy of its ranks was the manner in which
the IRGC conceived of itself and conveyed that conception to its members and
the public. Events such as Guard's Day—which presented guardsmen to Iranian
authorities in a grand parade of military potential, religious virtue, revolutionary dedication, and an unwavering willingness to die in the path of Khomeini—
were part of that effort. The Guards also employed less grandiose methods
to help shape self-perception and their public persona. The IRGC produced

various types of textual and visual materials to communicate its values to rank-and-file members and those outside the organization. Much of the Guards' work reflected the government's broader propaganda and cultural campaigns during the Iran-Iraq war.[4] Even so, the materials produced by the IRGC played an important role in forging its outward identity. Through texts and images, the organization articulated understandings of itself, its members, and the Iraq war. These productions—such as publications, photographs, and artwork—are crucial sites of the organization's self-conceptualization during the 1980s.

## The Islamic Model Army

From its establishment, the IRGC considered itself to be different from other militaries. Its leaders envisioned an organization that was Islamic in confessional identity and in deed. It was also to be revolutionary, and in certain respects, progressive and modern. The IRGC's leaders were not working with a blank slate in their attempt to engineer an ideal revolutionary Islamic force. Rather, their starting point was in part a reaction to what they perceived to be the pathologies that ran through secular militaries. In contrasting itself against these types of institutions—particularly the Shah's military and Marxist groups like the MKO—the IRGC crafted cornerstones of its organizational culture. Added to this were Islamic values and principles that the IRGC embraced and strove to integrate into their organization's practices.

The IRGC articulated these ideas in a March 1980 essay published in *Payam*, its biweekly news organ.[5] The IRGC explains that secular militaries have suffered from four major maladies: ignorance, moral corruption, rigid discipline, and the fostering of a low self-view or inferiority complex among the rank-and-file. These characteristics were the primary factors facilitating the oppressive impulses of militaries and the regimes they served. Ignorance of politics and immorality were especially harmful for soldiers, and at the root of the power of "colonialist and exploitative regimes." They directly link the banning of political and Islamic literature in the Iranian military under the Shah as an example of how autocratic regimes cultivate ignorance and immorality in their institutions. "Once a person is completely ignorant," they write, "he can be compelled [to commit] any crime." To the Guards, it was the lay soldier's ignorance that enabled the expansionary, imperial, and abusive policies of past militaries (they give several examples, including the Mongols and Ottomans), and the crimes of colonialist powers in the modern period. They blame centuries of ignorance and corruption in the states and institutions of the Islamic world for having enabled humiliations such as the crusades, the plague of autocratic regimes, conflict between the Shia and Sunnis, and ethnic divisions between Arabs, Persians, and Turks.[6]

Beyond those concepts, inequitable relations between commanding officers and subordinates is also highlighted as problematic. The harsh discipline of traditional militaries and abuse of subordinates by officers is singled out as especially damaging to armed forces. The article states:

> In militias and armies such as these individuals do not develop brotherly ties, camaraderie and mutual fondness, but on the basis of bias, the privilege and snobbery of the commanders over the subordinates becomes entrenched [*ostovar bashad*]. It is natural that such relationships will cause hostility and rancor [to develop] among the soldiers.

Not only does such rancor erode the esprit de corps of military units, it causes "senior commanders of armies to become self-indulgent [and in effect] force their subordinates into servitude so that they must blindly obey the upper-ranks and become spineless." They argue that this dynamic severely weakens military institutions, giving the example of the Persian Sassanid empire, which, despite its military's manifold advantages in resources and manpower, withered in the face of Arab Muslims whose ranks were unpolluted by institutionalized inequities and held together by belief in God. [7]

Beyond these ill-regarded traits, the article lists the *Islamic* principles the IRGC strives to put into practice. The discussion begins with a Quranic verse:

> God has verily bought the souls and possessions of the faithful in exchange for a promise of Paradise. They fight in the cause of God, and kill and are killed. This is a promise incumbent on Him, as in the Torah, so the Gospel and the Quran. And who is more true to his promise than God? So rejoice at the bargain you have made with him; for this will be triumph supreme.[8]

This verse instantly changes the conversation of what it means to be a military and a soldier. With it, the IRGC removes itself from the fold of traditional militaries and places itself within the domain of religion and the "cause of God." The secular goals of power and conquest are eschewed in favor of the rewards that can only come through service to God. In this case, that is the promise of heaven (*jannah*) and the willingness to "kill and [be] killed" in the path of their lord. As the organization writes, it will embrace "that which was commanded in the [above] verse so that we remember the necessary attributes and characteristics of jihad in the path of God."

The organization lists eight such attributes. The first of these is penitence (*al-ta'ibun*)—a term that evokes the penitent movement that arose in response to Imam Husayn's martyrdom at Karbala. The IRGC contrasts its understanding of this Islamic virtue from the Marxist practice of self-criticism (a practice vigorously adopted by the MKO and other revolutionary groups), and charges that this practice has made these groups dogmatic and "inflexible in the face of [changing] conditions." Islam, however, is "mobile and dynamic" and "Muslims are progressive and also realist." The authors stress that this does not mean that Muslims "change their color" to suit the moment, but rather "they always strive to transform the ruling conditions to benefit the fixed principles of God." They continue, the "revolutionary Muslim and mojahed in the path of truth is always considering his 'God,' aim, and ideological principles," which, the authors stress, can only be done by "implementing" and "safeguarding the principle of penitence."[9]

Beyond penitence, the IRGC lists seven more Islamic principles that its soldiers should embody. The organization lists spiritual devotion (al-'abidun), giving praise to God (al-hamidun), holding the fast (al-sa'ihun), bowing in submission to God (al-raki'un), prostrating in adoration to God (al-sajidun), propagating virtue and prohibiting vice (al-amrun b'il-ma'aruf wa al-nahun 'an al-munkir), and safeguarding Islamic lands (al-hafizun li-hudud allah) as the other pillars of the organization. These principles are all described as religious and spiritual acts that contribute to the welfare of one's spiritual condition and political awareness. For example, in describing the quality of giving praise, the organization writes,

> The mojahedin of Islam and the warriors in the path of Islam are alone in praising their God. They will never submit in the face of satanic foes, exploiters, despots, materialism, or hypocrisy. Nor will they don the garment of those inclinations. For they are neither greedy nor mercenaries, neither fearful nor spineless slaves, neither ignorant nor pawns.[10]

Each principle is similarly contrasted against the practices of secular militaries and packaged as an authentic Islamic element for an effective fighting force. They are the qualities required for the ideal Muslim warrior. In this way, the IRGC envisions its force to be Islamic, political, and spiritually pure.

These Islamic principles combined with the rejection of characteristics of secular militaries to form the organization's founding philosophy. They have had an important impact on the organization and its internal practices. For example, beyond the establishment of religious requirements for its troops, an egalitarian, fraternal ethos was central to the IRGC's organizational culture. Initially this led the IRGC to reject official ranks for its soldiers and commanders. Although commanders were of de facto higher rank and status than their subordinates, they held no formal ranking, and were often referred to with simple honorifics such as "brother" or "guard" (*pasdar*). The organization was later forced to adopt ranks after the war, but its commitment to Islamic fraternity has remained a core feature of the organization's culture and identity.

## Power of the Pen

The political and religious values of the IRGC were communicated in its publications. The organization's membership swelled in its early years, increasing from an estimated 10,000 guardsmen by the end of 1979 to 25,000 in mid 1980, 50,000 by the end of 1981, and up to 350,000 by 1986.[11] In addition, the IRGC took over command of the Basij popular militia, and was charged with the martial and ideological training of its ranks (which grew to an estimated three million by 1986).[12] The majority of these new guardsmen and basijis differed from their commanders in both experience and ideological sophistication. Though they lacked the years of activism and ideological commitment, new recruits shared a deep-rooted faith in Shia Islam and a zealous commitment to the revolution and Ayatollah Khomeini.[13] IRGC publications became a tool used by the organization to help build on these commonalities and educate its expanding ranks.

Central to this effort was *Payam-e Enqelab* (*Message of the Revolution*), a biweekly political journal that served as the organization's official newsletter (*organ*).[14] Though it was similar in both form and content to other political journals that emerged after the revolution, *Payam* was unique in that it was primarily aimed at the IRGC's rank-and-file. Like its sister publication, *Omid-e Enqelab* (*Hope of the Revolution*), which was geared toward the Basij, *Payam* used articles, interviews, posters, and other content to express the spiritual, ideological, and political values of the organization. After the Iraqi invasion, the journal focused on the organization's role in the war, offered narratives of important campaigns, and celebrated those killed in action. IRGC editors also reserved space in each issue for international news and coverage on resistance movements throughout the Third and Islamic worlds. *Payam* created a space in which a sense of identity and purpose could be fostered among IRGC members and among interested civilians.

The IRGC also produced various books, booklets, and pamphlets. After the Iraqi invasion, these publications began to focus on the geopolitical context of the war and its deeper connections to Islam and Shiite history. An example is the series *Let's Learn from the Quran*, which began publication in 1981. The first volume of this series, *War and Jihad in the Quran,* coupled Arabic Quranic passages related to the subjects of warfare and jihad with translations and explanations in Persian. The authors argue that the book's publication was in response to "the enemies [that] have [waged war] on the Quran and *hadith.*" By providing an entryway to the Arabic Quran through Persian translations, the authors claim that guardsmen will be armed with the "fist of the Islam" in their battle with the "infidels of the world" and the "infidel Iraqi Baathists."[15] The Persian translations also suggest the IRGC's awareness of their rank-and-file's general illiteracy of Arabic.

Other publications, such as those produced by the IRGC's Political Office, more directly dealt with the war. An example is *War and Transgression: The Imperialist Front against the Islamic Revolution,* which, with chapters such as "Imperialist France, a Colluder with Saddam?" and "Will America Protect Saddam?" situates the early Iraq war into a larger context of imperialist and Western threats to the Islamic Republic.[16] The Political Office also produced materials aimed at outside audiences, such as short-lived English and Arabic versions of *Payam-e Enqelab,* which instead of being translations of the journal's Persian edition were part of the Islamic Republic's coordinated white propaganda (*tablighat*) campaign aimed at influencing non-Iranian publics.[17] Similar publications include *A Glance at Two Years of War,* an English translation of a Persian IRGC report that summarizes the organization's operations, strategy, and victories through mid-1982.[18]

In addition to the Political Office, the IRGC's Public Relations and Educational units supervised the production of materials aimed at fostering ideological awareness among the ranks.[19] Later in the war, the IRGC established research centers and universities devoted to training guardsmen and producing materials on Islamic ideology, politics, and military science. In 1984 the Guards opened the Center for Investigation and Research in Qom, which produced "ideological and political" materials specifically geared to IRGC and Basij soldiers at the front.[20] As a collaboration between lay guardsmen and clergy from the Qom seminary, this center produced books such as *Wars of the Prophet,* which presented the battles fought by the Prophet Muhammad as parables for the war with Iraq in order to imbue the latter with a parallel sense of spiritual significance. Beyond this, the most important training initiative undertaken by Guards during the war was the founding of Imam Husayn University and its Institute of Military Sciences and Technology in Tehran, which opened in May 1986.[21]

## Wartime Cultural Activism

IRGC publications are an outgrowth of the organization's commitment to ideological and cultural activism. Six months into the Iraq war, the organization claimed that "90 percent" of its non-combat operations were devoted to promoting ideology. This work, which the IRGC defined as "cultural activities" (*fa'aliyyat-ha-ye farhangi*), was a broad-based effort of promoting the religious and political values championed by the organization, the IRP, and esteemed clergy like Ayatollahs Montazeri and Motahhari.[22] As cultural activism was a central duty of the IRGC throughout the war—and remains as such through the present—it is valuable to consider how the IRGC conceived of this effort. An example of this is provided in a February 1981 organizational review published in *Payam-e Enqelab*. This report, briefly discussed below, sheds light on how the Guards promoted their ideas, the mediums they found most valuable, and the material they found most convincing.

The IRGC divides this report into two sections focusing on the production and distribution of textual publications and of audio-visual materials. The report claims that IRGC units established over 2,400 libraries throughout Iran's major provinces during this period. In these and already existing libraries, the Guards donated 629,102 books and further distributed approximately 482,000 booklets throughout the country. In addition, Guards units produced approximately 440,000 publications, not including the organization's political journals. Many of these publications were donated pro bono publico. Others were sold as a source of revenue, resulting in 9.75 million *rials* in sales for IRGC units,[23] including three million in sales from the war-torn southwestern provinces.[24] Although the precise numbers are not mentioned, "ideological and political" publications were also given to "liberation fronts" outside of Iran.[25]

The audio-visual and "artistic" (*honari*) materials produced by the IRGC during this period includes several media types. Part of this initiative organized 4,049 film showings around the country and the production of eighty-five theatrical presentations. Provincial units also distributed nearly sixty thousand audio cassettes. These cassettes focused on various religious topics, such as excerpts from the Quran (6,000) and Ayatollah Khomeini's *Guardianship of the Jurisprudent* (3,000), but the most widely distributed cassette (21,000) included sermons of the martyred ideologue, Ayatollah Motahhari, whose work continued to grow in popularity among more conservative Khomeinists. The IRGC distributed these items directly throughout its local bases and through organized "art exhibitions," which sold books and cassettes, and held slideshow presentations for the public (the Guards held 1,620 such exhibitions during this period).[26]

The artistic medium most favored by the IRGC was the political poster.[27] Guards units produced and distributed roughly nine million sets of posters both within Iran and abroad. These posters—like the political posters produced by other official agencies and parties during the war—were often resized and altered to become the artwork for pamphlets, billboards, or even postage stamps.[28] IRGC posters (examples of which are discussed later) were commonly reproduced in issues of its official journals, particularly as inside and outside covers. Although they ranged in content and composition, the posters produced by the Guards generally depicted issues related to the political, religious, and martial dimensions of the war.

## Visual Identity

Similar to other revolutionary groups, such as the Mojahedin-e Khalq and the Mojahedin of the Islamic Revolution, the IRGC emblem is the primary enunciation of its organizational identity.[29] As mentioned earlier, the IRGC based its emblem on that of MIR and in so doing assumed a similar antagonistic stance vis-à-vis the Islamic left.[30] Like the MIR emblem, the IRGC emblem (see figure 7.1) depicts the Arabic negative article "*la*" in the center of the design, out of which extends a clenched fist holding a rifle.[31] The "*la*" stands for the Muslim

*Figure 7.1* Official emblem of the IRGC

proclamation of faith "*la ilaha ilallah . . .*" ("There is no God but God . . .") and the clenched fist holding the rifle stands for armed resistance. Above the rifle sits a verse from the Quran—"Prepare against them whatever arms and cavalry you can muster . . ."—which is used as a rallying cry for righteous militancy.[32] To the right of the "*la*" is the representation of a book, symbolizing the Quran, and to the right of that is the organization's name in Persian (i.e., Islamic Revolutionary Guards Corps). Out of the Quran extends a branch with leaves, suggesting both the desire for peace and the garden of heavenly paradise (*ferdows* or *jannat*). This is superimposed on a representation of the globe, expressing the organization's commitment to internationalism while downplaying its national focus. At the bottom of the image rests the Persian year of the organization's establishment (1357, or 1979).

Like the literary *emblemata* of early modern Europe, the emblems of modern political organizations are products of their time. Concerning the former, John Manning argues, "Grounded in a historical moment, emblems can be misunderstood, or be totally incomprehensible, unless there is an awareness of the immediate temporal context. Chronology, the moment of utterance, is a clue to meaning."[33] Although the designs created by Iranian revolutionary organizations are not as obtuse as the subject matter Manning is referring to, they are nonetheless steeped in the political and cultural moment from which they emerge. Their visual components are designed to be overt political statements. Yet, while emblems are static, the groups they represent are dynamic. As time passes, an organization may be forced, or simply choose, to alter its initial ideological platform to adapt to larger changes occurring within the sociopolitical context. Even though the political platform of an organization can be altered, emblems often remain unchanged. So, while an emblem reflects specific historical aspects of an organization, it is not necessarily an accurate reflection of the organization.

Such is true for the Revolutionary Guards. The IRGC's emblem was designed shortly after the establishment of the organization in 1979. Its designer, Mohsen Kolahduz, an original member of the IRGC's Command Council, also designed MIR's emblem.[34] The two emblems are not only products of the same historical moment, they stem from the aesthetics and abilities of a single individual. Further, both emblems were designed contemporaneously with the establishment of their respective organizations in early 1979. For the IRGC, this means that the chief fixture of its corporate identity was created before the organization had a clear function or place in post-revolutionary society. The emblem was designed to represent a militant, Islamic, and anti-leftist revolutionary organization, which is why it more closely resembles the standard of a resistance movement (out of which the IRGC in fact emerged) than a national military (which is what the organization ultimately became). A sense of revolutionism and resistance is also expressed in the political message of the emblem; themes increasingly at odds with the organization's growing political conservatism during this period.

Thus, as the IRGC became an official organ of the Islamic Republic and transformed into its leading military force during the war, it retained the guise of a resistance movement outside the system of state power. The emblem, in this manner, evokes the organization's political reality. That is, unlike other resistance organizations, the IRGC was not established to oppose a system; rather (as its name suggests) it was formed to oppose *opposition* to a system. Its resistance, then, can be seen as a perpetual state of being; an inseparable component of establishing or maintaining an idealistic Islamic society. Pro-regime militancy, in this scheme, is therefore an expression of the Guards' resistance: resistance to actual, perceived, and existential threats to the Islamic Republic and its revolutionary system (*nezam*).

## Iconology of the Self

As explained in the preceding chapters, the IRGC's roots extend deep into the revolutionary movement of the late 1960s and 1970s. Indeed, most of the IRGC's early leadership had been participants in that movement. It is not surprising then that, before the Guards developed a visual identity specific to the organization, its imagery retained some of the aesthetics of the Islamic anti-Shah guerrilla movement. Its emblem is one example of this; however, many portrayals of guardsmen in IRGC publications highlight this practice as well. I have chosen two related images that illustrate this point. These images, shown in figures 7.2 and 7.3, were found in *Payam-e Enqelab* throughout the 1980s. Although they appear in different versions (two of which I show as examples), they were consistently used as signifiers for the IRGC or the individual guardsman. They embody aspects of both IRGC identity and self-conception.

In these images, which seem to be based on a photograph, we see the same bearded individual holding a Kalashnikov rifle. He wears a nondescript military-style uniform, but lacks the insignia, accoutrements, and stance of a government soldier. The man holds a Kalashnikov rifle at his hip, appearing to be either discharging or ready to discharge the weapon. By aiming or firing the rifle in such a manner, the individual demonstrates a lack of proper martial training, and thus assumes the posture of a guerrilla militant. This does not discredit the individual. On the contrary, the man (like his Kalashnikov) evokes a revolutionary spirit. He is, in a sense, a prototypical Muslim resistance fighter.

*Figure 7.2* Guard icon (1981)

*Figure 7.3* Guardians icon (1985)

Yet this individual is not used to denote the general militant or even the Muslim revolutionary; he is employed as a specific and direct marker for the Revolutionary Guards. This is suggested by his uniform (which closely resembles that worn by members of the IRGC) and is made clear from the contexts in which these images appear. For instance, in one of the earliest printings of this image in *Payam-e Enqelab* it is placed directly next to a poem entitled "Guard" (*pasdar*).[35] The poem, an ode to the guardsman by the prominent revolutionary poet Hosayn Esrafili, in part reads:

> O who is proud to sacrifice himself
>    A scion of the *Sarbadaran*
> Within the clamor of machinegun fire,
>    You are found

Through extolling the virtues of the guardsmen, this poem highlights the same notions of militancy, Shiite identity, and resistance captured in the image. The author connects the war fighting of the guardsmen ("found in the clamor of machinegun fire") with the notion of an Iranian-Shiite tradition of resistance ("scion of the *Sarbadaran*")—a reference to an uprising of mostly Persian Shiites against Turko-Mongol rule in 14th Century northeastern Iran.[36] The image stands for a visualization of the poem's subject (the guardsman) if not an illustration. This is made obvious by the image's placement within the same text box as the poem and its blatant title. The editors make the connection for the reader unequivocal: the image in the box is a guardsman.

Just as this version of the image is meant to signify a guardsman, when multiplied, the image stands for the entire organization. The second example above illustrates this point. Here, *Payam*'s graphic designers inversed and triplicated the original image to make it appear to represent a broader force or even an armed brotherhood. In the example provided, the triplicated image—which is the more common of the two—is included in a section on poetry by rank-and-file guardsmen submitted to the journal for publication. If the meaning of the image was not plain enough to the reader, the editors include a text box below it stating: "Gifted to the Islamic Revolutionary Guards Corps." Thus, the editors indicate that the image signifies the IRGC.[37]

So what can these two images, which are akin to clip art, tell us about the organization? These images, after all, played a minor role in the pages of *Payam-e Enqelab*. They were not widely used in other materials and certainly did not gain the type of public attention that photographs of guardsmen did during the war. Nevertheless, I have chosen to discuss these particular images because they embody a certain Islamic-revolutionary aesthetic that lies at the heart of IRGC identity. They resemble the politically driven Muslim activists that founded the organization in the midst of revolution, but do not overly express the sacred or the righteous. These guards are not the same type of religious warriors the guardsmen became synonymous with in the war; rather they resemble the politically driven Muslim activists that founded the organization in the midst of revolution. In other words, these images emphasize the political and revolutionary roots of the guardsman and the organization. That these images were printed multiple times over several years indicates they continued to hold meaning for the editors and designers who employed them. They continued to signify the guards *to* the organization, even as the latter began to favor more overt religious motifs and symbols to describe its soldiers.

## Warriors of Karbala

As the visual examples have shown, the IRGC partly defined itself with a political and revolutionary aesthetic. However, with the onset of the Iraq conflict, guardsmen increasingly took on more of a sacred guise. Photographs of ragtag Iranian soldiers with headbands displaying religious slogans were ubiquitous in Iranian and international media during this period. Such photographs and similar artwork were used extensively in IRGC publications to capture the multitude of experiences and emotions related to fighting (living, praying, and dying) on the frontlines. Graphic designers also frequently altered photographs, transforming them into compositions that could more directly communicate the values of the organization and spirit of the war effort. An expressive, and overlooked, body of imagery adorns the pages of *Payam-e Enqelab*. These visuals are important in that they, perhaps more so than any other medium, epitomize how the IRGC conceived of itself and the war during this period.

Following the rhetoric of Ayatollah Khomeini and Iran's clerical leadership, IRGC productions framed the Iraq conflict as a war between Islam and its chief antagonists (i.e., America, Western imperialism, and Zionism).[38] Though many Islamic metaphors were used to describe the conflict, the most salient and powerful metaphor used was that of Imam Husayn and his final stand against the Umayyads at Karbala. This metaphor allowed for the war to be re-imagined as a modern Karbala, wherein Iran's forces were both reliving and redressing the Imam Husayn's heroic struggle against oppressive forces. As Hojjat al-Islam Fazlollah Mehdizadeh Mahallati, Khomeini's representative to the IRGC, explained:

> Our revolution emanates from Husayn's Karbala . . . and our dear Imam is the Husayn of our time . . . [When] we gaze upon our war fronts and upon the areas that the Corps controls, [we see that] these are [manifestations of] love for the Imam Husayn and that our path is the same path as the Imam Husayn.[39]

Entwined with the calls for the liberation of Jerusalem, the Karbala metaphor infused even more religious symbolism into the discourse fueling the Iraq conflict. In this scheme, Saddam Hussein's secular Baathist regime became seen as an obstacle in Iran's Islamic quest for emancipating Palestine from Zionist control. Karbala was more than a metaphor for the engagement with Iraq; its liberation was also something the IRGC believed could be achieved.[40] As the popular wartime slogan "the path to Jerusalem runs through Karbala" expressed: Karbala was considered both a destination and a way station in the Islamic revolution's drive against imperialism and Zionism.

Visual imagery played an important role in conveying these themes to rank-and-file guardsmen. For example, the cover of a December 1981 issue of *Payam-e Enqelab* depicts the quest for Jerusalem and the slogan "the path to Jerusalem runs through Karbala" (see figure 7.4).[41] The image shows a political map of the Middle East with Iran on the right side, Iraq in the middle, and Israel on the left.[42] Within Iran is a small photograph of a convoy of Toyota pickups transporting groups of guardsmen. Emanating from the guardsmen is a bold, rainbow-colored arrow that stretches through Karbala (a point on the arrow difficult to discern in the copy) and across Iraq and Jordan to Israel. The point terminates at a Star of David, within which sits a picture of Jerusalem's Dome of the Rock. Beneath the point in the arrow designating Karbala, and upon Iraq, is the phrase "the path of Jerusalem" (*tariq al-quds*) in Arabic.

The simple mechanics of this image allow for a clear communication of the slogan it visualizes. With the country of Jordan obfuscated and nearly consumed by the Star of David and the arrow, Iraq (or Karbala) is seen as the literal and figurative obstacle standing between the Muslim warriors of Iran (represented by the truckloads of guardsmen) and the liberation of Jerusalem (represented by the Dome of the Rock). The rainbow coloring of the arrow also suggests that the ultimate objective in this effort is peace and justice in the region.

A similar photograph from *Payam-e Enqelab* (see figure 7.5) approaches this idea from another perspective. In this image we see a familiar scene: a Toyota pick-up transporting a group of guardsmen seemingly to the warfront. Most of the guardsmen point their Kalashnikov rifles in the air in a confident, almost victorious manner. The guardsmen appear to range in age; some have full beards while others lack facial hair. True to the supply and equipment shortages that plagued the IRGC, each of the guardsmen wears a slightly different uniform. Some are wearing wool hats, some steel helmets, while some lack headgear altogether. Most of the men look in the direction from which they came, while another, who appears to be the youngest soldier, seems to gaze directly at the photographer or viewer. The driver of the pickup, who is leaning out of his window and gesticulating with his left hand, appears to be looking at or past a road sign.

*Figure 7.4* "Path of Jerusalem . . ."

*Figure 7.5* "Road to Karbala"

As Susan Sontag suggests, photographs "are a way of imprisoning reality, understood as recalcitrant, inaccessible; of making it stand still." But they can also "enlarge a reality that is felt to be . . . perishable, remote."[43] By itself, there is little remarkable about this photograph. It is similar to countless other wartime photographs that depict guardsmen on their way to the front, posing for cameras, exuding a sense of confidence and certainty in their mission. What makes this image more interesting is how the designers chose to "enlarge" the reality it captures by inscribing a deeper meaning to an otherwise familiar scenario. That is, the information on the road sign that the driver seems to be acknowledging has been altered. Although the original text on this sign is unknown, superimposed next to the IRGC emblem (an original part of the sign) is the phrase "the road to Karbala" written in red—the color most associated with martyrdom and sacrifice.[44] This simple yet evocative alteration adds a religious dimension to the image that would not otherwise be apparent. While this photograph captures these guardsmen "accurately" as soldiers in a modern war, by modifying the text on the sign the image also presents them as warriors traveling toward a destination that is as much spiritual as material. Here, Karbala is more than a metaphor for the war or a gateway to Jerusalem; rather, it is a spiritual condition, an aspiration of martyrdom, a victory in and of itself. In a sense, these soldiers can be seen as the reinforcements Imam Husayn never received, given a chance to rewrite or redress history by retaking, refighting, or simply re-experiencing Karbala through the Iraq war.

Iran's hope of a decisive victory over Iraq faded as the war dragged on. Iranian forces had some successes, such as the 1984 capture of Iraq's Majnun Island oil complex, but the heavy cost in blood and treasure injured Iranian morale. The breadth and severity of Iraq's aggression, which threatened to cripple the Iranian economy and terrorized Iranian population centers, dampened expectations.[45] However with the capturing of Iraq's strategic Faw Peninsula in February 1986, Iran's fortunes seemed to be improving. The capture of Faw rekindled hopes for a victorious conclusion to the war, and was touted as a key step toward liberating Karbala and Jerusalem. As one popular slogan put it: "God willing, as the victory of Khorramshahr has led to the liberation of Faw, a victory in Karbala will lead to an advance on Jerusalem."[46]

This renewed hope, and the melancholy that preceded it, is captured in an IRGC poster published in an April 1986 issue of *Payam-e Enqelab*.[47] This image (see figure 7.6), a photographic collage, shows a group of guardsmen seated on the ground, most of whom are gazing slightly to their right. It is unknown what seems to have captured their collective consideration, but one may assume that they are perhaps listening to a speech or being addressed by one of their commanders. The background of the image is abstracted and made to contrast with the center, which is an untouched rectangular section of the original photograph. This section, which is posited as a "clear" view into the photographed scene, invites the viewer to focus on a single soldier, a communications specialist, who rests his chin on his hand, appearing to be engaged with what lays before him. Below this soldier is a Persian phrase that reads: "Karbala is waiting . . ."

Outwardly, this poster uses a photographic composition to evoke the sentiment and expectations spelled out in the phrase "Karbala is waiting . . ." That is, the object of the guardsmen's collective gaze and imagination, the image tells us, is Karbala. The guardsmen seem to be aware that Karbala is in their future; it is, as the ellipses suggest, waiting . . . for them. If we look at this image in another way, and consider what Roland Barthes calls the "obtuse" meaning of images, it begins to suggest other possibilities.[48] The text tells us that "Karbala is waiting." Waiting, we assume, for guardsmen to liberate that consecrated land from Baathist control. However, if you look at their faces, it seems obvious that the guardsmen are waiting too. They are, perhaps, waiting to take their revolution and the divine justice it embodies to Karbala, to Jerusalem, and to the rest of the Muslim world. Waiting to fulfill what has been promised them by their religious, political, and military leaders. Waiting for victory; a victory that has so far eluded them; a victory that perhaps seems no closer now than four years prior.

While the success at Faw encouraged Iran's military leaders, the faces of these soldiers do not seem to exude confidence or hope. Rather they seem to express a sense of concern, melancholy, or even pessimism. Karbala, after all, is not only a destination, it is a spiritual reality; a condition that centuries of Shiite literature,

*Figure 7.6* "Karbala is waiting . . ."

poetry, and imagery suggest is one of divine intoxication.[49] If Karbala is still waiting, it is because these guardsmen have not reached or attained *it* yet. Such a reading might conflict with the graphic designer's original intentions, but it nonetheless speaks to the general mood and tenor of the composition—a mood more reflective of Iranian society during the final years of the war.

The feeling of pessimism, doubt, or melancholy evoked by this image was in some sense prophetic. The war, of course, ended in stalemate, leaving the economies and cities of both countries in ruin. The near-goal of liberating Karbala was not achieved, and the far-goal of emancipating the Palestinians and the holy city of Jerusalem was as distant as ever.[50] While Iran eventually succeeded in regaining its territory, it failed to topple Saddam and ignite an Islamic revolution among its coreligionists in Iraq. Thus, the metaphors that inspired the war effort and the rhetoric that mobilized millions of soldiers fell hollow. Yet, as the war failed to live up to the expectations of those fighting it, it succeeded in developing a novel class of national and spiritual heroes. That is, by the end of the war, the IRGC soldier and the Basij militiaman had come to assume a strong and powerful identity. No longer urban militants, but not yet purely professional soldiers, guardsmen and basijis emerged from the devastation of war as a new brand of fighter, a new breed of citizen, a new Iranian-Islamic archetype.

Although there are numerous visualizations of guardsmen and basijis from this period, the example in figure 7.7 vividly articulates how these soldiers came to be portrayed during and after the war.[51] This image, published soon after the

*Figure 7.7* Warrior of Karbala

conflict ended, encapsulates some of the key sentiments that have defined guards-men in postwar government-sponsored memorials, tributes, and literature. In this image, which appears to be either a painting or drawing—and may be based on a photograph—we see the profile of a guardsman. We know he is a guardsman or basiji by his uniform and headband, which bears an invocation to Imam Husayn in Arabic. The man holds his right hand over his heart in a sign of humility, devotion, and piety. These spiritual qualities are reinforced by the depiction of the shrine of Imam Husayn in Karbala, which hovers among clouds in the background.

The obvious theme of this image is the commemoration of Ashura, but the symbolism employed conjures up impressions of martyrdom and sacrifice.[52] This is denoted by the association to Imam Husayn and his martyrdom at Karbala, and suggested by the stylized clouds encircling both the shrine and the guardsman. Although these clouds are inspired by a style popularized through the minia-tures of early modern Iran—and are thus a particularly Iranian marker—clouds in general are a common motif in artistic depictions of martyrs.[53] Similar to how the Karbala metaphor was employed in wartime rhetoric and propaganda, this image portrays the guardsman as a modern incarnation of the Karbala hero. He represents the vast multitude of guardsmen and basijis killed during the Iraq conflict and serves as a bridge between those individuals and their spiritual ancestors. That is, just as Imam Husayn and his companions suffered martyrdom in the path of a cause deemed righteous, so too had the soldiers of Iran. Taken a step further, this parallel plays out in a perhaps unintentional irony: both the past and present Karbala narratives are essentially tragedies. Although Imam Husayn achieved a moral victory with his stand at Karbala, he lost both politically and militarily. Similarly, while Iran could claim a moral victory by at least regaining its territory and forcing Iraq to sue for peace, it failed to accomplish its broader strategic goals, and was unable to fulfill the many promises it had made to its soldiers and citizens throughout the war.

While this image may engender such a reading, particularly from a viewer far removed from the conflict and its horrors, it is at its heart a deeply spiritual com-position. Released from the context of warfare, and with depictions of militancy notably absent, the guardsman takes on a spiritual guise. Although we still con-ceive of him as a soldier, he is lionized for his religious devotion. He represents the hope and fidelity of those who were inspired to fight in a war for reasons reli-gious and patriotic. Like the heroes of Karbala, he is a willing martyr for whom the ultimate sacrifice is also the ultimate reward. The guardsman thus becomes a pillar of faith. No longer does homage to revolutionary militancy befit him; rather, within the reflection of his figure, the notions of spirituality, Shiite tradi-tion, and Iranian patriotism assume primacy.

# 8

# When Johnny Comes
# Marching Home

The Guards Corps sacrificed their lives so as to defend the boundaries of religion, honour and the country. It stood firm in the face of the
entire forces of arrogance. The services rendered by the Guards Corps
were so great that the Imam graciously said "I wish I were a revolutionary guard". . . . Today, you and I should follow the same line. We
should sincerely and virtuously support our great leader, His Eminence
Ayatollah Khamene'i. . . . Turning our back on the Velayat will lead to
the collapse of the system. . . . If the two trends of our revolution . . . join
forces, they would surmount every counter-revolutionary movement,
inside and outside the country. Otherwise, whichever group assumes
power would be thirsty for the blood of both revolutionary trends and
would crush both trends.[1]

—Ahmad Khomeini

Demobilization is a moment of potential crisis . . . veterans are the
unique element in this moment of crisis and [their] actions often determine its outcome.[2]

—Alec Campbell, *Irregular Armed Forces and Their Role in State*
*Formation*

The end of the Iraq war ushered in a period of uncertainty. As destructive as the
war had been, it had also been a unifying force for the Khomeinist movement.
The death of Ayatollah Khomeini on June 3, 1989, dealt another significant blow
to the revolutionary regime. With the war over and Khomeini's incontestable
authority no longer available to quell factional differences, the central stabilizing
factors in the Islamic revolution were lost. In the midst of this, Iran was faced
with the challenge of transitioning from a nation at war to a nation at peace.[3]
For eight years the war had been the central cause of the Islamic Republic. To
be a revolutionary and to be a true devotee of the Imam was to be a volunteer
guardsman or basiji on the front lines. The war not only forged the identities of
the IRGC, Basij, and other associated organizations, it had come to define the
values of an entire generation of combatants.

Now with the war over, the futures of these revolutionary armed forces and their members were in limbo. As neither the Guards nor Basij had a clear peacetime role, there were rumors that they would be either dissolved or absorbed into the regular military which remained mobilized to protect Iran's borders. This would have been the most direct and dramatic solution to demobilization. However, realizing the value of these ideologically committed institutions and the vast human resources they contained—not to mention the IRGC's political clout—Iran's leaders created new areas of involvement for these organizations and expanded their domestic responsibilities. The Iranian government partially addressed the problem of demobilization by providing the IRGC, Basij, and other veterans outlets for religiously and nationally imbued service. Such moves gave these groups a bigger stake in non-military affairs, and a stronger voice in post-war politics.

The promotion of Ali Khamenei to office of supreme leader was part of the growing disintegration of the Khomeinist movement. No longer united around Khomeini and the war, ideological differences within Iran's leadership became the main source of political contestation. Khamenei's promotion signaled which political faction held the upper hand: the conservative right. The conservatives were a loose coalition of the bazaari traditional merchant class, clerical organizations, religious associations, veterans groups, and governmental bodies that largely supported the "absolute" (*motlaqeh*) rule of the guardian jurist, favored traditional commercial practices, and opposed social liberalization. This faction dominated the clerical ranks of the Assembly of Experts and the Guardian Council, and was responsible for engineering the appointment of Khamenei to the office of supreme leader. Under Khamenei, and in an alliance with newly elected President Akbar Hashemi Rafsanjani and his modern-right faction, the right took the lead in forming Iran's postwar reconstruction policies—policies which often brought the rightist factions into conflict with the more populist-oriented left. While the latter faction retained many of the radical and populist commitments that were promoted in the early days of the revolution, it also became increasingly interested in social progress and democratic development. By the late 1990s the Khomeinist-left faction, which had previously been the more radical wing of the Khomeinist movement, took on the "reformist" (*eslahgara'i*) label and sought to open up Iranian society both socially and politically.

Disputes between these amorphous political currents intensified through the 1990s. With the election of the reformist cleric Mohammad Khatami as president in 1997, the fear of a less religious and more democratic Islamic Republic provoked widespread unrest among conservatives and far-right hardliners. The IRGC and Basij were among the most outspoken critics of reformism. Although many of the rank-and-file members of these organizations actually supported

Khatami's presidency and reformist agenda, the organizations themselves and their senior commanders were uncompromisingly aligned with Khamenei and his conservative constituency. IRGC and Basij war veterans considered reform to be a direct challenge to the Islamic values they had fought and sacrificed to protect. The ideas of social liberalization, democracy, civil society, and a more conciliatory approach to foreign affairs were seen as foreign intrusions that threatened Islam and Iran's Islamic system. These organizations, their members, and associated veterans' groups like Ansar-e Hezbollah (Helpers of the Party of God) viewed reformism—and the social liberalization efforts that preceded it— as a dangerous new enemy and worked to combat it and its proponents both rhetorically and physically. The right's postwar push for influence, which relied on the alignment of religious leadership and military-backed force, benefitted from the Islamic Republic's approach to demobilization. The result, witnessed in the conservative campaign against Khatami and reformism, was the monopolization of coercive power by the IRGC and its conservative patrons and the empowerment of militarism in Iran.

## Postwar Reconstruction under Rafsanjani

Ayatollah Khomeini's absence opened up the door to a new order of leadership in the Islamic Republic. Ali Khamenei now bore the titles of Supreme Leader and Guardian Jurist, but he was still considered a middle-ranking cleric, and despite his powerful allies he lacked a natural support base.[4] Khamenei alluded to his lack of clerical standing in his June 6, 1989, inaugural address, stating: "I am an individual with many faults and shortcomings and truly a minor seminarian."[5] This differentiated the nature of his religious authority from Iran's high-ranking and influential clergy, who attained their stations through the popular recognition of seminary students and lay constituencies. Khamenei's lack of standing within both the clerical and lay communities limited the scope and influence of his religious authority, particularly during the first few years of his tenure. This empowered President Rafsanjani, who—with the office of the prime minister abolished in 1989—strengthened the role of the presidency and exercised a greater measure of influence than his predecessors. Khamenei firmly backed Rafsanjani and allowed him to take the lead in shaping postwar policies. Khamenei's support was influential in the implementation of Rafsanjani's ambitious national reconstruction campaign (*towse'eh*) and first Five Year Plan. The alliance between the two leaders, which lasted through Rafsanjani's first term, created a form of "dual leadership" at the top of Iranian society.[6] However, as Khamenei began to establish his own alliances with the traditional right factions—including conservative clergy, bazaari merchants, and IRGC leadership—he took a sterner stance toward Rafsanjani and publicly criticized much of the policies of the latter's second term.

Cooperation between the two clerics brought together the major factions of the right: the traditional right (represented by Khamenei) and the modern right (led by Rafsanjani). Rafsanjani and the modern right promoted policies aimed at modernizing Iran's economic and industrial sectors, while tempering its radicalism in the areas of social and foreign affairs. This involved a move toward the privatization of state-owned industries, promotion of domestic manufacturing, strengthening and stabilization of the *rial*, and favoring expertise over ideological orthodoxy in managerial positions. In most of these areas, Rafsanjani and his cadre of technocrats were supported by the conservative clergy and the bazaari merchant class of the traditional right. However, the modern right also pushed for higher taxation, increased regulation of commercial markets, and a softening of austere Islamic social regulations. This brought Rafsanjani a fair amount of support from the left-leaning factions, but also brought him into conflict with the traditional right and hardline (far-right) factions—a conflict that ultimately ended the conservative alliance by 1995.

Conservatives were able to seize control of many governmental institutions and newly privatized bodies during this period. The most significant changes occurred in election laws. Reacting to conservative lobbying efforts, the Guardian Council clarified its reading of Article 99 of the constitution which regarded its role in overseeing elections. The Council's new reading, reached in December 1991, afforded the conservative-dominated body "approval supervision" of elections (a role that had been the mandate of the left-dominated Interior Ministry), a significant alteration from its previous role as "observer." Conservatives also sponsored laws in the summer of 1990 that changed election procedures to the Assembly of Experts in their favor. The new law gave the Guardian Council similar approval status over candidates to the clerical body, in that the religious qualifications (*ejtehad*) of the candidates had to be approved by either the conservative clerics of the Council or Khamenei. These two laws gave the Council unprecedented power in disqualifying candidates—based on ill-defined and unappealable accusations of an insufficient commitment to Islam, the guardian jurist, or personal moral failings—to all elected bodies and the Majles (parliament), which came under conservative dominance after the barring of hundreds of left-wing candidates in the 1992 and 1994 elections.[7] Khamenei took advantage of his position by appointing allies to the Guardian Council and other prominent posts, such as the appointment of former IRGC minister Mohsen Rafiqdust to head the powerful Foundation for the Oppressed and Wounded Veterans (*bonyad-e mostaz'afin va janbazan*) in 1989.[8] By appointing Rafiqdust, a member of the conservative bazaari Allied Islamic Society (*jam'iyat-e mo'talefeh-ye eslami*) and Rafsanjani's brother-in-law, Khamenei removed yet another prominent left-leaning activist (former Prime Minister Mir-Hosayn Musavi) from a position of influence.[9]

Part of Rafsanjani's reconstruction campaign was the streamlining of the defense and security sector. The three major domestic security organizations—the police, gendarmerie, and revolutionary committees—were merged to form the Law Enforcement Forces (LEF, *niru-ha-ye entezami*).[10] This measure was outwardly aimed at reducing redundancy, but it was also part of Rafsanjani's de-revolutionization plan. By bringing the security forces under the direct influence of the Ministry of Justice, and thus centralizing its command and bringing it under direct governmental control, the internal conflicts that arose from factionalism endemic to these organizations were reduced. The elimination of the revolutionary committees was also a blow to the radical left, which had considerable influence within them. The merger met stiff resistance from the left, such as from former Interior Minister Ali Akbar Mohtashami, who lambasted the decision to dissolve the revolutionary committees in a Majles session, saying, "if we lose the revolutionary committees, we will lose our revolutionary identity." [11]

Changes to the defense sector had a similar cause and effect. In 1989, Rafsanjani reorganized the Supreme Defense Council to form the Supreme National Defense Council (SNDC), which took the lead on military, security, and foreign policy decision making. He merged the IRGC Ministry with the Defense Ministry to form the new Ministry of Defense and Armed Force Logistics (MODAFL). Although the IRGC remained separate from the regular forces and retained a leading position in military matters, the loss of an independent ministry caused many to fear that the move presaged the organization's dissolution.[12] Like the establishment of LEF, the IRGC ministry merger was part of a larger process aimed at curbing radicalism, reducing redundancy, increasing professionalization, and asserting centralized state control over national defense.[13] This meant centralizing the command structure—achieved through the creation of MODAFL—and forcing professionalism on the IRGC. Toward the latter, Rafsanjani, backed by Khamenei, imposed a system of ranks on the IRGC parallel to those used by the regular military.[14] This move was publically supported by IRGC chief Mohsen Rezai and other conservative commanders, but it went against the founding revolutionary principles of the organization, which considered ranks and rigid hierarchical structure to be one of the most corrosive features of secular and imperialist militaries. By rejecting ranks at the outset of its establishment, the IRGC claimed to be creating an organizational culture that reflected its Islamic and revolutionary values.[15] Although the imposition of ranks was an unpopular development for guardsmen and basijis, Guards commanders emphasized that ranks were necessary for the organization's development. As Rezai explained, "If we want to make the IRGC a military force, then we must have grading [i.e., ranks]."[16]

Postwar reorganization also extended the IRGC's overall reach and domestic influence. Part of this was the result of the actual expansion of the IRGC. The massive Basij militia was upgraded into a standalone branch of the IRGC, and its name changed from the Basij of the Oppressed to the Basij Resistance Forces (*niru-ye basij-e moqavemat*).[17] The IRGC also established a special operations wing known as the Quds (Jerusalem) Force (*niru-ye qods*), which took over the work of the now-closed Office of Liberation Movements.[18] The IRGC now had five official branches: the ground, air, naval, Basij, and Quds forces. It had gained important footholds in domestic affairs with the Basij and in foreign policy with the Quds Force, but it was outside of military matters where the IRGC's most important development took place.[19] Rafsanjani encouraged the IRGC to utilize its unique resources and vast membership (especially war veterans from the Basij) in the postwar reconstruction campaign to help develop Iran's industrial capacity.[20] Rafsanjani's encouragement, as well as a possible understanding that the IRGC would be responsible for much of its own funding, brought the Guards into the center of Iran's industrial and economic arenas.[21] The IRGC had been involved in construction and commercial activities since early in its career, but postwar opportunities, particularly in the area of industrial development, opened up avenues for the organization to take a leading role in the country's reconstruction. Through the 1990s, the IRGC became the chief recipient of lucrative state contracts and formed a multi-billion-dollar industrial empire.[22] The organization articulated its focus on development during this period as an evolution in its militaristic mandate: "At this time when the frontlines against imperialism have become the trenches of economics and the spreading of development, [the Guards] are actively involved in this blessed arena and [their work] is markedly pronounced." [23]

The Khatam al-Anbia engineering firm (Seal of the Prophets, *Qaragah-ye sazandegi-ye khatam al-anbia*) became the IRGC's lead development agency. Established in 1990, Khatam (as it is often referred in English) brought together many of the IRGC's engineering and construction units into a single company to focus on national industrial and agricultural construction projects. It had undertaken 367 state-funded projects by 1995, including major industrial projects like the Mashhad-Sarakhs railway in northeastern Iran and the Kharkheh dam (Iran's largest dam and hydroelectric facility) in Khuzestan, and lesser projects in construction and agriculture.[24] Khatam and other IRGC affiliated firms became the leading contractors in the oil sector, undertaking significant projects like the Hamedan-Sanandaj pipeline.[25] By 2007, Khatam had completed 1,220 governmental projects and had 247 projects ongoing[26]—such as the development of the South Pars gas field.[27]

The IRGC grew increasingly involved in public works during this period through its affiliation with several charitable foundations (*bonyads*). Although the IRGC is best known for its connections to the powerful Foundation for the Oppressed and Wounded Veterans (Iran's largest financial institution) and Martyrs Foundation, it also worked with smaller organizations on public works projects—such as the Foundation for Mutual Assistance (*bonyad-e ta'avom*), which, for instance, the IRGC helped build a regional fishery complex.[28] Through its control of various shipping companies, the IRGC became a major importer of legal and illicit commercial goods.[29]

Through all of these endeavors, the IRGC became interwoven within Iran's economy. Consequently, the organization and its leaders—who profited from the lucrative government contracts and commercial importing—became involved in protecting their financial interests. Initially, this meant supporting Rafsanjani (who encouraged and enabled the IRGC's economic role) and most of his policies; however, as Rafsanjani took measures in his second term aimed at undermining the bazaari merchant's monopoly on commercial pricing, the IRGC joined the traditional right (to which many of its commercial interests were linked) in opposition.[30] Opposition to increased governmental over-sight of the commercial sector, as well as resistance to the relaxation of Islamic social policies (also initiated by Rafsanjani, with support from the left), moved the IRGC into a firm alliance with the traditional right and their patron, the Supreme Leader Ali Khamenei. By the mid-1990s, the IRGC actively worked against proponents of these issues, and became antagonistic toward reformism under Rafsanjani's successor, Mohammad Khatami, after his election in 1997.

## Propagating Virtue, Prohibiting Vice

Entrance into the various areas of development gave the IRGC a significant national role outside of its militaristic raison d'être. Extra-military enterprises helped legitimize the organization's continued existence in the early years after the war when questions regarding the future role of the organization and its possible dissolution were rife. Development work also provided the organization a partial solution to the question of demobilization. The issue of how to deal with massive amounts of war veterans is a recurring problem that has plagued postwar societies throughout history.[31] For Iran and the IRGC, this problem was compounded by a shattered national economy and an exorbitant number of poorly trained soldiers, who had little opportunity for employment at home. With funding scarce, it would have been impossible to train, arm, and absorb all basijis (many of whom were either too young, too old, or otherwise unfit to serve as proper military soldiers) into the IRGC or regular forces. The prospect of hundreds of thousands of unemployed war veterans presented an obvious problem for the IRGC and Iran's leaders. However, basiji veterans also comprised an extensive community of patriotic, religious, and loyal adherents to the supreme leader. This network, and the vast human resources it contained, was seen as too valuable to simply disband.[32]

With the support of Rafsanjani and Khamenei, IRGC commanders created new avenues of service for war veterans. Development initiatives were important in this regard, with guardsmen and basijis working in all areas (from engineers and architects to mechanics and laborers) of IRGC operations. The IRGC and Basij also focused on increasing their institutional presence in national and local security.[33] Thousands of guardsmen were moved into the LEF, as both rank-and-file soldiers and as officers appointed to top command positions.[34] Such employment measures were only a partial solution, and did not fully harness the Basij's unique attributes and ideological zeal. The Basij was seen as an important institutional vehicle for the defense of revolutionary values and the promotion of the "culture of the defense"—a term used to denote the ethos of religious and nationally motivated militancy and sacrifice fostered during the Iraq war.[35] The postwar program of the Basij emphasized the organization's responsibilities in defending local infrastructure (e.g., airports and public buildings), serving as security for governmental officials and clergy, and helping train all sectors of society in military matters.[36] Instead of being full-time soldiers living in and operating from military barracks, basijis were integrated into Iran's social fabric. Though some basijis served full-time, most had a looser commitment and participated in the organization while simultaneously pursuing their education or employment.[37] Through these part-time members, the Basij's presence in mosques, schools, guilds, professional organizations, factories, and farms was expanded. Universities were of particular importance to the organization, which established Basij student organizations as a way to promote the organization and its values on campus.[38]

Despite its foray into non-military areas, the Basij remained a martial force. As Basij commander, Brigadier General Ali-Reza Afshar, explained:

> The Basij can primarily be summed up in this way: it is an armed guardian and an armed defender of the dignity of the revolution. Wherever the enemy threatens, an armed basiji is present. In truth, the Basij is a military force. By military it is not meant that the Basij should only involve a small portion of society. Why? Because defense and jihad are essential parts of religion [foru'-e din] and the lawful charge of all the faithful. . . . This is the culture of the defense. In terms of logic, if a person is threatened he must act to defend himself. Even animals do this.[39]

Afshar stresses the militaristic (or "armed," mosallah) nature of the Basiji's activities and its position as a defender of the revolution. Concerning the latter,

Afshar was speaking to both the material and existential (i.e., cultural or ideological) threats to the regime and the values cultivated during the war ("culture of the defense," *farhang-e defaʿ*). While the Basij continued to have a military function, its main role became acting as the IRGC's front-line force against cultural and political change. As Afshar explained, the Basij was to confront threats reflexively and with armed force. The ability to legally use force made physical coercion the backbone of the Basij's power and influence in Iranian society.

The Basij's mandate was expanded to include law enforcement–type responsibilities.[40] Although the Basij (like the IRGC) had been involved in aspects of law enforcement since its inception, it was not until November 1993 that the Basij was granted the credentials to legally perform arrests.[41] The basis of the Basij's law enforcement role was the Islamic injunction "the propagation of virtue and the prohibition of vice" (*amr be maʿruf va nahy az monkar*). This injunction, also known as "commanding right and forbidding wrong," offers a simple but powerful prescription for regulating righteousness in Islamic society: every individual Muslim has the responsibility to both encourage morality within his community and to take an active role in preventing immorality. It has been an enduring subject of debate among Muslim theologians.[42] Early Shiite scholars debated whether the injunction was even applicable in the absence of the imam because only the infallible imam could implement the injunction with perfect justice. The majority of later Shiite jurists accepted its implementation with limitations regarding who could rightfully give permission to punish an immoral act, particularly if lethal force was required. After the revolution, most senior clerics followed Ayatollah Khomeini's thinking on the subject, which considered the granting of permission for physical or lethal punishment to be the exclusive domain of a qualified jurist. With establishment of the Islamic Republic, the implementation of the injunction became the domain of the state.[43]

The doctrine of "the propagation of virtue and the prohibition of vice" (or "morals policing," as I will call it) became a significant political tool in the post-revolutionary period.[44] This is particularly true with regard to the IRGC, who adopted these twin duties as one of its founding tenets:

> Propagating virtue and prohibiting vice are revolutionary principles that have become permanent elements of the doctrine of the Islamic Revolution. The mojahed and guardian of Islam must always oversee the carrying out of these Islamic commands and not allow the people, the state, or the powers to deviate from the Islamic line and principles. ... Propagating virtue and prohibiting vice are two principles that give Muslims—especially the faithful and mojahedin guardsmen—not only the right but also the duty and authority to carry out laws.[45]

Following the logic that Islamic organizations had the duty and authority to enforce legal codes, morals policing became a key justification for the IRGC and the Basij's domestic policing efforts. In 1992, the government expanded its role in morals policing by establishing the Office for the Vivification of the Propagation of Virtue and Prohibition of Vice (*setad-e ehya-ye amr be ma'ruf va nahy az monkar*)—which was charged with leading the regime's public morality campaign.[46] Headed by senior cleric Ayatollah Ahmad Jannati and staffed by basijis, this committee worked in conjunction with security forces, judicial authorities, and nongovernmental veterans' groups such as Ansar-e Hezbollah to implement this doctrine at the local level. As an ideologically committed organization with hundreds of thousands of members, the Basij, in the words of Hojjat al-Islam Ebrahim Ra'isi, Tehran's Revolutionary Court prosecutor, was considered "the most suitable revolutionary apparatus for the organization, coordination, and carrying out the propagation of virtue and the prohibition of vice."[47] In inaugurating the establishment of the new office, Brigadier General Afshar similarly proclaimed to Basij members: "You are the agents who will reform society and eradicate its vices."[48]

As morals policing was commonly upheld as the duty of each individual Muslim, its implementation by the state required some degree of professionalization.[49] In addressing a crowd of basiji morality agents, Ayatollah Mohammad Ali Movahedi-Kermani, Khamenei's representative to the IRGC, explained that the inherent "shades of transgression" made implementing the doctrine a delicate matter. Hence, he argued, the individuals who worked as morality police "must have a good track record. Must have outstanding Islamic morals and be admirable. Must be well-informed of the propagation of virtue and the prohibition of vice, sociology, [and] must know which type of people to strike against."[50] An IRGC textbook on the subject published by Movahedi-Kermani's office further explains that basiji morality agents should receive "precise and exact training" in religious jurisprudence (*fiqh*) from clerical authorities and be versed in the protocols of the propagation of virtue and the prohibition of vice before engaging in its implementation.[51] Despite the militaristic overtones of the Basij's morality mandate, Movahedi-Kermani reminded the organization that carrying out the doctrine was not akin to war; rather "the spirit of the propagation of virtue and the prohibition of vice is similar to the work of a compassionate doctor, such as the Prophet of God who was like a roaming physician searching for spiritual illnesses [to treat]."[52] In total, however, basijis only needed to undergo a two-week training course to qualify as morality police.[53]

Despite official guidelines for the training of morality agents, enforcement of the doctrine remained loosely defined. This is due in part to the implicit vagueness of the injunction, which in contemporary society can encompass aspects of civil law, Islamic law, and cultural politics. Examples of how the IRGC conceived of and conducted its morality operations elucidate some of these points. For example, a report issued by the political office of the provincial IRGC of Gilan (northern Iran) discusses its morals policing program. Local "basiji brothers and sisters" were split into two groups of five to six individuals and sent to places throughout the province to carry out morals policing. After two weeks, they reported the following successes: 1,100 immorally dressed (*bad-hejab*) individuals were given verbal warnings (a prerequisite to physical coercion); 120 individuals were detained and "guided" (*hedayat*) toward submitting confessions to untold offenses (all were later freed after posting bail); ten cases of irreligious figurines were confiscated and prevented from being sold; and thirty-two "seditious" individuals were arrested for insulting and provoking the basijis. The IRGC of western Tehran released a similar report. These basijis split into seventeen teams and coordinated their operations with the LEF and judicial authorities (*maraja'-e qaza'i*). After a two-month campaign they discovered and confiscated five illicit video caches, 251 illicit video tapes, three illicit cassette tape reproduction facilities, 465 illicit cassette tapes, 332 irreligious pictures, 32 bottles of liquor, 21 vials of opium, one cache of sidearms, and 135 bullets. Those teams arrested ninety-one individuals in connection to the above crimes, all of whom were later released after receiving religious guidance (*ershad*) from the basijis and posting bail.[54]

Through such operations, the Basij became involved in the enforcement of civil laws and religious morality at the local level. The regime's favorability of the Basij enabled it to extend its domestic presence in other areas as well. For instance, by the end of 1993 the Basij announced that it was active in "68% of all high-schools, technical-schools and teacher-training colleges and in more than 44% of boys' and girls' schools" ("more than 10,000 schools" altogether). The Basij claimed that these school chapters involved the recruitment of over a million new student members.[55] On the military and security side, Brigadier General Mohammad Zolqadr, the Chief of the Joint Staff of the IRGC, claimed in 1994 that one thousand Basij brigades had been formed throughout Iran.[56] A year later, Brigadier General Afshar announced that in Tehran alone, the Basij had expanded to 186 Ashura (male) battalions, 17 Zahra (female) battalions, and 50 student battalions.[57] The intended result of this growth was the transformation of the Basij from a popular volunteer militia to an extensive paramilitary organization with a strong social movement base. The main architects behind this expansion—IRGC commanders, conservative clerics, Khamenei, and initially Rafsanjani—positioned the Basij as a bulwark against the spread of social liberalization.

## Taking Back the Revolution

Morals policing was part of a concerted conservative political project aimed at eliminating manifestations of social liberalization. The IRGC had promoted social conservatism since its formation. After the war, the traditional right became increasingly passionate about protecting austere Islamic social mores in Iranian society. Rafsanjani's first-term economic policies were largely supported by conservatives, but his efforts to relax social restrictions were not.[58] An early example of this was the conservatives' vociferous protests to the 1992 platform of the High Council for Cultural Revolution (a governmental council headed by Rafsanjani). The council wanted to institute broad social reforms and minimize clerical influence in cultural affairs. Early causalities of rightwing outrage were Mohammad Khatami and Mohammad Hashemi (Rafsanjani's brother), widely considered the architects of the government's social liberalization measures. Khatami and Hashemi were forced out of their government posts and respectively replaced as cultural minister and head of television and radio by Mostafa Mir-Salim and Ali Larijani—both former guardsmen and members of the powerful traditional conservative coalition, the Allied Islamic Society (jam'iyat-e mo'talefeh-ye eslami). Under Larijani, Mir-Salim, and other officials appointed by Khamenei (such as Ayatollah Jannati as the head of the morals policing office, Guardian Council member, and Tehran's Friday prayer leader), conservatives developed methods to confront social liberalization in all its forms. Central to this was the empowerment of hardline veteran activists—such as basijis and hezbollahis (a general term for unaffiliated far-right activists)—through morality policing endeavors. The Basij and IRGC worked in concert with the traditional right to combat leftist and modern-rightist influence in the postwar era. Through a confluence of shared values and interests, these organizations became a fixed element of the conservative camp and the leading forces against reform.[59]

Clashes over policy intensified in Rafsanjani's second term. In Rafsanjani's economic agenda, he proposed increased taxation and other measures that were seen as weakening the bazaari's traditional monopoly of the commercial sector. The traditional right split with the president on this issue. Now at odds with traditional conservatives, Rafsanjani was forced to rely on the support of his modern-right faction and on the left, which helped the latter promote its social and democratic reform agenda. In a political partnership, those two factions worked together to curb the growing power of the traditional conservatives and their hardline supporters. Despite the barring of numerous left-leaning candidates by the Guardian Council, the modern-right and pro-reform axis made significant gains in the 1996 Majles elections. Although the conservatives retained a majority in the Majles, and dominated most government and security institutions, they were unable to stem the pro-reform movement.

The election of Mohammad Khatami in May 1997 made reformism a formidable force in Iranian politics. The election came as a shock to conservatives and reformists alike. With the backing of the supreme leader, the Guardian Council, prominent clergy, powerful bazaari leaders, and the commanders of the IRGC and Basij, many observers had assumed that the conservative candidate, Majles Speaker Ali Akbar Nateq-Nuri, was all but assured victory.[60] Khatami's election and the popular social forces that brought him to office—dubbed the 2nd of Khordad movement after the date of the election in the Iranian calendar—simultaneously announced hope for his supporters and confirmed the conservatives' worst fear: the modernist Islamic ideologies of Rafsanjani and the reformists were succeeding.[61]

Leading up to and after Khatami's election, conservatives vigorously attacked what they deemed to be the ideological tenants of an emergent (or returning) "liberal" movement.[62] Conservatives and hardliners charged "liberals" (or the modern-right and reformist axis) with leading a Western-backed conspiracy to destroy the revolution. Liberals, conservatives argued, were actively working to discredit Islam by openly questioning the validity of the guardianship and by promoting Western social mores and political practices such as democracy.[63] Conservatives feared liberals were striving for a détente with the United States and were thus leading Iran back toward foreign control. These themes were summed up in the central conservative claim that liberals were at the head of a Western "cultural invasion" (*tahajom-e farhangi*) that was undermining the revolution's Islamic character. Warning against the "cultural invasion" of Western values became a rallying cry for anti-reform activism.[64]

The IRGC and Basij became the front line defense against reformism and its backers.[65] After the Rafsanjani and pro-reform axis made gains in the 1996 Majles elections, Majles Speaker Nateq-Nuri announced that "liberals" posed a "serious threat to the revolution," adding:

> If liberal ideology becomes dominant in the country, Islamic laws will not be implemented and we shall return to the helplessness and dependency of former times. . . . This is not a superficial danger. Nor has it ended. Because of this, it is necessary for basiji volunteer(s) and hezbollahi forces to eradicate this ideology by being vigilant and continuously present in different arenas. . . . Any ideology that prevails over the next Majlis will also prevail over the next government. The Majlis with a liberal government would prepare the way for [trampling] the values and principles of the revolution.[66]

Charged with combating liberalism, the Basij worked to understand this ideology and the cultural invasion that lay behind it. An article published in a Basij research journal argues that the foundation of cultural invasion is the spread of Western thought in Islamic societies. The author, Mohammad Hosayn Jamshidi, identifies the ideologies and "principles" (osul) that form the intellectual basis for anti-Islamic, liberal policies as humanism, rationalism, scientism, secularism, materialism, naturalism, individualism (fard-gara'i, esalat-e fard), and utilitarianism (esalat-e sud). By outlining and discussing the intellectual elements of liberalism, this article presents a "scientific" view of the Western cultural threat to Islam in Iran. Jamshidi's conclusion is unequivocal: "Cultural invasion is a type of culture war."[67]

Using similar logic, Mohsen Rezai made numerous speeches to the IRGC and Basij telling them to be vigilant in their defense against liberalism. Rezai described liberalism as a cancerous disease that would eat away at the revolution from within. He referred to the positions of the left and modern right as a form of "American Islam," which aimed to spread Western values under the guise of Islamic modernism. In contradistinction to liberals, true revolutionaries, Rezai argued, were those who were faithful to Islam, the institution of the guardianship, and the revolutionary forces (i.e., IRGC and Basij).[68] After Khatami's election, Rezai continued to emphasize the importance of the guardianship and Khamenei's leadership to the revolutionary system: "If the policies of the leader are implemented by the whole country, there will be no reason for enemy cultural combatants to profit from a cultural vacuum and permeate [vared shodan] our society."[69] Thus, in Rezai's view, the only remedy for the disease of liberalism was total obedience to the institution and views of the supreme leader.

The IRGC and Basij's role in defending revolutionary culture was more than an ideological endeavor. Commanders were careful not to explicitly call for these organizations to employ physical violence as means of combating liberalism. Instead, they issued general statements that spoke to the organizations' responsibilities to protect Islam, the guardianship, and revolutionary values. The tone and context of these statements, however, did not hide the notion that preventing the spread of liberalism would require physical coercion. As Mohammad Baqer Zolqadr, IRGC joint chief of staff, argued:

> The Guards Corps is not merely a military force which sits in its barracks waiting for the enemy's military attack; the status of the Guards Corps in the constitution is to safeguard and protect the values of the revolution. Therefore, it cannot look indifferently at cultural onslaught and the sinister influence of the lackeys of the West and of the liberals in the ranks of this sacred system. . . . In the name of [reform], some people want to . . . weaken all the fundamentals and values of this

revolution, for the preservation of which so many martyrs and disabled veterans have sacrificed their lives; and they want to please [imperialist] arrogance by turning their backs on the sacred aspirations of the revolution.[70]

Mohsen Rezai made similar arguments and pledged that the IRGC and Basij should not allow liberals to undermine the Islamic tenets of the revolution. In a July 1996 speech to the Basij, Rezai warned: "The liberals have no right to take advantage of the political nobility and tolerance of the revolutionary forces." He continued:

> The basijis are duty-bound to defend the values of the revolution, the leadership and the clergy, and there is no doubt that they will perform this duty under any condition whatsoever. . . . While maintaining their serious presence in the arenas of the revolution, the basiji and revolutionary forces should not allow themselves to be drawn into violence. . . . The activities of the basij forces should be within the framework of the law.[71]

Both Zolqadr and Rezai emphasize the IRGC and Basij's obligation to combat all manifestations of liberalism. As military organizations, physical coercion is implicitly part of that responsibility. Rezai reminds basijis that they should strive to avoid violence and operate within the law. However, under the law, the Basij could legally engage in violence and physical coercion through its broad mandate of morality policing. In this way, Rezai's call for legal and nonviolent action is more a call for the institutionalization of activism rather than an argument against coercive violence. Rezai is reminding his audience to not act outside the legal bounds of their organization to combat liberalism—something basijis had been accused of doing—but to do so through available institutional mechanisms.[72]

Nongovernmental groups were even less encumbered by issues of legality and the facade of impartiality. Surrounding the Majles and presidential elections, there was a surge in violence involving Ansar-e Hezbollah and other hezbollahi gangs. Ansar-e Hezbollah began as a veterans' association devoted to advancing veterans' rights and social conservatism. The group has been mischaracterized as an IRGC apparatus due to its veteran membership and close association with local Basij units.[73] However, the group was not beholden to IRGC commanders. Ansar's activities were coordinated by its civilian and clerical patrons, particularly former IRGC commander Hosayn Allahkaram, the group's founder, and Guardian Council secretary Ayatollah Jannati, its chief clerical overseer.[74] With the backing of powerful clerics and the supreme leader, the group served as an outlet for veterans activism and an agent of the conservative establish-ment.[75] Employed as "pressure groups," Ansar and other hezbollahi gangs were organized by powerful bazaari leaders and influential clergy to harass the con-servative right's political opponents and their constituencies.[76] Ansar activists were involved in numerous incidents of violence, including several clashes with student groups on university campuses, and the May 1996 torching of Tehran's Qods cinema, which the group claimed was in response to the screening an "un-Islamic" film.[77]

Khatami's landslide victory—he received nearly 70 percent of the vote—was terrifying for conservatives. It symbolized reformism's appeal to not only the general public, but also to the rank-and-file of the security forces. Reports suggested that large numbers of guardsmen and basijis openly supported Khatami in the election.[78] Even though the IRGC and Basij retained a core of veterans committed to conservative social values, other veterans and the postwar generation had largely become supportive of Khatami's message of change.[79] Such evidence seems to have convinced Khamenei and conserva-tive leaders that they had failed to act decisively enough against the spread of liberalism. The door was opened for hardliners, who advocated more extreme measures against liberalization, to take a leading role in rightist political activ-ism. In the case of the IRGC, Khamenei asked Mohsen Rezai, the architect of the organization's conservatism, to step down. Rezai was appointed to the Expediency Discernment Council (a governmental body that serves as an intermediary between the Majles and the Guardian Council) in what was in effect a forced retirement. Rezai vowed to continue his involvement in the "cultural struggle [*mobarezeh-ye farhangi*] of the country," but he was otherwise sidelined from power. His replacement was Yahya Rahim Safavi, the IRGC deputy commander and a decorated war veteran. Khamenei's appointment of the more hardline Safavi was seen as an endorsement of the far right and its uncompromising politics.[80] The leadership change suggested a new direc-tion for the IRGC's political role and served notice that Rezai's more cautious approach to political activism was no longer favored by the supreme leader. With the support of Khamenei and other powerful conservatives, Safavi and a new cadre of hardline staff commanders led the IRGC into direct opposition with the Khatami government.

Through 1998 and 1999, hardline elements collectively worked to intimidate and destroy the reformist project. Key Khatami allies such as Tehran's mayor, Gholam-Hosayn Karbaschi, and Interior Minister Abdollah Nuri were impris-oned on trumped up charges. Several reformist newspapers were shut down.[81] And a wave of vigilantism led to a series of attacks and murders on journalists and intellectuals.[82] These acts provoked vigorous denunciations from reformist leaders and the reformist press. Hardliners countered with accusations that the reformists were serving the interests of Iran's enemies and unleashing dissension in society. The IRGC responded to this dissent with a more threatening tone. In a February 1999 speech to Basij battalions in Yazd (central Iran), IRGC chief Safavi warned his troops:

> The enemy declares that there are power and political struggles in Iran, while no such thing exist(s) in the country. Using your political-revolutionary vigilance, be wary of the internal and external sedition and await orders from the leader [Khamenei]. Once an order is given by the leader, the seditious individuals will not be able to survive.[83]

Turmoil erupted after the July 1999 closing of *Salam*, a reformist newspaper. The paper was shut down after it had published a document suggesting the existence of a conservative conspiracy to censor the pro-Khatami press. Outrage over the closing and the suspicion of an anti-reformist cabal led to a July 8 protest by student activists on the campus of Tehran University. In response, hezbollahi activists stormed a student dormitory and indiscriminately attacked students, throwing some out of windows. Though Khamenei criticized the assailants and called for justice, news of the incident sparked a series of anti-conservative and anti-Khamenei student protests throughout the country.[84] Each demonstration was met with a counter-demonstration led by student basijis and hezbollahis. As the protests intensified, so too did the rhetoric of conservative leaders, who criticized the students for spreading disunity and for undermining Islam and the position of the guardianship. On July 12, the IRGC and Basij had moved into cities and campuses throughout Iran to provide security and prevent further uprisings.[85] The same day, a letter signed by twenty-four senior IRGC and Basij commanders was delivered to President Khatami threatening aggressive action if the disturbances were not stopped. The letter was leaked to the conservative *Jomhuri-e Eslami* newspaper and published. In it, senior commanders criticized Khatami for allowing his supporters to run amok and freely disparage the supreme leader. Arguing the protests would lead to the destruction of the guardianship and Iran's Islamic culture, the commanders emphasized Khatami's duty to veterans and to the families of martyrs to protect revolutionary values. The commanders cautioned, "You know full well that despite our capabilities, we are impotent because of [the] concern with expediency." They continued with an ultimatum:

> How long should we observe the situation with tears in our eyes? How long should we suffer in silence and practice democracy through creating chaos and insulting each other? How long should we have revolutionary patience while the system is being destroyed? . . .

Mr. President: If you do not make a revolutionary decision and if you do not fulfill your Islamic and national mission today, tomorrow will be far too late. It is unimaginable how irretrievable the situation will become.

In the end, we would like to express our utmost respect for your Excellency and to declare that our patience has run out. We cannot tolerate this situation any longer if it is not dealt with.[86]

The implication was clear: if the president did not take action, the IRGC would bypass his authority and do it itself. Such a provocation not only threatened Khatami's standing, it threatened the foundation and sanctity of the presidency in Iran. It was a proclamation of the IRGC's arrival as a political heavyweight. It would no longer be ignored.

# The War on Terror

States like these, and their terrorist allies, constitute an axis of evil, arming to threaten the peace of the world. By seeking weapons of mass destruction, these regimes pose a grave and growing danger. They could provide these arms to terrorists, giving them the means to match their hatred. They could attack our allies or attempt to blackmail the United States. In any of these cases, the price of indifference would be catastrophic.

We will work closely with our coalition to deny terrorists and their state sponsors the materials, technology and expertise to make and deliver weapons of mass destruction. . .

And all nations should know: America will do what is necessary to ensure our nation's security. We'll be deliberate, yet time is not on our side. I will not wait on events while dangers gather. I will not stand by as peril draws closer and closer. The United States of America will not permit the world's most dangerous regimes to threaten us with the world's most destructive weapons.

Our war on terror is well begun, but it is only begun.[1]

—George W. Bush

The attacks of 9/11 changed the course of American foreign policy in the Middle East. President George W. Bush's cautious assessment of the region was transformed into a hurried effort to confront terrorists and terrorist-supporting states. The neoconservative architects of Bush's policies recognized the opportunity 9/11 afforded them to implement their vision of a democratic Middle East less hostile to Israel and Western values.[2] The administration's blueprint for post-9/11 foreign policy was laid out in the president's January 29, 2002, State of the Union address. President Bush emphasized the need to combat terror around the world and proclaimed that the US strategy in the "war on terror" would be to target states that harbored and supported terrorists. He charged that beyond Al Qaeda there was an "axis of evil" comprised of Iraq, Iran, and North Korea— states that not only supported terrorism but whose attempts to develop weapons of mass destruction threatened democracy and freedom around the globe. These were not empty threats. Bush's admonitions soon translated into a military invasion of Iraq in March 2003. The quick collapse of Saddam's regime and the fall of the Taliban in 2001 served notice to the remaining axis of evil states that Bush was willing to use military force to advance his geopolitical agenda.

The IRGC and Iran's hardliners benefited greatly from these policies. After Saddam's Iraq, no state was seen as more antagonistic to American interests than Iran, and no element inside Iran was considered a more direct threat to American influence in the region than the IRGC. From its ballistic missile program to its support for Hezbollah in Lebanon and Hamas in Gaza, the IRGC and its subsidiaries were considered the main vehicles of Iranian aggression. Yet the war on terror not only failed to contain the IRGC, it was a boon to the organization and both directly and indirectly encouraged its political involvement, domestic expansion, and entry into Iraq. As US policies provided the space and means for the expansion of IRGC influence abroad, the Bush administration's hostile rhetoric created the perception in Iran that a US attack was imminent. Further, suspicions of US covert operations in Iran gave credence to the notion that America was actively trying to topple the Islamic regime. This legitimized the IRGC's paranoid politics and foreign adventurism, further marginalized reformists, and fueled the policies of Mahmoud Ahmadinejad's hardline government.

## Axis of Evil

The 9/11 attacks inspired a rare display of sympathy for the United States across Iran. Spontaneous candlelight vigils from Tehran to Shiraz accompanied statements from President Mohammad Khatami condemning terrorism and the attacks.[3] The goodwill was short lived. As Washington began building up a campaign against the Taliban and Al Qaeda in Afghanistan, Iranian pundits warned against any American military action in the Muslim world. A news site connected to the conservative Islamic Propagation Organization warned: "Any unilateral military action against innocent Afghans may help to boost the image of Uncle Sam at home, but it will surely tarnish the US image on the international arena for its flagrant violation of international law."[4] While condemning the 9/11 attacks, the reformist *Aftab-e Yazd* newspaper argued that 9/11 "should not become an excuse to make the world insecure and create warlike events."[5] Yet, as Iran was condemning American aggression, Khatami's administration was quietly exploring ways in which Iran could assist the effort against the Sunni fundamentalist Taliban. Iran had been actively supporting Afghanistan's Northern Alliance for years, and had almost gone to war with the Taliban after the murder of eight Iranian diplomats in Mazar-e Sharif in 1998. Iran had a vested interest in seeing the Taliban overthrown in favor of its allies in the Northern Alliance.[6]

Soon after 9/11, the Bush administration dispatched Ryan Crocker—then a senior US State Department official—to engage in secret meetings with Iranian diplomats in Geneva and Paris. The two sides discussed potential US operations to uproot the Taliban in Afghanistan. According to Seyed Hossein Mousavian, then the head of the SNSC's Foreign Relations Committee, the Iranian delegation was "pursuing two objectives":

> First, we sought ways to unseat the Taliban and eliminate extremist terrorists, namely al-Qaeda. Both of these groups . . . were arch enemies of Iran. Second, we wanted to look for ways to test cooperation with the Americans, thus decreasing the level of mistrust and tension between us. During these meetings, neither party pursued the subject of Iran-US relations. Nonetheless, we did the groundwork for significant, mutual cooperation on Afghanistan during these meetings, resulting in Iran's assistance during the attack on the Taliban.[7]

Iran's delegation consisted of three ambassadors and one anonymous "member of the security establishment responsible for Afghanistan"—likely a member of the IRGC's Quds Force.[8] It became apparent to Crocker through these deliberations that Iran's delegation answered to Qassem Soleimani, the Quds Force chief. The Iranians eagerly shared intelligence on Taliban positions. In one meeting, the lead Iranian negotiator gave Crocker a map that identified Taliban locations. Crocker recounted the exchange in an interview with the *New Yorker's* Dexter Filkins. He recalled the Iranian saying: "Here's our advice: hit them here first, and then hit them over there. And here's the logic . . ." Crocker asked if he could take notes, to which the Iranian diplomat responded: "You can keep the map." At one point the lead Iranian negotiator told Crocker that Soleimani was "very pleased with our cooperation."[9] The diplomatic exchanges bore fruit. Crocker recalls giving his Iranian counterparts the location of an Al Qaeda operative living in the eastern Iranian city of Mashhad. The Iranians detained the operative and later turned him over to Afghanistan's post-Taliban government.[10] The IRGC's help might have also extended to the battlefield. Mousavian writes that through the Quds Force's close ties with the Northern Alliance (America's Afghan allies against the Taliban), the IRGC had been "actively involved in organizing" the victory over the Taliban in Herat (western Afghanistan), and Soleimani himself had been "key in organizing" the Northern Alliance's advance into Kabul.[11]

President Bush's axis of evil speech in January 2002 ended any budding trust. Crocker, who was stationed at the US embassy in Kabul, met with an incensed Iranian diplomat the next day. "You completely damaged me," the diplomat told him. "Soleimani is in a tearing rage. He feels compromised." Crocker was further told that Soleimani had begun considering a "re-think" of Iran's relationship with the United States.[12] Mousavian recalls Soleimani telling him that "he had suspected that the US request for our help might have been a tactical move and not intended to lead to long-term cooperation." Washington's apparent insincerity left Iranian diplomats and President Khatami feeling "betrayed."[13]

Despite such overtures by Iran—and despite the US intelligence community's suggestion that Iran could be engaged on the Afghan and potential Iraq wars—the Bush administration rebuffed Tehran's offers and took an uncompromising line against the Khatami government.[14] The inclusion of Iran in the axis of evil provoked a backlash across Iran's political spectrum. It also provided hardliners added fodder to criticize Khatami's pro-Western policies. Supreme Leader Ali Khamenei castigated American foreign policy as "the greatest evil" and claimed that he was "proud" that "the most cursed of the world's satans" placed the Islamic Republic within the axis of evil.[15] An editorial by Hosayn Saffar-Harandi in *Kayhan*, the leading hardline daily, argued that Bush's statements were evidence of America's ingrained antagonism toward Iran and proof that the reformists' attempts to improve relations with Washington were not only misguided, but detrimental to national security. He charged that since the reformists had also criticized Bush's statements they implicitly admitted to their naiveté and strategic failings. Saffar-Harandi claimed that America's actions vindicated the conservative and hardliner position vis-à-vis the West, writing:

> After five years of misrepresentation and enduring all kinds of insults and accusations, the critics of 2nd Khordad Front now feel vindicated. It has now become clear that as the result of unilateral efforts to make friends with the foreigners and to open a dialogue with them, one cannot close one's eyes to international realities and to have vain hopes that the satanic nature of America and her allies would change.[16]

By contending that Khatami had misjudged the nature of American foreign policy, hardliners were able to paint themselves as the more realist political camp. Their vocal declarations against a détente with Washington, once seen as ignorant and alarmist by reformists, were now trumpeted as reasonable and informed.

Hardliners used Bush's comments and the prospect of an American attack as added justification to undercut Khatami and his already weak government. Despite being reelected by an overwhelming majority in the summer of 2001, Khatami was a near-powerless leader. Conservatives continued to control the most important state institutions and used their influence to block all significant attempts of political and social reform initiated by the president.[17] An example of Khatami's political impotence occurred the day after his re-election when

Ansar-e Hezbollah stormed a pro-Khatami celebration. The anti-reform activists arrested many of the president's supporters and injured numerous bystanders, including BBC journalist John Simpson.[18] Khatami's lack of support within the police (who either participated in the attack or stood aside) evinced his broader alienation from the security services. As the war on terror began to take shape, growing anxiety spawned numerous attacks on pro-Khatami elements and on others with perceived pro-Western biases.

Most dramatic was a string of murders committed by a small group of basijis in 2002. The six basijis—all morality agents—admitted to killing five individuals. They were suspected in thirteen additional murders, all in the Kerman area. Each of the victims had been killed on the basis of "prohibiting vice" and in an attempt to stomp out the "cultural invasion" of Western immorality. A young couple engaged to be married were killed because they had been suspected of having engaged in premarital sex. Another woman was buried up to her chest and stoned to death for suspected adultery.[19] In the subsequent trial the accused justified their killings by claiming the victims were sinners whose immorality was punishable by death under Islamic law (*mahdur al-dam*). They identified prominent hardline cleric Ayatollah Taqi Mesbah-Yazdi as the religious authority whose guidance on the matter they had followed. The six defendants were found guilty and sentenced to death. However, the Supreme Court in Tehran refused to accept the ruling and sent the case back to another regional court in Kerman to be retried. After two more trials and two more guilty verdicts, a fourth trial in 2007 ultimately found the accused not guilty and acquitted them of their crimes. The court agreed with the defendants that the victims had indeed been immoral Muslims whose actions were justifiably punished by death.[20] The Supreme Court accepted the ruling. Because the six had been licensed morality police, they were seen as having carried out their civic duty. The judiciary's role in acquitting the basijis signaled that right-wing vigilante activism had the tacit support of both state institutions and the supreme leader, whose silence on the rulings was taken as implied support for the defendants.

Pressure on Khatami's government increased after Iran's secret nuclear enrichment program was made public in the fall of 2002. Although information on Iran's enrichment facility in Natanz and a heavy water plant in Arak was disclosed to the International Atomic Energy Agency (IAEA) in August of that year by the National Council of Resistance of Iran (the political front for the Mojehedin-e Khalq), US officials did not seize upon the issue until December.[21] As a signatory to the nuclear Non-Proliferation Treaty (NPT), Iran's failure to disclose its secret facilities (themselves legal under the NPT) put Iran in violation of its international agreements. Consequently, Iran was compelled by the United States, the so-called EU-3 of Britain, France, and Germany, and the IAEA to make additional concessions on its nuclear program, including the suspension of its enrichment program and allowing for snap inspections of its facilities by IAEA monitors.[22] Those demands were made alongside the Bush administration's aggressive rhetoric toward Iraq, which was accused of harboring a secret WMD program and of supporting terrorism. Even though both Khamenei and Khatami denied Iran had any intention of developing nuclear weapons and argued that such weapons were against Islamic law, Iran knew that American intelligence had evidence suggesting Iranian scientists possessed designs for a suspected nuclear device.[23]

The Khatami administration found itself in an impossible situation. Any apparent compromise with the West over Iran's nuclear program would be vociferously opposed by hardliners. Further, the Bush administration's justification for the invasion of Iraq made the continuation of nuclear enrichment risky. Europe's clear objection to Iran's enrichment activities, backed by the implied military threats of the United States and Israel, gave Iranian leaders few options of resolving the crisis outside of succumbing to Western demands. Khatami's cabinet began to pursue a deal with Washington. This effort culminated in a proposal faxed to the US State Department by the Swiss ambassador to Iran, Tim Guldimann, who was in charge of American affairs in Tehran.[24] The contents of the fax contained the outline of a proposed resolution to Iran's nuclear situation—a text purportedly approved by both Khatami and Khamenei.[25] Iran demanded a non-aggression pact with the United States, "rectification" of Iran's status (e.g., removal from the axis of evil and an end to hostile rhetoric), abolishment of all sanctions against Iran, "full access to peaceful nuclear technology, biotechnology, and chemical technology," recognition of Iran's special relationship to the Shiite shrine cities of Najaf and Karbala in Iraq, recognition of Iran's "legitimate" regional security interests, and repatriation of MKO terrorists from Iraq to Iran. In exchange, Iran would fully cooperate with the IAEA, accept additional protocols and effectively prove that it did not have an active nuclear weapons program or have any intention to start one, take action against Al Qaeda members in Iran, coordinate with the United States to ensure a stable, secular, and democratic Iraq, cease material support for Palestinian militant organizations including Hamas and Islamic Jihad, encourage Hezbollah to become a solely political organization in Lebanon, and accept the Saudi Arabian initiative for a two-state solution in Israel and the Palestinian territories.[26]

Reaction to the missive in the Bush administration was mixed. Dick Cheney and John Bolton rejected the offer immediately, considering it a weak attempt from a nation obviously frightened by America's recent military success in Iraq. The offer was proof that their strategy to reshape the Middle East through the use of force was working.[27] Others in the State Department, particularly Richard Haass, the director of policy planning, who advised Secretary of State Colin Powell that the offer might be worth pursuing. While not convinced of the proposal's provenance, Haass felt that the only way to find out if it had merit would be to pursue it through diplomatic channels. Secret talks were already taking place between Iranian diplomat Mohammad Javad Zarif and US ambassador to Afghanistan Zalmay Khalilzad on possible ways to share intelligence on terrorist organizations. Zarif wanted Washington to exchange Iranian MKO members in Iraq—who had been disarmed by US forces shortly after the defeat of Saddam—for Al Qaeda suspects in Iran that had been detained after fleeing the US invasion of Afghanistan. The Bush administration was not willing to exchange terrorist suspects, but it asked Iran to interrogate its Al Qaeda suspects for information about a rumored operation developing in the Persian Gulf. If Iran had had any intelligence on such an attack it did not share it with Washington. On May 12, 2003, four bombs exploded in an American housing complex in Riyadh. Bush administration officials were convinced that the Al Qaeda suspects in Iranian custody had been aware of the operation. They blamed Iran for not investigating the matter. All talks with Tehran were promptly called off and the proposal was killed. What might have been an opportunity to fundamentally shift the relationship between the United States and Iran died on the vine.[28]

With a direct deal no longer possible, the EU-3 and the IAEA were left to work out a resolution with Iran. Khatami's position, however, had grown more tenuous. While attempting to placate the conservative opposition with bold refusals to compromise Iran's nuclear ambitions, Khatami was also negotiating with the West in search of a compromise.[29] When Khatami agreed in November 2004 to temporarily halt enrichment as a goodwill gesture during talks with the EU-3 and the IAEA, he was immediately slammed by conservatives. Mohsen Rezai, Expediency Council secretary and former IRGC chief argued that Khatami's diplomats had given Europe too much "top secret" information on Iran's nuclear program and had undermined Iran's "deterrence" capabilities.[30] In a speech to IRGC commanders, senior cleric Ayatollah Nuri-Hamadani charged that by agreeing to cease enrichment Khatami's administration had helped advance America's plot against Iran.[31] Prominent hardline cleric Hojjat al-Islam Mohsen Doagu called the agreement the "worst in the history of the Islamic Republic" in a Friday prayer sermon.[32] The hardliner onslaught against Khatami undermined his attempts to reach compromise with the West. It also spurred their political revival.

## Electing Ahmadinejad

By marginalizing Khatami, conservatives were paving the way for their own return to dominance in the electoral realm. Aided by mass disqualifications of reformist candidates and low voter turnout, conservative politicians took the majority of seats in the 2003 Municipal Council elections and in the 2004 Majles elections. They then set their sights on the next year's presidential election.[33] The election of June 2005 was the first since 1997 that would not include Mohammad Khatami as the reformist candidate.[34] Without Khatami the reformists lacked a consensus leader. The bulk of reformists threw their support behind two political veterans: former Majles Speaker Mehdi Karrubi and cabinet minister Mostafa Moin. While both of these individuals had strong reformist credentials, neither possessed the popularity, charisma, or public recognition of Khatami. The weak field of candidates opened up the door for the return of Akbar Hashemi Rafsanjani. Rafsanjani presented himself as a moderate candidate who could bring balance to Iran's ideological divide. Already one of Iran's most influential figures, most political analysts and pre-election polls predicted Rafsanjani the likely winner of the 2005 presidential race.

Hardliners saw the presidential campaign as a way for the fundamentalist or "principlist" (*osulgara*) coalition to capture the government. They too, however, lacked a candidate with the sufficient standing to challenge Rafsanjani. Candidates included former IRGC chief Mohsen Rezai, secretary of the Supreme National Security Council and former guardsman Ali Larijani, and Mahmoud Ahmadinejad, Tehran's little-known mayor of two years and a former guardsman and basiji. The leading candidate was Mohammad Baqer Qalibaf— a former IRGC air force commander, Tehran's police chief, and the rumored preference of Khamenei. Qalibaf had gained notoriety and reformist scorn for leading the crackdown on student protestors in 1999. He presented himself as a candidate with modern and youthful sensibilities.

Qalibaf's use of "nationalist" (i.e., non-Islamic) symbols and modern attire in courting the youth vote gained him detractors among hardline leaders. Those suspicions led to a quiet but substantial shift of support to the unheralded Ahmadinejad.[35] As a former guardsman and avid supporter of war veterans, Ahmadinejad had already formed a staunch support base among the Basij. A pre-election poll conducted by the University of Tehran's Basij student association found more basijis favored Ahmadinejad than any other candidate (the reformist Moin came in second).[36] Despite the backing of basijis across Iran, Ahmadinejad did not have the explicit endorsement of either the Basij or the IRGC. This was due to the IRGC's official neutrality in political matters and because the organization was likely split between the four candidates that came from its ranks: Qalibaf, Rezai, Larijani, and Ahmadinejad. Instead of endorsing a specific candidate, IRGC counseled its members on the characteristics an ideal candidate should have. Khamenei's representative to the Guards, Ayatollah Mohammad-Ali Movahedi-Kermani, highlighted six attributes voters should look for in choosing the next president. The model candidate would be: (1) someone who above all else heeds the religious demands of the people and is accountable to them; (2) someone who is obedient to the supreme leader and serves at his pleasure; (3) someone who lives a modest life and understands the suffering of the poor and dispossessed; (4) someone who will lessen the gap between the wealthy and impoverished; (5) someone who speaks on welfare and the economy at least as much as piety, attainment, chastity, and truth; and (6) someone who does not seek to attract votes with empty slogans.[37] Beyond these qualities—all of which characterized Ahmadinejad—guardsmen and basijis were to vote their conscience.

There was widespread trepidation that the IRGC would interfere in the election process. Part of this stemmed from comments made by the Guardian Council that volunteers from the Basij would be in charge of protecting polling stations on election day.[38] This worried reformist leaders who publicized the issue with the hopes of discouraging possible machinations. Interior Minister Abdol-Vahed Musavi Lari confronted the Guardian Council on this point and warned of possible interference by state "military" organs—a clear reference to the IRGC and Basij.[39] IRGC leaders countered these accusations with a calculated media effort. Ayatollah Movahedi-Kermani assured the public that the IRGC was a non-political institution that did not harbor bias for any presidential candidate.[40] The Basij Public Relation's office took this a step further and promised the militia would personally lead investigations into any suspected election fraud should any take place.[41] Such statements did not mean that members of these institutions would not vote or campaign for their favored candidate. On the contrary, an IRGC spokesman promised that members of both organizations would participate in the elections en masse as voting was both their right and civic duty.[42] Principlists argued that a high election turnout would be a powerful counter to American aggression. That made voting a particularly patriotic endeavor for members of IRGC and Basij.[43]

The first round of voting ended on June 17, 2005, with Rafsanjani leading with 6.1 million votes (just over 20 percent of votes cast), Ahmadinejad in second with 5.7 million, and Karrubi in third with 5 million. While Rafsanjani and Karrubi's numbers generally followed those in pre-election polls, Ahmadinejad's strong showing came as a surprise. Questions regarding Ahmadinejad's numbers arose on election night as a discrepancy of 6 million votes between the results given by the Guardian Council (which claimed 21 million votes had been cast) and the Interior Ministry (which claimed 15 million votes had been cast) had been announced on state television.[44] Why the Guardian Council was even involved in election results, which had previously been overseen by the Interior Ministry, was not clear. That the conservative Guardian Council's numbers seemed to favor Ahmadinejad further cast suspicion on the results. Karrubi instantly claimed that the Basij and IRGC had committed election fraud—an accusation the IRGC vigorously rejected.[45] He pointed to the province of South

Khorasan as a "most peculiar" ('ajibtar) example, which with 270,127 eligible voters had registered 298,000 votes.[46] Rafsanjani also registered a protest with Khamenei and informed the supreme leader that he intended to withdraw from the race. Khamenei publically praised the election and condemned Karrubi's accusations. He also convinced Rafsanjani to stay in the running on the basis that a withdrawal would feed into American propaganda.[47]

In the runoff election on June 23, Ahmadinejad trounced Rafsanjani by nearly 6 million votes. Although turnout was less than the first round (60 percent versus 63 percent), Ahmadinejad somehow managed to capture nearly all of the votes that had previously gone to other hardliners while also gaining many of the votes that had gone to reformists.[48] Rafsanjani on the other hand, despite being endorsed by leading reformist organizations and first-round candidate Mostafa Moin, did only marginally better in the second round. While Ahmadinejad had developed a larger support base between the first and second rounds by playing to populist sentiment (an impressive feat for less than a week of campaigning), accusations of widespread voter fraud continued. Rafsanjani issued a statement protesting the results and warned that "divine retribution" (enteqam-e elahi) awaited those responsible for the election fraud.[49]

Suspicions were rife that the Basij and IRGC had been behind Ahmadinejad's sudden rise. With fears of these organizations tampering with the voting process expressed by the interior minister even before the elections took place, and with the Basij in charge of guarding voting facilities and encouraged to fully participate in the voting process, such suspicion was not surprising. The curious role of the Guardian Council in the election process and public praise for the results by Khamenei and other conservative clergy (despite the public protests of the reformist candidates, interior minister, and Rafsanjani), further strengthened the notion that a cabal had brought Ahmadinejad to power.[50] The existence of a plot might have merit. Citing well-placed sources, Iranian journalist Kasra Naji claims that conservative and hardline politicians met with the supreme leader at his residence a few nights before the first round. At the meeting the group decided on supporting Ahmadinejad over Qalibaf due to the latter's questionable commitment to hardline positions. Basijis, most of whom did not become aware of the plan to support Ahmadinejad till the morning of the first round election, were enlisted to ensure that he got a substantial number of votes. Naji cites one basiji who admitted to voting numerous times in the first round using the birth certificates of deceased Iranians.[51] The existence and dimensions of a plot are impossible to determine. What is clear is that the IRGC and Basij actively worked toward the election of Ahmadinejad in both rounds— something all but admitted to by IRGC commanders.[52] The IRGC issued an official statement praising Ahmadinejad's election:

Undoubtedly, the winners of this great and historic test are each and every proud and pious Iranian who, despite propaganda attacks and the psychological operations of the American and Zionist media and broadcasting organizations, accepted the invitation of the wise and learned leader of the Islamic Revolution, Grand Ayatollah Khamene'i (blessed be his excellency), and in an unprecedented act of public participation, suitably determined the destiny of the country and themselves.... The hegemon[ic] powers of the world will try to use different methods to portray this everlasting epic as colorless, but this will not be forgotten in the historical memory of this nation and other free and great nations.[53]

With Ahmadinejad's election, the IRGC witnessed one of its own reach the country's highest elected office. It gained an outspoken and uncritical supporter in the president. Ahmadinejad demonstrated his gratitude to his supporters by giving ten out of twenty-five seats of his first cabinet to IRGC and Basij members and several more to war veterans.[54]

## An Iran Ascendant

As aggressive US policy encouraged a revival of hardline power in Iran, policies toward other states in the region and globally helped facilitate the expansion of Iranian influence outside its borders. For instance, the antagonistic relationship between the Bush administration and Hugo Chavez in Venezuela opened up the door for Chavez to seek closer ties with other international partners. Iran's relationship with Chavez had grown stronger during Khatami's presidency. Ahmadinejad promoted Iranian-Venezuelan relations as a new anti-imperialist front. Strengthening Iranian-Venezuelan relations was more than simple political showmanship, however, as both oil-rich countries increased investment in each other's infrastructure and commercial enterprises. In 2007 the Chavez regime listed Iran as its second largest investor after the United States, with $9.1 billion invested annually.[55] In 2006 Iran's semi-official Petropars firm was awarded a lucrative contract by Chavez to develop drilling operations in an off-shore Venezuelan oil field.[56] Tehran and Caracas also increased military cooperation which provided the IRGC a limited presence in South America.[57]

The expansion of Iranian influence in the Middle East was more pronounced. In Lebanon, Bush administration policies inadvertently helped bolster Hezbollah and, by extension, the IRGC's influence in that country. Following the assassination of Rafiq Hariri in February 2005 by suspected Syrian agents, the Bush administration joined a popular movement in Lebanon in calling for

Syria to end its military occupation.[58] Backed by Christian and Sunni politicians, the so-called Cedar Revolution led to the end of the almost thirty-year Syrian military occupation of Lebanon. It was hailed by Washington as a sign of the global spread of freedom and a serious blow to Hezbollah.[59] The Syrian occupation enabled Hezbollah operations against Israel. But it also constrained the group's power. That became evident in the aftermath of the July 2006 war between Israel and Hezbollah. Even though Israel was able to inflict significant damage on Hezbollah, it was unable to achieve its stated aim of destroying the terrorist organization. By simply outlasting its enemy on the battlefield, Hezbollah claimed to have defeated Israel twice—first in forcing Israel to quit its eighteen-year occupation of southern Lebanon in 2000 and secondly in the 2006 war—something no Arab state could claim to have done. With Syria's military no longer able to curb Hezbollah's ambition, the organization followed the 2006 war with an aggressive push for power.[60] In May 2008, after a nearly eighteen-month boycott of the government, Hezbollah was able to win a concession from the Lebanese government which gave the organization a veto over executive decisions.[61] Hezbollah used its political influence to promote a domestic agenda at odds with the Cedar Revolution, including stymieing the UN investigation into Hariri's assassination.

As its main benefactor, Hezbollah's assent in Lebanon gave the IRGC a stronger foothold in Lebanese politics and in the geopolitics of the Palestinian-Israeli conflict. American policies toward the latter provided the IRGC another opportunity to advance its agenda. In 2005 the Bush administration began pushing for democratic elections in the Palestinian Territories. The January 25, 2006, election did not produce the result Washington was hoping for. In a rejection of the perceived corruption of the secular Fatah organization, Palestinians gave the Islamist Hamas organization a resounding victory.[62] Hamas, like Hezbollah, describes itself as a militant resistance organization and is listed by the US State Department as a proscribed terrorist group. Instead of recognizing the results and supporting the Palestinian democratic process it had advocated, the Bush administration quickly called for a boycott of Hamas and cut off all funding to its government. The Bush administration continued to support Fatah; however, the vacuum created by its abandonment of financial support for the Hamas-led administration opened the way for Iran to step in. Buoyed by a steep rise in oil prices, Iran was able to become the leading financial supporter of the Hamas-led government. Through its patronage of Hamas, Iran gained another client able to influence the Palestinian-Israel issue.[63]

American policies toward Lebanon and Hamas benefited the IRGC. The US occupation of Iraq had an even greater impact on the organization's foreign influence. Although the US military presence in Iraq was designed to indirectly put pressure on Iran, it also made US forces vulnerable to Iranian retaliation. Prior to the occupation, IRGC commanders made clear that it would target American interests and troops in the region in response to any aggression against Iran. Following the axis of evil speech, IRGC Brigadier General Mohammad Zolqadr warned:

> If the Americans show madness and attack us, we will not defend our-selves only within our borders. We have a long and powerful arm, and we can threaten American interests anywhere. There is no need for us to go very far. There are many American assets in the Persian Gulf. Sixty to 70 per cent of world energy is produced here. Well, this place is under our observation and within our reach. Of course, we do not wish to threaten anyone, but if our security is violated, no other place will have security either. We have the ability to respond with force to such threats. Afghanistan lacks an army, it lacks naval borders, and it lacks the ability to hit a strategic target. It is natural that such a country can be easily eliminated. Iraq also shares some of the same characteristics. We must stress that through immaturity and naivety, the Americans are in danger of creating a major incident in the world. We think that they are mainly engaged in a political bluff, but if they wish to act they will involve the world in a serious crisis. They may be able to start an inci-dent in Iran, but its continuation will in no way be under their control.[64]

Zolqadr intimates Iran's ability to strike at Western targets outside of its bor-ders. In part he is suggesting that if attacked Iran would turn toward the same instruments of terrorism that the Bush administration had accused Iran of spon-soring. However, with the presence of US forces in Iraq, added implications of such a strategy became evident. In Iraq, the IRGC was able to utilize its close ties to expatriate organizations such as the Supreme Council of Islamic Revolution in Iraq (known as the Supreme Islamic Council of Iraq or SICI after 2006) and the Badr Organization (which had functioned as a part of the IRGC dur-ing the Iran-Iraq war). The IRGC also patronized other Shiite militias to help it advance its interests in Iraq and keep pressure on American forces.[65] Iran's threat of retaliation against American targets became a key element in its approach to deterrence. By later demonstrating that US forces were susceptible to Iranian-sponsored attacks, Iran was able to use the threat of escalating violence in Iraq as a deterrent to an American attack against Iran's nuclear facilities.

Iran began activities in Iraq shortly after the March 2003 invasion, but it was not until Ahmadinejad took office that Tehran took a more aggressive approach to pursuing its interests in that country.[66] The first evidence of poten-tial Iranian involvement in the fighting in Iraq came from British command-ers who began to notice that Iranian-manufactured explosives were being used by Shiite militants in southern Iraq. By March 2006, Defense Secretary Donald Rumsfeld accused the IRGC's Quds Force of fomenting violence in Iraq through its support of Shiite militias.[67] Soon Iranian involvement was suspected in various attacks against coalition forces. In response, US forces were given the green light to arrest and detain any Iranian operatives found in Iraq, and after January 2007 were authorized to kill or capture suspected Iranian agents.[68] Several Iranians had been arrested under the suspicion of providing aid to Iraqi insurgents in cross-border smuggling operations through 2006. The most publicized incidents were raids on two Iranian offices in Irbil in northern Iraq on January 11, 2007. After the raids, American officials claimed to have detained five Quds Force commanders on the suspicion of aiding the Iraqi insurgency.[69] Iraqi foreign minister Hoshyar Zebari protested the arrests, claiming that the Iranians were diplomats. US officials countered that the detainees had been in charge of mediating IRGC support to Iraqi militant groups.[70]

Tehran denounced the arrests and claimed the officials detained were part of its diplomatic mission to Iraq. Less than two weeks later, five American soldiers were captured in Karbala. The soldiers had been meeting with Iraqi counterparts at an office of the Supreme Islamic Council of Iraq, when armed militants stormed the meeting. The attackers wore Iraqi and American uniforms and carried official identification badges. They had entered the building unhampered. After a brief exchange of gunfire, the militants captured the American soldiers and spirited them away. US forces hurried to track down the assailants and rescue the hostages. They found the soldiers about thirty miles away. All five were found dead of gunshot wounds. Evidence at the scene suggested that the Americans had been killed during a failed escape attempt.[71]

American officials suspected that Iran was behind the attack.[72] The number of US soldiers captured—the same number as Iranians detained in Irbil—did not seem coincidental. Some suspected Iran might have engineered the kidnappings to compel a hostage exchange with Washington—a tactic Iran and Hezbollah honed during the Lebanese civil war.[73] Tehran declared it had no knowledge of the incident. The IRGC implied otherwise. In a February 12 editorial in the IRGC weekly news organ *Sobh-e Sadeq*, Ali Rahimi, a senior member of the IRGC's Political Office, suggested that the Karbala raid had been in response to the arrest of Iran's diplomats in Irbil.[74] In another incident on March 24, the IRGC arrested fifteen British sailors for purportedly entering Iranian territory while on patrol in the Shatt al-Arab. The sailors were held for two weeks, but eventually released. The provocativeness of the incident led some to suspect that it might have also been in reaction to the Irbil five. However, as the UN Security Council voted to place further sanctions on Iran's nuclear program the very next day, the incident could have been related to that matter.[75] The kidnapping of former FBI agent Robert Levinson—who disappeared from Iran's Kish Island on March 8—may also have been blowback to the Irbil arrests.[76]

The Karbala attack exposed the IRGC's role in Iraq. At the center of the case was Qais Khazali, a former lieutenant of Muqtada al-Sadr who broke away from al-Sadr's Mehdi Army and formed his own militant organization with the IRGC's support. Quds Force operatives had been active in Iraq since 2003 supporting allies such as the Badr Organization and other Shiite militant groups that were active in resisting the US occupation. Khazali's group—Asaib Ahl al-Haq (League of the Righteous)—was one of the militias that formed close ties to the IRGC. Better known at the time by US forces as part of the shadowy "Special Groups" that emerged from the Sadrist movement, Khazali's militia received extensive support from the IRGC. His fighters often traveled to Iran for training within specialized IRGC camps. With deeper knowledge of tactics, explosives, and weaponry, Khazali's group distinguished itself from the broader Shiite resistance. It was more aggressive and more effective than other Shiite militias.[77]

The Quds Force enlisted members of Lebanese Hezbollah to assist its operations. Ali Musa Daqduq was the lead Hezbollah operative in Iraq. According US officials, Daqduq—along with Yussef Hashim—was sent to Iran in 2006 to assist the IRGC in the training of Iraqi militants. The Quds Force soon deployed him to help train militants in Iraq. Once in Iraq, Daqduq began to work closely with Khazali's Asaib militia—including at the operational level. Within a few months, the investigation into the Karbala attack led to the arrests of Qais Khazali, his brother Laith Khazali, and Daqduq in Basra. The three were captured in safe house together in a raid by British forces. Also discovered at the time was a cache of materials that detailed both the IRGC's direct support to Asaib Ahl al-Haq and the group's attacks on US and coalition forces. In addition to training, the Quds Force had funded Khazali's operation with sums ranging between $750,000 to $3 million dollars a month. The materials also linked Quds to the Karbala attack. It reportedly provided intelligence to Khazali in the form of "detailed information on the activities of American soldiers in Karbala including, shift changes and the defenses at the site" to assist in the operation.[78] Daqduq was the alleged mastermind of the Karbala operation, but the IRGC's fingerprints were also all over it.[79]

The IRGC's overall strategy in Iraq was to advance Iran's interests through the subversion of American influence in Iraq. This was a two-pronged approach. The first part centered on support to client groups such as Khazali's Asaib Ahl al-Haq, Kitaib Hezbollah (Hezbollah Brigades), and other Shiite militias that refused to enter into the political process. These militias regularly targeted American and coalition forces throughout the occupation and were a mechanism that provided

Iran leverage with the Iraqi government and the United States. The second part was more aboveboard. The IRGC continued its close relationship with Kurdish groups, the Supreme Islamic Council of Iraq, the Badr Organization, and the Dawa party, all of which participated in the Iraqi political process. These organizations comprised much of post-Saddam Iraqi officialdom. Through these relationships the Islamic Republic and IRGC had contacts of influence within both Iraqi state and in the underground resistance.[80]

The utility of the IRGC's support to the Shiite insurgency became evident in March and April 2008. During this period, Iraqi state security forces under the direction of Prime Minister Nuri Al-Maliki began a campaign to root out anti-governmental Shiite militant groups in Basra. These groups had amassed considerable influence in the area and had begun to undermine the already tenuous authority of the Iraqi government. Al-Maliki's ambitious plan initially floundered due to the inexperience of his troops, their unwillingness to engage fellow Iraqi Shiites in battle, and the tenacity of local Basra militants.[81] Unable to achieve his goals militarily, Al-Maliki was forced to send a team to negotiate a ceasefire with the Basra groups in Qom, Iran. The man behind the deal, as first reported by McClatchy's Leila Fadel, was Quds Force chief Qassem Soleimani.[82] Part of the agreement included an offer by Maliki to absorb Badr Organization militants into Iraq's security forces—a move that further entwined pro-Iranian and IRGC-linked elements with the Iraqi government.[83]

Soleimani's role in the Basra ceasefire highlighted Iran's growing influence in Iraq. It also signaled Soleimani's emergence as a powerbroker. Recognizing his own rising stock, in May 2008 Soleimani sent a letter to his "counterpart" in Iraq, US General David Petraeus, suggesting that the two meet to discuss Iraqi security.[84] Petraeus dismissed the letter, but Soleimani's message was clear: Iran had amassed considerable power in Iraq and would have to be engaged for stability in that country to be achieved. That event was the high watermark of Iranian influence in Iraq during the first half-decade of the US occupation. It came on the heels of a partial reversal of Bush administration policy which had renewed limited contacts with Iranian diplomats over Iraqi security. Through 2007 and 2008, Ryan Crocker (now US ambassador to Iraq) held three meetings with his Iranian counterpart, Hassan Kazemi Qomi, in Baghdad. Although these discussions were confined to issues of Iraqi security, that they even took place was in sharp contrast to the Bush administration's rhetoric and refusals to engage in unilateral talks with Ahmadinejad's government. They marked success for the IRGC. By inserting itself into the ground war through the patronage of Shiite militant groups, the IRGC had forced the American and Iraqi governments to the negotiating table.

# The Specter of War

With Iranian clients gaining ground throughout the Middle East, Yahya Rahim Safavi announced in September 2007 that, in "geopolitical" and "military" terms, Iran had become an "extra-regional power."[85] Less than a year later, Safavi's successor as IRGC chief, Mohammad Ali Jafari, attributed Iran's rise in part to America's missteps in the region.[86] Iran's regional footprint was a double-edged sword. The IRGC's influence in Iraq and its ability to escalate violence in that country gave Iran a certain amount of leverage over the United States. However, the IRGC's support for militant groups also strengthened the Bush administration's case against Iran. Thus, even despite the findings of the November 2007 National Intelligence Estimate that Iran no longer had an active nuclear weapons program, the Bush administration continued to suggest that military action against Iran remained a possibility.[87] The prospect of another elective war in the Middle East spurred sectors of the American public to speak out. An illustration of this is the number of books written by academics, intellectuals, and ex-officials between 2005 and 2007 that warned of the Bush administration's designs for military confrontation with Iran.[88] These books paralleled the articles written by prominent American journalists such as David Sanger, Nicholas Kristof, David Ignatius, and Seymour Hersh, which indicated that military action against Iran was a growing possibility. Hersh's articles in particular, published in the *New Yorker* between 2005 and 2008, described plans for an attack against Iran in detail.[89]

With opposition to Middle East wars mounting within the American public, an attack on Iran and the start of perhaps another protracted conflict would likely have required an act of congress. The US Senate nearly offered the Bush administration such consent in the form of amendment 3017 of House Resolution 1585. In its submitted form, amendment 3017—co-sponsored by Senators John Kyl (Republican from Arizona) and Joseph Lieberman (Independent from Connecticut)—made a clear case for military action against Iran.[90] Quoting the congressional testimonies of Gen. Petraeus and Ambassador Crocker, the amendment produced evidence of Iran's support for insurgent groups in Iraq and claimed that Iran—through the IRGC's Quds Force—was turning "Shia militia extremists in Iraq into a Hezbollah-like force that could serve [Iranian] interests." The amendment argued that it was vital to American national security to prevent Iran from achieving its objectives in Iraq, charging that "it should be the policy" of the US government "to combat, contain, and roll back the violent activities and destabilizing influence" of Iran and its "proxies" in Iraq. It further called for the "prudent and calibrated use of all instruments of American national power in Iraq, including diplomatic, economic, intelligence, and military instruments, in support of the [above] policy . . . with respect to [Iran] and its proxies." Equally significant, the amendment argued that on the basis of its training of and support for Shiite insurgents in Iraq, the IRGC should be designated "as a foreign terrorist organization under section 219 of the Immigration and Nationality Act" and placed on the list of "Specially Designated Global Terrorists, as established under the International Emergency Economic Powers Act and initiated under Executive Order 13224."[91] The implications of these sections caused a vigorous debate on the Senate floor including a denunciation by Sen. Jim Webb (D., Virginia) who asked for the amendment to be withdrawn on the grounds that its wording and the listing of the IRGC as a terrorist organization could be used by the Bush administration as de facto congressional support for military action against Iran.[92]

In order to get the amendment passed on September 26, 2007, last-minute revisions were made which deleted the sections that called for potential military action against Iran. However, the section that designated the IRGC as a terrorist organization remained.[93] Although the amendment stopped short of adding the IRGC to the State Department's list of foreign terrorist organizations (which would have had more extensive ramifications), it enabled the Treasury Department to target the Guards' financial holdings outside of Iran. Iranian officials and the IRGC considered the move another step toward an American war with Iran.[94]

Iranian authorities already contended that an American campaign to undermine the Islamic Republic was underway. Pro-democratic activism within Iran was seen as part of an American effort to encourage a "velvet revolution" against the regime, which led to the arrests of several academics and journalists through 2009. Iranian authorities pointed to the uptick in terrorist attacks and violence arising from Iran's minority ethnic populations as evidence of American-sponsored attempts to destabilize the country. Iranian forces had sporadically done battle with ethnic insurgent groups and criminal smuggling networks along the country's periphery for decades, however since 2005 there had been a steep increase in the frequency and boldness of attacks.[95] The most serious terrorist incidents were linked to Sunni organizations operating within the minority ethnic Baloch communities of southeastern Iran and across the border in Pakistan. The People's Resistance Movement of Iran (*jonbesh-e moqavemat-e mardomi-e iran*)—better known as Jondollah (Army of God)—claimed responsibility for numerous attacks against the Iranian government, including the February 2007 bombing of an IRGC transport vehicle, the June 2008 assassination of a district prosecutor in Saravan near the Iran-Pakistan border, the kidnapping and eventual executions of sixteen guardsmen in summer and fall 2008, the kidnapping of Quds Force commander Zarif Shaybani in March 2009, and the bombing of a Shiite mosque in Zahedan in May 2009.[96] The April 2008 bombing of a religious center (*hosayniyyeh*) in Shiraz used by the Basij and a local hardline Mahdist organization known as the Rahpuyan was also linked to Baloch militants.[97]

Iranian authorities saw the hand of foreign powers in all of these attacks.[98] Government officials directly blamed American intelligence for supporting Jondollah and for participating in its operations.[99] Even though such accusations were a reflexive response to all anti-regime activism by Iranian authorities, an article published in the *New Yorker* on June 30, 2008, by Seymour Hersh lent credence to Iranian suspicions. In the article, which describes American plans for military action against Iran, Hersh suggests that the Bush administration was supporting groups such as the Kurdish Pjak organization, the Mojahedin-e Khalq, and Jondollah in a similar way as it had the Northern Alliance against the Taliban in Afghanistan.[100] For Hersh, American support for ethnic insurgencies was a prelude to a more substantial military engagement with Iran. Regardless of the veracity of Hersh's information, anonymous-sourced articles such as his fed into the Islamic Republic's perception that the Bush administration was seeking war with Iran.

To prepare for a possible conflict, the IRGC began to rethink its approach to strategic defense. This process began under IRGC chief Yahya Rahim Safavi in late 2005, but it took on more urgency under Safavi's successor, Brigadier General Mohammad Ali Jafari, who was appointed by the supreme leader in September 2007.[101] (The change in command caused speculation that Safavi had fallen out of favor with the Khamenei. However, Safavi's subsequent appointment as senior military advisor to Khamenei suggested that he retained the latter's confidence.) A signal that Jafari's star was on the rise had come in 2005 when Khamenei entrusted the then IRGC ground forces commander to head the newly established Center for Strategic Studies (*markaz-e motale'at-e rahbordi-e sepah*)—a think tank tasked with updating IRGC military doctrine. Jafari was promoted to this position based on his expertise in insurgent warfare, experience he had gained by leading irregular ground operations during the Iran-Iraq war.[102] Jafari's promotion to top IRGC commander was likely due to his extensive background in both operations and strategic affairs—valuable qualities with the prospect of war on the horizon.[103]

After taking office, Jafari began to restructure the IRGC and Basij into more mobile, more decentralized, and more "asymmetrical" (*na-motaqaren/na-hamtaraz*) military forces. A key element of this effort was the expansion of the IRGC's command structure, strategic centers, and areas of responsibility.[104] In July 2008, Jafari announced that thirty-one new provincial commands would be established—one for each of Iran's provinces and two for greater Tehran. These commands would enable each province the capability to organize and execute its own specific defense strategy without having to depend on orders and planning from IRGC central command in Tehran.[105] Jafari took a similar approach to IRGC naval operations and expanded the organization's purview over the maritime domain by bringing the Persian Gulf directly under IRGC command—an area of operations that had been previously split between the IRGC and regular navies.[106] He established a new strategic studies center and operational training facility for IRGC special naval forces in Bandar-e Anzali on the southwestern Caspian Sea coast to formulate irregular tactics to defend against the American naval threat in the Gulf.[107] Additionally, Jafari announced the formation of a separate IRGC missile command unit to help facilitate the effective utilization of Iran's ballistic missiles in the case of war—a capability Jafari considered central to Iran's overall strategic defenses.[108]

Jafari also expanded the role of the Basij. The most significant reform was Jafari's decision to bring the Basij directly under his command. Although the Basij already operated as a branch of the IRGC, its focus was split between military duties and non-military (e.g., ideological and cultural) activism. By bringing the Basij into his portfolio, Jafari initiated a process that would see the Basij distanced from military affairs in order to concentrate on domestic security operations and political activism.[109] To this end, six hundred new Imam Hosayn battalions (armed Basij units) were established and integrated into each of the thirty-one new provincial commands, thereby expanding the Basij's presence in regional defense and local security.[110] This move was partly aimed at increasing the professionalization and effectiveness of the Basij as a security organ; however, it was also aimed at bringing a greater measure of the Basij's cultural and ideological strengths into the IRGC.[111] As Jafari expanded the Basij's security profile, he repositioned the organization as the cultural core of the IRGC. Examples of the latter can be seen in the Basij's continued expansion in cultural and ideological areas. Jafari appointed Hosayn Taeb—a former seminary student of Ayatollah Khamenei and the commander of the cultural faculty of Imam Hosayn University—to head the Basij partly on the basis of his long history with ideological work.[112] The establishment of a new "specialized" headquarters under the Basij Student Organization aimed to bridge the expanded security capacities of the Basij with its ongoing ideological activism in civil society.[113] These developments were a clear indication that Jafari did not intend to dilute the Basij's ideological base in favor of greater professionalization. If anything, the new structure under Jafari placed the Basij in the position to better animate the ideological resolve of the IRGC and its place in Iranian society. If war was ever to come to Iran, Jafari ensured that the Basij would be the core of the resistance.

# Big Bang, Big Crunch

If the officials of [Iran] get daunted by the bullying of the arrogant powers and, as a result, begin to retreat from their own principles and make
concessions to those powers, these concessions will never come to an
end. First, they will pressure you into recognizing such and such an illegitimate regime, then they will force you not to call your constitution
Islamic. They will never stop obtaining concessions from you through
pressure and intimidation, and you will be forced to retreat from your
values and principles step by step! Indeed, the end to U.S. pressure
and intimidation will only come when Iranian officials announce they
are ready to compromise Islam and their popular government of the
Islamic Republic.[1]

—Ali Khamenei

Iran's 2009 presidential election arrived at an auspicious moment. The new president of the United States, Barack Obama, promised to reverse his predecessor's
reckless foreign policy in the Middle East. Iranians were inspired by his message
of hope and change. Some took comfort in the fact that Obama's middle name—
Hussein—was the same as Shiism's greatest hero and third imam. Even the new
president's last name, as it was spelled in Persian, was seen as symbolic. The three
syllables, when separated, spelled out "He [is] with us." Obama's first message to
Iran, the March 21 message that marked the beginning of the Persian new year
(*nowruz*), an Iranian national holiday, reiterated his commitment to decreasing
tensions and improving ties between the two countries:

> So in this season of new beginnings I would like to speak clearly to Iran's
> leaders. We have serious differences that have grown over time. My
> administration is now committed to diplomacy that addresses the full
> range of issues before us, and to pursuing constructive ties among the
> United States, Iran and the international community. This process will
> not be advanced by threats. We seek instead engagement that is honest
> and grounded in mutual respect.[2]

Any potential opening soon crumbled in the face of Iranian intransigence and the mass protests that followed June's disputed presidential election. Iranian security forces, led by the Revolutionary Guards and the Basij, brutalized demonstrators, using violence and terror to regain order and stop the pro-democracy movement in its tracks. Instead of engaging President Obama, Iran's authorities—fearing the post-election unrest was part of a Western plot to overthrow the regime—were antagonistic. Iran's unwillingness to compromise on the nuclear issue led the United States and the international community to ramp up sanctions. This approach favored economic pressure over military confrontation to compel Iranian nuclear concessions. At the same time, a hard-edged covert campaign was also unleashed on Iran. Nuclear scientists were assassinated in public, and sabotage struck nuclear facilities. Iran blamed Israel for these attacks, but also saw the United States, Saudi Arabia, and other foreign entities as complicit.

As pressure on Iran mounted, the Middle East exploded in a wave of popular protests. Iran's response to the Arab Spring was inconsistent. It supported protestors when they challenged the regimes of its rivals and condemned those that threatened its allies. These policies heightened tensions between Iran and Saudi Arabia, putting the two countries on opposite sides of the region's unfolding crises. The combination of sanctions, the assassinations, and political feuds fueled by the Arab Spring backed Iran into a corner. It began to lash out with plots and attacks against Saudi and Israeli officials in several countries, including in the United States. The spasm of violence appeared rash and hot-blooded. Much of it was linked to the IRGC and its Quds Force division, which, through a series of bumbling plots and botched attacks, exposed Iran's campaign of retaliation.

## "Death to the Dictator!"

As Iran's 2009 presidential election season began, there was little reason to think the outcome would be much different than 2005. The principalists seemed to be in full control of their destiny and Ahmadinejad retained the favor of the supreme leader. Ahmadinejad's main challenge appeared to come from fellow hardliners. Growing discontent with the president's poor management of the country, and the economy in particular, sparked speculation that another regime insider such as Tehran Mayor Mohammad Baqer Qalibaf or Parliament Speaker Ali Larijani would run against Ahmadienejad. Ultimately, however, Larijani and Qalibaf stood back and supported Mohsen Rezai, the former IRGC chief. Rezai was still a prominent conservative, and a critic of Ahmadinejad's inept leadership. "I am the representative of people who are fed up with crankiness, adventurism, and disorganization," Rezai claimed in the run up to the election. "The people in this resource-rich country deserve a life without tension or economic problems."[3] But despite the support he received from some powerful hardliners, Rezai's lack of national popularity (many still associated him with the troubles of the Iran-Iraq war) afforded him little chance of unseating the incumbent. Rezai (like Qalibaf and others) also did not appear to have the backing of the supreme leader. Khamenei continued to show support for the president, and even intimated in a public address in August 2008 that Ahmadinejad should be prepared to remain in office.[4] Although he later qualified that remark, Khamenei's preference for Ahmadinajad was apparent.[5] Whether because of this, or because no willing, more popular challenger existed among them, the prinicipalists seemed resigned to Ahmadinejad staying put.

Little was expected from the reformists. Mehdi Karrubi was running again, though, as his 2005 tally suggested, he did not have the national recognition to realistically threaten Ahmadinejad. Mohammad Khatami was encouraged to run, but with the likelihood slim to none that he could pass vetting by the Guardian Council, he and the majority of reformists threw their support behind Mir Hosayn Musavi. Musavi was a curious figure who had kept a low profile since his tenure as prime minister during the Iran-Iraq war. His clashes with then president Khamenei were still remembered, as was his ability to steer Iran's economy during its bleakest period. Yet, even though he was associated with the reformists, his politics were not well known. Because of this, Musavi was able to rebrand himself as a champion of change. By challenging Ahmadinejad in televised debates and promising reform in his speeches, Musavi managed—in just four weeks—to electrify a legion of supporters and spawn a burgeoning movement. He galvanized public opinion and injected an unexpected enthusiasm into a wide swath of voters. Many who had soured on Ahmadinejad and others with more reform-minded ideals all found something hopeful in Musavi. By the end of May, poll numbers showed strong support for Musavi in Iran's major cities, and particularly in Tehran. While a few polls showed Ahmadinejad with some solid numbers, when voting began on June 12, only four weeks into a short campaign season, Musavi was arguably Iran's most popular personality and seemed poised to be its next president.

In the midst of Musavi's surging popularity, rumors of a secret plan to secure the election for Ahmadinejad and concerns about interference from the IRGC began to emerge. In late May, a supposedly confidential letter providing election guidance by Hojjat al-Islam Ali Saidi, the supreme leader's representative to the IRGC, became public. The letter—reportedly written in response to an inquiry by the IRGC ground forces commander—stated that the supreme leader had been "clear" that Ahmadinejad "should be re-elected." It continued, "It is thus binding on the esteemed commanders of the IRGC ground forces to heed the repeated counsels of his eminence and to notify the personnel under their command."[6] The letter was picked up by Iranian media, sparking alarm. When asked by an Iranian reporter about the authenticity of the letter, Saidi did not deny—or confirm—writing it. The IRGC's public relations department, however, rejected that the letter had come from Saidi, claiming it was a forgery designed to foment accusations against the organization.[7] Whether the letter was authentic or not, it echoed the views made by Saidi's predecessor, Ayatollah Movahedi-Kermani, in his guidance to the IRGC ahead of the 2005 presidential election, and was therefore not unprecedented.[8] It also fit with the prevailing tenor of IRGC commentary on the 2009 election. The organization consistently criticized reformists for their dubious allegiances. It also stressed that firm commitments to the supreme leader and the revolutionary system (along with similar qualities) were perquisites for any suitable presidential candidate—positions that amounted to thinly veiled advocacy for the incumbent.[9]

Another controversial document emerged a week before the election. An open letter sent to media outlets by purported anonymous whistleblowers from the Interior Ministry warned of a plot inside the ministry to rig the election. The letter revealed that a senior ayatollah (rumored to be Ayatollah Mesbah Yazdi) had warned election officials from the Interior Ministry in a closed meeting that Ahmadinejad's challengers should not win. The senior ayatollah was quoted as telling officials: "If someone is elected the president and hurts the Islamic values that have been spread [by Mr. Ahmadinejad] to Lebanon, Palestine, Venezuela, and other places, it is against Islam to vote for that person. We should not vote for that person, and also warn people about that person. It is your religious duty as the supervisors of the elections to do so."[10] Though its provenance was uncertain, and would never be confirmed, the letter raised concern in the election camps of Ahmadinejad's rivals.

Even without a grand scheme to rig the vote, the election process was marked with problems. The Interior Ministry officials overseeing the government's election headquarters included Kamran Daneshjou and Brigadier General Ali-Reza Afshar, both former IRGC commanders, noted hardliners, and Ahmadinejad loyalists. On the ground, Basij units were dispatched to guard certain ballot boxes and run voting areas across Iranian cities. Two days before the election, Ahmadinejad claimed on national television that his challengers were planning to cause trouble if they lost. More ominously, IRGC commander Jafari warned that any attempt at a "velvet coup" would not be tolerated. It was also announced on election day that two hundred thousand security forces would be deployed to Tehran's streets after 5:00 p.m. to keep order—a unprecedentedly high number for an Iranian election.[11]

As reformists had hoped, turnout was high and in-house exit polls showed strong support for Musavi. The Musavi camp was confident of victory.[12] However, the official results announced on Iranian television that night gave victory to the incumbent. In the final results, Musavi received 23 percent of the vote to Ahmadinejad's 63 percent. To the citizens that turned out en masse to vote for Musavi, the numbers were stunning. Not only did the official tally not reflect the visibly strong turnout for Musavi, it did not resemble any past election. Provincial variances in participation, a hallmark of Iranian elections, had been erased. Mehdi Karrubi, an ethnic Lor, who had received 440,247 votes in his native Lorestan province in 2005, received only 44,036 votes in 2009. Mazandaran and Yazd provinces recorded turnout above 100 percent of possible voters, an inconsistency also found in the 2005 election (e.g., in South Khorasan).[13] Numerous other irregularities were reported. Some ballot boxes were never opened. Some ballots were cast in the name of deceased Iranians. Other ballots that were among the counted appeared to be crisp and unused, suggesting they had never been folded into a ballot box. A Musavi office in north Tehran was attacked by a group of plainclothes basijis. An unknown number of polling stations closed early, while others ran out of ballots and were not resupplied.[14] These were just some of the issues reported. But the final results were the most problematic. The reported figures were simply unbelievable, and suggested to the candidates and their supporters that the vote had been rigged. Something likely conceived and carried out at the highest levels.

Musavi, Karrubi, and Rezai all protested the election and called for an investigation.[15] Their supporters took to the streets in massive, nationwide protests. Over the next several days, demonstrations overwhelmed security forces and triggered clashes. The scenes in Tehran evoked the revolutionary turmoil of 1978 and 1979, and made the student protests of 1999 seem small and isolated in comparison.[16] Police in riot gear were the front line of security. They confronted the protesters with brute force, beating them back with truncheons, shields, and tear gas. Those tactics sparked chaos in the streets and turned a nonviolent, popular display of discontent into a furious assembly. A small fraction of demonstrators responded to the aggression by throwing rocks, bottles, and tear gas canisters at police. Clashes intensified after Basij units and volunteers from Ansar-e Hezbollah joined the fray. They penetrated crowds on the backs of motorcycles and unleashed violence to disperse demonstrators. As the violence escalated the intensity and size of the protests grew. Images of basijis, many in plain clothes, beating protesters with iron rods, bats, and clubs were prolifically shared on social media and broadcast via international news networks. A subset of the militiamen began to use handguns. They seemed to fire indiscriminately into the crowds and into the air, fomenting panic in the streets and rage from the protesters. In one gruesome incident, demonstrators clashed with occupants of a Basij base in Tehran. What began as a protest against the Basij's viciousness devolved into a fuming back-and-forth between the protestors and the base's militiamen. Some from the crowd threw stones and other projectiles at the building. Militiamen responded by firing rifles from the roof. A witness estimated that around three hundred shots were fired in all, half into the crowd and half into the air. Several demonstrators died at the scene. That night, two Tehran hospitals received the bodies of forty dead civilians from the protests, many with multiple bullet wounds.[17] Instead of becoming another Jaleh Square, the incident passed as one of many nameless episodes of carnage.

The chilling murder of Neda Agha-Soltani on June 20 thrust the Basij's ruthlessness into the spotlight. Neda was a twenty-six-year-old student returning home from a piano lesson with her teacher. Stuck in traffic because of the protests, Neda and her teacher got out of their vehicle and mixed with the demonstrators. As she stood there, a gunshot struck Neda, tearing through her aorta and lung. Phone cameras captured video of the immediate aftermath. Neda collapsed to the ground bleeding profusely. A doctor in the crowd rushed to her side and tried to help, but with such a severe wound, nothing could be done. Neda quickly bled to death. Witnesses saw the man who had fired the shot that killed her. When demonstrators confronted him, he was heard yelling, "I didn't want to kill her!"[18] An identification card taken from the man identified him as Abbas Kargar Javid, a member of the Basij's Devotees of Fatimah Zahra unit of western Tehran. In addition to counter-protest activities, Javid had also allegedly worked as an election day monitor for the Guardian Council.[19]

Iranian authorities rejected that Javid was the killer, and instead linked the murder to a number of usual conspiracies (e.g., Zionists, the MKO, foreign media, etc.). At one point hardliners claimed that the actual culprit had been Arash Hejazi, the doctor who was seen on video trying to save Neda's life. The murder gained widespread attention when video of the incident went viral on social media and was broadcast on international news networks such as CNN and BBC. Gruesome and tragic, it was one of numerous acts of callous violence committed by Iranian security forces during the post-election crisis, much of which was attributed to the IRGC and Basij. The most extreme reports of abuse came from those protestors who had been arrested. Torture and sexual violence were frequently used against detained protestors, particularly at the IRGC's Kahzirak detention center outside of Tehran. In one report, a fifteen-year-old boy recounted how he had been raped in front of other detainees. During the assault, IRGC prison guards had told the boy that they were "doing this for God" and warned the other boys to cooperate or they would receive the same treatment. When the victim reported the abuse to his interrogator, the interrogator had the teenager bound again and raped so he would "learn not to tell such tales anywhere else." In an interview with Britain's Channel 4 News, a former basiji claimed that the raping of detainees was allowed to IRGC and Basij members as sort of gift for their role in combating the protests. When the former basiji objected to the practice to his commander, the latter replied: "This is Fath Al

Moin [aid to victory]. It's a worthy deed. There's nothing wrong with it. Why are you complaining?"[20]

Iranian officials acknowledged that some abuses against detainees had taken place. Qorban-Ali Dori-Najafabadi, the prosecutor general, admitted that a few "painful accidents which cannot be defended" had occurred and that "those who were involved should be punished."[21] Iran's police chief, IRGC Brigadier General Esmail Ahmadi Moghaddam, announced (in response to the deaths of several detainees) that three prison guards had been arrested for excessive beatings at Kahrizak and that the head of the detention center had been dismissed and jailed.[22] There was no admission of rape. In a call to Majles Speaker Ali Larijani, Mehdi Karrubi decried the treatment of protestors and asked to meet with top officials to present them with evidence of "sexual abuses in some prisons." Musavi similarly claimed that "establishment agents" were guilty of raping and abusing prisoners. These accusations were immediately dismissed by Larijani and other top officials. Ayatollah Ahmad Khatami, Tehran's Friday prayer leader, lambasted Karrubi and denounced his allegations as a gift to Iran's enemies and "a deviation."[23]

The involvement of the IRGC in the crackdown on protesters was decisive and controversial. While the Basij and irregulars from Ansar-e Hezbollah confronted demonstrators on the streets, the IRGC assumed command of the broader counter-protest campaign. The IRGC had been closely linked to Ahmadinejad since his 2005 election, and the organization's involvement further consecrated its bias. Musavi and Karrubi denounced the IRGC's perceived role in yet another disputed election just as protestors began to call for an end Khamenei's rule. "Death to the Dictator!" became the protest movement's most provocative slogan. The IRGC rejected the accusations repeatedly, and early on framed them as "lies" intended to incite public opinion against it and the Basij.[24] Years later, Mojtaba Zolnur, Khamenei's former deputy representative to the IRGC, shed some light on the organization's calculus in countering the unrest. Zolnur, who had spent much of his career in IRGC intelligence, claimed in a January 2014 interview with Iran's *E'temad* newspaper that the protocol regarding internal crises was simple: if a threat to the revolution could not be handled by lead agencies (e.g., the police in 2009), then the IRGC would step in. Zolnur claims the Supreme National Security Council approved the IRGC's intervention—a distinction that Zolnur stresses to argue that the Guards did not act outside of the official chain of command—and did so because the protests had grown beyond the Law Enforcement Force's control. He claims the IRGC's goals were straightforward: "to stop the destruction" and to "disperse the crowd." The IRGC "did not initiate any clashes," and only "confronted aggressors . . . not protestors." The mid-level cleric who later left the IRGC to run as a parliamentary candidate acknowledged that passions of the moment might have led to abuses, but assured the interviewer that protocols exist within the organization to reprimand and punish anyone that committed aggravated abuses.[25]

To Zolnur, the 2009 protests were an existential threat "under the direction of foreigners" to "overthrow the revolutionary system [*nezam*]."[26] IRGC chief Jafari expressed a similar perspective, telling a group of his commanders in an undated video that the potential return of the reformists in 2009—"those opposed to the revolution and the values of the revolution"—had been a "red line" for the organization.[27] These themes—that the post-election unrest threatened the very fabric of the revolution and had been planned by foreign powers—were consistently used by the IRGC to justify its involvement in the crackdown. IRGC officials maintained this line from the beginning and through the duration of the protests associated with what became known as the Green Movement. They deemed the disorder a premeditated foreign-based plot, a "velvet revolution" orchestrated to sow chaos and topple the regime. On June 17, the IRGC released a statement that claimed it had evidence the demonstrations were "pre-planned," received outside support, and were fueled by Western-based Persian news agencies ("Radio Zamaneh, Radio Farda, and BBC Persian, etc."). The IRGC called the claims of a rigged election "a pretext to cause insecurity and agitation in the country," and further declared: "These organized centers benefit from financial and technical support by American and Canadian companies and media, and the American and British intelligence agencies."[28] On August 10, IRGC political chief, Yadollah Javani, called for the arrest of Musavi and other protest leaders, arguing: "any current and any individual . . . that in cooperation with America, this Great Satan, tries to overthrow the Islamic system [*nezam*] and establish a secular system in its place must be punished for subversion and treason."[29] Later that month, Jafari told a group of Basij members that the "plot" was engineered "by spy networks and counter-revolutionary groups based outside Iran but certain people inside Iran also became involved."[30]

The fear of foreign machinations against the revolution is as old as the revolution itself. This anxiety runs at the core of the IRGC, shapes its decision-making, and forges its politics. Worries of counter-revolutionary plots in 1979, years of fighting Saddam and his supporters, the Bush administration's War on Terror, axis of evil speech, and general hawkishness toward Iran, and mistrust of the Obama administration, hardened this paranoia to such a degree that conspiracies against the system were recognized everywhere and in nearly everything. The regime's reaction to the protests that began in June 2009 was rooted in that insecurity. The statements of IRGC officials affirm this; however, more illustrative are exchanges between Maziar Bahari—a Canadian-Iranian journalist jailed on June 21 as part of the crackdown in Tehran—and his IRGC interrogator, whom Bahari called Rosewater. Bahari's recollection of first meeting his interrogator is surreal:

"Can you tell me why I'm here, please?"

"You know why. Because you are an agent of foreign intelligence agencies," he [the IRGC interrogator] began.

I [Bahari] was completely caught off guard. *Of what?* "Could you let me know which ones?" I managed to say.

"Speak louder!" He shouted. . .

"I was wondering if you could be kind enough to let me know which organizations," I repeated.

"CIA, MI6, Mossad, and *Newsweek.*"

"Do you mean *Newsweek* magazine?"

"Yes. Your 'magazine' is part of the American intelligence apparatus. . . Don't think you can cheat us or misguide us. We know everything about you. We know you are the mastermind of Western media in Iran."[31]

In another exchange, the IRGC interrogator asked Bahari about a dinner he had had with eight fellow journalists at the home of the *New York Times* correspondent Nazila Fathi:

"You are part of a very American network, Mr. Bahari. Let me correct myself: you are in charge of a secret American network, a group that includes those who came to that dinner party."

"It was just a dinner."

"It was not a dinner! It was a *mahfel!*" This word, which means "cabal," suggested that I was part of a group of seditious reformists and journalists conspiring against the Islamic Republic. "A very American dinner," he went on. "A very American *mahfel.* It could have happened in . . . *New Jersey.*"

The strangeness of the accusation was unsettling. New Jersey?

"You've been to New Jersey, haven't you, Mr. Bahari?". . .

"Well, yes, sir. New Jersey's not a particularly nice place," I said, trying to sound conversational.

"I don't care if it's nice. All I know is that it is a godless place, like the one you were trying to create in this country. With naked women and Michael Jackson music!" He paused. "Your own New Jersey in Tehran." His questions were having a weakening effect. I felt dizzy all of a sudden. I tried to muster the strength to answer him. "I'm sorry. I don't understand."

"You were planning to eradicate the pure religion of Mohammad in this country and replace it with 'American' Islam. A New Jersey Islam. Tell me," he said, "did any of the women at the dinner party have their veils on?"

"No."

"Then don't tell me that you didn't have a secret American network. A *New Jersey* network."[32]

## The Soft War

Post-election turmoil confirmed to the IRGC that the revolution was in danger from external enemies and their domestic proxies. The size and scope of the demonstrations, and the intense international focus, pressure, and condemnation that came with the regime's forceful response, made the urgency of this threat even more acute. The potential for a "velvet revolution" such as those that had occurred in Ukraine (2004) and Kyrgyzstan (2005) was now considered a distinct possibility in Iran, and something the United States and other enemies were actively trying to achieve. As IRGC chief Jafari later warned: "We have to know that devils, including the foreign ones, have mobilized to confront the Islamic system and defeat the spirit of the revolution. . . . [But] without the guardianship of the jurist, the Islamic Republic will be destroyed."[33] At stake therefore was the soul of the revolution. The principles fought and died for during the war, and the system the IRGC had been entrusted to safeguard. Thoughts that the unrest could have defeated the revolution terrified Iran's leadership.

The IRGC poured untold resources into preventing future domestic challenges. The term "soft-war" became a catch-all for any dissent that had a social and political basis. The IRGC stood up new units to counter the soft-war, such as the Strategic Ammar Base headed by former Basij commander Mehdi Taeb. It also invested in media and cyber capabilities to gain an edge in the information war it believed was being waged against Iran. Reorienting the Basij was at the heart of this campaign. The Basij was the IRGC's front line against social and political change. It played a decisive role in the 2009 post-election crisis, but its brutality also escalated tensions and pushed Iran to the brink of popular revolt. Its crude tactics further eroded what little confidence much of Iranian society had in the militia. In order to improve its effectiveness and refurbish its tarnished brand, the IRGC began to restructure the Basij. The plan aimed to widen its appeal and better position it to fight the soft-war.

To oversee this project, Khamenei appointed Brigadier General Mohammad Reza Naqdi as the Basij's new commander.[34] Soon, Naqdi—a stern figure, who wears a *keffiyeh* in solidarity with the Palestinian movement (a fashion popular within the Basij and IRGC)—began a press tour to explain the changes the organization would undergo. Framing it as a response to the "wisdom" and objectives set forth by the supreme leader, Naqdi advanced a general plan that would transition the militia away from martial activities and expand its efforts in society, scientific research, and culture work. This, along with a corresponding name change, was an attempt at a rebrand of the organization. The "Basij Resistance Force" became the "Basij Organization of the Oppressed" (literally the "Organization of the Mobilization of the Oppressed," *sazman-e basij-e mostazafin*), a name that echoed the organization's original, pre-war ethos. The new name connoted the militia's long-standing involvement in social and cultural causes, particularly those of the poor and marginalized classes. As Naqdi explained,

> The word 'force' [*niru*] has military connotations, and the Basij is an entity which goes far beyond just military affairs ... the Basij will [now] have a stronger presence in the social, scientific, and development arenas, and will make efforts to ensure continual and systematic progress and development of the country.[35]

The switch was intended to improve the Basij's image—one stained by its involvement in post-election violence—by showing it as a less military, more inclusive entity.[36] Naqdi claims that restructuring the Basij had long been an objective of the supreme leader, but was only now being put into practice. "We investigated it and discovered that the military appeal [was exclusionary] and that the high amount of work needed to [maintain] military discipline was hindering the process [of this shift]," he said. "We also realized that the [martial] language used in the Basij was the reason why other people were less attracted to this force."[37] To make the organization appeal more to everyday Iranians, the Basij broadened its recruitment and scope of activities. To enlist and retain more brain power, Naqdi explained that the organization would change its requirements and provide suitable work for professionals. This would allow scientists, academics, clerics, and others—those who shared the ideals of the Basij but had no interest in the type of activities younger basijis took part in—to join the organization and be engaged in its efforts for the long term.[38] Another requirement change, as IRGC chief Jafari later explained, was firearm instruction, which was removed as part of the Basij's basic training regimen to entice young people who "fear working with weapons" to join the organization.[39] The aim of these broad changes, Naqdi explains, was for the Basij to help the IRGC fulfill the constitutional responsibility of safeguarding the revolution by growing its ranks and expanding its activities into all spheres of Iranian life. The overall goal was the establishment an "ideal Islamic society." With a larger Basij, Naqdi argues, "the principles and values [of the revolution] will be safeguarded ... The greater the number of people in the Basij, the more the revolution will benefit."[40]

Unlike the IRGC and Iran's other military and security forces, the Basij does not take conscripts. It is an all-volunteer organization that vets its prospective members and their families along ideological and religious lines before they are allowed to join. Once in, Basij members undergo ideological, religious, and political training and are policed internally to ensure their continued conformity with regime orthodoxy—e.g., firm devotion to the supreme leader and the concept of clerical rule, the two pillars of Iran's Islamic system.[41] Because of this, Basij members are considered by the regime to be the most faithful and loyal members of Iranian society.[42] During the 2009 demonstrations, there was some speculation that a segment of IRGC officers and rank-and-file members were sympathetic to the opposition and angry with the crackdown. The scope of any such dissent is unknown, but its existence was real. IRGC chief Jafari acknowledged that fact by admitting some in the organization had supported the protests.[43] In and of itself, that is unsurprising. The IRGC is a large organization. Its rank-and-file members are predominantly conscripts who hold a range of views consistent with those found in general Iranian society.[44] But such divisions, even if limited, were problematic. In order to avoid heterodoxy within its ranks, the IRGC prioritized the recruitment Basij members.[45] Even with the reorganization of the Basij, Naqdi reiterated that it would remain the central source of recruitment for the IRGC ground forces.[46] The militia had also become an important supplier of manpower to the IRGC navy and likely to other specialized units.[47] Along with the children of IRGC members, basijis were a main target of IRGC recruiters.[48] The Basij thus retained a strong connection to the IRGC's military activities, even as its stated focus turned toward social and cultural activism.

The 2009 "sedition" influenced revisions in the Basij's training materials. Understanding the threat of "soft-war" became a subject of focus. Basij course books described soft-war as a project designed in the West and championed by Iran's rich upper classes.[49] (Such class warfare is common in the Basij. Its commanders routinely stress the differences between Iran's rich and poor to motivate the activism of their members, many of whom come from poorer backgrounds.[50]) A Basij report entitled *Overcoming Sedition* investigates this conspiracy from a social science perspective. Its author compares the 2009 unrest to the pro-democracy revolutions in Georgia, Ukraine, and Kyrgyzstan—all seen as manifestations of "velvet coups" engineered by the West and carried out with cooperation by opportunists and spies in those countries.[51] Drawing from the supposed confessions of a spy arrested during the demonstrations, and that of other political detainees, the author identifies a number of "elements" (*bazu*, literally "arms") that laid the groundwork for the attempted 2009 "velvet coup d'état." The human rights lawyer and Nobel Prize winner Shirin Ebadi is seen as the head of the female and ethnic-minority angles of this conspiracy through her advocacy of human rights. Labor activists, nongovernmental organizations, and university students comprise other elements. Prominent intellectuals, such as the philosopher Abdol-Karim Soroush, are seen as providing the intellectual cover for the project, and undermining the foundations of the Islamic revolution, through alternative perspectives on Western cultural influence in Iran (*gharbzadeghi*).[52] To confirm links between the conspiracy, the opposition, and America, the author provides quotes from prominent reformists and intellectuals (e.g., Said Hajjarian and Kian Tajbakhsh) on a variety of topics to show their inherent commitment to Western ideals that clash with the tenets of the Islamic system.[53] The argument gets so convoluted that a statement by Musavi claiming that members of the Baha'i religion—an Iranian minority community maligned as a boogeyman, agent of foreign imperialism, and universal scapegoat in ways similar to how anti-Semitic conspiracies were used to galvanize populist sentiments in nineteenth and twentieth century Eastern Europe—"have a right to their beliefs" is seen as proof that Musavi received support from "liberals, nationalists, and the enemies of the Islamic system."[54] The gist of the report is that the United States has engineered a complicated and widespread project to destroy the revolution from the inside:

> [By] hiring middlemen and elements that could carry out its meddlesome policies. . . . By engaging in widespread psychological operations and fighting over every issue large or small, by emphasizing widespread fraud and making the government appear illegitimate, [the United States] attempted to cause division [in Iranian society], suggest the existence of a crisis, organize a group of supporters, and give rise to a caustic and bipolar environment.[55]

The 2009 sedition was thus seen as another episode in Iran's long-standing struggle against the United States. By restructuring the Basij, the regime wanted to fight this challenge by developing young minds into devoted champions of the Islamic system, so firm and convinced of their beliefs that they would be immune to the "psychological operations" and meddling of foreign enemies. Yet, even as the organization championed this side of the Basij, it did not abandon its security role. Neighborhood Basij units—the building blocks of the organization's urban-based force—continued to conduct security functions, such as stop-and-search "street" operations.[56] The organization also established the Imam Ali Battalions, a specialized counter-protest division developed in response to the 2009 unrest.[57] By late 2012, IRGC chief Jafari claimed that with the Imam Ali Battalions, the Basij had formed one hundred security-focused units and four hundred military-ready units (Imam Husayn Battalions) throughout the country. These units—along with the more socially and culturally focused Ashura and Bayt al-Muqaddas battalions—share the broadly defined responsibility of countering "soft-war" threats in all major arenas (i.e., social, cultural, economic, etc.).[58] They also represent the Basij's continued, robust presence in Iran's domestic security infrastructure.

# Springtime

Iran's post-election crisis was a foreshock. Less than two years later, similar controversies ignited waves of popular revolt across the Arab world. Egypt, Tunisia, Libya, Syria, Bahrain, and Yemen were the hardest hit. The so-called Arab Spring sent shockwaves throughout the Middle East and overturned autocratic regimes once thought unshakeable. Iran witnessed these convulsions with mixed emotions. The spread of democracy was empowering Islamist groups, such as the Muslim Brotherhood in Egypt and Annahda in Tunisia, and toppling or putting at risk political foes. But protests also threatened Syria, Iran's closest state ally, and led to the harsher repression of Shiite communities in Bahrain and Saudi Arabia. Seeing the pro-democracy movement spread in the region would have been unsettling for Iran's leaders. The demonstrations looked and sounded too similar to those in 2009 for Tehran to feel at ease. Unsurprisingly, just as they lauded an enlivening of the spirit of Islam, Iran's leaders warned of foreign hands manipulating populations against their rulers. The pick-and-choose approach to the Arab Spring led to bipolar policies. As Iran cheered the protests in Egypt, Bahrain, Tunisia, and Syria, it jeered those in Syria, calling the protestors terrorists and part of a foreign plot against the resistance. Tehran backed Assad's brutal crackdown. It condemned the use of violence against protestors elsewhere.

Iranian officials initially hailed the political upheaval in the Arab world. The supreme leader set the tone, calling the protests in Tunisia and Egypt evidence of "oppressed" (*mazlumaneh*) Muslim populations waking up and taking a stand against Western imperialism. In a February 2011 sermon, he argued that these movements were inspired by Iran's Islamic revolution and a blow to the "puppet rulers that obey the West" and their irreligiousness.[59] Brigadier General Hossein Salami, IRGC deputy commander, similarly claimed:

> Today a political hurricane has started in the region and Americans are now facing a vast and extensive front and are completely paralyzed and unable to control the flames of its wrath. . . . Today revolutionary people have pervaded on Islamic lands and have risen against the colonial and American policies and the United States' lights [i.e., allies] are being turned off one by one.[60]

Yahya Rahim Safavi—military advisor to Khamenei and former IRGC chief—boasted that with the "developments in Egypt and other Islamic Arabic countries . . . an Islamic Middle East has been formed."[61] Behind the veneer of self-confidence was a more deep-seated unease. Basij commander Naqdi warned that the West would try to replicate what was happening in Tunisia and Egypt in Iran. Playing off the story of Mohammed Bouazizi, the desperate Tunisian fruit monger who set himself on fire in protest of government corruption and sparked the Arab Spring,[62] Naqdi crudely warned: "Western intelligence organizations are looking to find a retard to set fire to himself in Tehran and trigger events like those that have occurred in Tunisia and Egypt. They too are retarded if they think that they can succeed in reproducing such events in Iran."[63]

Early returns from the Arab Spring did benefit Iran. Longtime foe Hosni Mubarak was embattled and was forced aside, giving the Muslim Brotherhood a short-lived opportunity to rule Egypt. Islamists gained a stronger position in Tunisia, winning seats in parliament, and becoming an influential bloc in the country's politics. Mass demonstrations also spread to the majority Shiite population in Bahrain, embroiling the tiny island nation in tumult and posing a stiff challenge to the legitimacy of the Sunni Al Khalifa ruling family. Across the causeway in Saudi Arabia—Iran's foremost rival in the Arab world—youths in Qatif and other largely Shiite towns in the country's Eastern Province took to the streets calling for greater political and religious freedoms.[64]

The exploding pro-democracy movement was posing a serious challenge to Iran's rivals in the region (Egypt, Saudi Arabia, and to a lesser extent Bahrain), giving rise to Islamist political groups in Egypt and Tunisia, and shedding light on the marginalized and repressed Shiite populations of Bahrain and Saudi Arabia—all positives for Iran. But Arab Spring protests also challenged Iranian interests. Most worrisome was the spiraling rebellion threatening Bashar al-Assad in Syria. Assad was Iran's closest state ally and a vital intermediary for its support to Hezbollah in Lebanon. Syria had been Iran's only friend in the region during the eight-year war with Iraq, and the two countries had maintained close relations. The Assad regime's extreme brutality transformed Syria's nascent populist, pro-democracy protest movement into a mostly Sunni-Arab rebellion against the Alawite-dominated regime.[65] By the end of 2012, Assad was engulfed in a full-scale civil war against rebel groups supported by the West and funded by Saudi Arabia, Qatar, and private donors in Kuwait and Bahrain.[66]

A similar dynamic arose in Libya, where Muammar Qaddafi's all out war against peaceful demonstrators ignited a country-wide rebellion. International condemnation of Qaddafi's actions spurred action from Western Europe and the United States, leading to a military intervention in support of the rebels. The toppling of Qaddafi's regime—and his murder at the hands of the rebels— upped the ante for potential Western intervention in response to other Arab Spring–induced civil unrest. Western condemnation of Assad's crackdown, and calls for him to step down, including from President Obama, made the Baathist regime appear to be in equal danger of foreign military action.[67] Iran's leaders denounced foreign involvement in Libya, but voiced support for the protestors. They saw the foreign pressure on Assad as a direct threat to their interests.[68]

Demonstrators in Bahrain and Saudi Arabia also faced stiff repression. Fearing a cascading crisis, and the rise of a potentially Iran-linked radical Shiite movement, the Saudi-led Gulf Cooperation Council (GCC) agreed to intervene. In Operation Peninsula Shield, the GCC sent heavily armed military units and security personnel into Bahrain. The peaceful protest movement was violently crushed. Bahrain became militarized, with checkpoints, bunkers, and armed encampments dotting the capital, Manama, and other Shiite villages across the Island.[69] Saudi authorities similarly put down protests in its Eastern Province, arresting scores of youth and some prominent Saudi Shiite clerics in the process.[70]

Iranian officials denounced the carnage taking place in Bahrain. They noted the hypocrisy of Western governments, who turned a blind eye to the plight of Shiites in Bahrain and Saudi Arabia, but intervened against Qaddafi and condemned Assad. The IRGC's hardline base was incensed. The Basij called the military intervention a "massacre of Bahrain's Muslims," conducted under the direct order of the United States by its "servants" in the region.[71] Basij student groups called for the expulsion of Saudi and Bahraini ambassadors from Iran, seeing those country's repressive actions against Shiites as part of the West's long-standing conspiracy against Islam. These "crimes" they argued, "are being carried out by the same people who spoke of the people, of freedom, and human rights. However, now they are providing a green light to the perpetrators of the massacre of Muslim and freedom-loving people in Bahrain."[72] Another student group pledged their willingness to go to Bahrain and "don the robe of martyrdom" in "defense of Islam and the Muslims of Bahrain."[73] IRGC political director Yadollah Javani used language harkening back to the early days of the revolution, calling the pro-democracy uprising in Bahrain a "liberation movement" and pledging Iran's support.[74] An editorial in the IRGC-affiliated *Javan* newspaper used the powerful metaphor of Imam Husayn's heroic stand against Umayyad forces, calling the violent repression in Bahrain "a replay of the events in Karbala" that would spread beyond the island's borders. The editorial ends with a question indirectly aimed at Iran's government: "why are other Islamic governments preventing the martyrdom-seeking youth, who are prepared to depart for Bahrain and take part in jihad against the occupying American mercenaries, from going?"[75]

The landscape of the region was changing. This created opportunities for Iran. It also brought peril. The unrest in Syria and Western pressure on Assad was at the very least worrisome. The interventions in Libya and Bahrain increased the potential for outside involvement in Syria. Iran blamed its Arab neighbors for complicity in an American and Zionist campaign to crush Islamic movements in the region. Saudi Arabia's leading role in crushing the peaceful protests in Bahrain was especially egregious to Iranian authorities, who took the intervention against its co-religionists as a deeply personal affront. Iran felt that it had to respond. The IRGC's top brass set the tone for a more proactive approach to the Arab Spring. In an April 2011 interview, IRGC chief Jafari slammed the intervention in Bahrain as an act of imperialism. He called it a foolish move that engendered the demise of the Al Saud monarchy. He also alluded that Iran would not let it go unanswered:

> One must have revolutionary patience. That is to say, for Iran to act like Saudi Arabia would not be difficult, because Iran's military capability is not at all comparable to that of a country such as Saudi Arabia; but, Iran does not need to do so. Rather, one must wait for the hand of divine revenge. God willing, to avenge in the near future the crimes they have committed.[76]

It was not clear at the time, but Jafari was signaling a turn toward a forward-leaning posture to counter Iran's rivals and safeguard its regional interests. The implications of this move would take Iran from the margins of the regional upheaval to the heart of the storm. Tehran and Riyadh were on opposing sides in the Arab Spring. Their political differences, rooted in a toxic stew of conflicting sectarian chauvinisms and strategic interests, thrust the two into hostilities and eventually into a proxy war. Although mostly concealed by the secret nature of the operations, Iran began to lash out in a covert campaign. This included a Quds Force–linked assassination of a Saudi consulate official in Karachi in May 2011.[77] But it was not until a far more audacious plan was uncovered in the United States that Iran's escalating feud with its neighbor was exposed.

The plot to kill the Saudi ambassador to Washington was disclosed in October 2011 by US Attorney General Eric Holder, who said it was "directed and approved by elements of the Iranian government and, specifically, senior members of the Quds Force."[78] At the center of the case was Mansour Arbabsiar, an Iranian-American used car salesman from Texas, who acted as a middle-man between agents in Iran and hired assassins associated with a drug cartel in Mexico.[79] The plot was an uncharacteristically bold and risky venture for Iran. It also appeared far-fetched. Iran's intelligence minister Heydar Moslehi vigorously denied that his country had had any connection to Arbabsiar, dismissing the matter as a "foolish plot" designed by the United States.[80] American analysts and commentators were skeptical.[81] The Obama administration seemed incredulous that Iran would try something so provocative on US soil. Secretary of State Hillary Clinton remarked: "The idea that they would attempt to go to a Mexican drug cartel to solicit murder for hire to kill the Saudi ambassador—nobody could make that up, right?"[82] It was a scheme straight out of Hollywood. US officials were certain it was real.

Arbabsiar had no history of politics or extremism. He was a Jack Daniel's drinker, womanizer, and small-time businessman who fancied himself a deal maker.[83] He was also in a state of financial and personal ruin. Divorced and broke, he returned to Iran. There he became reacquainted with Abdol-Reza Shahlai, a cousin and childhood friend from their days growing up in Kermanshah, a provincial city in western Iran. Shahlai was now a senior Quds Force commander. He had made a name for himself during the US occupation of Iraq, and was soon the group's point man in Yemen.[84] Through stories about selling cars across the border in Mexico, Arbabsiar mentioned to his cousin that he had contacts with some drug dealers in that country. Intrigued, Shahlai inquired about whether they could enlist these contacts to do some work for Iran. Shahlai brought in Ali Gholam Shakuri, a Quds Force colonel, and eventually they settled on the idea of kidnapping or killing the Saudi envoy to the United States, Adel Al-Jubeir.[85]

With Shakuri as his handler in Iran, Arbabsiar was given $15,000 to travel to Mexico and put the plan into motion. Through previous contacts, Arbabsiar was introduced to a purported associate of the Los Zetas cartel, with whom he eventually forged an agreement: in exchange for a $1.5 million payment, the contact—known as "Junior" (or "CS-1" in official US documents)—would hire a four-man team to organize and carry out the assassination. (They also discussed a scheme to import opium from Iran, but this apparently did not get off the ground.) Fortunately for Al-Jubeir, Arbabsiar's man in Mexico doubled as an informant for the US Drug Enforcement Agency (DEA). The DEA was alerted to the plot early, and federal agents monitored the scheme as it unfolded. Captured phone conversations between Arbabsiar and the informant exposed discussions on the plan. The Quds Force apparently wanted Al-Jubeir targeted alone, but when the informant mentioned that this would be too difficult given the size of the envoy's security detail, they settled on a public hit. The plan was to strike Al-Jubeir at his favorite DC haunt, the see-and-be-seen Café Milano in Georgetown, an institution frequented by Washington insiders and visiting foreign dignitaries. The informant told Arbabsiar that the bomb blast required for this type of operation would likely kill dozens of innocents. "They want that guy [Al-Jubeir] done [killed], if the hundred go with him f**k 'em," Arbabsiar was recorded as saying. The informant pressed Arbabsiar, telling him that high-level US officials routinely eat at that restaurant and could also be killed. "No big deal," was Arbabsiar's response.[86] Arbabsiar then cleared this plan and its potentially high causality rate with Shakuri and another "senior Qods Force official" in Iran.[87]

When enough evidence had been collected, including money transfers from Quds Force–linked accounts to dummy accounts set up by US authorities, Arbabsiar was arrested. He admitted to his role in the plot and agreed to help the FBI collect further intelligence on his handlers. During this time, Arbabsiar participated in orchestrated phone calls between him and his contacts in Iran while federal agents were in the room. In one of these calls, Arbabsiar spoke to Shakuri telling him that everything was set and asking if he should go forward with the assassination. Using coded language, Shakuri replied "Buy it [kill him], yes. Buy all of it."[88] Arbabsiar stopped cooperating with the FBI shortly thereafter, worrying that his collaboration could put his family in danger.

The legal prosecution of Arbabsiar went forward. [89] He was convicted for his role in the murder-for-hire scheme in May 2013 and sentenced to twenty-five years in prison, the maximum time allowed. After the sentencing, US Attorney for the Southern District of New York, Preet Bharara, called Arbabsiar "an enemy among us . . . the key conduit for, and facilitator of, a nefarious international plot concocted by members of the Iranian military to assassinate the Saudi ambassador to the United States and as many innocent bystanders as necessary to get the job done." The fifty-eight-year-old Arbabsiar took responsibility for his actions, stating: "Whatever I did wrong, I take responsibility for it. I can't change what I did. I have a good heart. I never hurt anyone." Adding, "My mind sometimes is not in a good place."[90]

## The Instruments of Coercion

Iran's aggression toward Saudi Arabia was not only triggered by differing agendas, it was an outgrowth of the wider, immense pressures Iran was under.[91] The Arab Spring and the regional turmoil it brought forth came at a difficult time for Iran. Although the Obama administration had struck a softer tone, in 2010 it began to ramp up tough economic sanctions. The nuclear issue remained an area of concern for the United States and the sanctions were put in place to induce an Iranian compromise. The combination of unilateral US sanctions and more broad-ranging sanctions supported by the UN Security Council (UNSC) had a destructive effect on Iran's economy. Sanctions were not the only culprit— Ahmadinejad's ill-conceived fiscal policy, mismanagement, and long-standing systemic corruption in Iran all contributed to its economic morass. Indeed, while other countries in the region dealt with corruption and mismanagement, Iran's economy had deteriorated to such an extent that by 2013 it was the only country in the Middle East and North Africa predicted by the International Monetary Fund to experience negative growth.[92] Sanctions preventing Iran from engaging in the international banking system and selling its oil and gas put a considerable strain on the country's resources.

The IRGC was also targeted with sanctions. In February 2010, the US Department of Treasury announced sanctions against the IRGC's Khatam al-Anbiya engineering division, four of its subsidiary companies, and its head commander, Brigadier General Rostam Qassemi. By freezing its assets and designating it a proliferator of weapons of mass destruction, Executive Order 13382 intended to expose "Khatam al-Anbiya's subsidiaries [to] help firms worldwide avoid business that ultimately benefits the IRGC and its dangerous activities." [93] In June 2011, the Treasury placed sanctions upon an IRGC port operating firm (the Tidewater Middle East Company) and Iran Air for facilitating illicit weapons shipments and providing material support to the IRGC. An Iranian business man and his shipping business were also sanctioned for providing material support and weapons shipments to Lebanese Hezbollah on behalf of the IRGC. Explaining its continued focus on the IRGC, the Treasury Department stated: "The IRGC continues to be a primary focus of US and international sanctions against Iran because of the central role it plays in all forms of Iran's illicit conduct, including Iran's nuclear and ballistic missile programs, its support for terrorism, and its involvement in serious human rights abuses."[94] In December of that year, the Treasury placed sanctions on Hassan Firouzabadi, the Chairman of the Joint Staff of Iran's armed forces, and Abdollah Araqi, the deputy IRGC ground force commander, for human rights abuses committed by the IRGC and Basij during the 2009 post-election crackdown.[95]

The IRGC was similarly targeted by the international community for its links to Iran's nuclear and ballistic missile programs. The UN Security Council adopted resolution 1929 in June 2010, which among other measures sanctioned Iran's ballistic missile program (which is led by the IRGC) and banned all countries from providing a wide range of foreign military assistance, including certain weapons sales, financing, and training. It also froze the funds of the IRGC and Iran's state shipping company, the Islamic Republic of Iran Shipping Lines.[96] The European Union separately designated IRGC-affiliated companies for their involvement in Iran's ballistic missile and nuclear programs.[97] These measures extended sanctions already placed on the IRGC and its subsidiaries, such as UNSCRs 1737 and 1747, the 2007 US State Department designation of the Quds Force for providing material support to the Taliban and other terrorist groups, and the Treasury Department's designation of Qassem Soleimani and four other top IRGC commanders.[98]

Sanctions were not the only tool used to pressure Iran. A campaign of sabotage and murder was unleashed against Iran's nuclear program. The Stuxnet virus was one such attempt by Iran's adversaries to disrupt the nuclear program from the inside. The malware program—which later spread to public computers around the world—worked by manipulating a security flaw in certain Siemens machines used in the operation of the centrifuges at the Natanz enrichment facility. The program altered the speed of rotation of uranium centrifuges, intermittently accelerating them to the point of failure while masking that activity from monitoring systems. By June 2010, a third of the centrifuges at Natanz had broken or become inoperable through this process. [99]

As Iran dealt with this problem, a murderous campaign against its scientists began. The assassinations, which occurred from January 2010 to February 2012, targeted scientists linked to Iran's nuclear program. Masoud Ali Mohammad, a nuclear physicist at Tehran University, was the first victim. He was murdered by a remote-detonated bomb near his home in Tehran. A few months later, a nuclear engineering professor at Tehran's Shahid Beheshti Universty was killed in morning traffic on his way to work. A motorcyclist rode up beside Majid Shahriari's vehicle and attached a magnetic "sticky bomb" to the driver's side door. The explosion killed Shahriari and seriously injured his wife, who sat in the passenger seat. That same morning, Fereydoon Abbasi Davani, an IRGC scientist, was injured in a similar magnetic explosive attack, but survived. (Davani was hailed as a national hero, and later become the head of Iran's Atomic Energy Agency.)[100] In July 2011, Darioush Rezaienejad, a thirty-five-year-old researcher in electrical engineering at Tehran's Khajeh Nasir Tusi University of Technology, was gunned down next to his wife outside their home. Motorcycle-borne assailants fired five shots at Rezaienejad, killing him instantly and possibly injuring his wife. The two were reportedly on their way to pick up their daughter from a nearby kindergarten.[101] In January 2012, Mostafa Ahmadi Roshan, a thirty-two-year-old academic and supervisor at the Natanz enrichment facility in Esfahan, was killed along with his driver in another magnetic bomb attack.[102]

Iran was understandably enraged. Conspiracies about foreign involvement were rife. Along with Stuxnet, the murders suggested to Iran—and outside observers—that a coordinated campaign to undermine the nuclear program was underway. Iranian authorities pointed a finger at the usual suspects. In December 2010, Iranian intelligence indicated that Mossad, the CIA, and MI6 were all behind the killings.[103] Iranian authorities made a number of arrests, uncovering the purported terrorist cells behind the killings. After arrests of individuals charged with the Rezaienejad murder, Iran's intelligence minister Heydar Moslehi said all the perpetrators involved in the assassinations had been working in conjunction with the Mossad, CIA, and other foreign "intelligence services."[104] Moslehi directly implicated Mossad saying that Israeli agents had provided training and logistical support to the culprits at "bases within the territories of one of Iran's western neighbors"—most likely a thinly veiled reference to Saudi Arabia.[105]

To authorities in the Islamic Republic, nearly everything that is seen to go against public order can be traced to foreign intelligence. They see a cabal involving the CIA, Mossad, and M16 as the hidden hand manipulating events, people, culture, world events, and domestic politics designed to weaken the revolution. Iran has blamed so many problems of its own making on foreign operatives, that many of its claims are rightfully seen as baseless and summarily dismissed by critical observers. But the beauty of all-encompassing conspiracy theories is that sooner or later something will confirm their existence. That is the case here. In these instances—sabotage and assassinations—Iran's suspicions were warranted. The sophistication of the attacks, the intelligence required for their effective planning and execution, and the professional, cold-blooded manner in which the killings were conducted, all suggested the capabilities and sensibilities of foreign state-sponsored actors.

Western reporters lent credence to this notion and affirmed Iran's accusations. Over time the suggestion that Israel and the United States had engaged in efforts to damage Iran's nuclear program through a variety of methods began to gain currency. David Crist, a US Department of Defense historian, claims that Israeli officials proposed "extreme measures such as assassinations of Iranian scientists and supporting armed opposition groups inside Iran" to the Bush administration as a means of countering Iran's nuclear program. Bush officials "completely rejected these schemes" but along with Israel and possibly some European nations, became involved in a series of other, non-lethal activities that stayed "within the limits of American legality."[106] Citing anonymous sources in the Obama administration, David Sanger confirmed in the *New York Times* that Stuxnet (along with other unknown cyber attacks) had been a joint venture by the United States and Israel to disrupt Iran's nuclear program.[107] That idea was also put forward by national security reporters Dan Raviv and Yossi Melman, who further claimed based on Israeli intelligence sources that the Mossad had been solely behind the string of assassinations of Iran's scientists and had conducted other acts of sabotage, including the massive November 2011 explosion that flattened a military facility outside Tehran. The explosion killed Brigadier General Hassan Tehrani-Moghadam, an IRGC war hero and the architect of its missile program, and at least sixteen subordinates.[108] As they mourned the loss of their comrade, IRGC officials claimed the explosion was an accident.[109] Israel's logic for these activities, Raviv and Melman argue, was to send "a loud and clear message to Iranians and scientists of other nations . . . don't help Iran go nuclear. Otherwise, your career could be cut short by a bullet or a bomb."[110]

## Knives Out

The pressure against Iran provoked a response. Whether out of vengeance or to send a message of resolve to its enemies, Iran engaged in a number of provocative acts outside its borders. Several were failures and ended in little publicized arrests or accusations.[111] Iran denied involvement in every case. But events across three countries in February 2012 thrust its campaign into the open. On the thirteenth of that month, attacks on Israeli diplomatic vehicles occurred in New Delhi and Tbilisi just hours apart. The next day an accidental explosion in Bangkok blew an Iranian cell's cover. The investigations into these incidents revealed that Iran's pushback against its enemies did not stop after the DC debacle. Instead, Iran was leaning in, responding to perceived Israeli aggression in tit-for-tat strikes against its officials.

The attack in New Delhi was a near miss. As a Toyota Innova minivan stopped at a traffic signal, a motorcyclist that had been following it placed a magnetic "sticky bomb" on its rear side and sped off. The explosion seriously injured the vehicle's occupants, which included the wife of the Israeli defense attaché and her driver, who were on their way to pick up the woman's children from school.[112] A few hours earlier, a similar magnetic bomb was discovered under an Israeli embassy vehicle in Tbilisi, Georgia. Its driver, who had just dropped off his child at a local school, noticed the device after the car had been making an odd sound. He alerted Georgian police, who defused the explosive.[113]

Authorities in India and Georgia rushed to find out who was behind these attacks. A series of explosions in Bangkok the next afternoon led to a break in the case. The first explosion rocked a house in the city's residential Sukhumvit neighborhood. The three Iranian nationals inside quickly gathered their stuff and fled in different directions. Masoud Sedaghatzadeh managed to make it to the airport and fly to Kuala Lumpur. The next morning he was detained by Malaysian authorities while trying to board a flight to Iran. Another suspect, Mohammad Khazaei, also tried to board a flight to Kuala Lumpur, but was arrested by Thai police. The third, Saeed Moradi, fled barefoot with a large backpack and two small magnetic explosives, one in each hand. Conspicuously injured by the blast, Moradi attempted to hail a taxi. When the car failed to stop (or the driver refused to take him), Moradi threw a bomb at the taxi, destroying part of the car and further injuring himself. Local police rushed to the scene. Moradi threw his other explosive at a police vehicle. But either out of weakness from injury or because the bomb accidently hit a tree and bounced back (accounts differ) the device exploded at Moradi's feet and blew off his lower legs.[114]

The resulting Thai investigation concluded that the Iranian nationals had intended to hit Israeli diplomats in Thailand with the explosives, a plan derailed by the accidental detonation of one of the bombs.[115] In addition to Sedaghatzadeh,

Khazaei, and Moradi, Thai authorities claimed that another Iranian national, Leila Rohani, under whose name the apartment had been rented, was involved. Rohani fled to Iran via Kuala Lumpur and avoided arrest. The investigation found similarities between the magnetic explosive devices used in the Bangkok bombings with those used in Delhi and Tbilisi. Thai investigators also discovered links between the operatives in the three countries, evidence strongly suggesting the incidents were connected and coordinated. Sedaghatzadeh, the purported leader of the cells, was the linchpin. After he was arrested, Malaysian authorities discovered that his "passport included visas both for India and Thailand" and that a notebook he was carrying had the "phone numbers for many of those identified in [the] Tbilisi, Delhi and Bangkok" attacks as well as other relevant contacts in Tehran.[116] This was the first break in the case and became part of the evidence used to convict Khazaei and Moradi in May 2013. Both were found guilty in Thai court on explosives charges. Khazaei was sentenced to fifteen years in prison. Moradi, who had the added charge of attempted murder, received a life sentence. Sedaghatzadeh remained in prison in Kuala Lumpur where he appealed an extradition order. Thai authorities did not directly implicate Iran in the attack.

Indian officials arrived at similar conclusions. Their investigation into the New Delhi bombing centered on Houshang Afshar Irani, an Iranian national who was suspected of placing the bomb on the diplomat's vehicle. Irani left India immediately after the attack and returned to Iran after spending a day in Kuala Lumpur. Two other Iranian nationals and a local Indian journalist were also suspected of aiding the plot through earlier reconnaissance and logistics. Those Iranian nationals had returned to Iran well before the attack took place. The Indian journalist, Syed Mohammed Kazmi, was arrested and charged in the conspiracy. Kazmi and his family vigorously maintain his innocence and claim that he is little more than a fall guy.[117] Although Indian police concluded that the culprits all had ties to the IRGC, local Indian agencies were less specific, and blamed a "security entity" of the Iranian regime for the attack.[118]

Georgian officials have released less information about the failed Tbilisi bombing, but investigators in India and Thailand found conclusive links between all three attacks. This includes phone records, travel documents, money transfers, and the explosive devices used, which employed the same magnetic strips. The similarities in the timing, targets, and background of the suspects in the three attacks also indicate a connection. Building on this evidence, an investigation done by the *Guardian* newspaper in London, which "scoured witness statements, police evidence and court documents," concluded that all three plots had been "co-ordinated [by] a group of roughly 12 Iranians, with preparations involving reconnaissance missions, house and transport rentals and target surveillance over a period of at least 10 months."[119] The sophistication of the operations, their use of Iranian nationals, the fact that several suspects returned to Iran without facing any legal repercussions there, and the symbolic use of the same type of magnetic "sticky bombs" that were used to kill Iranian scientists, strongly suggest official Iranian involvement. As one Western security official remarked, "The question is not was this Iran-backed or Iran-organised but who in Iran was running all this."[120]

Drawing mostly from Israeli intelligence sources, Matthew Levitt alleges that the attacks were part of a larger campaign by the IRGC to hit Western targets. Quds Force coordinated some of these activities with Hezbollah, but also worked alone. Hezbollah was tasked with looking for soft targets (e.g., the 2012 bombing of a bus in Brugas, Bulgaria, that killed eleven Israeli tourists) and the Quds Force led the more complex effort of targeting foreign officials. The motivations for the groups were to some degree shared, such as avenging the assassination of Imad Mughniyeh—the head of Hezbollah's terrorism wing, who was killed in a Damascus car bombing in February 2008—but Iran's motivations were probably more personally tied to the assassination of its scientists and other pressures. The incidents in February 2012 fell to "Unit 400," a Quds Force unit in charge of special external operations, and green lit by the unit's commander, Majid Alavi.[121]

Available public evidence lends credence to the broad outlines of Levitt's assertions, but not the behind-the-curtain details. Given the findings of investigators into these attacks, it is uncontroversial to conclude that some segment of the Iranian state was involved in a broad campaign of political violence during this period. Iranian operatives were involved in this campaign and appeared to be advancing a policy of retaliation. The targeting of foreign officials is clearly related to Iran's troubles with Saudi Arabia and Israel, and in the context of the manifold pressures facing Iran, is not all that surprising. What is less definitive is what part the IRGC had in these matters. Levitt and others argue that the IRGC was not only involved but at the helm of the events. This is supported by the findings of US authorities regarding the DC plot, and has been strongly intimated by Thai and Indian authorities as well. It is therefore reasonable to conclude that the IRGC, through the Quds Force, was a key element in this campaign if not the architect.

# In Defense of the Family of the Prophet

[The United States] aims to portray the Islamic Republic of Iran as a Shi'i republic and tries to set it against the great Sunni community. This is a very dangerous plot which their politicians are currently trying to carry out. . . . We should do our utmost to thwart the arrogant powers in their goal. All Muslims should be aware and vigilant. Our nation, our elite and scholars and our dedicated and diligent clergymen should all be careful not to say or do anything that would be conducive to the enemies' plot.[1]

—Ali Khamenei

The Shia-Sunni conflict is at once a struggle for the soul of Islam—a great war of competing theologies and conceptions of sacred history—and a manifestation of the kind of tribal wars of ethnicities and identities, so seemingly archaic at times, yet so surprisingly vital, with which humanity has become wearily familiar. Faith and identity converge in this conflict, and their combined power goes a long way toward explaining why, despite the periods of coexistence, the struggle has lasted so long and retains such urgency and significance. It is not just a hoary religious dispute, a fossilized set piece from the early years of Islam's unfolding, but a contemporary clash of identities. Theological and historical disagreements fuel it, but so do today's concerns with power, subjugation, freedom, and equality, not to mention regional conflicts and foreign intrigues. It is, paradoxically, a very old, very modern conflict.[2]

—Vali Nasr, *The Shia Revival*

The Arab Spring presented a number of challenges to the Islamic Republic. Beyond the problem of ascendant pro-democracy movements, popular revolts were undoing the regional status quo. Iran could either benefit from the inevitable change or lose ground. The major players in the region all understood the moment through the same calculus of self-interest. They had a vested concern in managing the outcomes of the unrest and looking for ways to steer events to their benefit. This led Iran and its rivals into a fierce competition for dominance.

The potential for a fundamental political reorientation in the Middle East was at its most acute since the fall of the Soviet Union. The region was going to change. How and to what end was the question. The Islamic Republic saw peril and opportunity. As Quds Force chief Qassem Soleimani explained in May 2011, the unfoldment of the Arab Spring was as critical to the future of the revolution as the war against Saddam. "Today, Iran's defeat or victory will not be determined in Mehran or Khorramshahr, but rather, *our borders have spread*. We must witness victories in Egypt, Iraq, Lebanon, and Syria."[3] In order to safeguard its interests and counter its enemies, Tehran had to look beyond its borders. If it failed to help determine the future course of the Middle East, Iran's enemies would be the beneficiaries.

Soleimani was not speaking rhetorically. He was expressing an evolving view in the IRGC that it not only had the responsibility but the ability to advance Iran's agenda outside its borders. The IRGC had learned with the fall of Saddam that it could successfully exploit power vacuums for strategic gains. Syria's civil war and the war against ISIS in Iraq were new entryways for the organization. Under the direction of Soleimani, the IRGC led Iran's campaigns of assistance in both countries. These were in large part strategic efforts designed to protect Iran's allies and equities from hostile forces. But their resilience was rooted in religion. The IRGC framed its involvement in both countries in religious terms. In Syria, the IRGC was defending the shrine of Sayyida Zaynab—a mosque built near Damascus that Shiites believe houses the remains of Zaynab bint Ali, a sister of the Imam Husayn and revered hero in Shiism—and in Iraq, it was safeguarding the holy shrines of the imams and the Shia population. As the IRGC saw it, these conflicts were part of a larger war waged by Sunni Arab states and the West against Iran and its allies. It was a war intrinsically against Shiism and the family of the Prophet. To defeat the jihadist scourge and its Sunni Arab benefactors, the IRGC mobilized pro-Iranian, pro-Shiite supporters in Syria and Iraq. These relationships helped Iran advance its agenda and expand its influence. They also intensified sectarian hatreds.

## In Defense of Sayyida Zaynab

Tehran could not afford to lose Bashar al-Assad. The Assad regime was not only Iran's closest ally, it was fundamental to Iran's interests in the Western Mediterranean. Support for Hezbollah, Hamas, and the leverage these relationships afforded Tehran vis-à-vis Israel and the United States hinged on having access to Syrian military bases, land routes, airports, and port facilities. It had been through Syria that Iranian-supplied rockets reached Hezbollah in Lebanon— rockets that were effectively deployed against Israel in the 2006 war. Iran had also relied on Syrian intelligence, such as monitoring facilities in the Golan, for information on Israeli military movements, including near the Lebanon border. Even more, many senior Iranian leaders held a deep emotional attachment to the Assad regime. Hafez al-Assad harbored Iranian dissidents before the revolution and facilitated their ties to Palestinian militants in Lebanon. Syria was Iran's only friend during the Iran-Iraq war, and helped it pressure Saddam during that conflict by cutting off Iraqi oil access to the Mediterranean. As bitterness toward the West and Saudi Arabia hardened during the war, Syria garnered the enduring gratitude of Iran's leadership. This is especially true for the IRGC, which has overseen Iran's military ties with Damascus and its relationship with Hezbollah. As Sayyed Hassan Entezari, a mid-ranking IRGC officer who served in Syria during its civil war, explains:

> [Bashar] was the one who protected the resistance line in the region and established a connecting bridge between Iran, Hezbollah and Hamas. What Arab country do you know that has provided such a connection for Iran? Syria even supported Iran during the war, even if they were members of the Baath Party. . . . All Arab states embargoed Iran during the war, but it was Hafez al-Assad who stayed beside Iran. We got most of our weaponry through Hafez al-Assad. Nobody can deny this support from al-Assad. He was a supporter of Iran and when this war and intrigue happened to them, how could we abandon them and not support them?[4]

Gradually over the three decades, Syria became a cornerstone of the Islamic Republic's deterrence strategy. Without access to Syria, Iran's ability to resupply Hezbollah and threaten Israel would be in jeopardy. If Iran were no longer able to credibly threaten Israel through its clients, then its deterrence efforts vis-à-vis Israel and the United States would be severely degraded. It is unsurprising then that Iran's leadership saw the unrest in Syria and foreign intervention in support of the rebels as inimical to its strategic interests. Former Basij commander Mehdi Taeb was unambiguous about this point in a September 2013 interview:

> Syria is the 35th province and a strategic province for [Iran]. . . . If the enemy attacks and aims to capture both Syria and Khuzestan, our priority would be Syria. Because if we hold on to Syria, we would be able to retake Khuzestan; yet if Syria were lost, we would not be able to keep even Tehran.[5]

Qassem Soleimani expressed a similar perspective, claiming the movement against Assad was part of a much larger Western plot to sow division in the

Middle East and weaken "Iran's place in the region."[6] The threat to Syria was existential for Iran. The stakes could not be higher. The IRGC's response was correspondingly robust.

Even though the initial protests against Assad cut across ethnic and sectarian lines, the rebel movement spawned by those protests gradually became dominated by Sunni Arabs. Assad's tactics encouraged sectarian polarization. The Baathist regime had long portrayed itself as the protector of the country's minority populations. Along with the Alawite clans that controlled much of the state, Christians, Druze, and other minority communities saw the regime as a bulwark to Sunni domination. As the government cracked down violently on the protestors, hatred for the Alawites that controlled much of the state rapidly increased. Assad also employed largely Alawite gangs known as *shabiha* (ghosts) to retaliate against Sunnis for taking part in the protests. The shabiha began rampaging through Sunni communities, brutally killing and torturing men, women, and children. Fury grew among Sunnis. Rebel leaders began to call for revenge against regime supporters and Alawites in particular. The increasingly sectarian language alienated Alawites and other minority groups from the rebellion. As armed conflict took hold and spiraled into civil war, the lines that divided Syrian society had been set. Alawites, Christians, and Druze mostly supported Assad, as much out of fear of Sunni dominion as out of any genuine favor for the regime. Much of the urban Sunni elite that had benefited from Baathist rule also sided with Assad in hopes that the status quo could be preserved.[7]

On the other side were the Sunni militants—from former army officers and conscripts to Islamists and foreign jihadists—that began forming armed rebel groups. The rebels initially enjoyed widespread sympathy in international fora. The United States supported them, affirmed that Assad should go, and allowed Gulf states—particularly Saudi Arabia and Qatar—to fund and arm the rebels to that end.[8] Turkey and Jordan, whose borders swelled with Syrian refugees fleeing the violence, became staging grounds for the rebellion. Turkey emerged as the most important conduit for the arms, financing, and foreign fighters that supplied rebel factions. Support for the rebels was widespread and came through numerous state and private channels. But without the introduction of foreign state military forces, the level of assistance remained below the threshold needed to topple the Assad regime. Rebels were able to liberate territory all over Syria, but they could not effectively take the fight to Assad's strongholds in Damascus and the western mountains.

Assad benefited from air superiority, a hardening of his constituency, and parochial divisions in the rebel camp. He also benefited from outside support. The backing of Russia and China prevented major action by the United Nations Security Council, and probably helped discourage US military intervention. Russia continued to resupply the Syrian military, and both it and China provided financial aid to Damascus.[9] Iran became more intimately involved. It is unclear precisely when or how Iran's intervention in Syria began, but a broad-based effort that included military, security, intelligence, and financial assistance appears to have been in full swing by March 2011.[10] Much of Iran's effort was covert and something its leaders denied. But by May, the US Treasury Department began exposing Iranian entities for aiding the Assad regime. The Treasury Department's designations, based on US and allied intelligence channels, provide an outline of Iran's involvement. The Quds Force was the first to be designated by the Treasury for its role in Syria. Qassem Soleimani and another Quds commander, Mohsen Chirazi, were sanctioned in May 2011 for "complicity . . . in the human rights abuses and repression of the Syrian people." Soleimani was listed for being the "conduit of Iranian material support" to Syrian intelligence, while Chirazi was targeted for his role as the head of the IRGC's operations and training in Syria. [11] The next month, the Treasury designated the commander of Iran's Law Enforcement Forces, Esmail Ahmadi-Moghaddam, and his deputy, Ahmad Reza Radan, for providing "expertise to aid in the Syrian government's crackdown on the Syrian people."[12]

Between October 2011 and September 2012, the Treasury designated Iranian airlines on four separate occasions for facilitating the transfer of weapons, material aid, and IRGC personnel to Syria. Iran's Mahan Air was the first to be listed "for providing financial, material and technological support" as well as "transportation, funds transfers and personnel travel services" to the Quds Force. Mahan Air reportedly helped transfer weapons to Syria and Hezbollah in Lebanon, was a front for Quds business transactions, and ferried IRGC personnel to and from Syria and Iraq.[13] In March 2012, similar designations targeted the Iranian cargo line Yas Air and other Quds-linked entities and individuals involved in facilitating "lethal aid" transfers to the Levant and parts of Africa.[14] Months later, the Treasury identified 117 aircraft that Iran had used in this effort. According to the designation, these aircraft "operated by Iran Air, Mahan Air, and Yas Air" had used "deceptive measures when shipping such items to Syria, by using a combination of passenger and cargo flights and declaring illicit cargo as humanitarian and other licit goods." The report uses the example of a Yas Air flight detained by Turkish authorities in March 2011 to illustrate the campaign. The Syria-bound flight had "listed 'auto spare parts' on its cargo manifest" but was instead carrying "weapons including Kalashnikov AK-47 assault rifles, machine guns, nearly 8,000 rounds of ammunition, as well as an assortment of mortar shells."[15]

Iranian planes were reportedly delivering supplies to Syria on "an almost daily basis."[16] After the embarrassing seizure of the Yas Air flight, Iranian aircraft avoided Turkish airspace and began using Iraqi airspace instead. With the departure of US forces from Iraq at the end of 2011, Iraqi airspace became open to Iranian military flights. Although the Nuri al-Maliki government in Baghdad was pressured by Washington to no longer allow such Iranian flights to pass over Iraq, little was done about it. Iraq's transportation minister, Hadi al-Ameri, was also the head of the Badr Organization, a close personal friend of Qassem Soleimani, and one of the IRGC's principal allies in the country. He likely provided the cover needed for Iranian assistance to continue. Under al-Ameri, Iraqi authorities interdicted a small handful of Iranian flights, but these inspections identified no illicit cargo and were probably prearranged events staged to ward off US pressure.[17]

Aside from facilitating that effort, the IRGC was on the ground in Syria advising and training Assad's military. In May 2012, Quds Force officer Esmail Qaani acknowledged that Iranian units were providing assistance to Syrian forces. He did not specify what that entailed, but did claim that the Iranian advisors were having an ameliorating affect and that a lot more civilians would have been killed by Syrian security forces had they not intervened.[18] It is difficult to imagine that Assad's merciless onslaught could have been any more severe. However, Iran's crackdown in 2009 was in comparison less murderous and more effective. Assuming the IRGC drew from its experience, it is possible that they counseled Assad against using too much aggression or tried to reign in his forces at times. How effective they were is unclear, as Assad's forces did not shy away from savagery against the Syrian people. Such statements do not unburden the IRGC from complicity in Assad's repression, but they do suggest that the organization recognized that his brutality was counterproductive and had intensified the rebellion.

To whatever extent the IRGC was involved in shaping events on the ground, its greatest impact likely came through the development of pro-Assad paramilitary forces. The effectiveness of Assad's military had been degraded by mass defections of Sunni commanders and conscripts. The remaining force was racked by divisions and inexperienced in urban and counter-insurgency warfare. The shabiha gangs were likewise ineffective in war even if their allegiance to Assad was firm. Assad faced a stark demographic reality: Sunni Arabs made up at least 60 percent of the country, and Alawites were closer to 10 percent. Even with superior military technology, the rebel's ability to draw support from the Sunni Arab population gave them a potentially significant manpower advantage. The Baathist regime was in need of forces that could defend neighborhoods, man checkpoints, and take part in urban assaults. It needed armed units that could operate beyond the confines of conventional military tactics and confront the rebels with less predictable, more asymmetrical methods. The IRGC excelled in these areas. Instead of trying to retrain or restructure the Baathist Syrian Arab Army, the IRGC spearheaded the establishment of a paramilitary force modeled on the Basij. As Mehdi Taeb, former Basij commander, explained in February 2013: "Syria had an army but it was not able to manage the war inside Syrian cities. This is why Iran suggested that it forms a Basij force to manage urban war." Taeb further claims that Syria's new militia forces took over urban operations from the regular military, which began to concentrate on areas better suited to its capabilities.[19]

In September 2012, IRGC chief Jafari provided a few details on the campaign. Jafari implied that the IRGC had helped form and train "popular forces" that were operating parallel to Assad's military. Jafari referred to this organization as the "People's Army" (*jaysh al-sha'abi*), which already had fifty thousand troops active throughout the country.[20] A year later, Taeb stated the number had increased to sixty thousand.[21] Another IRGC official put the number at seventy thousand in May 2014.[22] The IRGC's role in organizing these forces earned it another designation from the US Treasury Department. The designation charges that the IRGC began providing "training, advice, and weapons and equipment" to the militia since mid-2012, and "provided routine funding worth millions of dollars." It also claims that the militia was initially most active in Damascus and Aleppo, and that it operated both unilaterally and in conjunction with regular regime forces.[23]

By mid-2013, there were numerous reports of Iranian commanders overseeing the training of Syria militia members inside Syria and in Iran. Syrian officials began referring to the militia as the National Defense Forces (NDF), which by 2013 had become a mainstay in most major operations in the war. IRGC commanders, however, generally referred to it by other names, such as the People's Army, the Popular Defenses, the National Forces, and the Syrian Basij. Interviews with a few of these militiamen conducted by *Reuters* reporters in Homs Province sheds some light on their training. *Reuters* found that most of the recruits had come from Alawite and Shiite backgrounds, with a smaller proportion coming from Syria's other minority communities, particularly Christians and Druze. The recruits appeared to operate in their home regions, creating a system of local and provincial units with loose, centralized command structures similar to the Basij. Training was limited and seems to have concentrated on core fundamentals and tactics. A Christian recruit who underwent training in Iran offered some details: "It was an urban warfare course that lasted 15 days. The trainers said it's the same course Hezbollah operatives normally do. . . . The course teaches you the important elements of guerrilla warfare, like several different ways to carry a rifle and shoot, and the best methods to prepare against surprise attacks." The training described was specialized, and included separate training for ground warfare, anti-air support, and sniping. The Iranian trainers spoke in Arabic, but some also relied on translators. Hezbollah members were also present at the base, some serving as instructors others as students. The training for the Lebanese was separate and appeared unequal to the Syrians. As one Syrian put it, "I think their training was tougher than ours." The recruits claimed that the training was more effective than what they had received back home, and had sharpened their fighting abilities and know-how. The recruits said that the Iranian trainers stressed certain principles of war. One point highlighted by the Iranians was that retreating in the face of insurmountable pressure was preferable to being killed. "If you lose the position but survive, you can recoup and regain the site another day. If you die, your position will eventually be lost." Recruits asserted that their commanders in Syria had demanded the opposite—retreating was not an option. Unethical behavior such as looting, always a popular pastime for armed groups in ungoverned spaces, was strictly forbidden. "If you joined [to loot] and not defend your country, you will die an ugly death and go to hell," a recruit was told. The sectarian elements of Syria's civil war were also rejected by the Iranian trainers, who emphasized that the militiamen were fighting to defend their country, not to defeat Sunnis. According to a Christian recruit, this sentiment was not shared by the Alawites in the camp, who wanted to "kill the Sunnis and rape their women in revenge."[24]

Syria's Baath Party had intermittently used paramilitary forces since the 1960s, and it is probable that a loose collection of already established pro-Assad militias was the starting point for the IRGC's venture.[25] But no corollaries to previous Baathist entities were mentioned by Iranian leadership. For them, the militia was first and foremost an imprinting of the Basij and Basij culture on sympathetic, mostly Muslim Syrians. Mehdi Taeb referred to the militia as the "Syrian Basij" and its members as "hezbollahis," a term that connotes Shiite religiosity and ideological perspectives in line with the Islamic Republic.[26] IRGC commander Mohammad Hosayn Sepehr emphasized similar points, claiming: "Basij culture and thought have spread throughout Syria," and that this "divine culture" had become a bulwark to foreign powers.[27] In October 2014, Iran's ambassador to Damascus, Mohammad Reza Rauf Shaybani, reiterated that Syria's "popular defense" (*defa'-e mardomi*) forces were modeled on Iran's Basij. He said that the militia was involved in the protection of the sacred Sayyida Zaynab shrine and fighting against jihadist terrorist groups. That same month an Iranian Basij commander was reported to have been killed near Aleppo.[28]

The IRGC's main motivation for establishing the NDF probably centered on wanting to help Assad safeguard his regime from collapse. Other incentives might have also played a role. As the IRGC understands, armed forces are a key to power and influence. The IRGC used armed force to outflank Khomeini's opponents in 1979, crush its opposition in the 1980s, weaken reformism in the 1990s, and to stop the Green Movement in 2009. Through its relationship with Hezbollah, the IRGC gained influence in Lebanese politics and a foothold in the conflict with Israel. Iran's defense ministry has even called Hezbollah "Iran's representative on [Lebanon's] border with Israel."[29] Similarly, the IRGC used client militant networks to undermine the US occupation of Iraq. The Iraqi militants under its sway gave it so much influence that Iran was seen as having a hand in the departure of American forces in December 2011.[30] Having a client base in Syria could afford Iran similar utility. Sayyed Hassan Entezari, an IRGC officer who served in Syria until he was shot in the spine in a firefight with rebels, spoke of the NDF's potential: "It is true that war has a brutal face and many of [Syria's] economic and social structures have been damaged. But if we look at this from another angle, there is a similarity between Iran's presence [in Syria] and how Hezbollah [was founded]."[31] Such an objective was also intimated by Hosayn Hamedani, the former head of Tehran's provincial IRGC command, in May 2014. Subsumed within a larger plan to rebuild Syria after its war concludes, Hamedani boasted that "Iran has established a second Hezbollah in Syria." He added that the force was composed of "Alawite, Shiite, and Sunni" youth and divided into 42 groups and 128 units active in all Syrian cities and provinces.[32] Hamedani was in a position to know. A few months later, he was identified by Mohsen Kazemayni—the former's successor as commander of the Mohammad Rasulollah Corps of provincial Tehran—as the IRGC's point man for the training and organization of paramilitary forces (jaysh al-watani) in Syria.[33]

Iran's support brought an untold number of IRGC personnel to Syria. In February 2014, Reuters cited a recently retired IRGC commander and an Iranian official close to the IRGC in reporting that there were a "few hundred" commanders from the Quds Force and other IRGC divisions in Syria, as well as "thousands" of Basij militiamen involved in training and advising missions.[34] These numbers appear reasonable given the scale of the effort, which theoretically included oversight of pro-Assad militias across the country. Advising those troops throughout Syria alone would require a sizeable delegation of advisors and trainers. This footprint made IRGC members accessible targets for rebel forces. Syria's rebels considered Iran complicit in their oppression, and held as much antipathy for the IRGC as they did Assad's military. In one incident, an uncertain number of guardsmen were taken hostage in August 2012 when a bus full of Iranians was stopped by a rebel group associated with the Free Syrian Army. The bus was the last in a convoy of six carrying Iranian passengers from the Damascus International Airport to the Al-Faradis Hotel, a spot popular with Iranian tour groups. The forty-eight captured Iranians had entered Syria as part of a pilgrimage group organized by the Samen al-Aemmeh travel agency, which specializes in religious tourism for IRGC and Basij members. The agency is also a subsidiary of Samen al-Aemmeh Industries, an IRGC front company designated by the US Treasury and the UN Security Council for its role in Iran's nuclear program.[35] Iranian officials admitted that some of those captured were guardsmen, but maintained they were pilgrims and not there in a military capacity. The Syrian captors provided several IRGC identification cards taken from the Iranians as proof that the detainees were active-duty soldiers. Iranian sources—an employee of Samen al-Aemmeh and a guardsman stationed in Syria—confirmed to Farnaz Fassihi of the *Wall Street Journal* that everyone on the bus had been a member of the Guards or Basij and had been deployed to Syria to assist with the IRGC's training mission.[36] US State Department spokeswoman Victoria Nuland similarly implied that all the detainees were guardsmen. In January, the rebels released the Iranian hostages in exchange for 2,130 prisoners of the Assad regime.[37] Iranian media reported that at least seven of the released Iranians were IRGC members.[38] The deal was brokered by Turkey and Qatar, and is suggestive of the importance of the hostages and the weight of the IRGC's influence in Damascus.

IRGC soldiers were clearly present on the ground in Syria. But were they involved in combat? Iranian authorities repeatedly denied that they were, despite evidence that confirmed the IRGC's at least limited involvement in lethal operations. The clearest indication of such activity, and the most illuminating view into the IRGC's training mission, came through videos found in the camera of an IRGC filmmaker killed by rebels near Aleppo in August 2013. The videos were shot by Hadi Baghbani, an IRGC videographer who was on his second trip to Syria to document the work of a Quds Force unit commander, Esmail Ali Taqi Heydari, and his Iranian troops.[39] Heydari's unit, which included around twelve Iranians, was assigned to a local branch of the National Defense Force called the Sayyida Ruqayya Brigade—a name that honors a daughter of the Imam Husayn who died in Damascus at the age of four while imprisoned by the Umayyad Caliph Yazid. The videos—released to the media by Syrian rebels and later compiled as part of an investigative documentary by the BBC—were probably intended as internal documentation of IRGC activities or as footage for a promotional video for Syria-bound troops. As such, they provide an intimate perspective into some of the work IRGC advisory teams were engaged in and their life at the front.

Footage shows a close-knit Iranian unit. All of its members lived together in a house in an Aleppo suburb, where they are shown eating, praying, and laughing together. In one scene, they joke about being martyrs and the need to say extra prayers for protection. In another scene, when Baghbani is being given a tour of a part of Aleppo that runs adjacent to rebel-held territory, his driver talks about how dangerous the area is and quips, "You can see why I said some prayers earlier!" The passenger responds flatly, "You have to say your prayers around here."

Other footage shows Heydari and his men at the local NDF headquarters, which seemed to serve as their main base of operations. In one clip, we see a communications room manned by a uniformed Iranian who seems to be monitoring radio messages and maintaining contact with other area units. Another scene shows the Iranians in a prayer room listening to a sermon by a Shiite cleric. The twelve men are seated in two rows before the standing cleric. They range in age, with at least half appearing older, with grey hair. This suggests that advisors included both experienced, long-serving IRGC members—possibly including retired officers—and younger soldiers. Heydari explains that the main responsibility of these men was to advise and train their Syrian counterparts. He mentions that many of the Syrians had previously attended training in Iran, and as a result worked well with the Iranian advisors. The Iranians are clearly in a leadership role.

In an interview with Baghbani, Heydari reveals his perspectives on the events in Syria. He explains that the conflict has been misunderstood. It is not a civil war between competing factions. It is a war "between Islam and the infidels," a battle of "good versus evil." As proof of this, the unit commander lists the supporters of each side. Those supporting Assad include the supreme leader, Hassan Nasrallah, Lebanese Hezbollah, as well as Iraqi and Afghan "mojahedin." Those supporting the rebels are "Saudi Arabia, Qatar, and Turkey," who benefit from the financial backing of the UAE, United States, Britain, France, and "other Europeans." Even if unintended, the sectarian implication of Heydari's description is unavoidable: to him, this is a fight between Shiites and Sunnis. The Shiites are on the side of God, the Sunnis, who are backed by the West, are on the side of the infidels.

But overt sectarianism does not come through in other parts of the video. Heydari presents the Iranians as a positive force in the conflict. He believes their presence has decreased the abuses of the Syrian military, which he says is disrespectful and abusive to the local population. Stemming from this attitude, Heydari says that it was the "mistakes" made by the Syrian government at the outset of the uprising that have "led to all this." He holds up the Islamic Republic as more benevolent, implying that the irreligiousness of the Syrian government was at the root of its problems. "Islam has taught us to be kind," he says. Heydari contends that the Iranians hold themselves to a higher standard and are considerate to the locals. Footage showing him handing out candy to a few small boys during a drive through a village is meant to illustrate that point. But even here the picture is quickly muddled. As Heydari explains that the presence of the Iranians has brought security to the area and led to the return of "humans" to their homes, his passenger sarcastically responds, "there are still no humans here, they're Arabs!" revealing some degree of chauvinism by the Iranians.

According to Heydari, the Iranians are active and not passive in the conflict. In explaining their activities, the unit commander says that the Iranians are regularly involved in nighttime reconnaissance operations aimed at intelligence gathering and identifying enemy positions. Once enemy positions are identified, Heydari lists three ways they typically respond. They either strike those positions with artillery, plant mines and roadside bombs along the routes traveled by rebels, or they conduct a raid to destroy the enemy post. "We do this quite often," Heydari says of armed raids.

It is in this capacity that Heydari's unit is called to defend a pro-Assad base known as the "Poultry Farm," which is reportedly being approached by a rebel detachment. The Iranians meet up with an NDF squad as they race to shore up defenses. Heydari explains that the Poulty Farm is near a strategic hill, which if captured would enable the rebels to dominate the entirety of southern Aleppo. At the base, Heydari and his deputy Yahya—both of whom speak Arabic—take charge of the gathered Syrian militiamen, around forty-five in all. They are all in military uniforms and armed. One of the NDF militiamen wears a green headband with a Shiite invocation on it reminiscent of the Basij. Heydari, his deputy, and Baghbani—who is also in uniform and armed—gather up a group of about twelve others and head out on foot to defend the right flank of the base. As they walk through open farmland they are ambushed by a larger, heavily armed unit of the Liwa al-Dawud rebel group that was lying in wait. Heydari, Baghbani, and at least four others are killed.

Iranian media covered the funerals of Heydari and Baghbani, who were both buried with full IRGC honors in their home town of Amol in northern Iran just days after their deaths. They were hailed as martyrs who died "defending the holy shrine of Sayyida Zaynab" in Damascus. This was a standard line for all Iranians killed in Syria, at once magnifying their deaths as a spiritual sacrifice in the defense of the honor of the sacred family of the Prophet while also obscuring the actual—and generally never reported—circumstances of their deaths. Between 2012 and 2014, Iranian press reported dozens of fatalities of servicemen in Syria; most were part of the IRGC, and all were heralded as martyrs in service to Sayyida Zaynab.

The highest-ranking official killed in Syria was Hassan Shateri, a senior Quds Force officer and its Lebanon representative. He had been traveling between Damascus and Beirut on February 13, 2013, when he was killed, probably by Syrian rebels.[40] Shateri's death received widespread attention in Iran. Khamenei eulogized Shateri, saying he had "tasted the sweet syrup of martyrdom." Potentates, clergy, and top military officials attended his funeral, as did Jihad Mughniyeh, the son of Hezbollah's slain terrorism chief.[41] Qassem Soleimani praised the service of Shateri and his work in Lebanon. He held him up as an archetypal Islamic soldier. He "was greater than any man, city, province or even country. Indeed, he will be considered a symbol of Shiism," Soleimani said. "Martyrs like [Shateri] continue to insure the revolution and its Islamic school. They will always reside in our hearts."[42]

Shateri had been the head of Lebanon operations and the IRGC's lead liaison with Hezbollah. His presence in Syria was probably connected to the growing role of Hezbollah in the fight against the rebels. According to the US Treasury Department, Hezbollah's assistance to Assad's forces began in early 2011. Lebanese militants worked with the IRGC in the training of Syrians and took part in limited military operations.[43] Some Hezbollah deaths were reported in the fall of that year, but it was not until 2012 that the group began moving into Syria to protect strategic border crossings and Shiite villages. Hezbollah secretary general Hassan Nasrallah acknowledged his troops were active in border areas in May 2012, and by 2013 Hezbollah was operating openly in many parts of Syria. The group was an effective auxiliary force for the Assad regime, expelling rebels from the key strategic town of Qusayr in June 2013, leading operations in the Qalamoun region, and helping secure gains in Homs and Damascus.[44]

Hezbollah's controversial support for Assad imposed steep costs on the organization and severely undermined security in Lebanon. By spring 2014, it was reported that around five hundred Hezbollah fighters had been killed in combat in Syria, including some senior commanders.[45] Another report documented 313 funerals for Hezbollah fighters who had been killed in Syria between 2012 and March 2014.[46]

Hezbollah's intervention sparked a wave of terrorism and sectarian violence in Lebanon. Suicide bombings and other attacks hit Hezbollah and Shiite targets. Sectarian armed clashes intermittently broke out in the northern city of Tripoli and in other parts of the country. Iranian interests were targeted as well. In one attack, Iranian officials were hit in a double-suicide bombing in front of Iran's embassy in Beirut. The attack killed Iran's cultural attaché Hojjat al-Islam Ebrahim Ansari, the wife of an Iranian diplomat, and twenty-two others.[47] At least 150 more were injured, including five Iranian security personnel.[48] It appeared that Iran's ambassador to Lebanon, Ghaznafar Roknabadi, had been the intended target. Roknabadi was rumored to be closely connected to the IRGC's operations in Syria and to Hezbollah, and had been scheduled to leave the embassy with Ansari at the time of the first explosion.[49] Iranian Foreign Ministry officials quickly blamed Israel.[50] Hezbollah chief Hassan Nasrallah pointed a finger at Saudi Arabia, saying the assault was "linked to Saudi Arabia's rage against Iran over its failure" to defeat Assad in Syria.[51] A Lebanon-based jihadist organization, the Abdullah Azzam Brigades, took credit for the assault, announcing it had been conducted by "two Sunni heroes of Lebanon."[52] Lebanese authorities arrested the group's leader, Majid Muhammad bin al-Majid, a Saudi national who soon died in detention, further inflaming tensions.[53] A few weeks later, two car bombs exploded close to the Iranian cultural center in a Shiite neighborhood in Beirut, killing six and injuring 129 Lebanese citizens, including a number of children at a nearby orphanage. The Abdullah Azzam Brigades again took responsibility, calling for Hezbollah to withdraw its fighters from Syria.[54] These attacks are emblematic of the violence that began to ravage Lebanon since Hezbollah's intervention in Syria. Through the end of 2014, Syria-linked attacks had caused deep divisions and mistrust among confessional communities in Lebanese cities and rural areas such as the Bekaa Valley, threatening a return to the communalism that drove the country's long civil war.[55]

Like Iran, Hezbollah had a strategic stake in Assad's survival. But its entrance into Syria's civil war magnified the sectarian dimensions of the conflict. When Iraqi Shiite militias began to operate in Syria in early 2012, it had become evident that Assad's regime was being propped up by a broad, transnational Shiite alliance led by Iran and the IRGC. By October 2012, leaders of Iraqi Shiite organizations told *New York Times* reporters that Iran was sending their members to Syria, some after having trained in Iran first. Young men were being encouraged to join the fight to help protect the Sayyida Zaynab shrine from Sunni extremists. Militants and weapons traveled over land in tour buses disguised as pilgrimage groups. Recruitment among Iraqi Shia played to their communal identity and hatred for Sunni extremists. Their involvement in the Syrian conflict was endorsed by Iraqi politicians and Shiite religious authorities. Qom-based Grand Ayatollah Kazem Haeri, the point of emulation (*marja'*) for many of the Iraqi militants, ruled in December 2013 that fighting in Syria was religiously permissible. "The battle in Syria is not for the defense of the shrine of [Sayyida Zaynab] but it is a battle of infidels against Islam and Islam should be defended," he argued. He also assured potential volunteers that those who died would be received as martyrs in the afterlife.[56]

The militants that traveled to Syria did so through IRGC clients, particularly Asaib Ahl al-Haq, Kataib Hezbollah, Liwa Abu al-Fadl, and the Badr Organization. These militias, some of which cut their teeth fighting US forces in Iraq, were mostly concentrated in the areas around the Sayyida Zaynab shrine. The shrine, which is situated in a Shiite neighborhood that already included Iraqi, Iranian, and Afghan ex-patriots, was both a symbolic target for Syrian rebels and a strategic one due to its proximity to a highway connecting the capital with Damascus International Airport. The shrine was close to a number of contested areas in outer Damascus and fighting there led to mounting deaths for the Iraqis. The bodies of militants killed in action would return to Iraq via Iran, and then often be buried in Shiite cemeteries in the holy cities of Najaf and Karbala. By March 2014, several burials were occurring daily. As one Najaf gravedigger told Martin Chulov of the *Guardian* newspaper, "There have been more of their bodies coming back from Syria than ever before. There are easily around 500 of them buried here. We have been getting around three each day for the past month alone."[57] These numbers only included fighters from Asaib Ahl al-Haq, and were thus just a portion of an unknown number of Iraqis killed. Iran reportedly paid $5,000 to the families of each martyr and covered burial costs for those who could not afford them.[58]

Martyrs were celebrated through visual memorials posted to Facebook pages associated with Iraqi militant groups. These posters hailed the fallen as Shiite heroes who died in the defense of Holy Zaynab and the family of the Prophet.[59] They became a prominent fixture of the growing number of Arabic Facebook pages devoted to the Syrian conflict, the wider war against Sunni extremists in Lebanon and Iraq, the Iranian regime, and Shiism. Khamenei was heavily featured in these pages. He was hailed as the political and spiritual head of their movement. Hezbollah and the IRGC also occupied a revered place, but were seen as equal to the Iraqi militias. In one visual composition that was circulated, the face of Khamenei floats in the heavens above the Earth, which lies behind him. Along Earth's arc are the emblems of major Shiite militant groups: the Badr Organization is in the center, and flanked by the IRGC and Kataib Hezbollah on the right, and Lebanese Hezbollah and Asaib Ahl al-Haq on the left. The image gives the impression of a united, global Shiite militant front under the divine guidance of Iran's supreme leader.[60] Such images created the sense of a broad political movement with a deeply spiritual and distinctly Shiite worldview. But the Facebook community was relatively small, and appeared to be mostly engineered by the Iraqi militias, the IRGC, and Hezbollah. The pages were thus as much evidence of the insularity of the movement as of any wider, grassroots appeal.

These pages intensely concentrated on Shiite identity, and made no attempt to hide overt sectarianism. They made the battle lines clear: devout Shiites under the guidance of Iran's leader were at war with Sunni extremists, Saudi Arabia and other Arab states, Israel, and America. But more than this, these pages and the entities behind them seemed to be advancing the concept of a transnational Shiite movement. One that was defending Shiite interests in the Middle East and reclaiming their rightful place in the region. This idea was being put forward in Iran as well. In one article published by a hardline newspaper, the militants supporting Assad and defending the Sayyida Zaynab shrine against a "warmongering cult" were seen as an "international Shiite army (*sepah*)." Referring to the involvement of Iraqi militants in Syria, the article says: "This issue can be the beginning of a great transformation in the mobilization of popular Shiite forces in the region." Such forces will not only make an impact in the Syrian conflict, their influence will move beyond that country's borders and produce a "fundamental change in all lands dominated by the Axis of Resistance."[61]

Despite the IRGC's insistence and perhaps sincere belief that it was not involved in a sectarian war in Syria, the coalition of foreign forces it had assembled was almost entirely Shiite. For Lebanese Hezbollah and Iraqi militants, this was a battle for Shiite interests. What is more, the IRGC began to recruit Shiites from other countries and pay them to fight in Syria.[62] The largest contingent, probably numbering in the hundreds, came from Afghanistan and Afghan immigrants in Iran.[63] The office of Ayatollah Mohaghagh Kaboli, a senior Afghan cleric in Qom, described the recruitment effort: "They [the IRGC] find a connection to the refugee community and work on convincing our youth to go and fight in Syria. . . . They give them everything from salary to residency."[64] One Afghan captured by Syrian rebels near Aleppo claimed that he had been released from an Iranian prison in exchange for agreeing to fight in Syria and a $600 monthly stipend. He said that there were 450 Afghan militants in Syria, organized into three 150-man battalions. In December 2013, *Fars News* announced that the "Devotees of Fatima (*fatimaiyun*) Brigade" had been formed by Shiites in Kabul and was defending the Sayyida Zaynab shrine.[65] Another report suggests the Fatima Brigade included "Pakistani, Azeri and other Asian fighters" in addition to Afghans.[66] Afghans might have been traveling to Syria because they genuinely believed in the cause. But because Afghans in Iran are generally poor and part of a marginalized refugee community with high unemployment and uncertain residency status, it is unsurprising that the IRGC would use incentives such as legalized residency for recruitment. Offering citizenship or legal residency is not an uncommon incentive for armed forces to use. It is a hallmark of the French Foreign Legion and something the US military uses to encourage the service of undocumented immigrants as well.[67]

## A Return to Karbala

The IRGC's campaign in Syria was wholly supported by the leadership in Tehran. That unity of mission continued after the election of President Hassan Rouhani in June 2013. Rouhani brought with him a pragmatic approach to foreign policy, one less confrontational and more mature than Ahmadinejad's. The change in government opened up the door to reengagement with the United States. Though secret talks between Tehran and Washington had begun a few months before Rouhani's election, the new tone set by his administration enlivened the diplomatic process.[68] Led by Rouhani's foreign minister, the University of Denver–educated diplomat Mohammad Javad Zarif, Iran took part in a new series of talks with the P5+1 to seek compromise on its nuclear program and an end to sanctions. These talks came at an otherwise awkward time. The United States and its Arab partners were engaged in a proxy war against Iran-backed forces in Syria. Added to this, in July 2014 another short, brutal conflict broke out between Hamas and Israel in Gaza. In these areas, Iran's policies were unchanged. It was unflinchingly committed to Assad, Hamas, and to the destruction of Israel. Rouhani needed a partner willing to look past these significant areas of disagreement in order to make progress on the nuclear issue and had one in his American counterpart. It became clear that the nuclear issue was a priority for President Obama. Solving it would prevent the United States from having to go to war with Iran, increase trust between the two sides, and possibly open up new areas of compromise in the region.

Although Rouhani brought a change in tone, his policies in Syria were an extension of his predecessor's. His government maintained the same line: Assad was fighting a war for survival against terrorists, and the West and certain Arab governments were supporting the terrorists to further their own anti-Iran, anti-resistance, pro-Zionist interests. Just weeks into Rouhani's tenure, Iran was almost thrust into potential conflict with the United States when it appeared Obama might order strikes against Assad after it was determined that Syrian government forces had used chemical weapons against civilians—crossing Obama's previously stated "red line."[69] Iranian officials warned against American intervention. IRGC chief Jafari threatened that any US military action against Assad would spark a much wider war in the Middle East. Qassem Soleimani was more explicit, warning: "Syria is our red line. The land of Sham is our ascension to heaven and it will be the graveyard of the Americans."[70] When Russia stepped in and brokered a deal to destroy Assad's chemical weapons stockpile via the United Nations, Obama decided against military action. This legitimized Russian and Iranian positions in Syria, and decreased international pressure on the pro-Assad camp. The IRGC continued its course in Syria unaltered.

The rise of the Islamic State in Iraq and al-Sham (ISIS) and its push into Iraq in the summer of 2014 gave credence to Iran's position. Terrorists were indeed part of the war against Assad. Having been at least indirectly emboldened by Arab states' support to Syria's rebels, the jihadist organization had been able to take over significant territory in two countries and exercise the pretensions of state. Jihadists had been active in Iraq since the US occupation and had gradually ratcheted up suicide bombings and other attacks on civilians since American forces left the country. Sunni jihadists considered Shiites their primary enemy and the root of Islam's problems. Sunni ex-Baathists, tribesmen, and other Islamists similarly resented the Shia's rise to power in Iraq and felt increasingly marginalized by the Shia-led government in Baghdad. Jihadists repeatedly struck Shiite and government targets with the aim of sparking a broader communal war.

ISIS's success in Iraq would not have been possible without the sectarian policies of Iraqi prime minister Nouri al-Maliki and his heavy handed response to jihadist violence. By collectively punishing Sunni communities suspected of harboring extremists through extra-judicial killings and the arrest of thousands, Maliki fell for the jihadists' trap.[71] The Shiite militias that had arisen during the US occupation through mostly Iranian patronage, acted as auxiliaries to Maliki's forces and were responsible for the worst reports of violence against

Sunni civilians. In an April 2014 incident, Shiite militiamen gathered up and executed dozens of young Sunni males after driving jihadists out of Buhriz, a village twenty-five miles north of Baghdad in Diyala Province.[72] Sunni communities began to rebel against Maliki's repression, leading to mass protest camps throughout the heavily Sunni Anbar Province. Iraqi government forces dealt with those protests with Saddam-like savagery. Through the winter and early spring of 2014, Maliki's largely Shiite forces stormed through camps in places such as Fallujah and Ramadi, killing and displacing large numbers of civilians. According to the United Nations and the Health Committee of the Provincial Council of Anbar, the civilian death toll in February alone was over a thousand, with some four hundred thousand more displaced.[73]

Iraq's Sunnis were primed for revolution, and ISIS—an outgrowth of Al Qaeda's Iraq affiliate—was the catalyst. [74] ISIS—also known derisively in the Middle East by its Arabic acronym "Daesh"—took advantage of the chaotic security situation and began moving assets and troops into Western Iraqi cities from its stronghold in eastern Syria. ISIS cells made incremental advances across Iraq through the spring and exploded into prominence in June when its fighters seized much of Western Iraq, including Mosul, the country's second largest city. As its victories mounted, it appeared that ISIS—whose forces were now armed with stockpiles of American-made weapons, vehicles, and artillery taken from routed Iraqi forces—would push into Baghdad, the Shiite south, and Kurdistan in the north. Flush with new recruits, weaponry, and hundreds of millions of dollars looted from Iraqi banks, ISIS grew in confidence and pretense. Its leader, Abu Bakr al-Baghdadi—a former small time preacher turned militant who spent four years in prison during the US occupation—changed the organization's name to simply the Islamic State and declared himself caliph of the Muslim world. [75] Through this move he aimed to restore the most potent symbol of Sunni leadership. The caliphate had not been occupied since Kemal Mustapha Ataturk abolished the office after World War I and its restoration had long been a goal of Islamist and jihadist organizations. With its capital in the eastern Syrian city of Raqqa, the Islamic State controlled a wide swath of territory straddling two countries and held authority over millions of people.

The specter of a jihadist state in the heart of the Middle East galvanized a massive international effort against the self-proclaimed caliphate. The group's savagery made this decision easy. It murdered men, women, and children by the thousands, sold non-Muslims into slavery, and attempted to destroy any who opposed its firestorm—including fellow Sunnis. Its mission was simple: kill Shiites, purge any signs or adherents of that religion and of any non-Sunni faith from the lands under its control, and establish a utopian state that would operate under its cherry-picked, blood-thirsty interpretation of Islamic law. Unlike in Syria, Iran and the United States were on the same side in Iraq. Both moved to save Iraq from collapse, but Iran's intervention was immediate and unflinching, whereas the United States was hesitant and made its support contingent on Maliki stepping down. Pressure against Maliki was mounting from within his Shiite base too. The massive and embarrassing failures of the Iraqi military, which disintegrated in the face of ISIS forces, exposed Maliki for having appointed corrupt and incompetent commanders on the basis of loyalty. He had put Iraq on the course to civil war and the whole country was now paying the price. Grand Ayatollah Ali Sistani, Iraq's most senior Shiite religious authority, came out against Maliki even as he called for volunteers to join the fight against ISIS.[76] Iran seemed initially disinclined to abandon Maliki, who had been a trusted ally, but when Maliki began losing the faith of important Shiite constituents, Iran did not step in the way. Hayder al-Abadi was chosen as the Dawa Party's candidate to replace Maliki as prime minister in August. Iran was one of the first countries to congratulate his victory—thus offering its endorsement.[77]

By early June, the IRGC was rapidly moving assets, advisors, and troops into Iraq. Early reports suggested that Quds Force and IRGC elite commando (*saberin*) units had entered the country to support Iraqi forces.[78] Within weeks, the IRGC's support had grown substantially. Intelligence and communications units along with drone operators took up shop in Baghdad's Rasheed Air Base, which became a special control center for the IRGC. With signals intelligence equipment and *Ababil* surveillance drones in Iraqi skies, the IRGC was able to monitor Islamic State communications and troop movements. In addition, the IRGC began to transfer military weapons and supplies to Iraq state forces, Shiite militias, and Kurdish peshmerga fighters.[79] Kurdish forces were battling ISIS on multiple fronts, such as in Baiji, Sinjar, and outside Kirkuk—a city now occupied by pershmerga after Iraqi troops retreated under ISIS pressure. Kurdish Regional Government president Massoud Barzani heralded Iran as the first to heed to its requests for support, sending two cargo plane loads "full of weapons" to help supply peshmerga fighters.[80]

IRGC assistance to Iraq included two Soviet-era Sukhoi Su-25s and one Su-25B close ground support military aircraft. The planes were delivered to Iraq in July and began to fly combat missions over Fallujah, Ramadi, and Baiji soon after. Originally sold to Iraq by the Soviet Union, the aircraft were later flown to Iran in 1991 to protect them during the Gulf War. Iran confiscated the planes as reparations for Saddam's invasion of it eleven years earlier and made them a key part of the IRGC's air fleet. In returning the planes to Iraq, the IRGC denied its pilots would be operating them.[81] But it was unlikely that Iraqis, who were no longer trained on the aircraft, could fly them in combat so quickly.[82] This suggested that IRGC pilots were flying combat missions themselves and thus taking part in the fighting. While Iranians did not appear to be directly engaged in other areas of combat, the IRGC's growing presence as advisors on the front lines led to early causalities. The first reported death was that of Colonel Shoja'at Alamdari Murjani, an IRGC pilot and drone operator, who was killed in June near the Imam Askariyeen Shrine in Samarra by an ISIS mortar attack.[83] Murjani joined his comrades killed in Syria as a martyr who died in "defense of the holy shrines"—a euphemism that now was used by Iranian officials to describe IRGC involvement in both countries—and given a funeral with full military honors.[84]

Like in Syria, the Islamic Republic's involvement in Iraq was in part a strategic decision. Iran had cultivated close ties with Baghdad since the fall of Saddam, and had relied on that relationship to help mitigate its regional alienation. Iraq was an important trading partner for Iran and open to Iranian commercial interests. Iraq had become one of Iran's closest allies. Speaking on Iran-Iraq ties, Qassem Soleimani said: "Because of [Iran's] Shiite clerical leadership (*marja'iyyat*), Iraq was able to free itself from America's clutches. If it were not for [Iran's] clerical leadership, who else could have managed this?"[85] In other words, Iran had intervened to drive out US forces from Iraq and it would do so again with ISIS. Iran had long accused Saudi Arabia and other Arab states of supporting anti-government militants in Iraq and the rise of the Islamic State appeared to be a culmination of that effort. As Ali Saidi, the supreme leader's representative in the IRGC, explained: "Saudi Arabia tried very hard to ruin the situation in Syria, and Qatar also invested a lot in this situation . . . Today they feel that all of their conspiracies have failed in Syria. They have started a new front in Iraq."[86] Iran could not afford to lose its only friend in the region after Syria, nor could it see Iraq conquered by hostile, anti-Iran, anti-Shiite forces. Iran's long border with Iraq magnified the danger. But Iraq also housed the most important religious shrines in Shiism—sites ISIS was intent on destroying. This made the fight in Iraq more than a strategic or political contest. This was a defense of the family of the Prophet and an existential battle for the future of the Shiite faith. In June, Rouhani made Iran's pledge firm, saying that it would not "spare any effort" to defend Shiite holy sites.[87] That same month, Qom-based Grand Ayatollah Naser Makarem Shirazi issued a fatwa declaring the fight in Iraq a "jihad," and making defense of the shrines a religious duty for all Muslims. [88]

Grand Ayatollah Sistani's calls for volunteers to fight ISIS fell in line with this religious sentiment. Sistani was asking for all Iraqis—regardless of sect—to defend the country, but his message had unique resonance among the Shia. Iraqi militias took up the effort and began to establish volunteer divisions for the new recruits. While they still maintained a presence in Syria, Iraqi militants had begun gradually returning to Iraq in late 2013 as the fight against ISIS gradually moved across the border.[89] Departures from Syria spiked in June when thousands of Iraqi militants came home and reintegrated into militia ranks now at war with ISIS.[90] With the collapse of the Iraqi military in much of the western and northern parts of the country, the militias were well-positioned to take a leading role in the war. Every major Shiite militia and political party looked to take advantage of the quick influx of volunteers. The Supreme Islamic Council of Iraq, for example, announced in June the establishment of a fifty thousand man volunteer militia called the Ashura Brigades.[91] The IRGC was poised to have some involvement in the training of these new militants, which eventually coalesced into the Popular Mobilization Units (*al-hashd al-sha'abi*)—an umbrella organization overseen by Iraq's Interior Ministry and led by major Shiite militia commanders, including Hadi al-Ameri (Badr), Qais al-Khazali (Asaib Ahl al-Haq), Abu Mahdi al-Muhandis, and Shebl al-Zaidi (Kataib Imam Ali).[92] Basij commander Mohammad Reza Naqdi confirmed in November 2014 that Iran had been training Iraqis, and stated that because Iraq now had its own "basijis," Iranian forces would not be required in the fight against ISIS—an official line that mirrored what had been said about Iranian forces in Syria.[93] As early as June, Basij units had been reportedly deployed to different parts of Iraq. An Iraqi official told London's *Guardian* newspaper that 1,500 basijis had crossed the border to Khanaqin in Diyala Province and another five hundred had entered Badra Jassan in Wasit Province further south. This made the Basij another part of the IRGC's overall contingent in Iraq. Given the Basij's strengths, its troops most likely became part of urban-based units and had some role in training and advising Iraqi counterparts.[94] But even this type of activity could potentially place Basij members—like other IRGC and Quds troops—in a de facto combat role. Hamid Reza Zamani, a Basij member from Kerman Province who was killed "defending the Shrine of Imam Husayn" near Karbala in October, is an example of the ambiguity in which Iranian advisors served in Iraq. A picture of Zamani posted by a news agency closely associated with the IRGC shows him in an Iraqi military uniform—the same worn by Shia militiamen—holding an automatic rifle and standing in front of a 107-mm rocket system, suggesting that his role in Iraq might have transcended advice.[95]

The most prominent militias fighting ISIS in Iraq were also those most aligned with Iran's leadership. The Badr Organization, Kataib Hezbollah, Asaib Ahl al-Haq, and Liwa Abu Fadl al-Abbas quickly became a core part of the Iraqi government's campaign. These groups bolstered defenses in Baghdad, Samarra, and the Shiite south, and led operations in eastern Diyala as well as other areas. Along with the Kurdish peshmerga—which they often coordinated with in Diyala— the Shiite militias symbolized the sectarian and ethnic fault lines of Iraq's war. They also symbolized Iran's influence. Unlike after the fall of Saddam, when Iraqi groups allied with Iran—such as the Supreme Islamic Council—generally deemphasized patronage from Iran, Shiite militias were now open about receiving Iranian support. This was in part an artifact of the moment. Iraq was in trouble and clearly needed outside help. But it was also a sign of Iran's relationship with these groups which had developed into a close partnership built on shared ideology and religious identity. Jabar Rajabi, the representative for Asaib Ahl al-Haq and Kataib Hezbollah in Qom, exemplifies this point. Speaking to Iranian reporters, Rajabi pledged "the allegiance (*bay'at*) of the Islamic resistance groups of Iraq to the supreme leadership of his holiness Ayatollah Khamenei" and claimed that these groups followed the authority of Shiite leadership in Qom (as opposed to Najaf). Clarifying the basis of these commitments, Rajabi said that religion, not politics, was the determining factor in their relationship with Iran.[96] By announcing allegiance to Khamenei, Rajabi was marking the place of Iraqi organizations within a pro-Iranian fraternity that also included Lebanese Hezbollah, the most stalwart proponent of clerical rule outside of Iran.[97] Yet, even if the Iraqi groups were relative newcomers, Rajabi asserted that Iran's leadership treated all equally and made no distinction between the Iraqi groups, Hezbollah, or other, non-Shiite organizations such as Hamas. In Rajabi's articulation, however, this network has a clear Shiite coloring that makes the Sunni Palestinian organizations appear more marginal. Religious identity is paramount for Rajabi, so he is compelled to explain the inclusion of Sunni allies, Hamas and Islamic Jihad, by suggesting that Iran's support for them is based on the shared commitment of the liberation of Palestine. In this framing, Rajabi inadvertently implies the superiority of Shiite groups in the Iran network. Sunnis are supported but only insofar as they remain devoted to certain political aspirations, whereas Shiite groups are supported out of shared belief and religious kinship. [98]

At the helm of all this was Qassem Soleimani, the Quds Force chief. Soleimani was instrumental in facilitating the IRGC's entrance into the war, and utilized his close ties to Shiite militias and Kurdish forces in coordinating the fight against ISIS. But the rise of the Islamic State was a stain on his legacy, and especially of his handling of the Syrian war. Soleimani helped pro-Assad forces stop major rebel advances, and defend Damascus and Assad strongholds, but this strategy also included ignoring ISIS, allowing it to develop and gain strength.[99] That approach backfired. Soleimani underestimated ISIS, and it now controlled territory from eastern Syria to villages near the Iraq-Iran border. The deteriorating situation must have been worrisome for Soleimani's bosses in Tehran. Iranian leaders never criticized Soleimani publically, but some signs suggested faith in the seasoned commander might be slipping. Most significant was the introduction of Ali Shamkhani, an IRGC war hero and head of the Supreme National Security Council, as the Rouhani government's new point man in Iraq. Shamkhani attended high-profile meetings with Iraqi officials and was instrumental in the effort to get Maliki to step aside—particularly by enlisting Grand Ayatollah Sistani to help compel Maliki from office.[100] Soleimani was considered close to Maliki, so the move to replace him with Hayder al-Abadi was seen as a potential check on the Quds Force commander's influence. Shamkhani, an ethnic Arab from Khuzestan, also became the Iranian government's envoy to the

Arab world, and was seen in many ways as the antithesis of Soleimani—a more moderate, diplomatically-inclined statesman who benefited from his ethnic heritage in gaining the trust of key Arab leaders. In this capacity he traveled to Saudi Arabia, where he aimed to decrease tensions with Riyadh, dampen snowballing sectarianism, and find some common ground regarding ISIS.[101] In many ways his job was to repair the damage done by Soleimani—and Iranian policies more broadly—to Tehran's relations with Arab neighbors.[102]

With Shamkhani in the picture, rumors of unknown provenance began to spread that Soleimani would soon be replaced. One narrative suggested that Shamkhani had taken full control of the Iraq file in the SNSC and would now head Iran's support effort.[103] Another rumor suggested Hosayn Hamedani would take over ground operations in Iraq from Soleimani as he had in Syria.[104] An Iranian hardline news site dismissed these rumors as a Saudi plot.[105] A similar story suggested that Soleimani would be promoted to IRGC chief (replacing Ali Jafari) and Hamedani would become the new Quds commander.[106] Any inclination Iran's leadership might have had to sideline Soleimani quickly succumbed to the weight of inertia. Soleimani was either too influential at home or too influential in the field—probably both—to be circumvented. He owned Iran's operations in the Middle East and could not be simply rotated out. His was a business of personal connections and trust built on years in the trenches. He was a figure that commanded respect and engendered deep and abiding loyalty from his men. Soleimani was inseparable from the war, and Iran's interests resided in his success.

At least that is how it appeared. In response to the rumors or actual behind-the-scenes maneuvering against Soleimani, a sudden, almost guerilla public relations campaign emerged with the Quds Force chief as its star. Beginning in September 2014, photographs of Soleimani in the field in Iraq began to be leaked on social media. The images were initially circulated on Facebook pages associated with Iraq's Shiite militias but quickly spread. The pictures depicted him with Shiite and peshmerga commanders—especially Badr Organization head Hadi al-Ameri—in different battle zones. Others showed him holding firearms, having picnics, praying, shaking hands, and smiling with troops on the front lines. Soleimani was almost always shown in the same uniform: khaki pants, khaki sports cap, black-and-white keffiyeh, and khaki shoes. Sometimes he wore a jacket. Combined with his slight stature, the simple attire gave Soleimani the appearance of a humble, unassuming man. He had an avuncular quality that made him seem a man of the people without detracting from his innate authority. The images became so ubiquitous that a meme developed on social media depicting Soleimani in all sorts of places and with all sorts of people. Soleimani shaking hands with an astronaut on the moon. Soleimani seated behind Jacqueline Kennedy in a presidential motorcade. Soleimani as an attendee—along with Albert Einstein and other Nobel Laureates—of the 1927 Solvay Conference. His personage had gone from relative obscurity to fringe Internet cultural phenomenon in a matter of weeks. Gradually the photos of Soleimani in Iraq began to be picked up by Iranian media as evidence of his exploits—something that suggested his public relations campaign had become endorsed by Iranian officialdom.[107]

This was all incredibly unusual. Prior to the Syrian conflict, Soleimani had maintained a very private profile. He was the leader of Iran's main covert force and his image fit that role. He was described as shadowy, mysterious, and a master spy. Only a few photographs were even available of him. So the sudden release of dozens of photos over a few months was entirely out of character and appeared to be a very deliberate public relations effort—one seemingly spearheaded by Soleimani's team and later embraced by Iranian officials. Any rumors of Soleimani's demise as Iran's man in Iraq were being instantly and repeatedly repudiated with photographic evidence. Beyond that, a more profound message was being sent: Soleimani—and by extension, Iran—was doing more than any other to assist Iraq. He was literally on the ground, at the front lines, overseeing battles. He was the linchpin bringing together Shia and Kurdish forces to fight a common enemy. When others hesitated, Soleimani acted. He was now more than just a spy chief or organizer of militias. He was the single most important military commander in an international war—something of a mix between Che Guevara and Douglas MacArthur. The same Soleimani who was rebuffed by David Petraeus in 2008 was now essentially occupying the same role as the American general six years later. He was an equal to America's top commander. *Iran* was a military power. The world needed to know.

The media campaign was not simply a vanity project. There was substance behind what was being released. Soleimani was on the front lines. He was overseeing joint Shia and Kurdish operations in certain conflict zones. Iraqi officials attested to this. Iranian officials also boasted of Soleimani's work. IRGC aerospace commander Amir Ali Hajizadeh claimed, for example, that Soleimani with only seventy men had "stopped the advance of Daesh terrorists" into Erbil in the early part of the war.[108] Shia militias and Kurdish forces were beginning to record victories against the Islamic State, and photographs of Soleimani reportedly on the front lines of these battles were released to show his centrality to their success.[109] The first major victory was in the village of Amerli, where Shiite militias and Kurdish peshmerga succeeded in driving out Islamic State forces. The campaign benefited from US air support, which was most likely coordinated through the Kurds, but the militias and peshmerga did the heavy lifting.[110] Shiite and Kurdish forces under Soleimani's command had similar success driving out the Islamic State from the eastern Diyala villages of Jalawla and Saadia, roughly twenty miles from the Iranian border.[111] These battles included the first reported use of Iranian F-4 military aircraft, which provided air support for the ground forces. The use of the F-4s was an escalation probably prompted by the proximity of the fighting to Iran's borders. It was a bold assertion of Iran's place in the war. Regardless of frequency or effect, Iranian air assets were operating in Iraq in a manner parallel to that of US and allied air forces. Western pundits saw this as evidence of direct US-Iranian coordination. Both countries denied this, but in December 2014 Secretary of State John Kerry described the impact of Iran's military contributions as having a "positive" net effect in the broader war against the Islamic State.[112]

Iran was a formidable player in the war because of Soleimani. His close association with Shiite militias, however, was a mixed blessing. On the one hand, these relationships provided Iran credibility and influence in Iraq. Shared religious identity and ideological commitments gave Iran a strong connection to its Shiite clients, and a position in the war unmatched by other outside powers. It also gave the impression that Iran was pursuing a sectarian agenda. Support for Assad was based on friendship and politics, but Sunni Arabs saw it as a Shiite alliance against them. It did not matter that Assad's Baathist regime was secular, and that Alawites were religiously distinct from Twelver Shiites. Alawites were seen as Shia by Sunnis, and Hezbollah and Iran's backing of Assad confirmed that view. The IRGC also saw Alawites as part of the Shiite fold, even if they were largely ignorant of Shiite religious practices and beliefs. The situation in Iraq was clearer. Iranian officials, including IRGC commanders, partly described the conflict in strategic, non-sectarian terms. As they saw it, Iran supported the Kurds along with the Shia. The Islamic State was hostile to Iran, and Iran could not allow its belligerency to take root next door. Religious identity played a strong part in Iran's motivations, but so did territorial integrity, support for allies (both Shia and Kurd), and regional strategy.

The war was different for the Iraqi Shia. It was existential and very much sectarian. Jihadists were out to destroy all signs of Shiism in the Middle East, and they would kill every Shiite man, woman, and child to accomplish that. This fight was personal. Shiite militants had been battling Sunni extremists since the fall of Saddam and had cultivated an abiding hatred for the enemy. It was as much about identity as territory, and the militias maintained the same brutal tactics they were known for to ensure victory for their side. Interviews with Shiite fighters on the front lines of Diyala offer a glimpse of those perspectives. Gazing at the enemy's position, one fighter said: "This land [in between the Shiite militias and Islamic State forces] is what separates good from evil . . . Here you see the flag of Imam Husayn and there you see the black flags of ISIS." To him, this was a replay of the battles in Shiism's founding moments, stating: "This is the same history repeating itself." Another spoke of deep-seated mistrust of the Sunni population: "When I withdraw my forces now the Sunnis will come back and they will become an incubator for ISIS again. . . . When I liberate an area from ISIS why do I have to give it back to them? Either I erase it or settle Shia in it." A fellow militant added: "If it's for me I will start cleansing Baghdad from today. . . . We have not started sectarian war, we are just trying to secure our areas, but if the sectarian days come back then I am sure it will be won by us.[113]

# 12

# Epilogue

Russian aircraft began striking rebel positions on September 30, 2015. This followed weeks of Russian military buildup in western Syria, wherein a variety of tanks, aircraft, antiaircraft platforms, and hundreds of associated personnel were deployed to bases near the Assad stronghold of Latakia.[1] Moscow's intervention instantly changed the strategic landscape of the war. The loyalist, pro-Assad campaign, which had been dominated by the IRGC and its clients—Hezbollah, Iraqi militias, and Afghan mercenaries—was now led by a veto-holding member of the United Nations Security Council. Russia provided a counterweight to the United States. It could challenge Washington politically and in the skies over Syria. This provided a buffer for loyalist forces at the diplomatic level and on the ground. For Iran, it was now working in concert with a great power, and its enemies had little choice but to accept it.

Days before air strikes began, Russia announced that it had joined with Iran, Iraq, and the Assad regime to form a coalition against terrorism—one parallel to the US-led coalition but less tortured by contradictory policy.[2] Like Iran, Russia wanted to defeat all "terrorists" that had waged war against Assad, and saw no distinction between ISIS, jihadist groups such as Nusra Front and Ahrar al-Sham, and other Syrian rebels. As much as Russia's involvement aided Iran, it also put it in an uncomfortable position. Iran's leaders had steadily maintained their independence in regional affairs. Iran remained an active proponent of the Non-Aligned Movement, and never strayed from the "neither East nor West" principle of its revolutionary creed. Iran's leaders had long called for foreign powers to leave the Middle East, and for Muslim states to handle regional security themselves. Acquiescing to Russian involvement in Syria seemed to fly in the face of Iran's do-it-yourself credentials. Unsurprisingly, President Rouhani rejected that Iran was part of any coalition with Russia, stressing that the two countries were pursuing complementary but different tracks of support to Damascus.[3]

Distancing Iran from Russia allowed Rouhani to reaffirm his country's independence in the conflict, but that notion contradicted the reality on the battlefield. The IRGC did not seem to share Rouhani's misgivings, and were less allergic to the concept of a coalition. Mohsen Rezai, who had announced a return to the IRGC in April 2015,[4] praised Russia's air campaign and the "coalition" against terrorism.[5] He further called on Muslim states to join the coalition of Iran, Hezbollah, Syria, Iraq, and Russia, to "cleanse the region of [ISIS] terrorists [and] bury the extremist group in Iraq and Syria."[6]

The Rouhani government maintained that Russian intervention was coordinated directly between Damascus and Moscow.[7] However, it is likely that the IRGC was involved in the process. Qassem Soleimani traveled to Moscow in late July 2015 and reportedly held several meetings with Russian counterparts during that visit. Both Iranian and US officials acknowledged the trip took place, which contravened the 2007 UN travel ban on Soleimani. An Iranian official claimed that Soleimani was in Russia to discuss regional issues and weapons sales.[8] Given Iran and Russia's shared interests, Syria would have been at the heart of these talks. Russia's military buildup began only a few weeks later.

Soleimani's visit to Russia came on the heels of gradual but mounting losses for the pro-Assad camp. Syrian rebels took the northern towns of Jisr al-Shughour and Idlib, including the regime's most important military base in the area, in April and May. Loyalist forces had crumbled under rebel pressure, exposing the fragility of their defenses. The Syrian army was depleted and exhausted. Its numbers had fallen from 300,000 before the war to less than 100,000 troops, and desertions were on the rise.[9] The United States had also stepped up its role in Syria. It provided air support to assist the Kurdish People's Protection Units (YPG)—the Syrian branch of the leftist Kurdistan Workers Party (PKK)—in defending the northeastern city of Kobane from a massive ISIS advance. Washington looked to expand that effort to help Kurds and certain Arab rebel groups advance toward ISIS's capital of Raqqa.[10] Assailed from all sides, and faced with increasing US involvement, the Assad regime was in a precarious position. A Damascus-based diplomat claimed that "the Iranians" prompted Russia to act, telling Moscow bluntly that, if it did not intervene soon, Assad would fall.[11]

Coinciding with Russia's intervention, pro-Assad forces prepared for a ground campaign aimed at retaking Aleppo, Hama, and Idlib. The IRGC reportedly sent hundreds of additional troops to aid in the effort.[12] The troop increase was acknowledged by Iranian officials. In an interview with the *Guardian*, Iran's deputy foreign minister, Hossein Amir-Abdollahian, stated that, while there was "no [Iranian] fighting force, as such" in Syria, Iran had "decided to increase the number of our military advisers to help the fight against terrorists." "The number of officers and advisers is not important," he continued. "What is important is an unwavering will to fight against terrorism."[13] General Joseph Dunford, the chairman of the Joint Chiefs of Staff, reported in late October that the United States estimated the number of Iranian troops to be less than two thousand in Syria and more than one thousand in Iraq.[14] If those numbers were accurate, the deployment of hundreds of additional soldiers would have been a significant increase.

This was an escalation for Iran. As loyalist ground advances began, the costs of the IRGC's amplified involvement became apparent. In early October, the IRGC announced that its top-ranking commander in Syria, Brigadier General Hosayn Hamedani, had been killed near Aleppo.[15] Soon the IRGC reported the loss of two more senior commanders, Brigadier General Farshad Hasunizadeh, former commander of the IRGC's elite special operations Saberin Brigade, and Brigadier General Hamid Mokhtarband, the former commander of the Hazrat-e Hojjat 1st Brigade Headquarters of Ahvaz.[16] These deaths were followed by dozens more in the month of October, making it the bloodiest period of the war for the IRGC. Abdollah Baqeri, a prominent bodyguard to former president Mahmoud Ahmadinejad, and a member of the Ansar al-Mahdi personnel protection unit, was among those killed.[17] The remaining dead came from various ranks and parts of the IRGC, including the Basij, and included junior- to mid-level officers. They brought the IRGC's death toll in Syria to nearly 160 since 2013.[18]

Iranian officials hailed their martyrs. They attended funerals and met with the families of the fallen. Many of the deaths in October coincided with the holy month of Muharram, and the commemoration of Imam Husayn's martyrdom on Ashura, which added a spiritual narrative and significance to their stories. The head of the IRGC public relations office, Brigadier General Ramezan Sharif, played on the Ashura theme and announced in late October that given changing circumstances and certain (unspecified) victories in Syria, the organization had decided to send additional troops to assist counterparts in "various parts of the country."[19] Brigadier General Hosayn Salami, the IRGC's deputy commander, admitted that the organization had suffered an uptick in casualties, but downplayed the number as "not that much."[20]

The IRGC stressed the strategic importance of Syria and the need to defeat "takfiri" terrorists in explaining its growing involvement. Brigadier General Salami described the IRGC's assistance to the Syrian military as taking place at four different levels: technical and logistical, strategic, operational, and tactical. In these areas, the IRGC was aiding counterparts in the use and deployment of weapons systems, helping modernize the Syrian military and develop the paramilitary National Defense Force, and assisting Syrian commanders in operational planning and war fighting. Salami maintained that Iranian soldiers were serving in only advisory capacities.[21] But in revealing the involvement of Iranians at the tactical level, the IRGC deputy commander implied a role for Iranian troops on the frontlines. The close proximity of the IRGC to the fighting—as advisors to ground unit commanders—partially explained the rising death toll. But it also suggested that IRGC soldiers where intimately involved in the war. Regardless of whether Iranians were pulling triggers or simply assisting others in pulling triggers, they were part of the fighting and being killed in the process.

Despite heavy losses, the Russian-Iranian escalation had changed the dynamics of international diplomacy on Syria. With the backing of Moscow, Iran was invited for the first time to take part in multilateral discussions aimed at finding a political solution to the war. The talks, held at the end of October in Vienna, Austria, brought together major powers with the main outside players of the conflict. Iran had previously been barred from Syrian talks and Saudi Arabia lobbied passionately to keep Iran from attending. One could imagine the frustration of the Saudis. Its main enemy, the country that it blamed for the chaos and sectarianism in the region, was being afforded a position of legitimacy and given a prestigious platform to advocate its interests. Iran's reversal of fortunes meant that Saudi policy had failed and that its influence with the West was no longer sufficient to keep its neighbor isolated. To add insult to injury, the Saudi foreign minister, Adel Al-Jubeir, would be sitting across the table from representatives of a regime that had plotted to assassinate him four years earlier.

Hostility between Riyadh and Tehran had never been higher. Beyond the wars in Syria and Iraq, sectarian violence against the Shia in Saudi Arabia and elsewhere in the Gulf was spiking, and the Saudi-led war against the Iran-allied Houthis in Yemen was having a massive humanitarian toll. In early October, Ali Shamkhani, secretary of the Supreme National Security Council, blasted the Saudis for an indiscriminate bombing campaign, and argued that the sheer scale of civilian deaths was evidence of Saudi war crimes.[22] The Saudis meanwhile blamed Iran for continuing to send arms to Yemen's Houthi movement. In late September, the Saudi-led coalition interdicted an Iranian-manned fishing boat off the coast of southern Oman and discovered a cache of weaponry, including dozens of anti-tank artillery shells.[23] A month later, the Saudi Defense Ministry released aerial surveillance video purporting to show its jets striking boats off the coast of western Yemen. The Saudis claimed the boats were Iranian and carrying weaponry destined for the Houthis.[24] Iranian authorities did not comment on the matter.

As wars raged across the region, millions of Muslims from around the world gathered in Saudi Arabia to take part in the annual hajj pilgrimage to Mecca and Medina. During one of the traditional rites of the hajj in Mina near Mecca, a horrific stampede occurred within the massive procession of pilgrims. Over 2,100 pilgrims, including at least 465 Iranians, were killed in the incident and the chaos that followed. The tragedy reminded Iranians of the 1987 hajj disaster, which left 287 Iranians dead, and provoked a similar vitriolic response. Iran's supreme leader demanded a Saudi apology, and declared that the issue would "not be forgotten."[25] IRGC chief, Ali Jafari, announced that the IRGC was prepared to respond to Saudi Arabia at any time and place, and pledged that his forces would "take revenge [on] the Al Saud for the terrible crime."[26]

In addition to the dead, over sixty-five Iranians remained unaccounted for. Among them were Ghazanfar Roknabadi, Iran's former ambassador to Lebanon, and other unnamed officials. During his tenure in Lebanon, Roknabadi was rumored to have been heavily involved in supporting Hezbollah and IRGC operations in Syria. That prominent role made him a target, including in the 2013 suicide bombing attack on Iran's embassy in Beirut, which killed Iran's cultural attaché and twenty-two others. Roknabadi's disappearance was shrouded in mystery and confusion. Despite Iran's claims to the contrary, Riyadh denied the former Iranian official had even entered the country. Iranian officials slammed what they saw as Saudi obfuscation and hinted at sinister intentions. Deputy foreign minister Hossein Amir-Abdollahian claimed that Roknabadi had been seen by witnesses being "transferred to a Saudi ambulance" after the stampede.[27] Hossein Noushabadi, a deputy minister of culture in the Iranian parliament, said that Iran was exploring the possibility that Roknabadi had been detained by Saudi authorities, explaining:

> The fact that Saudi officials denied that Roknabadi and other pilgrims were initially among the list of pilgrims landed in Saudi Arabia indicates that they probably know where Mr. Roknabadi and others are. . . . [No] trace whatsoever has been found of these diplomatic figures among the dead or injured; it is far too obvious that there is a plot and that the fate had been sealed for Roknabadi somewhere in the power corridors of the Saudi regime. . . . The [highest] probability, thus, is that Mr. Roknabadi is now in the hands of a Saudi security body.[28]

Roknabadi was eventually confirmed dead by the Saudis. His body, which had been buried soon after his death, was returned to Iran in late November. Details of his death were not released, but they did not really matter. The bitter rivalry between Saudi Arabia and Iran was destined to continue. Incompatible agendas, myopic sectarian policies, and personal enmities fueled the divide. With mistrust so pervasive, there would be little hope for mitigation. Regional conflict was the new normal.

# 13

# Conclusion

One of the central arguments of this book is that the IRGC has contributed to the construction of the Islamic Republic. In the introduction, I situated this issue within the broader discussion of militaries in the war-making/state-making nexus. I argued that conflict in all its forms is fundamental to both the development of armed forces and the political formation of states. I also explored the shifting perspectives on unconventional or irregular armed forces in these areas. As the IRGC's career has shown, armed forces do much more than make war. It is involved widely in the Iranian state—politically, socially, culturally, economically—beyond the confines of military activity. That broad participation has left an indelible imprint on the Islamic Republic.

The IRGC is a product of conflict. From its genesis in the contentious politics that birthed the Islamic revolution to the wars in Syria and Iraq, conflict in all its forms has molded the organization into what it is today. The same factors have helped shape the Islamic Republic. The previous chapters have explored these issues from a variety of angles. We began by discussing the gradual emergence of the Islamic movement in Iran. The anti-Western, anti-secular politics that were at the heart of that movement were likewise the foundation of the IRGC's emergence. At the core was the belief that enemy forces were trying to destroy Islam and Islamic culture. These spiritual, cultural, social, and political forces had to be defeated for Islam and Islamic Iran to flourish. This dynamic of conflict—militating against the amorphous threats to Islam—is what has defined the IRGC's mission of safeguarding the revolution. A role that presumes the revolution will always need defending and necessitates a perpetual threat.

Threats to the revolution exist within a broad spectrum. The IRGC has specific enemies—Israel and the United States in particular—but has also considered itself in contradistinction to any number of political ideas, movements, and policies. Vague notions such as anti-revolutionism, cultural invasiveness, liberalism, secularism, the Baha'i religion, and moral corruption have been used at various times to portray Islam's enemies. The IRGC perceives its self-interests to be synonymous with the sanctity of the revolutionary system. Much of the organization's role in conflict springs from its desire to defend its equities and values and those of the revolution. Conflict is therefore integral to the organization. From its beginnings, the IRGC engaged in acts of coercion to crush its enemies and marginalize rivals to Khomeini. Its antipathy for the Mojahedin-e Khalq and other Marxists fueled its early activism. It enabled the organization's involvement in political activism, law enforcement, and security. It was also the impetus for the organization's development of intelligence and information operations. Such capabilities became institutionalized within the organization and became the foundation for its vast intelligence apparatus and media empire.

The IRGC was still a fledgling entity when the war began. Provincial insurgencies (especially in the Kurdish regions) had thrust the organization into military operations soon after the revolution. The war accelerated its progression as a military. Early on, the IRGC remained in the shadow of the regular military, which was more trusted by the government and more able to operate complex vehicles, artillery, and aircraft. The IRGC was used mostly as an adjunct ground force. But through its political clout, the purge of rivals in the government, the support of prominent clergy, and boldness on the battlefield, the organization transformed into a leader within Iran's military sector. This position was further consolidated after the war. The patronage of the new supreme leader, Ali Khamenei, protected the IRGC from the reforms of President Rafsanjani, even as the latter opened the door to the organization's expansion into non-military industrial construction and lucrative state contracting. Khamenei's patronage was repaid through political support. The IRGC advocated for the supreme leader and the interests of his hardliner constituency at both the ground and top levels. When pro-democratic reformism appeared on the scene under President Khatami, the IRGC assertively moved to stomp it out. The organization proved adept at suppressing the reformist movement through various means and even threatened to overstep the president's authority during the 1999 student protests. The turmoil of this period helped determine a place for the Basij in the postwar. Its militiamen became the IRGC's foot soldiers in domestic political contests. The militia could be used as a cultural enforcer, a pressure group, an institution of indoctrination, and a source of grassroots activism. It became the IRGC's agent of culture war.

Regional conflicts similarly enabled the IRGC's development outside of Iran. The Lebanese civil war and the Israeli occupation of southern Lebanon gave the organization an opportunity to expand its support for allies in Lebanon into a sustainable clientage. With the establishment of Hezbollah and lasting contacts with Palestinian groups, the IRGC emerged as a player in the region's most enduring conflict. It could influence the larger Palestinian-Israeli issue through its Lebanese and Palestinian clients. This gave the IRGC and the Islamic Republic a foothold in an issue of paramount importance to Israel and the United States. In

the wars that followed both 9/11 and the Arab Spring, the IRGC looked to replicate that success in Iraq and Syria. Its instrument was the Quds Force, which
has gradually emerged as one of the most important levers of Iranian power and
influence. The Quds Force's ability to cultivate allies in these countries and elsewhere has helped Iran expand its interests in the region through largely covert
means. Iran relies on its client groups to outmaneuver those of its regional rivals
and put pressure on its enemies in the process. As the spearhead in that effort,
Quds has become a pillar of Iran's strategic and foreign policy.

Viewed holistically, it is evident that much of what the Islamic Republic has
become has been determined by its experience with conflict. Conflict has driven
the IRGC's institutionalization as a military, security service, political entity,
sociocultural force, covert operator, economic conglomerate, media mogul, and
mechanism of foreign and strategic policy. How the organization has chosen to
navigate conflict has in turn had a profound impact on the Islamic Republic. The
IRGC has been deeply entwined in the Islamic system since its emergence as
Khomeini's vanguard. Without it, the Islamic Republic would not have developed as it has nor function as it does. From the supreme leader's reliance on the
organization as a instrument of coercion and grassroots activism to the country's
dependence on covert operations in achieving foreign policy goals, the Islamic
Republic and its particular way of being have been shaped by and through the
IRGC. Ayatollah Khomeini famously claimed that had it not been for the IRGC
there would be no revolutionary Iran. In many respects that is true.

I have advocated for a more nuanced perspective on religion in the IRGC.
There is no doubt that the IRGC is a religious organization. Faith and tradition are vital to its identity, culture, and politics. The impact of religion on the
group, however, is not clear-cut or consistent. Religion is malleable. How it is
emphasized, when it is evoked, and to what degree it shapes behavior are all in
part determined by political factors. As a political organization, the IRGC's religious views are as much a product of organic orthodoxy as of the navigation of
context. Religion and politics are continuously negotiated. And while ideology
provides parameters, it too is subject to change over time. I have emphasized the
connection between faith and identity because that is one area where the impact
of religion is pronounced. Less obvious, but equally important, is how religion
and religious identity have affected other aspects of the organization's behavior.

The IRGC was established by religious militants in close association with
Shiite clergy. They emerged out of a larger tradition of pro-clerical activism in
Shiism. The use of religious activism toward political ends has remained a core
feature of the organization. The same impulse that brought clergy and militants
together to revolt against the Shah has animated the IRGC's grassroots political activities for the entirety of its career. In the postwar period, the Basij has
most exemplified the enduring importance of that ground-level effort. More

than being driven by that tradition, the IRGC became the mechanism of its expression. Through the IRGC, the multi-polar universe of pro-clerical activism in Iran was centralized under the supreme leader. This deprived provincial and local clerics resources of coercion and helped ensure that competitors to the supreme leader could not easily arise from within the traditional religious community. It did not end the development of personal support networks which prominent clergy still rely on, but it did remove the potential for these networks to challenge those patronized by the state. From this perspective, rather than an aberration, we can view the IRGC as an evolution of the cleric-adherent relationship in Shiism. Iran might be its birthplace, but, with the formation of similar militant bodies in Lebanon and Iraq, this model could also bloom in other Shiite societies.

The supreme leader is what makes such centralization possible. By placing one cleric above all others, Iran's theocratic system invested the leader with spiritual and political authority. Those elements of power fundamentally changed how the leader would be conceived by his followers. One's obedience to the leader might be derived as much by the consequences of disobedience than authentic fidelity, but these are distinctions made at the individual level. As an institution, the IRGC expresses its devotion to the leader in distinctly religious terms. Khomeini and Khamenei have both been referred to with the honorific of *imam*, which in Persian is an allusion to the divine authority of the twelve Shiite imams. The leaders have not been seen as equals to those immaculate beings, but their authority is derived from a similar divinity. In the absence of the Hidden Imam, Iran's supreme leaders occupy the highest realms of authority achievable within Shiite society. Because of its proximity to the leader and occupation as his chief defender, the IRGC is cloaked in that authority. The organization's activities are inherently sanctioned by the leader and thus touched with the same essence of sacredness that he represents. So long as the leader does not publically disagree with the organization, its actions are essentially unimpeachable within the context of Iran's system. It is unsurprising that the IRGC and its members have retained faith in the leader. He is the source of their power and their guiding light. The spiritual implications of this relationship are unique, and differentiate the IRGC from other contemporary state military organizations.

The current supreme leader's political authority is confined to Iran, but, as we have seen, some client organizations outside the country proclaim their allegiance to him (e.g., Lebanese Hezbollah and Iraq's Badr, Kataib Hezbollah, and Asaib Ahl al-Haq). The depth of their commitment is difficult to determine. Iran relies as much on these groups to advance its agenda as these groups rely on Iran for funding and material support. These are mutually beneficial relationships rooted in a shared religious culture. Although the leader's connection to non-Iranian clients is inherently different from his relationship with Iranian institutions, he is important. At the very least, he is a symbol used to mark their political allegiances, religious leanings, and worldview. Beyond that he is their principal sponsor and a religious authority who adds legitimacy to their actions.

That is an asset to Iran and a danger. The Islamic Republic's greatest successes of exporting the revolution have come through the development of client armed groups in Shiite societies. Shared religious identity is the foundation for these relationships. Shiism is the ether through which Iran's influence is most effectively transmitted. But while common identity has brought clients closer to Iran, it also defines their role in regional conflicts. Iran sees these conflicts as an opportunity to reset the power balance of its neighborhood. Exploiting religious tensions for political gain has worked for Iran *and* its rivals. The resulting sectarianism will have long-term implications that are uncertain and probably underappreciated by all players involved. Iran's enemies are increasingly Sunni Arabs. Its allies are all (with the exception of Palestinian groups) either Shiites or considered to be Shiite (i.e., Alawites in Syria and Zaydis in Yemen) by Sunnis. Whatever Iran's political aims, the end result is that it is on one side of a sectarian war. Even as religion has provided opportunities for the advancement of the Islamic Republic's influence, it is also a principal source of its alienation.

As conventional militaries gain strength within a state, they are often confronted with a choice: whether to submit to civilian authority and limit involvement in the state or expand involvement into areas of governance. The latter model typified much of the developing world during the Cold War, and remains the backdrop for states such as Egypt, Pakistan, and Burma. So far in its career the IRGC has avoided committing to either model. Although the organization wields influence and power, it has remained obedient to the supreme leader. Its relationship with the government has also been mostly complementary. Incidents such as the 1999 letter to President Khatami and possible election rigging in 2005 and 2009 show the IRGC's willingness to interfere in aspects of governance; but they also reveal the limits of how far it has been willing to go. In general, the IRGC appears comfortable working within Iran's theocratic system even as the supreme leader has had to balance its interests with those of other important constituencies and institutions (such as prominent clergy and the elected government). In other words, the IRGC might not always get its way but it gets it often enough.

However, this does not mean the IRGC's position is sustainable. The organization faces four serious challenges. The first is an inherent tension between the IRGC's interests and the shifting values of the Iranian people. As Iran's last two presidential elections have shown, the appetite for pro-democratic reforms remains strong within the civilian population. The passion for change was evident in the massive protests that followed the disputed re-election of Mahmoud Ahmadinejad in 2009. The election of Hassan Rouhani in 2013 returned

optimism to those who favor moderating Iran's system and its foreign relations, and exposed the unpopularity of the candidates preferred by the IRGC
(i.e., Saeed Jalili and Mohammad Baqer Qalibaf). Rouhani, despite not being a
reformist, has increased the expectations of the Iranian people. These expectations clash with the IRGC's interests. For example, the organization's expansive
role in Iran's economy is unpopular and has garnered criticism from President
Rouhani and others. Social issues are another area of contestation. The IRGC's
continuous push to limit the freedoms of the Iranian people runs counter to the
trends in Iranian society. Even as Iranians seek more engagement with each other
and the outside world through social media, the IRGC leads a cyber-monitoring
effort that has put regular Iranians in jail for their online activity. This type of
authoritarianism is familiar in Iran, but, as the Arab Spring has shown, authoritarianism does not guarantee stability. If the current trajectory holds, tension
between the desires of the public and those of the IRGC will increase.

This leads to the second challenge: the problem of peace. The threat posed
by the United States has been the backdrop for much of the IRGC's career. The
organization has relied on the United States to serve as an omnipresent boogeyman bent on destroying the revolution. If the Islamic Republic were to reach
a rapprochement with the United States, America would no longer be a viable
scapegoat for the repression of Iranians. Within that context, Iranians will expect
more out of life and more freedoms from the regime. An argument could be
made that a rapprochement with the United States would have an ameliorating effect on Iran's behavior both internally and externally. Some sectors of the
regime, such as the reformists, would probably favor such change. The IRGC
and the hardline camp likely would not. This is because the IRGC's status in
the country is contingent on the existence of existential threats to the Islamic
system. If the United States is no longer a problem, the IRGC will need to find
a suitable replacement. Threats will need to be found outside Iran and within.
The IRGC already sees the social and cultural arenas as a battleground between
it and anti-Islamic forces. The need for a threat could see the IRGC place more
emphasis on these issues—and other scapegoats such as religious minorities—
than it already does. This means further repression of the Iranian people at a time
when they will be expecting more liberty, not less.

Dealing with outside threats will continue to be a problem. Outwardly, wars
in the Middle East of the twenty-first century have benefitted Iran. They toppled
its nearest enemies (Saddam in Iraq and the Taliban in Afghanistan) and created
opportunities for it to expand influence. The IRGC has been the spearhead of
that influence, working for decades in support of Hezbollah, creating a clientage in post-Saddam Iraq, helping keep Assad in power in Syria, and playing a
leading role in the fight against ISIS. Those efforts have strengthened Iran's ties
to its allies in the region, increased its political sway, and given it mechanisms to

affect events on the ground. But this has not come without costs. Iran's influence resides in its relations with mostly non-Sunni Arab groups, which has caused extreme resentment within Sunni Arab publics. The virulent anti-Iranian, anti-Shia views of ISIS is one outcome of that antipathy. Tensions with Arab states is another. Arab capitals—particularly in the Persian Gulf—view Iran's regional efforts to be a thinly veiled attempt at empire building.[1] That is, through its clients in Iraq, Syria, and Lebanon, Iran is gradually establishing a contiguous zone of Shiite-dominated polities from its borders to the Mediterranean. They fear that Iran's push for supremacy will inevitably destabilize all countries in the region, especially Shiite-majority Bahrain, as well as Saudi Arabia and Kuwait, which have sizeable Shiite minority populations. Those states saw Yemen, where forces loyal to the Zaydi Shiite Ansar Allah organization (also known as the Houthis, an IRGC ally) ousted the Yemeni president in January 2015, as an example of Iran's expanding ambitions. The ruinous Saudi-led war against the Houthis, which began in March 2015, is a dangerous outgrowth of that anxiety.

More problematic is that Arab states increasingly see Middle East politics through the lens of sectarianism. Iran is viewed as a sectarian actor with a sectarian agenda. Shiites have become a Fifth Column. This is not good for Iran, the IRGC, or the region. While the IRGC is distracted by its efforts in Iraq and Syria it is not adequately taking into account the long-term implications those actions. Iran needs good relations with Arab states if it is to have peace and prosperity at home. Even if ISIS were to be defeated, so long as sectarianism remains acute, new foes with anti-Shiite, anti-Iranian agendas will emerge. With hatreds hardening on all sides, Iran's pursuit of victory could be as fraught with peril as the risk of defeat. Fighting these enemies will require the IRGC to expend increasingly more resources outside of Iran's borders. It will continue to drain resources from Iranian state coffers and require more lives be lost. The IRGC is well-positioned to offer assistance, but it risks becoming overextended financially and militarily. Enduring conflict also raises the risk of escalation with one of Iran's neighbors. Iran can ill-afford a war against another state. A regional cold war will similarly restrain Iran's potential for economic growth, and could encourage efforts of destabilization from its enemies (e.g., through proxy warfare, terrorism, funding of ethnic minority insurgencies, or international political pressure). The Islamic Republic's continuing conflict with Israel could be similarly destructive.

Finally, the inevitable death or replacement of the supreme leader poses another potential hazard for the IRGC. Khamenei and the IRGC have had a strongly symbiotic relationship. More than his predecessor, Khamenei has overseen the IRGC's rise. He enabled the organization's expansion beyond the military sector, courted its activism, and sanctioned its foreign adventurism. In return, the organization has remained submissive to his overall decision-making and been an advocate for his policies. The leader is essential to the IRGC's place in Iran's system, and the IRGC is the foundation of the leader's power. The next leader will have a choice of whether to continue this dynamic or begin to change it. Barring serious disruptions to Iranian political dynamics (such as a rapprochement with the United States or a full-fledged war), the next supreme leader will enter office politically weaker than Khamenei is now. He will need support and would likely seek it from either Khamenei's hardliner base (including the IRGC) or the Iranian people. If the next leader relies heavily on the IRGC, that could give it more say in policy. Alternatively, if the leader sought a more popular mandate and looked to distance himself from hardliners to garner the support of the people, this could decrease the IRGC's influence. In either scenario, the IRGC will be faced with a difficult decision: push its agenda or restrain its ambition to secure stability during the transition.

Both carry risks for the organization. A leader predisposed to the IRGC could encourage the organization to maximize its influence. This could lead to more repressive behavior and provoke the Iranian people or other marginalized constituencies. It could also draw Iran further into regional conflicts. A leader less amenable to the IRGC would pose a threat to its interests. Attempts to constrain its influence could entice the organization into activism either from below through the Basij and associated groups or at the leadership level. This would be similarly destabilizing to Iran during an already vulnerable period. Either way, the IRGC runs the risk of provoking unrest out of ambition or creating it out of fear. The IRGC's challenge will be finding a way to best preserve the status quo while ceding some of its aspirations to maintain stability. I do not believe overthrowing the leader or attempting to rule Iran as a military junta would be an option for the IRGC. The leader is fundamental to the IRGC's self-conception and legitimacy. Its strength is contingent on the potency of the leader in Iran's system and his support for the organization. The IRGC knows it needs the leader. But whether it knows it or not, it also needs the Iranian people.

# NOTES

## Chapter 1

1. There was a good deal of reporting on this incident in both foreign and Iranian press. The details in the narrative I provide are drawn from primarily these sources: *ABNA*, November 29, 2011, http://www.abna24.com/persian/281116/print.html; Julian Borger and Saeed Kamali Dehghan, "Storming of British Embassy in Tehran Worsens Bilateral Relations," *The Guardian*, November 29, 2011, http://www.theguardian.com/politics/2011/nov/29/british-embassy-attack-iran-uk-relations; Robert F. Worth and Rick Gladstone, "Iranian Protestors Attack British Embassy," *The New York Times*, November 29, 2011, http://www.nytimes.com/2011/11/30/world/middleeast/tehran-protesters-storm-british-embassy.html; *Asr-e Iran*, November 29, 2011, http://www.asriran.com/fa/news/191445/; Julian Borger, "Iran: Quds Force leader Is Developing a Cult Status," *The Guardian*, December 1, 2011, http://www.theguardian.com/world/2011/dec/01/iran-quds-force-leader-cult; *Fars News Agency*, November 29, 2011, http://www.farsnews.com/newstext.php?nn=13900906001125; *Fars News Agency*, November 30, 2011, http://www.farsnews.com/newstext.php?nn=13900909000340; *Digarban*, November 30, 2011, http://www.digarban.com/node/3447; *Jahan News*, November 30, 2011, http://jah-annews.com/vglaa0n6049nou,..544k1kh6.html; and, *Tabnak*, November 29, 2011, http://www.tabnak.ir/fa/news/207030.
2. *Digarban*, August 23, 2012, http://www.digarban.com/node/8618; also, *Pyknet*, December 3, 2011, http://www.pyknet.net/1390/04azar/12/index12.htm.
3. The term "Hajj" or "Hajji" is as an honorific used for a Muslim man who has fulfilled the faithful Islamic duty of performing pilgrimage to Mecca and Medina, the sacred land of Islam's birth.
4. Afshon Ostovar, "Iran's Basij: Membership in a Militant Islamist Organization," *The Middle East Journal* 67, no. 3 (Summer 2013).
5. Saied Golkar, "Paramilitarization of the Economy: The Case of Iran's Basij Militia," *Armed Forces & Society* 38, no. 4 (2012).
6. Ostovar, "Iran's Basij."
7. While only a few works focus on the IRGC exclusively, most studies on post-revolutionary Iran provide some discussion of the organization and its participation in Iranian society. However, it should be noted that a few studies on post-revolutionary Iran have included substantial discussion and valuable insights on the IRGC. See particularly, Ali Ansari, *Iran, Islam and Democracy: the Politics of Managing Change* (London: Chatham House, 2006); Anoushirvan Ehteshami and Mahjoob Zweiri, *Iran and the Rise of Its Neoconservatives: The Politics of Tehran's Silent Revolution* (London and New York: I. B. Tauris, 2007); and, Mehdi Moslem, *Factional Politics in Post-Khomeini Iran* (Syracuse: Syracuse University Press, 2002).
8. See for instance, Anthony H. Cordesman, *Iran's Military in Transition: Conventional Threats and Weapons of Mass Destruction* (West Port: Praeger, 1999).

9. Sepehr Zabih, *The Iranian Military in Revolution and War* (London and New York: Routledge, 1988).

10. Nikola B. Schahgaldian and Gina Barkhordarian, *The Iranian Military under the Islamic Republic* (Santa Monica, CA: RAND, 1987).

11. See James A. Bill's commentary in *Iranian Studies* 26, no. 3–4 (1993): p. 403.

12. See for example, Juan R. I. Cole and Moojan Momen, "Mafia, Mob, and Shiism in Iraq: The Rebellion of Ottoman Karbala, 1824–43," *Past and Present* no. 112 (August 1986): pp. 112–143.

13. Ibid.

14. See Stephen Kinzer, *All the Shah's Men*.

15. Roozbeh Safshekan and Farzan Sabet, "The Ayatollah's Praetorians: The Islamic Revolutionary Guard Corps and the 2009 Election Crisis," *The Middle East Journal* 64, no. 4 (2010); also, Elliot Hen-Tov and Nathan Gonzalez, "The Militarization of Post-Khomeini Iran: Praetorianism 2.0," *The Washington Quarterly* 34, no. 1 (Winter 2011).

16. On modern praetorianism see, Amos Perlmutter, *Politics and Military Rulers* (New York: Routledge, 2013).

17. For example, Alfoneh, *Iran Unveiled*.

18. On the comitatus, see Christopher I. Beckwith, *Empires of the Silk Road: A History of Central Eurasia from the Bronze Age to the Present* (Princeton: Princeton University Press, 2009).

19. Ibid.

20. Sussan Babaie, Kathryn Babayan, Ina Baghdiantz-McCabe, and Massumeh Farhad, *Slaves of the Shah: New Elites of Safavid Iran* (London: I. B. Tauris, 2004).

21. On the religious aspects of Safavid kingship, see Kathryn Babayan, *Mystics, Monarchs, and Messiahs: Cultural Landscapes of Early Modern Iran* (Cambridge, MA and London, England: Harvard University Press, 2002); also, Said Amir Arjomand, *The Shadow of God and the Hidden Imam: Religion, Political Order, and Societal Change in Shi'ite Iran from the Beginning to 1890* (Chicago and London: University of Chicago Press, 1984).

22. See Charles Tilly's *Coercion, Capital, and European States, AD 990–1990* (Cambridge: Basil Blackwell, 1990); "Armed Force, Regimes, and Contention in Europe since 1650," in *Irregular Armed Forces and Their Role in Politics and State Formation*, eds. Diane E. Davis and Anthony W. Pereira (Cambridge: Cambridge University Press, 2003), pp. 37–81; and "War Making and State Making as Organized Crime," in *Bringing the State Back In*, eds. Peter B. Evans et al. (Cambridge: Cambridge University Press, 1985), 169–191. Also see Michael Mann's *The Sources of Social Power, Volume I: A History of Power from the Beginning to A.D. 1760* (Cambridge: Cambridge University Press, 1986); and *The Sources of Social Power, Volume II: The Rise of Classes and Nation States, 1760–1914* (Cambridge: Cambridge University Press, 1993).

23. Miguel Centeno, "Limited War and Limited States," in *Irregular Armed Forces and Their Role in Politics and State Formation*, eds. Diane E. Davis and Anthony W. Pereira (Cambridge: Cambridge University Press, 2003), pp. 82–95.

24. See, Samuel Huntington, *The Soldier and the State: The Theory and Politics of Civil-Military Relations* (Cambridge: Harvard University Press, 1959); Alfred Vagts, *A History of Militarism* (New York: Free Press, 1973); Alain Rouquie, *The Military and the State in Latin America*, trans. Paul E. Sigmund (Berkeley: University of California Press, 1987); and Karen Remmer, *Military Rule in Latin America* (Boston: Unwin Hyman, 1989).

25. Diane E. Davis, "Contemporary Challenges and Historical Reflections on the Study of Militaries, States, and Politics," in *Irregular Armed Forces and Their Role in State Formation*, eds. Diane E. Davis and Anthony W. Pereira (Cambridge: Cambridge University Press, 2003), pp. 8–10.

26. Ibid., 394.

27. Davis and Pereira, *Irregular Armed Forces*, pp. 14–15.

28. William Reno, "The Changing Nature of Warfare and the Absence of State-Building in West Africa," in *Irregular Armed Forces*, pp. 322–345.

29. Davis and Pereira are not unique for their disregard of cultural and religious forces in state and political development. Both Tilly and Mann, for instance, were criticized for deemphasizing the roles of religion and culture in their theoretical models. See for example the critique of

Mann's theory in John A. Hall and Ralph Schroeder, eds., *An Anatomy of Power: The Social Theory of Michael Mann* (Cambridge: Cambridge University Press, 2006). For a critique of Tilly, see Jack Goldstone's review of *Coercion, Capital, and European States*, "States Making Wars Making States Making Wars . . .," *Contemporary Sociology* 20, no. 2 (March 1991): pp. 176–178.

30. They do, however, argue against the Cold War typologies that linked state ideologies such as capitalism and communism with regime types such as democracies and authoritarianism.

31. The ability of some of these groups to establish effective means and systems of governance has been noted by some scholars. For instance, on the Taliban, see Carter Malkasian, *War Comes to Garmser: Thirty Years of Conflict on the Afghan Frontier* (New York: Oxford University Press, 2013).

## Chapter 2

1. Speech by Abu Sharif (Abbas Aqa-Zamani) to members of the Revolutionary Guards, *Payam-e Enqelab*, no. 5, March 1980, pp. 36–38.

2. For useful scholarly overviews of Shiism, see Moojan Momen's *An Introduction to Shi'i Islam* (Oxford: George Ronald, 1985); and Heinz Halm, *Shi'ism*, 2nd ed., trans. Janet Watson and Marian Hill (New York: Columbia University Press, 2004). Also, for a sociological history of Shiism in Iran, see Said Amir Arjomand, *The Shadow of the Hidden Imam: Religion, Political Order, and Societal Change in Shi'ite Iran from the Beginning to 1890* (Chicago: The University of Chicago Press, 1984).

3. For an overview of these traditions, see Moojan Momen, *Shi'i Islam*, 12–17.

4. Ibn Hanbal, *Musnad*, vol. 4, p. 281. Translation provided in Momen, p. 15.

5. al-Bukhari, *Sahih*, Kitab al-'Ilm, Bab 40, vol. 1, p. 41. Translation provided in Momen, p. 15–16.

6. For a traditional Shiite understanding of this and other foundational events in Shiite history see S. Husain M. Jafri, *The Origins and Early Development of Shi'a Islam* (Oxford: Oxford University Press, 2002).

7. For an interpretive history on succession and early Shiism, see Wilferd Madelung, *The Succession to Muhammad: A Study of the Early Caliphate* (Cambridge & New York: Cambridge University Press, 1997).

8. This story did not begin to appear in descriptions of the battle of Karbala until several centuries after the fact. See for instance, Heniz Halm, *Shi'a Islam: From Religion to Revolution* (Princeton: Markus Weiner Publishers, 1999), pp. 15–16.

9. Colonel Sir Lewis Pelly, *The Miracle Play of Hasan and Husain: Collected from Oral Tradition*, vol. 1 (London: W. H. Allen and Co., 1879), pp. 66 and 88.

10. Also see Marshall G. S. Hodgson, "How Did the Early Shi'a Become Sectarian?" *Journal of the American Oriental Society* 75, no. 1 (1955): pp. 1–13.

11. Halm, *Shi'a Islam*, pp. 8–16.

12. On the Ashura commemoration, see Yitzhak Nakash, "An Attempt to Trace the Origin of the Rituals of 'Ashura,'" *Die Welt des Islams* 33 (1993): pp. 161–181.

13. S. H. M. Jafri, *The Origins and Early Development of Shi'a Islam* (Oxford: Oxford University Press, 2002), pp. 222–233.

14. Halm, *Shi'a Islam*, p. 20.

15. This is not to say that other political revolts did not occur. See S. A. Arjomand's *The Shadow of the Hidden Imam: Religion, Political Order, and Societal Change in Shi'ite Iran from the Beginning to 1890* (Chicago: University of Chicago Press, 1984).

16. Denis McEoin, "Aspects of Militancy and Quietism in Imami Shi'ism," *Bulletin (British Society for Middle Eastern Studies)* 11, no. 1 (1984), pp. 18–20.

17. Shaykh al-Mufid, *Kitab al-Irshad*. Translation provided in Halm, *Shi'a Islam*, p. 37.

18. Said Amir Arjomand has written extensively on the Shiite tradition of occultation and to responses to the absence of the Twelfth Imam. See for instance, S. A. Arjomand, "Imam Absconditus and the Beginnings of a Theology of Occultation: Imami Shi'ism Circa 280–90 A. H./900 A. D.," *Journal of the American Oriental Society* 117, no. 1 (January–March 1997), pp. 1–12; "The Consolation of Theology: Absence of the Imam and Transition from Chiliasm

to Law in Shi'ism," *The Journal of Religion* 76, no. 4 (October 1996), pp. 548–571; and, "The Crisis of the Imamate and the Institution of Occultation in Twelver Shiism: A Sociohistorical Perspective," *International Journal of Middle East Studies* 28, no. 4 (November 1996), pp. 491–515.

19. See Andrew J. Newman, *The Formative Period of Twelver Shi'ism* (Richmond: Curzon Press, 2000).

20. On the development of Shiite jurisprudence, see Devin J. Stewart, *Islamic Legal Orthodoxy: Twelver Shiite Responses to the Sunni Legal System* (Salt Lake City: University of Utah Press, 1998); Hossein Modarressi, *Crisis and Consolidation in the Formative Period of Shi'ite Islam: Abu Ja'far Ibn Qiba Al-Razi and His Contribution to Imamite Shi'ite Thought* (Princeton: Darwin Press, 1993); and, Etan Kohlberg, *Belief and Law in Imami Shi'ism* (Aldershot, Hampshire, Great Britain & Brookfield, VT, USA: Variorum; Gower Pub. Co., 1991).

21. See for instance, Said Amir Arjomand, *Shadow of the Hidden Imam*.

22. See Kathryn Babayan, *Mystics, Monarchs, and Messiahs: Cultural Landscapes in Early Modern Iran* (Cambridge, MA: Center of Middle Eastern Studies of Harvard University, 2002); also, Sholeh Quinn, *Historical Writing during the Reign of Shah Abbas: Ideology, Imitation, and Legitimacy in Safavid Chronicles* (Salt Lake City: University of Utah Press, 2000).

23. On the emigration of Arab Shiite scholars to Iran, see Riba Abisaab's *Converting Persia: Religion and Power in the Safavid Empire* (London: I. B. Tauris, 2004); also see Andrew J. Newman, "The Myth of the Clerical Migration to Safawid Iran: Arab Shiite Opposition to 'Ali Al-Karaki and Safawid Shiism," *Die Welt des Islams* 33 (1993): pp. 66–112.

24. For more on the role of Shiite scholars in Safavid Iran, see Arjomand, *Shadow of the Hidden Imam*, pp. 122–159.

25. On the spread of Shiism through popular culture in Iran during the Safavid period, see Kathryn Babayan's *Mystics, Monarchs, and Messiahs*.

26. See Meir Litvak, *Shi'i Scholars of Nineteenth-Century Iraq: The 'Ulama' of Najaf and Karbala*. Cambridge: Cambridge University Press, 1998.

27. For a comparative treatment of the institution of the Marja through the contemporary period, see Linda S. Walbridge, ed., *The Most Learned of the Shi'a: The Institution of the Marja' Taqlid* (Oxford: Oxford University Press, 2001).

28. The Shiite Qajar dynasty ruled Iran between 1796 and 1925.

29. Nikki R. Keddie, *Modern Iran: Roots and Results of Revolution* (New Haven: Yale University Press, 2003), p. 61.

30. See Nikki R. Keddie, *Religion and Rebellion in Iran: The Tobacco Protest of 1891–1892* (London: Cass, 1966); also, Hamid Algar, *Religion and State in Iran, 1785–1906: The Role of the Ulama in the Qajar Period* (Berkeley: University of California Press, 1980), pp. 184–221.

31. On the roots and development of political Islam, see Nikkie R. Keddie, *Sayyid Jamal Al-Din Afghani* (Berkeley: University of California Press, 1972); Immanuel Sivan, *Radical Islam: Medieval Theology and Modern Politics* (New Haven: Yale University Press, 1990); Brynjar Lia, *The Society of the Muslim Brothers in Egypt: The Rise of an Islamic Mass Movement 1928–1942* (Reading: Ithaca Press, 1998); Vali Nasr, *The Vangaurd of the Islamic Revolution: The Jama'at-i Islami of Pakistan* (Berkeley: University of California Press, 1994); and Gilles Kepel, *Jihad: The Trail of Political Islam* (Cambridge, MA: The Belknap Press of Harvard University Press, 2003).

32. On the constitutional revolution, see Mangol Bayat, *Iran's First Revolution: Shi'ism and the Constitutional Revolution of 1905–1909* (Oxford: Oxford University Press, 1991); also, Janet Afary, *The Iranian Constitutional Revolution, 1906–1911* (New York: Columbia University Press, 1996).

33. Translation provided in S. A. Arjomand, "Traditionalism in Twentieth-century Iran," in *From Nationalism to Revolutionary Islam*, ed. S. A. Arjomand (Albany: State University of New York Press, 1984), p. 201.

34. See Arjomand, "Traditionalism in Twentieth-century Iran."

35. On the rise and rule of the Pahlavi dynasty, see Homa Katouzian, *State and Society in Iran: The Eclipse of the Qajars and the Emergence of the Pahlavis* (London: I. B. Tauris, 2000); Cyrus Ghani, *Iran and the Rise of Reza Shah: from Qajar Collapse to Pahlavi Rule* (London: I. B. Tauris, 1998); Stephanie Cronin, ed., *The making of Modern Iran: State and Society under Riza Shah*

*1921–1941* (London: Routledge Curzon, 2003); Ervand Abrahamian, *Iran between Two Revolutions* (Princeton: Princeton University Press, 1982).

36. The best and most complete treatment of the life and career of Mohammad Reza Pahlavi is Abbas Milani's *The Shah* (New York: Palgrave MacMillan, 2011).

37. For the life and work of Khomeini, see Baqer Moin, *Khomeini: Life of the Ayatollah* (London: I. B. Tauris, 1999); also see Vanessa Martin, *Creating an Islamic State: Khomeini and the Making of a New Iran* (London: I. B. Tauris, 2003).

38. Ruhollah Khomeini, *Kashf-e Asrar* (1943). Translation provided in Arjomand, "Traditionalism in Twentieth-century Iran," p. 205.

39. Ibid.

40. Ibid.

41. See Moin, *Khomeini*.

42. See Nikki R. Keddie and Mark J. Gasiorowski, eds., *Neither East nor West: Iran, the Soviet Union, and the United States* (New Haven: Yale University Press, 1990); Miron Rezun, *Soviet Policy in Iran from the Beginnings of the Pahlavi Dynasty until the Soviet Invasion in 1941* (Alphen aan den Rijn: Sijthoff & Noordhoff International, 1981); Martin Sicker, *The Bear and the Lion: Soviet Imperialism and Iran* (New York: Praeger, 1988); and David B. Nissman, *The Soviet Union and Iranian Azerbaijan: The Use of Nationalism for Political Penetration* (Boulder: Westview Press, 1987).

43. Keddie, *Modern Iran*, p. 110.

44. For a detailed narrative of the AIOC and its impact on Iranian politics and society, see Stephen Kinzer, *All the Shah's Men: An American Coup and the Roots of Middle East Terror* (Hoboken: John Wiley and Sons, Inc.), 2003.

45. Interview in Kinzer, *All the Shah's Men*, p. 67.

46. See Homa Katouzian, *Musaddiq and the Struggle for Power in Iran*. (London: I. B. Tauris, 1990).

47. On the Fada'iyan-e Islam, see Adele K. Ferdows, "Religion in Iranian Nationalism: The Study of the Fadayan-i Islam" (PhD diss., Indiana University, 1967); Farhad Kazemi, "The Fada'iyan-e Islam: Fanaticism, Politics, and Terror," in *From Nationalism to Revolutionary Islam*, ed. S. A. Arjomand (Albany: State University of New York Press, 1984); Davud Salek, *Sevvomin parchamdar: Zendaginnameh-ye shahid Sayyed Mojtaba Navvab Safavi* (Tehran: hawzah-e honari, 1999); and Davud Amini, *Jam'iyat-e fada'iyan-i eslam va naqsh-e an dar tahavvulat-e siyasi-e ejtema'i-e Iran* (Tehran: entesharat-e markaz-e asnad-e enqelab-e eslami-e Iran, 2002).

48. Kazemi, "Fada'iyan-e Islam," p. 161.

49. Translation provided in Kazemi, "The Fada'iyan-e Islam: Fanaticism, Politics, and Terror," p. 162.

50. See Amini, *fada'iyan-e eslam*, pp. 314–316; also, Richard P. Mitchell, *The Society of Muslim Brothers* (New York and Oxford: Oxford University Press, 1993), p. 126, no. 60.

51. *Rahnema-ye Haqa'eq*, trans. A. K. Ferdows, p. 123.

52. For a detailed study on the 1953 coup d'état, see Mark J. Gasiorowski, "The 1953 Coup D'etat in Iran," *International Journal of Middle East Studies* 19, no. 3 (August 1987), pp. 261–286; also see Kinzer, *All the Shah's Men*.

53. See Ervand Abrahamian, *Iran between Two Revolutions*.

54. See Amini, *fada'iyan-i eslam*, pp. 322–339.

55. See Hamid Dabashi, *Theology of Discontent: The Ideological Foundation of the Islamic Revolution in Iran* (New York: New York University Press, 1993).

56. On Shariati's life, activism, and intellectual work, see Ali Rahnema, *An Islamic Utopian: A Political Biography of Ali Shariati* (London: I. B. Tauris, 2000).

57. Frantz Fanon, *Wretched of the Earth*, trans. Constance Farrington (New York: Grove Press, Inc., 1968), p. 61.

58. Ervand Abrahamian, "The Islamic Left: From Radicalism to Liberalism," in *Reformers and Revolutionaries in Modern Iran: New Perspectives on the Iranian Left*, ed. Stephanie Cronin (London: Routledge, 2004), p. 269.

59. Ali Shariati, *Red Shi'ism*, trans. Habib Shirazi (Tehran: Hamdani Foundation), p. 8.

60. See Shariati, *Red Shi'ism*.

61. Abrahamian, "The Islamic Left," p. 269.

62. See Rahnema, *An Islamic Utopian*, pp. 287–296.

63. Interview with Mohsen Makhmalbaf, in Hamid Dabashi's *Close Up: Iranian Cinema, Past, Present and Future* (New York and London: Verso, 2001), pp. 167–168.
64. For more on the history and ideology of the MKO, see Ervand Abrahamian's *Radical Islam: The Iranian Mojahedin* (London: I. B. Tauris, 1989); also, Kenneth Katzman, "The People's Mojahedin Organization of Iran," in *Iran: Outlaw, Outcast, or Normal Country?*, ed. Albert V. Benliot (Huntington: Nova Science Publishers, 2001).
65. The MKO became split during this period, resulting in competing Marxist-Maoist and Islamist revolutionary factions. See Abrahamian, *Mojahedin*, pp. 145–169; also, regarding the release of MKO members from prison in the build up to the 1979 revolution, see 170–185.
66. See Mohammad G. Majd, *Resistance to the Shah: Landowners and Ulama in Iran* (Gainesville: University Press of Florida, 2005).
67. Ruhullah Khomeini, *Islam and Revolution: Writings and Declarations of Imam Khomeini (1941–1980)*, trans. Hamid Algar (North Haledon: Mizan Press, 1981), pp. 177–180.
68. On Khomeini's political thought, see Ervand Abrahamian, *Khomeinism: Essays on the Islamic Republic* (Berkeley: University of California Press, 1993).
69. Ibid., pp. 62–63.
70. Ibid., p. 149.
71. Abrahamian, *Khomeinism*, p. 31.

## Chapter 3

1. Khomeini's January 1979 interview with Giancesare Flesca in Neauphle-le-Château, France. See "Khomeini Comments on Islamic Republic, Gas, Oil," *L'Espresso* in Italian, January 28, 1979, in *FBIS-MEA*, February 7, 1979.
2. Khomeini's March 9, 1979 speech in Qom, see "Khomeyni Speech at Qom Cemetery," *Tehran Domestic Service in Persian*, in *FBIS-MEA*, March 9, 1979.
3. Arjomand, *Turban*, pp. 114–119.
4. Reports differ on the precise number killed at Jaleh Square.
5. Andrew Scott Cooper, "Declassified Diplomacy: Washington's Hesitant Plans for a Military Coup in Pre-revolution Iran." *The Guardian*, February 11, 2015, http://www.theguardian.com/world/iran-blog/2015/feb/11/us-general-huysers-secret-iran-mission-declassified.
6. Zabih, *Military*, pp. 69–78.
7. Nikki Keddie argues that the Homafaran and leftist guerilla groups were the chief elements in the military victory of the revolution. See *Modern Iran: Roots and Results of Revolution* (New Haven and London: Yale University Press, 2003), p. 238. Also see S. A. Arjomand, *The Turban for the Crown: The Islamic Revolution in Iran* (New York & Oxford: Oxford University Press, 1988), pp. 124–127.
8. Arjomand, *Turban*, pp. 124–127.
9. Alireza Mahfoozi, in an interview recorded by Zia Sedghi, April 7, 1984. Paris, France. Iranian Oral History Collection, Harvard University, p. 19.
10. Zabih, *Military*, p. 73.
11. In a February 2008 interview with the Persian daily *Hamshahri* in Tehran, Ayatollah Ali Akbar Hashemi Rafsanjani states that Khomeini ordered the establishment of the Revolutionary Council in the months leading up to the revolution, and that its original members were Ayatollah Motahhari, Ayatollah Beheshti, Ayatollah Musavi-Ardebili, Hojjat al-Islam Bahonar, and Rafsanjani himself. He also mentions that Khomeini intended that additional members should be added to these five, but does not mention any names. Shaul Bakhash lists these individuals as: Abolfazl Zanjani, Mehdi Bazargan, Ibrahim Yazdi, Yadollah Sahabi, Ahmad Sadr Hajj Seyyed Javadi, Kazem Sami, Ezzatollah Sahabi, Mostafa Katiriai, Naser Minachi, Aali Nasab, Hajj Kazem Hajji Tarkhani, Lieutenant General Ali-Asghar Mas'ud, and Lieutenant General Valiollah Qarani. See interview with Akbar Hashemi Rafsanjani, *Hamshahri*, in *FBIS*, February 19, 2008.
12. Arjomand, *Turban*, pp. 134–136; Also see Shaul Bakhash, *The Reign of the Ayatollahs: Iran and the Islamic Revolution* (New York: Basic Books, 1984), p. 51.
13. The army in particular suffered great losses. Major General Qarani, the army's Chief of Staff under the Provisional Government, commented on this point on February 20: "I inherited an army which in Tehran did not contain even one soldier, and which, because of treachery

by some of the former military leaders, had its barracks emptied of arms and in most cases destroyed by fire." See "Qarani on Army's Disintegration," Tehran Domestic Service in Persian, February 20, 1979, in *FBIS-MEA*, February 21, 1979.

14. *Sepah dar gozar-e enqelab: majmu'eh-ye ettela'iyeh, bayaniyeh, akhbar va . . .sepah.* Jeld-e avval. Tehran: Mo'avenat-e ravabet-e 'omumi va entesharat-e sepah, 2011, pp. 49–50. On the unification of IRGC's early command, see Ali Alfoneh, *Iran Unveiled: How the Revolutionary Guards Is Turning Theocracy in Military Dictatorship* (Washington, DC: AEI Press, 2013), pp. 10–14.

15. "Tehran Communications, Mosque Attacked," Tehran Domestic Service in Persian, February 14, 1979, in *FBIS-MEA*, February 15, 1979.

16. Ibid and Dasht-e Qazvin Transmitter Besieged," Tehran Domestic Service in Persian, February 14, 1979, in *FBIS-MEA*, February 15, 1979.

17. "Palestinian Report on Iran," *BBC World Summary of Broadcasts*, February 9, 1979.

18. Emphasis added. "Khomeyni Calls on Soldiers," Tehran Domestic Service in Persian, February14, 1979, in *FBIS-MEA*, February 15, 1979.

19. "Guardian Corps to Be Established," Tehran Domestic Service in Persian, February 21, 1979, in *FBIS-MEA*, February 21, 1979.

20. Ibid. Without the original Persian transcript of this interview, it is impossible to know whether the term translated as "corps" by FBIS was indeed the Persian "*sepah*" or not; however, it is reasonable to assume it was.

21. "Bazargan Addresses Nation on Government Problems," Tehran Domestic Service in Persian, February 28, 1979, in *FBIS-MEA*, March 2, 1979.

22. "Guards Operations Commander Interviewed," Beirut *As-Safir* in Arabic, December 1, 1979, in *FBIS-MEA*, December 4, 1979.

23. Ibid.; "Khomeyni Calls on Soldiers," Tehran Domestic Service in Persian, February 14, 1979, in *FBIS-MEA*, February 15, 1979.

24. "More on Entezam," Tehran Domestic Service in Persian, March 4, 1979, in *FBIS-MEA*, March 5, 1979.

25. Ibid.

26. For instance, in Entezam's April 8 press conference, he says: "As long as the army of the revolutionary guards has not been properly formed and has not started its activities, the weapons will not be collected up. . . . The revolutionary guards have been recruited under regulations similar to those used in the armed forces and are at the moment being trained." See "Amir Entezam's 8th April News Conference," *BBCSWB*, April 10, 1979.

27. Schahgaldian lists several individuals (including civilian leaders and clergy) who controlled personal armed contingents associated with the Revolutionary Guards. See Schahgaldian, *Iranian*, pp. 65–67.

28. "PLO Delegation to Mashhad," March 23, 1979, in *FBIS-MEA*, March 27, 1979.

29. "Navy Arrests Escapees," Abadan International Service in Arabic, March 5, 1979, in *FBIS-MEA*, March 6, 1979.

30. "Revolutionary Guards' Announcement," Tehran Domestic Service in Persian, March 24, 1979, in *FBIS-MEA*, March 27, 1979. The coverage of this story by the BBC includes a transliteration of the term "Command Headquarters," however I altered their rendering to conform to the style used in the present study. See "Iran: In Brief; Appeal to inform on 'counter-revolutionary elements,'" *BBCSWB*, March 21, 1979.

31. See Ali Danesh Monfared, *Khaterat-e Ali Danesh Monfared*, ed. Reza Bastami. (Tehran: Markaz-e esnad-e enqelab-e eslami, 2005), p. 91. Monfared, the Guards' lead commander at the time, specifically mentions that Taleqani's wife was a "non-Iranian," which apparently added to the suspicions surrounding the Marxist activist. See also, Rafiqdust, *Khaterat*, p. 174.

32. Mojtaba Taleqani began his activist career as a member of the MKO, but later (in 1975) split from the organization on ideological grounds. He discusses his embrace of Marxist ideology and the inadequacy of Islam as a revolutionary doctrine in a letter to his father (c.1975). For the text of the letter, see Abrahamian, *Mojahedin*, pp. 157–162.

33. Mehdi Saidi, *Sazman-e mohjadein-e enqelab-e eslami: Az tasis ta enhellal (1357–1365)* (Tehran: Markaz-e Asnad-e Eslami, 2007), p. 85.

34. "Protest Leader Marks Open Split on Iran's Policies," *The Globe and Mail*, April 16, 1979.

35. Abrahamian refers to this incident as "the first skirmish" between leftist organizations (especially the MKO) and the Khomeinist wing of the post-revolutionary regime. See, Abrahamian, *Mojahedin*, p. 190.

36. "Iranian Islamic Revolutionary Council's Call for Taleqani's Return," *BBCSWB*, April 16, 1979.

37. "Khomeini Orders Revolutionary Committees Purged," *The Washington Post*, April 20, 1979, Final edition.

38. "Remarks by Khomeyni on the Future of Revolutionary Committees," *BBCSWB*, April 21, 1979.

39. "Iran: In Brief; Chief Public Prosecutor's Announcement (text)," *BBCSWB*, April 17, 1979.

40. "Amir Entezam's 19th April Press Conference," *BBCSWB*, April 21, 1979.

41. "Bazargan's 24th April Address to the Iranian People," *BBCSWB*, April 26, 1979.

42. Ibid.

43. "The Islamic Revolution Guards Corps," *BBCSWB*, May 9, 1979.

44. For instance, numerous MIR activists, such as Mortaza Alviri and Hasan Hamidzadeh, simultaneous held positions of responsibility in the IRGC, the committees, and in MIR. See Saidi, *Sazman*, p. 89.

45. Schahgaldian, *Iranian*, pp. 65–67.

46. Mohsen Rafiqdust, *Khaterat-e Mohsen Rafiqdust*, vol. 1, ed. Davud Qasempur (Tehran: Markaz-e esnad-e enqelab-e eslami, 2004), pp. 174–182. Rafiqdust singles out Hajj Aqa Jaber-Ansari as a key individual who helped financially support the IRGC during this period. Also see Monfared, *Khaterat*, pp. 87–88.

47. "Revolutionary Guards Corps Established in Iran," Tehran Domestic Service in Persian, May 5, 1979, in *FBIS-MEA*, May 7, 1979. This announcement followed a similar declaration by Ayatollah Khomeini, which was published in the revolutionary newspaper *Enqelab-e Eslami* (Tehran) on May 6, 1979. See Sepehr Zabih, *The Iranian Military in Revolution and War* (London and New York: Routledge, 1988), p. 225, no. 3.

48. Rafiqdust, *Khaterat*, p. 174.

49. Ibid.

50. Ibid., p. 175.

51. Ibid.

52. Ibid.

53. Ibid., p. 176.

54. Abu Sharif and Ali Duzduzdani were both early leaders of the hezbollahi movement in Iran.

55. Also see Alfoneh, *Iran Unveiled*, pp. 7–10.

56. Rafiqdust, *Khaterat*, p. 181.

57. Ibid.

58. Katzman makes a similar argument, suggesting MIR played a "crucial role" in the formation of the IRGC. See Katzman, *Warriors*, pp. 32–34.

59. Saidi, *Sazman*, p. 89.

60. Ibid.; Makhmalbaf interview, pp. 179–182.

61. Saidi, *Sazman*, p. 89.

62. "Amir Entezam's 8th April News Conference," *BBCSWB*, April 10, 1979. In this press conference, Entezam states, "The Mojahedin of the Islamic Revolution is part of the organization of the revolutionary guards."

63. "Iran: In Brief; The Aims of the Mojahedin," *BBCSWB*, April 10, 1979.

64. *Badr* means "full moon," but in this instance it is likely a reference to the first major battle between the Muslims and the Meccans at Badr (north of Mecca) in 624 CE.

65. For a social and intellectual history of the MKO, see Ervand Abrahamian's *Radical Islam: The Iranian Mojahedin* (London: I. B. Tauris, 1989). On the group's post-revolutionary development, see Kenneth Katzman, "The People's Mojahedin Organization of Iran," in *Iran: Outlaw, Outcast, or Normal Country?*, ed. Albert V. Benliot (Huntington: Nova Science Publishers, 2001). Also, on the group's connection to Ali Shariati, see Ali Rahnema, *An Islamic Utopian: A Political Biography of Ali Shariati* (London: I. B. Tauris, 2000).

66. See, for example, the reflections of Makhmalbaf in Hamid Dabashi's *Close Up: Iranian Cinema, Past, Present and Future* (London and New York: Verso, 2001), pp. 164–181.

67. Maziar Behrooz, "The Revolution and the Guerilla Movement," in *Reformers and Revolutionaries in Modern Iran: New Perspectives on the Iranian Left*, ed. Stephanie Cronin (London: Routledge, 2004); and Abrahamian, *Mojahedin*, p. 201.

68. Behrooz, "Guerilla Movement," pp. 201–202.

69. Makhmalbaf interview, p. 173.

70. Ibid., p. 173–178.

71. Ibid., p. 173–174.

72. Ibid., p. 178.

73. Katzman, *Warriors*, pp. 31–32. Also, see Mohsen Rezai's official biography, *Zendegi-e doktor-e Mohsen Reza'i dar yek negah*, www.rezaee.ir.

74. Ibid.

75. Alfoneh, *Iran Unveiled*, pp. 9–10.

76. Saidi, *Sazman*, p. 79–80. Also, Abrahamian, *Mojahedin*, p. 211.

77. For more on the graphic elements and meanings of the MKO's emblem, see Abrahamian, *Mojahedin*, pp. 102–103.

78. Michael M. J. Fischer and Mehdi Abedi suggest that the usage of the "*la*" negative article in this form is influenced by Ali Shariati and his publications, which bore the negative article "on the cover of all of his books and published lectures." See Fischer and Abedi, *Debating Muslims: Cultural Dialogues in Postmodernity and Tradition* (Madison: The University of Wisconsin Press, 1990), p. 344.

79. Q: 25:57 ". . . so that men may stand by justice . . ."

80. The IRGC's emblem will be discussed in a later chapter.

81. "Le Monde: Antileft Feeling Heightens in Iran," Paris, *Le Monde* in French, May 5, 1979, in *FBIS-MEA*, May 11, 1979.

82. "Iran: In Brief; Those Responsible for Gharani's Murder," *BBCSWB*, April 26, 1979.

83. "Khomeini Vows Deaths Will Not Hold Iran Back," *The Washington Post*, May 3, 1979.

84. Ayatullah Murtaza Mutahhari, *Fundamentals of Islamic Thought: God, Man and the Universe*, trans. R. Campbell (Berkeley: Mizan Press, 1985), p. 56.

85. "Iranian Rightists Break Up Play; Attack Playwright and Audience," *The Globe and Mail*, May 17, 1979.

86. "Leading Iranian Newspaper Shuts after Attack by Khomeini," *The Washington Post*, May 13, 1979.

87. "Iranian Rightists Break Up Play; Attack Playwright and Audience," *The Globe and Mail*, May 17, 1979.

88. "Khomeini Blames U.S. for Assault on Aid," *The Washington Post*, May 27, 1979.

89. "Ayatollah, Aid of Khomeini, Shot in Tehran; Moslems, Leftists, Clash at U.S. Embassy," *The Washington Post*, May 26, 1979.

90. Ibid.

91. In a June 4 interview, MKO leaders Masud Rajavi and Mansur Mansuri articulated their support for Khomeini: "Ayatollah Khomeini is the guide of the revolution and we have a good relationship with him . . . [He is] a guide and a strong uncompromising leader against imperialism." See "Mujahidin Khalq Leaders on Relations with Authorities, U.S," *An-Nahar al-'Arabi wa ad-Duwali* in Arabic, June 4, 1979, in *FBIS-MEA*, June 8, 1979.

92. "Constitution for Cherikha-ye Feda'i-ye Khalq Proposed," *Kayhan* in Persian, in *FBIS-MEA*, May 27, 1979.

93. Mahfoozi acknowledges that the Fadai worked with Turkmen farmers on these issues and helped establish councils to push for land reform. However, he denies that the Fadai armed the Turkmen. See Alireza Mahfoozi interview, pp. 8–9.

94. "Khomeyni Representatives to Form Guards Corps in Ahvaz," Tehran Domestic Service in Persian, May 10, 1979, in *FBIS-MEA*, May 11, 1979; "Khuzestan Revolutionary Guardians Corps to be Established," Tehran, *Keyhan* in Persian, May 17, 1979, in *FBIS-MEA*, June 5, 1979; "Kermanshahan Guards Corps Being Formed," Tehran Domestic Service in Persian, May 17, 1979, in *FBIS-MEA*, May 23, 1979. On the clashes, see "Iran Arabs, Khomeini Forces Clash Violently; Arabs Seeking Autonomy Clash Violently with Khomeini Forces," *The Washington Post*, May 31, 1979; "Armed Men Attack Kermanshah Revolutionary Court," Baghdad INA in Arabic, in *FBIS-MEA*, June 8, 1979.

95. Ibid.
96. "Criticism of Baghdad Radio," Tehran in Arabic for abroad, June 2, 1979, *BBCSWB*, June 4, 1979.
97. "Iran Premier Calls Leftists Traitors to Islamic Regime," *The Globe and Mail*, July 3, 1979.
98. The Guards began releasing statements during this period calling on the public to disarm and for citizens to inform the local IRGC of those who refused to turn in their weapons. For example, the newly established Guards unit of Qazvin released this statement in early July 1979: "It [the IRGC of Qazvin] thereby wishes to inform all those who bear arms, whether they be ordinary individuals or the former city guards, that in the next 48 hours they should hand over their weapons to the staff of the Islamic Revolutionary guards of the city of Qazvin, on Sa'di Avenue, next to Dispensary No.1; otherwise they will be dealt with in accordance with the regulations." See "Qazvin City Guards Replaced by Revolutionary Guards," Tehran Domestic Service in Persian, July 11, 1979, in *FBIS-MEA*, July 12, 1979.
99. This included the major leftist-Islamist MKO, whose leadership, in a 4 June interview with an Arab journalist, said: "Since the imperialist interests have not been touched, we will not give up our arms." See "Mujahidin Khalq Leaders on Relations with Authorities, U.S.," Paris *An-Nahar al-Arabi wa ad-Duwali* in Arabic, in *FBIS-MEA*, June 8, 1979.
100. "Measures Reported Following Attack on Qom Guards Center," Tehran Domestic Service in Persian, July 7, 1979, in *FBIS-MEA*, July 12, 1979.
101. "Mojahedin-e Khalq Wants Open Talks on Arms-Carrying," *Ettela'at* in Persian, August 27, 1979, in *FBIS-MEA*, September 6, 1979.
102. Ibid. Even though the MKO suggested they would abide by Khomeini's decision, they clearly intended to remain armed. The MKO state "the decision of the imam [*sic*] and the government is the one by which our organization will ultimately abide especially as we are confident that they will never allow us to remain undefended against the threats of the people's enemies, imperialism's helpers, and SAVAK, who have pursued us for years."
103. Ibid.
104. "Bazargan's 1st August Message to the Nation," Tehran Home Service in Persian, August 1, 1979, *BBC Summary of World Broadcasts*, August 3, 1979.
105. *The Associated Press*, August 7, 1979, p.m. cycle.
106. Abrahamian, *Mojahedin*, p. 195.
107. *The Associated Press*, August 13, 1979, a.m. cycle.
108. *The Associated Press*, August 14, 1979, a.m. cycle.
109. "Revolution Guards to Insure Security at Friday Prayers," Tehran Domestic Service in Persian, September 13, 1979, in *FBIS-MEA*, September 14, 1979.
110. "Montazeri Interviewed on Muslim Solidarity, Gulf Ties," Paris *An-Nahar al-'Arabi wa ad-Duwali* in Arabic, October 22–28, 1979, in *FBIS-MEA*, October 29, 1979.
111. "Abadan Guards Fast in Support of Palestinians," Abadan Domestic Service in Persian, October 15, 1979, in *FBIS-MEA*, October 17, 1979.
112. "Army Chief Comments," Tehran Domestic Service in Persian, September 3, 1979, in *FBIS-MEA*, September 4, 1979.
113. "Guards Commander Outlines Plan for Taking Mahabad," Tehran Domestic Service in Persian, October 25, 1979, in *FBIS-MEA*, October 26, 1979.
114. "U.S. Embassy Held by Iranian Students in Bid to Get Shah," *The Globe and Mail*, November 5, 1979.
115. Katzman, *Warriors*, pp. 36–37. Katzman specifically mentions MIR's Behzad Nabavi and IRGC commander Javad Mansuri as having possible links with this student group.
116. Arjomand, *Turban*, p. 139.
117. On the constitutional debates and the role played by Khomeinist-aligned clergy during this process, see Bakhash, *Ayatollahs*, pp. 75–88.
118. Arjomand, *Turban*, p. 139.
119. Bakhash, *Ayatollahs*, p. 89.
120. Arjomand, *Turban*, pp. 139–141.
121. Ibid., p. 139.

## Chapter 4

1. "Khomeyni's 26th September Message to Iranians and Iraqis," Tehran in Arabic for abroad, September 27, 1980, *BBC Summary of World Broadcasts*, October 1, 1980.
2. S. P. Mackenzie, *Revolutionary Armies in the Modern Era: A Revisionist Approach* (London: Routledge, 1997), p. 2.
3. Abol Hassan Bani-Sadr, *My Turn to Speak: Iran, the Revolution & Secret Deals with the U.S.* (New York: Brassey's, 1991), p. 74. Also see Axeworthy, p. 192.
4. "Khomeyni's 26th September Message."
5. Ibid.
6. The successes of Iran's air force during the war is one of the less appreciated facets of the Iran-Iraq conflict. Michael Axeworthy stresses this point in *Revolutionary Iran*, pp. 189–202 (passim). Also see Tom Cooper and Farzad Bishop, *Iran-Iraq War in the Air, 1980–88* (Atglen, PA: Schiffer Military History, 2000); and Tom Cooper and Farzad Bishop, *Iranian F-14 Tomcat Units in Combat* (Oxford: Osprey Publishing, 2004).
7. Bani-Sadr, *My Turn*, p. 74.
8. *A Glance at Two Years of War* ([Tehran?]: Islamic Revolution's Guards Corps [Political Office]), 1982, pp. 40–41.
9. "Iranian Revolutionary Guards' Military Communique," Tehran home service, October 30, 1980, *BBC Summary of World Broadcasts*, November 1, 1980.
10. For example, see "Iranian Revolutionary Guards' Military Communique," Tehran home service, October 30, 1980, *BBC Summary of World Broadcasts*, November 1, 1980. Although the Iranians and Iraqis routinely exaggerated the successes and minimized the losses of their operations throughout the war for propaganda purposes, descriptions of the tactics used in (but not necessarily the outcomes of) these limited operations early in the war were less embellished.
11. *Two Years of War*, p. 42.
12. For Ali Shamkhani's letter, see Mehdi Ansari et al., *Khorramshahr dar jang-e tulani* [*Khorramshahr during the Long War*], vol. 3 (Tehran: Markaz-e Asnad-e Dafaʾ-e Moqaddas [Sepah-e Pasdaran-e Enqelab-e Eslami], 2008), p. 454.
13. "Ragged Iranian Fighters in Khurramshahr," *The New York Times*, October 6, 1980.
14. Ibid.
15. Yahya Rahim Safavi, *Az jonub-e lobnan ta jonub-e iran: Khaterat-e sardar-e Sayyed Rahim Safavi*, ed. Majid Najafpour (Tehran: Markaz-e Asnad-e Enqelab-e Eslami, 2004), p. 260.
16. Ibid., pp. 223–224.
17. Ibid., pp. 262–263.
18. The Supreme Defense Council was established on October 13, 1980.
19. O'Ballance, *Gulf War*, pp. 62–63.
20. See interview with retired Iraqi Major General Aladdin Hussein Maki Khamas, November 11, 2009, in Kevin M. Woods et al., *Saddam's Generals: Perspectives of the Iran-Iraq War* (Alexandria, VA: Institute for Defense Analyses, 2011), p. 132.
21. "Montazeri Preaches against US and Jewish 'Plots' in Iran," Tehran home service, December 5, 1980, *BBC Summary of World Broadcasts*, December 8, 1980.
22. "Resolution Issued by Shiraz Revolution Guards," Shiraz regional in Persian, February 21, 1981, *BBC Summary of World Broadcasts*, February 25, 1981.
23. IRGC Political Office, *Two Years of War*, p. 65.
24. "Montazeri Questions Iran's War Tactics: Message to Ahvaz," Tehran home service, December 31, 1980, *BBC Summary of World Broadcasts*, January 3, 1981.
25. "Islamic Clerics Denounce Bani-Sadr over Conduct of the War with Iraq," *The New York Times*, January 5, 1981.
26. O'Ballance, *Gulf War*, p. 67.
27. O'Ballance, *Gulf War*, p. 40.
28. O'Ballance, *Gulf War*, p. 58.
29. O'Ballance, *Gulf War*, p. 59.
30. Arjomand, *Turban*, p. 145.
31. *Payam-e Enqelab*, no. 59, May 29, 1982, p. 73.
32. David Menashri, *Iran: A Decade of War and Revolution* (New York: Holmes & Meier, 1990), p. 179.

33. "Purge of Revolutionary Guards Called for in Khomaini Speech," *The Globe and Mail* (Canada), April 2, 1981.
34. The IRGC unit in Garmsar was temporarily closed in December 1980 for this reason. See "Suspension of Garmsar Revolution Guards Unit," Tehran home service, December 1, 1980, *BBC Summary of World Broadcasts*, December 4, 1980.
35. The problem of IRGC transgressions was ongoing, as were attempts to deal with it. The issue was commonly raised by Iran's leadership, such as in this January 1982 statement by then President Ali Khamenei, addressed to senior IRGC commanders: "To recognize the main and true status and position of the corps and to act within the duties allocated to the corps—no more and no less. Interfering in the duties of others is not in the interests of any revolutionary institution or foundation. The corps should not act outside the limits of the duties allocated to it." See "Iranian President's Advice to the Revolution Guards Corps," Tehran home service, January 19, 1982, *BBC Summary of World Broadcasts*, January 21, 1982.
36. Abrahamian, *Mojahedin*, pp. 216–217.
37. Bakhash, *Ayatollahs*, pp. 162–165; also, Menashri, *Iran*, pp. 180–181.
38. "Revolution Guard's Statement on Tehran Clashes: 'Anti-Islamic Groups,'" Tehran home service, June 20, 1981, *BBC Summary of World Broadcasts*, June 22, 1981.
39. Arjomand, *Turban*, pp. 169–170.
40. Abrahamian, *Mojahedin*, pp. 220–222.
41. Bakhash, *Ayatollahs*, pp. 236–239.
42. Abrahamian, *Mojahedin*, pp. 243–261; also, Katzman, "People's Mojahedin."
43. *Two Years of War*, pp. 63–64.
44. O'Ballance, 67.
45. Hiro, *Longest War*, 53.
46. O'Ballance, pp. 66–67.
47. O'Ballance, p. 68.
48. *Two Years of War*, p. 64.
49. O'Ballance, pp. 79–81.
50. *Payam-e Enqelab*, no. 56, April 17, 1982, p. 9.
51. *Payam-e Enqelab*, no. 59, May 29, 1982, p. 26.
52. *Payam-e Enqelab*, no. 59, May 29, 1982, p. 27.
53. *Two Years of War*, p. 89. Here the IRGC dates the beginning of OBM as April 22, 1982.
54. O'Ballance, pp. 83–84.
55. This is a line in the call to prayer distinct to Shia Islam. Islamic traditions favored by Shia Muslims recount that the Caliph Umar removed this line from the call to prayer because he thought it could discourage Muslims from partaking in his military campaigns against Persia. It is thus a symbol of Shia identity that is also salient in the context of war. See, for example, Sayyid Moustafa al-Qazwini, *Inquiries about Shi'a Islam* (Ahlubayt Organization, 2013), http://www.al-islam.org/inquiries-about-shia-islam-sayyid-moustafa-al-qazwini/issues-pertaining-practice-prayers); also see Momen, *Shi'i Islam*, pp. 178–179.
56. Emphasis added. *Payam-e Enqelab*, no. 59, May 29, 1982, p. 28.
57. *Two Years of War*, p. 90.
58. *Payam-e Enqelab*, no. 60, June 12, 1982, p. 19.
59. O'Ballance, p. 93.

## Chapter 5

1. Davud Ghaffarzadegan, *Fortune Told in Blood*, trans. M. R. Ghanoonparvar. Austin: The Center for Middle Eastern Studies and the University of Texas at Austin, 2008, p. 6.
2. On Khomeini's possible misgivings, see Ali Alfoneh, "The War over the War," *AEI*, September 30, 2010.
3. There is some controversy on who advocated for the war to continue into Iraq. At the time, Mohsen Rezai, Ali Sayyad Shirazi, and Ali Akbar Hashemi Rafsanjani were seen as among the most hawkish of Iran's military and civilian leaders, and those who most clearly advocated for continuing the war into Iraq. In his memoirs, however, Rafsanjani frames himself in a more

passive role, and indicates military commanders were the ones primarily responsible for convincing Khomeini to take the fight into Iraq. See Axeworthy, *Revolutionary Iran*, pp. 226–228.

4. Anthony H. Cordesman and Abraham R. Wagner, *The Lessons of Modern War, Volume II: The Iran-Iraq War* (Boulder, CO: Westview Press, 1990), p. 5.

5. Cordesman and Wagner, *Lessons of Modern War*, pp. 50–51.

6. IRGC Political Office, *Jang va Tajavoz: Jebhe-ye impirialisti 'alayh-e enqelab-e eslami* (Tehran: Daftar-e Siyasi-e Sepah-e Pasdaran-e Enqelab-e Eslami, 1981).

7. Cordesman and Wagner, *Lessons of Modern War*, p. 53; also, Helen Chapin Metz, ed., *Iraq: a Country Study* (Washington, DC: GPO for the Library of Congress, 1988).

8. Cordesman and Wagner, *Lessons of Modern War*, p. 5.

9. Cordesman and Wagner, *Lessons of Modern War*, p. 49.

10. Cordesman and Wagner, *Lessons of Modern War*, p. 357.

11. It is likely the United States was fully aware of Saddam's use of chemical weapons against Iran during the war. For instance, see Shane Harris and Matthew M. Aid, "Exclusive: CIA Files Prove American Helped Saddam as He Gassed Iran," *Foreign Policy*, August 26, 2013, http://www.foreignpolicy.com/articles/2013/08/25/secret_cia_files_prove_america_helped_saddam_as_he_gassed_iran.

12. O'Ballance, pp. 93–94.

13. Cordesman and Wagner, *Lessons of Modern War*, pp. 183–184.

14. Gary Sick, "Iran's Quest for Super Power Status," *Foreign Affairs*, Spring 1987.

15. "The Ministry of the Revolution Guards," Tehran home service, November 11, 1982, *BBC Summary of World Broadcasts*, November 16, 1982.

16. *Payam-e Enqelab*, no. 147, October 12, 1985, p. 11.

17. "IRGC Commander Denies Rift with Army," *IRNA*, September 19, 1985, *BBC Summary of World Broadcasts*, September 23, 1985.

18. Schaldagian, p. 69.

19. One figure, given by IRGC minister Mohsen Rafiqdust, put the number of Basij at the front at six to seven hundred thousand in 1985. See Schaldagian, pp. 93–94.

20. Ian Brown, *Khomeini's Forgotten Sons: The Story of Iran's Boy Soldiers, Child Victims of Saddam's Iraq* (London: Grey Seal Books, 1990), pp. 38–40.

21. Ibid., p. 88.

22. Ibid., pp. 88–89.

23. Ibid., pp. 89–90.

24. Ibid., pp. 86–87.

25. Ibid., p. 93.

26. The campaign against Iranian shipping, and Iran's more limited retaliatory measures, was dubbed the "tanker war." On this, see Hiro, pp. 129–152.

27. S. Taheri Shemirani, "The War of the Cities," in *The Iran-Iraq War: The Politics of Aggression*, ed. Farhang Rajaee (Gainesville: University Press of Florida, 1993), pp. 32–40.

28. Cordesman, pp. 187–188.

29. Cordesman, p. 203; O'Ballance, p. 166.

30. See for instance the will and testament of Mohammad Safavi, *Payam-e Enqelab*, no. 128, January 19, 1985, p. 33.

31. "Rafsanjani Praises Iranian Revolution Guards," Tehran home service, January 9, 1985, *BBC Summary of World Broadcasts*, January 11, 1985.

32. "Khomeyni's Revolution Anniversary Message," Tehran home service, February 11, 1985, *BBC Summary of World Broadcasts*, February 13, 1985.

33. *Payam-e Enqelab*, no. 147, p. 6.

34. Ibid.

35. O'Ballance, *The Gulf War*, pp. 174–175.

36. O'Ballance, *The Gulf War*, p. 174.

37. Cordesman, p. 200.

38. Hiro, p. 170.

39. See interview with Mahmud Hojjati, deputy commander of Reconstruction Jihad, *Payam-e Enqelab*, no. 164, June 21, 1986, pp. 14–17.

40. *Payam-e Enqelab*, no. 160, p. 25.
41. Emphasis added. *Payam-e Enqelab*, no. 161, p. 46.
42. *Payam-e Enqelab*, no. 161, pp. 48–49.
43. Cordesman, p. 227.
44. "Iranian Revolution Guards Corps Minister Discusses War with Iraq," Tehran home service, March 23, 1986, *BBC Summary of World Broadcasts*, March 25, 1986.
45. "Iranian Revolution Guards Corps Minister Discusses War with Iraq," Tehran home service, March 23, 1986, *BBC Summary of World Broadcasts*, March 25, 1986.
46. *Payam-e Enqelab*, no. 160, p. 25.
47. *Payam-e Enqelab*, no. 160, p. 25.
48. "Iranian Guards Corps Commander on 'Large-Scale' Plans to Step Up War," Tehran home service, May 31, 1986, *BBC Summary of World Broadcasts*, June 3, 1986.
49. "Iranian Guards Corps Commander on 'Large-Scale' Plans to Step Up War," Tehran home service, May 31, 1986, *BBC Summary of World Broadcasts*, June 3, 1986.
50. On US involvement in the tanker war against Iran, see Lee Allen Zatarain, *Tanker War: America's First Conflict with Iran, 1987–1988* (Philadelphia and Newbury, England: Casemate, 2008).
51. See interview with Ali Akbar Ahmadian, Staff Commander of the IRGC navy: "Iran Guard Corps Commanders Discuss Military Capabilities," Tehran home service, September 24, 1987, *BBC Summary of World Broadcasts*, September 29, 1987.
52. Ibid.
53. "Iranian Guard Commander Says 'Time Has Come' to Deliver Blow to USA," Tehran home service, September 22, 1987, *BBC Summary of World Broadcasts*, September 24, 1987.
54. "'Mecca Massacre': Rafsanjani Addresses March in Tehran on Revenge," Tehran home service, August 2, 1987, *BBC Summary of World Broadcasts*, August 4, 1987.
55. On the Halabja massacre, see Joost R Hiltermann, *A Poisonous Affair: America, Iraq, and the Gassing of Halabja* (New York: Cambridge University Press, 2007).
56. Rafsanjani memoirs cited in Axeworthy, p. 270.
57. Hiro, pp. 207–210.
58. Ray Takeyh, *Guardians of the Revolution: Iran and the World in the Age of the Ayatollahs* (New York: Oxford University Press, 2009), p. 105.
59. Ibid., pp. 103–104.
60. "Khomeyni Decree Appoints Rafsanjani as Armed Forces Acting C-in-C," Tehran home service, June 2, 1988, *BBC Summary of World Broadcasts*, June 4, 1988.
61. Ibid.
62. See for example Rafsanjani's Friday prayer sermon on June 3, 1988, "Rafsanjani on War with Iraq 'No Compromise or Surrender,'" Tehran home service, June 3, 1988, *BBC Summary of World Broadcasts*, June 6, 1988.
63. For a fuller discussion of this process, see Axeworthy, pp. 277–282.
64. Khomeini's letter was originally released by Ayatollah Montazeri in his memoirs. See Hosayn-Ali Montazeri, *Khaterat-e Ayatollah Hosayn-Ali Montazeri* (Los Angeles: Ketab Corp, 2001), p. 571–572. Rafsanjani later also released the letter in September 2006, which caused much controversy in Iran. Anticipating renewed criticism for his role in the war and its conclusion, Rezai responded to the release of the letter by claiming that his report was intended to advocate for a long term strategy, and to provide Rafsanjani with a range of options. See Rezai's comments to *Fars News*, September 29, 2006, http://www.farsnews.com/newstext.php?nn=8412240198.
65. Axeworthy, p. 278.
66. "Iranian IRGC Commander Endorses Cease-Fire Decision," *Tehran home service*, July 21, 1988, *BBC Summary of World Broadcasts*, July 23, 1988.
67. Vahe Petrossian, "Iran Makes 'Shooting Gallery' of Abandoned Column of Mojahedin: Girls and Women among Thousands of Rebels Killed in one of the Gulf War's 'Worst Slaughters,'" The *Guardian* (London), September 5, 1988.
68. See, *Payam-e Enqelab*, issues 219–221 (August 13–September 10, 1988).

## Chapter 6

1. *Payam-e Enqelab*, no. 5, April 1980, p. 39.
2. *Payam-e Enqelab*, no. 4, March 19, 1980, p. 37.
3. Ibid., p. 32.
4. Ibid., pp. 35–36.
5. Ibid.
6. Fred Halliday, "Three Concepts of Internationalism," *International Affairs* 64, no. 2 (Spring 1988): pp. 187–198.
7. Ibid.
8. On the ideological and political contours of Third Worldism, and its relationship to socialism, see Mark T. Berger, "After the Third World? History, Destiny and the Fate of Third Worldism," *Third World Quarterly* 25, no.1 (2004).
9. "Foreign Minister Denies Iran Seeks to Export Revolution," *The Washington Post*, October 4, 1979.
10. "Export Revolution, Iran President Urges," *The Globe and Mail*, February 5, 1980.
11. "Ambassador to Kuwait on Bahrain, Rohani, PLO," Kuwait KUNA in Arabic, October 3, 1979, *FBIS-MEA*, October 4, 1979.
12. "Montazeri Son Accuses Rohani of Being CIA Agent," Kuwait KUNA in Arabic, July 18, 1979, *FBIS-MEA*, July 19, 1979.
13. Laurence Louer, *Transnational Shia Politics: Religious and Political Networks in the Gulf* (New York: Columbia University Press, 2012), pp. 179–180.
14. Much of Montazeri's pre-revolutionary career in Lebanon was followed by Iranian intelligence and preserved in numerous SAVAK documents. See *Shahid Hojjat al-Islam Mohammad Montazeri* (Tehran: Markaz-e Barresi-e Asnad-e Tarikhi-e Vezarat-e Ettela'at, 2006/2007).
15. "Foreign Ministry Protest by Would Be Lebanon Fighters Reported," Tehran *Ettela'at* in Persian, December 15, 1979, *FBIS-MEA*, December 1979. Prior to this incident, Iranian authorities issued a warrant for Montazeri's arrest after he and five hundred supporters attempted to seize an aircraft to fly to Libya for that country's anniversary celebration. See "Montazeri Interviewed on Muslim Solidarity, Gulf Ries," Paris *An-Nahar wa Ad-Duwali* in Arabic, October 22–28, 1979, *FBIS-MEA*, October 29, 1979; and "'Volunteer' Force Eyeing Lebanon," *The Globe and Mail*, December 5, 1979.
16. "Iranian Volunteers Ween in Lebanon," *The Globe and Mail*, January 5, 1980.
17. "Ayatollah Montazeri's Statement on His Son," Tehran home service in Persian, September 18, 1979, *BBCSWB*, September 20, 1979.
18. Hosayn-Ali Montazeri, *Khaterat-e Ayatollah Hosayn-Ali Montazeri* (Los Angeles: Ketab Corp, 2001), p. 249.
19. "Ayatollah Montazeri Notes Political Nature of Islam," Tehran Domestic Service in Persian, September 28, 1979, *FBIS-MEA*, October 1, 1979.
20. Ibid.
21. On this point, Khomeini said: "When we say we want to export our revolution, this is what we have in mind, this is what we want to export: we want to export the same spirituality which has emerged in Iran. . . . We do not want to draw our swords and take our guns and attack. . . . We want to export our revolution, our cultural revolution and our Islamic revolution to all Islamic countries. Once this revolution is exported, wherever it is exported, it will solve problems. What you must first do is to awaken your peoples [as Iran has done in] its revolution." See "Khomeyni Addresses Representatives of Liberation Movements," Tehran Domestic Service in Persian, August 9, 1980, *FBIS-MEA*, August 11, 1980.
22. Emphasis added. "Montazeri Interviewed on Muslim Solidarity, Gulf Ties," Paris *An-Nahar wa Ad-Duwali* in Arabic, October 22–28, 1979, *FBIS-MEA*, October 29, 1979.
23. For instance, at an IRGC seminar in Shiraz, a resolution was passed that proclaimed "unquestioning support for the velayat-e faqih," the clergy, and Ayatollah Khomeini. "Resolution Passed by Shiraz Revolution Guards," Shiraz regional in Persian, February 21, 1981, in *BBCSWB*, February 25, 1981.
24. Mehdi Moslem, *Factional Politics*, pp. 47–50.

25. The Persian text of Mohsen Rezai's resignation letter as well as a facsimile of the handwritten letter can be found in Saidi, *Sazman*, pp. 137–40, and pp. 294–96 for the facsimile.
26. Ibid., pp. 137–140.
27. Ibid.
28. For the political divide between the conservative and radical-revolutionary factions during this period, see Moslem, *Factional Politics*, pp. 50–67. Also see Alfoneh, *Iran Unveiled*, pp. 217–218.
29. This commitment appears in the IRGC's first official charter. *Payam-e Enqelab*, no. 47, December 12, 1981, p. 2.
30. Ibid.
31. Ibid.
32. *A Glance at Two Years of War*, ([Tehran?]: Islamic Revolution's Guards Corps [Political Office], 1982), p. 97.
33. Ibid.
34. Muhammad Baqir al-Hakim, *Ahadith mukhtara*, p. 11, cited in Jabar, *Shi'ite Movement in Iraq*, p. 252.
35. Jabar, *Shi'ite Movement in Iraq*, pp. 253–54.
36. This duty is listed in the IRGC's first official charter, *Payam-e Enqelab*, no. 4, March 1980, p. 37.
37. After a meeting with Ayatollah Montazeri in Qom, IRGC Commander Mohsen Rezai said: "It has been arranged that the ideological section of the corps be supervised by a canonist [Shiite cleric], who in addition to having the ideal religious qualifications should have perfect knowledge of current political and revolutionary issues." "The Revolution Guards in Iran," Tehran home service, October 29, 1981, *BBCSWB*, October 31, 1981.
38. "Iran Revolution Guards' 'Liberation Movements Unit,'" *BBC Summary of World Broadcasts*, February 6, 1981.
39. The IRGC developed extensive ties with several different Shiite militant groups in Afghanistan. However, factionalism and a lack of organization within the Afghan groups limited Iran's impact in that country. For Iran's involvement in this regard, see Nimatullah Ibrahimi, "The Failure of a Clerical Proto-State: Hazarajat, 1979–1984" (working paper series no. 2, Crisis States Research Center, London: Destin LSE, 2006). Also, Montazeri's and the IRGC's roles in assisting Afghan Mojahedin organizations are discussed in the confessions of Sayed Ebrahim, a member of the Afghan Sazman-e Fedayan-e Islam, see "Confession by Captured Insurgent Trained in Iran," Kabul home service, March 17, 1985, *BBC Summary of World Broadcasts*, March 30, 1985.
40. "Iranian Military to Fight for Lebanon," Tehran home service, June 7, 1982, *BBCSWB*, June 9, 1982.
41. "Iran: In Brief; Khameneh'i on training and help for Lebanon," Tehran home service, June 17, 1982 *BBC Summary of World Broadcasts*, June 19, 1982.
42. Other reports put this number at around 1,500. "Iran's Guards Rally to Beirut," *Newsweek*, June 28, 1982.
43. For an overview of Iranian-Lebanese interaction during this period, see H. E. Chehabi, ed., *Distant Relations: Iran and Lebanon in the last 500 years* (New York: St. Martin's Press, 2006), pp. 180–230. Also see Haleh Vazeri, "Iran's Involvement in Lebanon: Polarization and Radicalization of Militant Islamic Movements," *Journal of South Asian and Middle Eastern Studies* 16, no. 2 (Winter 1992).
44. Roschanack Shaery-Eisenlohr, *Shi'ite Lebanon: Transnational Religion and the Making of National Identities* (New York: Columbia University Press, 2008), pp. 94–99.
45. Much of Chamran's experience in Lebanon (including his relationship to Musa al-Sadr and the establishment of Amal) has been posthumously compiled from his writings, interviews, and speeches. See, for instance, Mostafa Chamran, *Lobnan*. ([Tehran?]: Bonyad-e Shahid-e Chamran, 1983). On Chamran's impact on the Shiite community of southern Lebanon, see Shaery-Eisenlohr, *Shi'ite Lebanon*, pp. 89–118.
46. Shaery-Eisenlohr, *Shi'ite Lebanon*, pp. 101–103.
47. Amal had partially been established to protect the interests of the southern Lebanese Shiites from the Palestinian organizations that had taken control of that area. This lead to an ongoing violent conflict between the two sides during the Lebanon's civil war. See, *Shi'ite Lebanon*, pp. 96.

48. Sayyed Ali Akbar Mohtashami, *Khaterat-e siyasi-e Sayyed Ali Akbar Mohtashami*, vol. 2 (Tehran: Khaneh-ye Andisheh-ye Javan, 2000), p. 108.
49. Safavi discusses his experiences in Lebanon in his memoirs. See Yahya Rahim Safavi, *Az jonub-e lobnan ta jonub-e iran: Khaterat-e sardar-e Sayyed Rahim Safavi*, ed. Majid Najafpour (Tehran: Markaz-e Asnad-e Enqelab-e Eslami, 2004), pp. 95–107.
50. Ibid., p. 105.
51. Ibid., p. 106.
52. A notable exception is the Popular Front for the Liberation of Palestine-General Command (PFLP-GC) which, under Ahmad Jibril, received limited Iranian support through the 1990s.
53. A sizeable literature on Lebanese Hezbollah in English has already been produced. Of the key monographs on the subject, see Hala Jaber, *Hezbollah: Born with a Vengeance* (New York: Columbia University Press, 1997); Ahmad Nizar Hamzeh, *In the Path of Hezbollah* (Syracuse: Syracuse University Press, 2004); Judith Palmer Harik, *Hezbollah: The Changing Face of Terrorism* (London and New York: I. B. Tauris, 2004); Joseph Alagha, *The Shifts in Hezbollah's Ideology: Religious Ideology, Political Ideology, and Political Program* (Amsterdam: Amsterdam University Press, 2006); and Augustus Norton, *Hezbollah: A Short History* (Princeton: Princeton University Press, 2007).
54. Hamzeh, *Path of Hezbollah*, pp. 24–26.
55. Ibid., p. 25.
56. Hamzeh, *Path of Hezbollah*, p. 25.
57. On Iran's connection to terrorism and hostage-taking in Lebanon during this period, see Magnus Ranstorp, *Hizb'allah in Lebanon: The Politics of the Western Hostage Crisis* (New York, St. Martin's Press, 1997). For the CIA's investigation into the US embassy bombing, see Robert Baer, *See No Evil: the True Story of a Ground Soldier in the CIA's War on Terrorism* (New York: Three Rivers Press, 2002).
58. Daniel Byman, *A High Price: The Triumphs and Failures of Israeli Counterterrorism* (New York: Oxford University Press, 2011), pp. 217–219.
59. Adam Goldman and Ellen Nakashima, "CIA and Mossad Killed Senior Figure in Car Bombing," *The Washington Post*, January 30, 2015, http://www.washingtonpost.com/world/national-security/cia-and-mossad-killed-senior-hezbollah-figure-in-car-bombing/2015/01/30/ebb88682–968a-11e4–8005-1924ede3e54a_story.html.
60. "Iranians fighting in Lebanon" (interview with Mohsen Rezai), *BBCSWB*, November 24, 1983.
61. Interview with Brother Mosleh, IRGC commander in Lebanon, *Payam-e Enqelab*, no. 138, June 8, 1985, p. 70.
62. Ibid., pp. 70–71.
63. Ibid., p. 73.
64. Ibid.
65. "Leaflets and Songs Show Iranian Link to Beirut's 'Party of God,'" *Christian Science Monitor*, April 29, 1985. This process continued through the early 1990s, by which time the vast majority of IRGC troops had been removed from Lebanon. See Hamzeh, *Path of Hizballah*, pp. 69–71.
66. Moslem, *Factional Politics*, pp. 47–70.
67. For a detailed discussion of the form and content of the debates that fostered the factionalism of this period, see Moslem, *Factional Politics*, pp. 47–81.
68. David Menashri, *Iran: A Decade of War and Revolution* (New York and London: Holmes & Meier, 1990), pp. 374–378.
69. Ibid.
70. On Iran's covert arms purchases from the US and Israel, see Trita Parsi, *Treacherous Alliance: The Secret Dealings of Israel, Iran, and the U.S.* (New Haven and London: Yale University Press, 2007); Ray Takeyh, *Hidden Iran: Paradox and Power in the Islamic Republic* (New York: Times Books, 2006), pp. 103–110; and Gary Sick, *October Surprise: America's Hostages in Iran and the Election of Ronald Reagan* (New York: Times Books, 1991).
71. Parsi, *Treacherous Alliance*, pp. 113–123.
72. Katzman, *Warriors*, pp. 150–152.
73. Montazeri, *Khaterat*, p. 339.

74. Menashri, *Decade of War*, pp. 379–382.
75. Ibid.
76. Montazeri discusses these events in his memoirs. See Montazeri, *Khaterat*, pp. 335–346. Also, for exchanges between Khomeini and Montazeri regarding the arrest of Mehdi Hashemi, see Baqer Moin, *Khomeini*, pp. 277–293.
77. Parsi, *Treacherous Alliance*, pp. 123–126; also, Menashri, *Decade of War*, pp. 379–380.
78. "Hundreds of Montazeri supporters arrested," *BBCSWB*, November 14, 1986.
79. Katzman, *Warriors*, pp. 147–160.
80. Montazeri had been elected in 1985 by the Assembly of Experts to be Khomeini's successor. His vocal criticism of the violent political suppression under the Khomeini regime led to a fallout between the two senior clerics. For exchanges between the two, see Moin, *Khomeini*, pp. 262–298.
81. "Montazeri statement on Muslim unity and export of the revolution," *BBCSWB*, 1 November 1988.

## Chapter 7

1. *Payam-e Enqelab*, no. 4, March 19, 1980, p. 38.
2. On the general religious requirements of serving in the IRGC and Basij after the war, see *Qanun-e Moqararat-e Estekhdami-e Sepah-e Pasdaran-e Enqelab-e Eslami*. ([Tehran?]: Edareh-ye Koll-e Qavanin va Moqararat-e Keshvar, 1995/1996), pp. 5–8.
3. Rafiqdust, *Khaterat*, 184. While it could be argued that green is the default color for most militaries around the globe, Mohsen Rafiqdust stresses that the color green was specifically chosen for its Islamic symbolism.
4. On the use of visual propaganda during the revolution and under the Islamic Republic, see Chelkowski and Dabashi's *Staging a Revolution*; and, Lynn Gumpert and Shiva Balaghi, eds., *Picturing Iran: Art, Society and Revolution* (London: I. B. Tauris, 2002).
5. *Payam-e Enqelab*, no. 4, March 19, 1980, pp. 32–34.
6. Ibid., p. 33.
7. Ibid.
8. Q9:111, Al-Tawbah [Repentence]. As is customary in this style of writing, the IRGC includes only the opening statement of this verse in the article. Translation from Ahmed Ali, *Al-Quran: A Contemporary Translation* (Princeton: Princeton University Press, 1994), p. 174.
9. Ibid., pp. 33–34.
10. Ibid., p. 34.
11. Schahgaldian, *Iranian*, p. 94.
12. Ibid., p. 69.
13. Katzman argues that it is in part due to the Guards' ability to assimilate "non-ideological groups" such as conscripts that demonstrates the organization's political resiliency. See Katzman, *Warriors*, pp. 8–9.
14. *Payam-e Enqelab* began publication in March 1980 and has continued with intermittent breaks through the present.
15. Preface to *Jang va Jehad dar Quran* (Tehran: Vahed-e Amuzesh: Setad-e Markazi-e Sepah-e Pasdaran-e Enqelab-e Eslami, 1981).
16. *Jang va Tajavoz: Jebhe-ye impirialisti 'alayh-e enqelab-e eslami* (Tehran: Daftar-e Siyasi-e Sepah-e Pasdaran-e Enqelab-e Eslami), 1981.
17. The Propaganda Staff of the newly established Supreme Defense Council of Iran issued an order soon after the invasion which required all government organs to pursue a coordinated propaganda effort. See "Directive Issued by Iranian Propaganda Office," Tehran home service, October 16, 1980, *BBCSWB*, October 18, 1980.
18. *A Glance at Two Years of War* ([Tehran?]: Political Office: Islamic Revolution's Guards Corps [Tarjomeh: Setad-e Tablighat-e Jang-e Sepah]), 1982.
19. *Payam-e Enqelab*, no. 4, March 19, 1980, p. 37.
20. *Jang-ha-ye Payambar* (Tehran: Vahed-e Amuzeshi-e `Aqidati-e Siyasi-e Sepah-e Pasdaran-e Enqilab-e Eslami, 1984), pp. 3–4.
21. *Payam-e Enqelab*, no. 162, May 10,1986, p. 48.

22. *Payam-e Enqelab*, no. 26, February 16, 1981, p. 46.

23. Because of the fluctuating value of Iranian currency during this period, it is difficult to come to a precise rate of exchange with the US dollar; however, 9.75 million *rials* in 1981 was probably around 10,000 USD.

24. Ibid., pp. 47–48.

25. Ibid., p. 54.

26. *Payam-e Enqelab*, no. 26, pp. 48–51.

27. On the role of political posters and visuality more broadly during the revolution and Iraqi conflict, see Peter Chelkowski and Hamid Dabashi, *Staging a Revolution*; Gumpert and Balaghi, eds., *Picturing Iran*; William Hanaway, "The Symbolism of the Persian Revolutionary Posters" in *Iran Since the Revolution: Internal Dynamics, Regional Conflicts, and the Superpowers*, ed. Barry Rosen (New York: Columbia University, 1985); Michael M. J. Fischer and Mehdi Adebi, *Debating Muslims* (Madison: University of Wisconsin Press, 1990); and Annabelle Sreberny-Mohammadi and Ali Mohammadi, *Small Media, Big Revolution: Communication, Culture, and the Iranian Revolution* (Minneapolis: University of Minnesota Press, 1994). For a discussion on the influence of Iranian political posters on those produced by Shiite organizations in Lebanon during that countries civil war, see Zeina Maasri's *Off the Wall: Political Posters of the Lebanese Civil War*, foreword by Fawwaz Traboulsi (New York: I. B. Tauris, 2009). And for discussions of the political poster as a genre, see Jeffrey T. Schnapp, *Revolutionary Tides: The Art of the Political Poster 1914–1989* (Milan: Skira, 2005); and Margaret Timmers, ed., *The Power of the Poster* (London: V&A Publications, 1998).

28. Chelkowski, "The Art of Revolution and War: The Role of the Graphic Arts in Iran," in *Picturing Iran*, pp. 128–129.

29. For a detailed discussion of MIR's emblem, see Saidi, *Sazman*, pp. 78–79.

30. This is especially true in regard to the IRGC's antagonism toward the Mojahedin-e Khalq.

31. Fischer and Abedi suggest that the usage of the *"la"* negative article in this form is influenced by Ali Shariati and his publications, which bore the negative article "on the cover of all of his books and published lectures." See, Michael M. J. Fischer and Mehdi Abedi, *Debating Muslims: Cultural Dialogues in Postmodernity and Tradition* (Madison: University of Wisconsin Press, 1990), p. 344.

32. Q:8:20

33. John Manning, *The Emblem* (London: Reaktion Books, 2004), p. 10.

34. Rafiqdust, *Khaterat*, p. 184.

35. The image and poem are published in *Payam-e Enqelab*, no. 24, June 17, 1981, p. 81.

36. The Sarbardaran uprising was one of the many historical events re-imagined as proto-revolutionary after the Islamic revolution. On the Sarbardaran period, see John Masson Smith Jr., *The History of the Sarbadar Dynasty: 1336–1381 A.D. and Its Sources* (Paris: Mouton, 1970). Also see H.R. Roemer, "The Jalayirids, Muzaffarids, and Sarbadars," in *The Cambridge History of Iran, Volume 6: The Timurid and Safavid Periods*, eds. Peter Jackson and Laurence Lockhart (Cambridge: University of Cambridge Press, 1986).

37. This image is published in *Payam-e Enqelab*, no. 139, June 22, 1985, p. 73.

38. On Khomeini's wartime rhetoric and its relationship to the images produced during the war, see Chelkowski and Dabashi, *Staging*, pp. 272–291.

39. Interview with Hojjat al-Islam Mahallati, *Payam-e Enqelab*, no. 135, April 27, 1985, p. 31.

40. Hiro, *Longest War*, p. 177.

41. This slogan was a popular theme in IRGC wartime imagery. For instance, an IRGC billboard displayed at the warfront during this period shows a guardsman carrying the Islamic standard toward a depiction of Imam Husayn's shrine in Karbala, and behind or *through* that shrine is the Dome of the rock. Above this scene is the phrase "the path to Jerusalem passes through Karbala" in Persian. A photograph of this billboard is published in Chelkowski and Dabashi, *Staging*, p. 286.

42. *Payam-e Enqelab*, no. 47, December 12, 1981, cover.

43. Susan Sontag, *On Photography* (New York: Picador USA; Farrar, Straus and Giroux, 2001), p. 163.

44. *Payam-e Enqelab*, no. 50, January 23, 1982, inside back cover.

45. Hiro, *Longest War*, pp. 129–152.

46. *Payam-e Enqelab*, no.162, May 24, 1986, back cover.

47. *Payam-e Enqelab*, no.159, April 12, 1986, back cover.

48. Roland Barthes, *The Responsibility of Forms: Critical Essays on Music, Art, and Representation*, trans. Richard Howard (Berkeley and Los Angeles: University of California Press, 1991), pp. 54–59.

49. On the development of the Karbala metaphor and associated rituals in Shiite Islam, see Kamran Scott Aghaie, *The Martyrs of Karbala: Shi'i Symbols and Rituals in Modern Iran* (Seattle and London: University of Washington Press, 2004), pp. 3–14. Also see Syed Akbar Hyder, *Reliving Karbala: Martyrdom in South Asian Memory* (Oxford: Oxford University Press, 2006).

50. By this I mean the notion of a direct military confrontation with Israel was mostly shelved by Iranian leaders after the war. However, Iran continued to support organizations such as Hezbollah and Hamas, which remained engaged in direct armed conflict and terrorism against Israel.

51. This image is published in *Payam-e Enqelab*, no. 220, August 27, 1988, p. 32.

52. On the visuality of Muharram and Ashura, see Chelkowski and Dabashi, *Staging*, pp. 70–85.

53. For instance, see the collection of martyrdom posters in Abulfazl A'li's *Honar-e Grafik dar Enqelab-e Eslami*, pp. 69–83.

## Chapter 8

1. "Khamenei and Ahmed Khomeini on importance of Revolutionary Guards' role," *Voice of the Islamic Republic of Iran* (Tehran), January 28, 1990, *BBCSWB*, January30, 1990.

2. Alec Campbell, "Where Do All the Soldiers Go? Veterans and the Politics of Demobilization," in *Irregular Armed Forces and Their Role in State Formation*, eds. Diane E. Davis and Anthony W. Pereira (Cambridge: Cambridge University Press, 2003), p. 97.

3. On the problems of demobilization, see Campbell, "Where Do All the Soldiers Go?," pp. 96–117. For the role of demobilization in state formation, see Charles Tilly, *Coercion, Capital, and European States, AD 990–1990* (Cambridge, MA: Blackwell, 1990); and Michael Mann, *States, War, and Capitalism* (Oxford: Blackwell, 1988).

4. The lack of an appointed successor—and with the previous successor Ayatollah Montazeri disgraced and marginalized—presented the regime with its most serious threat since the invasion of Saddam Hussein's forces. The Assembly of Experts, the clerical body charged with selecting the next Supreme Leader, recognized that no suitable candidate existed who was both politically untarnished and possessed the necessary religious standing (*marja' al-taqlid*) mandated by the constitution. The Assembly ultimately promoted Iran's president Ali Khamenei, a mid-level cleric, to the role of Supreme Leader. Although Khamenei was considered politically viable for the position he lacked the proper religious credentials for the office. This forced the Assembly to alter the constitution to enable Khamenei's succession, thus reshaping one of the fundamental principles of Khomeini's concept of the "Guardianship of the Jurisprudent." On Khomeini's succession, see David Menashri, *Post-Revolutionary Politics in Iran: Religion, Society, and Power* (London and Portland: Frank Cass, 2001), pp. 13–32. Also see Maziar Behrooz, "The Islamic State and the Crisis of Marja'iyat in Iran," *Comparative Studies of South Asia, Africa and the Middle East* 16, no. 2 (1996).

5. Karim Sadjadpour, *Reading Khamenei: The World View of Iran's Most Powerful Leader* (Washington, DC: Carnegie Endowment for International Peace, 2009).

6. Mehdi Moslem, *Factional Politics in Post-Khomeini Iran* (Syracuse: Syracuse University Press, 2002), p. 151.

7. Moslem, *Factional*, 157–160. Also, on the third and fourth Majles, see Bahman Baktiari, *Parliamentary Politics in Revolutionary Iran: The Institutionalization of Factional Politics* (Gainesville: University Press of Florida, 1996), pp. 145–234.

8. On the role and function of the bonyads in post-revolutionary Iran in general and Rafiqdust's tenure as head of the *Bonyad-e mostaz'afin va janbazan*, see Suzanne Maloney, "Islamism in Iran's Postrevolutionary Economy: The Case of the Bonyads," in *Gods, Guns, and Globalization: Religious Radicalism and International Political Economy*, eds. Mary Ann Tétrault and Robert A. Denemark. International Political Economy Yearbook, vol. 13 (Boulder: Lynne Rienner Publishers, 2004), pp. 191–217. Also see Moslem, *Factional*, pp. 42–46.

9. "Rafiqdust Replaces Musavi at Foundation for the Oppressed," Tehran home service, September 6, 1989, *BBCSWB*, September 7, 1989.

10. "Karrubi Re-elected Majlis Speaker; Security Forces to Merge," *Voice of the Islamic Republic of Iran* (Tehran), June 12, 1990, *BBCSWB*, June 13, 1990.

11. Majles debates, June 19, 1990, cited in Moslem, *Factional*, p. 192.

12. "Khamenei Denies Rumours of Dissolution of Guards Corps or Armed Forces," *Voice of the Islamic Republic of Iran* (Tehran), November 20, 1989, *BBCSWB*, November 22, 1989.

13. "Iran Guards Corps Official Discusses Planned Restructuring," *Voice of the Islamic Republic of Iran* (Tehran), January 16, 1990, *BBCSWB*, January 18, 1990.

14. "Military Ranks for Guards and Basij Personnel," *Voice of the Islamic Republic of Iran* (Tehran), May 6, 1990, *BBCSWB*, May 8, 1990.

15. *Payam-e Enqelab*, no. 4, March 1980, p. 33. In this March 1980 article on the tenets of IRGC ideology, the Guards distinguish their organization from traditional (secular) militaries by lambasting the corrosive nature of hierarchy and ranking systems. "Ungodly and autocratic" armies are criticized for stressing "rigid discipline and blind obedience" among their ranks. These characteristics, they authors, lead to the "ignorance," "moral corruption," and "low self-esteem" (*khod kam bini*) of soldiers, which in turn pacifies the ranks into obeying the corrupt policies of imperialist nations. "Were not the massacres in Vietnam, Algeria, Palestine, Eritrea, etc., committed by these very same ignorant and weak-kneed people?", the authors asks. They also argue that the hierarchical structure of armies encourages the "privilege and snobbery of commanders," prevents brotherhood and camaraderie, and fuels "hostility and rancor" among subordinates. The authors continue that these characteristics are not only descriptive of modern (imperialistic, autocratic, socialist, and revolutionary) armies and militias, but that they were at the root of the collapse of historical empires, particularly that of the ancient Sasanids. Thus, the Guards argued that a rank-free organization would be able to avoid these pitfalls. Further, by following Islamic principles, fraternal bonds between commanders and regular soldiers would be fostered.

16. "Guards Commander on Grading and on the New Basij and Qods Forces," *Voice of the Islamic Republic of Iran* (Tehran), April 17, 1990, *BBCSWB*, April 20, 1990.

17. Saeid Golkar, *Captive Society: The Basij Militia and Social Control in Iran* (New York: Columbia University Press, 2015), p. 17.

18. While the official name of the Quds Force is *Niru-ye Qods*, it is sometimes referred to in the Persian press as Sepah-e Qods (Quds Corps).

19. The establishment of the Quds Force centralized the IRGC's foreign operations under a single command. While the Iran took a more pragmatic approach toward foreign affairs in the postwar period, it continued to develop and deepen contacts abroad. The military side of these endeavors was largely under the IRGC's command, and after 1990, was part of the Quds portfolio. In a April 1990 interview, Mohsen Rezai explains the reasoning behind the Quds Force's establishment and its areas of responsibilities: "[T]he Qods Force, which is for assisting Muslims, Islamic states or Islamic governments, should they ask for help in training or advice. That is now a global custom. If an Islamic state, government or people need to be put through some training, well, the corps will go there and give them training; it will take measures to provide training support for world Muslims or Islamic states. There was a need for a force to perform this task, and the Eminent Leader commanded the corps to set it up. This force is now being set up and is mainly for helping Islamic governments and Islamic nations when there is a need to train them and transfer experience to them." See Rezai's interview with *Voice of the Islamic Republic of Iran* (Tehran), April 17, 1990.

20. "Rafsanjani Urges IRGC to Play a Role in Iran's Reconstruction and Development," *Voice of the Islamic Republic of Iran* (Tehran), January 7, 1992, *BBCSWB*, January 9, 1992.

21. Mohsen Sazegara, a founding member of the IRGC and critic of the present Islamic Republic regime, argues that the IRGC was asked by Rafsanjani to produce much of its funding in the postwar period. See Sazegara, "Sepah va seh enheraf," http://www.sazegara.net/persian/archives/2006/07/060723_154435.html.

22. For an overview of the IRGC's commercial endeavors, see Frederic Wehrey et al., *The Rise of the Pasdaran: Accessing the Domestic Roles of Iran's Islamic Revolutionary Guards Corps* (RAND

National Defense Research Institute, 2009), pp. 55–75, http://www.rand.org/pubs/monographs/MG821.html.

23. *Payam-e Enqelab*, no. 349, November/December 1996, pp. 23.

24. *Payam-e Enqelab*, no. 336, April 19, 1995, pp. 12–17. The Kharkheh dam was completed in 2002 and is said to be the sixth largest earthen dam in the world. See http://www.payvand.com/news/01/apr/1077.html.

25. "Development Projects Implemented by IRGC," *Voice of the Islamic Republic of Iran* (Tehran), January 15, 1994, *BBCSWB*, January 25, 1994.

26. Wehrey et al., *Pasdaran*, p. 61.

27. "Qaragah-ye sazandegi-e khatam al-anbia dar towse'eh-ye maydan-e pars-e jonubi sherkat kardeh ast," *Aftab*, July 11, 2004, http://www.aftab.ir/news/2004/jul/11/c2c1089539101.php.

28. *Payam-e Enqelab*, no. 336, p. 13.

29. "New Shipping Company to Operate in the Gulf," *Voice of the Islamic Republic of Iran* (Tehran), January 25, 1993, *BBCSWB*, February 2, 1993. Also, on the Guards illicit and black market activities, see Wehrey et al., *Pasdaran*, pp. 64–66.

30. On the relationship between Rafsanjani and the bazaari merchant class during his presidency, see Ali M. Ansari, *Iran, Islam, and Democracy: The Politics of Managing Change* (London: Chatham House, 2006), pp. 52–79. Also, on the history and place of the bazaari merchant class in Iran, see Arang Keshavarzian, *Bazaar and State in Iran: The Politics of the Tehran Marketplace* (Cambridge: and New York: Cambridge University Press, 2007).

31. Campbell, "Where Do All the Soldiers Go?," pp. 96–117. Also, for an interesting comparison to the Iranian case on the issue of demobilization and the role of veterans in a postwar period, see Norma Kriger, *Guerilla Veterans in Post-War Zimbabwe: Symbolic and Violent Politics, 1980–1987* (Cambridge and New York: Cambridge University Press, 2003).

32. For instance, see "Khamenei and Ahmed Khomeini on Importance of Revolutionary Guards' Role," *Voice of the Islamic Republic of Iran* (Tehran), January 28, 1990, *BBCSWB*, January 30, 1990.

33. *Omid-e Enqelab*, no. 243, October/November 1991, pp. 18–19; also, *Payam-e Enqelab*, no 334, January 1995, pp. 12–14.

34. "Some 5,000 Revolution Guards to Be Transferred to Law Enforcement Forces," *Voice of the Islamic Republic of Iran* (Tehran), February 6, 1992, *BBCSWB*, February 8,1992.

35. On the state's efforts to promote these sentiments through various government organs and media, see Farideh Farhi's "The Antinomies of Iran's War Generation," in *Iran, Iraq, and the Legacies of War*, eds. Lawrence G. Potter and Gary Sick (New York: Palgrave Macmillan, 2004), pp. 101–120.

36. The latter is in connection with the formation of a "20 million man army," the goal of a massive popular defense force called for by Khomeini in 1979.

37. "IRGC Commander on Basij Grading System," *Voice of the Islamic Republic of Iran* (Tehran), November 26, 1991, *BBCSWB*, November 28, 1991.

38. "Iran Commanders on Duties and Organization and Guards Corps and Basij Forces," *Voice of the Islamic Republic of Iran* (Tehran), December 29, 1990, *BBCSWB*, January 4, 1991.

39. *Omid-e Enqelab*, no. 240, September 6, 1991, p. 20.

40. *Payam-e Enqelab*, no. 301, February 3, 1993, p. 51.

41. "Basijis to Begin Judicial Activities," *Voice of the Islamic Republic of Iran* (Tehran), November 21, 1993, *BBCSWB*, November 22, 1993.

42. For an exhaustive study of this injunction in Islamic thought, see Michael Cook's *Commanding Right and Forbidding Wrong in Islamic Thought* (Cambridge: Cambridge University Press, 2000). For a more general discussion, see Cook's *Forbidding Wrong in Islam: An Introduction* (Cambridge: Cambridge University Press, 2003).

43. On classical Shiite debates on the subject see Cook's *Commanding Right*, pp. 252–301; for contemporary debates, see pp. 530–549.

44. Most of the contemporary discussions in Iran are based on the views of Ayatollah Khomeini. For a prime example of how Khomeini's thoughts on the subject are presented in the postwar period, see *Amr beh ma'ruf va nahy az monkar az didgah-ye Imam Khomeini* ([Tehran?]: Mo'asseseh-ye tanzim va nashr-e asar-e Imam Khomeini, 1998). For works on the subject that are either influential or directly related to the IRGC and Basij, see Ayatollah Morteza

Motahhari, *Rahbari-e nasl-e javan* ([Tehran?]: Kanun-e khedamat-e farhangi-e alast, 1982), pp. 90–115; The Center of Islamic Research of the IRGC, *Amr beh ma'ruf va nahy az monkar* ([Tehran?]: Namayandegi-e vali-e faqih dar sepah, 1997); and Mohammad Eshaq Mas'udi, *Pazhuheshi dar amr beh ma'ruf va nahy az monkar: Az didgah-ye qor'an va ravayat* (Tehran: Sazman-e tablighat-e eslami, 1999/2000).

45. *Payam-e Enqelab*, no. 4, March 1980, pp. 33–34.
46. "New Committee Formed for 'Propagation of Virtue and Prohibition of Vice," *Voice of the Islamic Republic of Iran* (Tehran), July 19, 1992, *BBCSWB*, July 22, 1992.
47. *Payam-e Enqelab*, no. 301, February 3, 1993, p. 51.
48. Ibid.
49. For instance, on morals policing as a duty of all Muslims, Ayatollah Jannati explains in a Friday prayer sermon: "It is the duty of every individual Muslim to propagate virtue and prohibit vice—wife with regard to her husband and husband to wife; children towards father and father to children. In organisations, subordinates should exercise it towards superiors and superiors towards subordinates. There is no distinction here. If a catering servant sees that a boss is doing something which is prohibited, he must—provided he is observing the necessary conditions—engage in prohibiting vice. One cannot say [to the servant] 'What has it got to do with you?'" See "Jannati Warns against Allowing Too Many Foreign Specialists," *Voice of the Islamic Republic of Iran* (Tehran), July 24,1992, *BBCSWB*, July 27, 1992.
50. Speech on morals policing to the Basij by Ayatollah Movahedi-Kermani, *Payam-e Enqelab*, no. 301, February 3, 1993, p. 50.
51. The Center of Islamic Research of the IRGC, *Amr beh ma'ruf va nahy az monkar* ([Tehran?]: Namayandegi-e vali-e faqih dar sepah, 1997), pp. 7–8.
52. *Payam-e Enqelab*, no. 301, p. 50.
53. "Basijis Will Receive Training on Propagating Virtue and Prohibiting Vice," *Voice of the Islamic Republic of Iran* (Tehran), November 18, 1992, *BBCSWB*, November 20, 1992.
54. *Payam-e Enqelab*, no. 299, December 1, 1992, pp. 32–33.
55. "Basij Resistance Force Official Says One Million Students Recruited," *Voice of the Islamic Republic of Iran* (Tehran), December 5, 1993, *BBCSWB*, December 7, 1993.
56. "IRGC Commander Says 1,000 Basij Brigades Formed in the Country," *Voice of the Islamic Republic of Iran* (Tehran), July 16, 1994, *BBCSWB*, July 18, 1994.
57. "New Commander of Tehran's Basij Resistance Forces Will Have Over 250 Battalions," *Voice of the Islamic Republic of Iran* (Tehran), July 29, 1995, *BBCSWB*, July 31, 1995.
58. Moselm, *Factional*, pp. 187–88.
59. Anoushirvan Ehteshami and Mahjoob Zweiri, *Iran and the Rise of Its Neoconservatives: The Politics of Tehran's Silent Revolution* (London and New York: I. B. Tauris, 2007), pp. 16–20.
60. Menashri, *Post-Revolutionary*, pp. 85–89; Ansari, *Iran and Democracy*, pp. 108–109; Moslem, *Factional*, pp. 240–251.
61. On a critical survey of the reformist thought, see Ansari, *Iran and Democracy*, pp. 141–168.
62. "Liberalism" as a term employed by the conservatives in the postwar era was seen by some as a reawakening of the "liberal" ideologies of the Bazargan provisional government.
63. The election of Khatami was seen as a direct challenge to the leadership of Khamenei who had openly endorsed Nateq-Nuri. This symbolic challenge to Khamenei was compounded by the views of reformist leaders, such as Mohsen Kadivar, who openly questioned the "absolute" (*motlaqeh*) authority of the guardian and suggested that the latter's authority should stem from the will of the people. Other Islamic intellectuals, such as Abdolkarim Soroush, argued for new understandings of Islam's relationship to democracy and civil society, which provided little room for the unchecked authority of the supreme leader. After his election, Mohammad Khatami made similar, though less overt claims, such as suggesting the guardian jurist should play more of a supervisory role in society and be held accountable to the laws and mandates of the constitution. Reformist positions were also taken up by Khamenei's chief rival, Ayatollah Montazeri, who spoke out against the "absolute" reading of the guardianship and supported Khatami's reformist initiatives.
64. Farhang Rajaee, *Islamism and Modernism: The Changing Discourse in Iran* (Austin: University of Texas Press, 2007), pp. 166–171.

65. See for instance, Office of the Supreme Leader's Representative to the IRGC, *Amr be ma'ruf va nahy az mokar* ([Tehran?]: Nemayandegi-e Vali-ye Faqih dar Sepah, 1997), pp. 5–8.

66. "Majlis Speaker Says Liberal Majlis a 'Serious Threat' to Revolution," *IRNA* (Tehran) in Persian, April 30, 1996, *BBC WM*, May 1, 1996.

67. Mohammad Hosayn Jamshidi, "Tahajom-e farhangi," *Basij: Majallah-ye elmi-e pazhuheshi*, no. 7/8 (Summer/Fall 1995), pp. 21–40.

68. *Payam-e Enqelab*, no. 344, July 1996, pp. 22–25.

69. *Payam-e Enqelab*, no. 356, August/September 1997, p. 16.

70. "Official Says Guards Corps Will Act to Protect Revolutionary Values," *Kayhan* (Tehran) in Persian, May 21, 1996, *BBCWM*, May 29, 1996.

71. "Basij Will Not Let 'Liberals' Weaken Government, Says Iranian Guards Commander," *IRNA* (Tehran) in Persian, July 9, 1996, *BBCWM*, July 10, 1996.

72. Basijis were involved in numerous incidents involving undue violence against moral offenders in the name of morals policing. See for instance, "Militants in Iran Renew Their Attacks on Western Influences," *The New York Times*, May 9, 1996.

73. For instance, in this otherwise excellent article, Ansar is referred to as a "unit" of the IRGC. See, Matthew C. Wells, "Thermidor in the Islamic Republic of Iran: The Rise of Muhammad Khatami," *British Journal of Middle Eastern Studies* 26, no. 1 (May 1999): p. 36.

74. A valuable narrative of Ansar's formation and its anti-reformist activities is provided by the legal statement (or "confessions," *e'terafat*) of Amir Farshad Ebrahimi—a former Basiji and early Ansar member. See, "Matn-e e'terafat-e Amir Farshad Ebrahimi," *Mihan*, no. 59, January 2003.

75. For a discussion of Khamenei's support for Ansar's activism, see "Ali Khamenei, Ansar-e Hezbollah, va eteqad beh r'ab," *Mihan*, no. 57, October 2002.

76. Ebrahimi claims that senior clerics paid Ansar members to violently disrupt reformist events. See "Matn-e e'terafat-e Amir Farshad Ebrahimi."

77. Although the group apologized for its involvement in the Qods cinema attack in a statement released two days after the event, it claimed that it had acted in defense of revolutionary values and recommitted itself to the protection of hezbollahi culture. See *Resalat*, May 8, 1996.

78. See for instance, Ansari, *Iran and Democracy*, p. 108.

79. Farhi, "War Generation."

80. Mohsen Rezai's farewell speech to the IRGC, *Payam-e Enqelab*, no. 356, August/September 1997, pp. 16–17.

81. On the attacks against the pro-Khatami press, see Adam Tarock, "The Muzzling of the Liberal Press in Iran," *Third World Quarterly* 22, no. 4 (August 2001): pp. 585–602.

82. For a detailed narrative of these events, see Kaveh Basmenji, *Tehran Blues: Youth Culture in Iran* (London: Saqi, 2005), pp. 221–261.

83. "Islamic Guards Ready to Cut 'Sedition' on Khamenei's Order," *IRNA* (Tehran) in Persian, February 11, 1999, *BBC WM*, February 12, 1999.

84. Menashri, *Post-Revolutionary*, pp. 146–147.

85. For narratives of the July 1999 protests, see Basmenji, *Tehran*, pp. 250–258; also, Menashri, *Post-Revolutionary*, pp. 142–150.

86. "Military Commanders Give an Ultimatum to President Khatami," *Jomhuri-ye Eslami* (Tehran) in Persian, July 19, 1999, *BBC WM*, July 20, 1999. (Emphasis added.)

## *Chapter 9*

1. President George W. Bush, State of the Union Address, January 29, 2002. A transcript of the speech is available here: http://www.washingtonpost.com/wp-srv/onpolitics/transcripts/sou012902.htm

2. Takeyh, *Guardians*, pp. 209–212.

3. See for example, "Khatami Condemns Terrorism, Calls for Global Fight against It," *Vision of the Islamic Republic of Iran Network 1* (Tehran) in Persian, September 22, 2001, *BBCWM*, September 22, 2001.

4. "UN Should Be Invited to Intervene," *Tehran Times*, September18, 2001, http://old.tehran-times.com/Index_view.asp?code=71850 (accessed April 15, 2009).

5. "Paper Fears Terror Response Will Create Further Violence," *Aftab-e Yazd* (Tehran) in Persian, September 15, 2001, *BBCWM*, October 3, 2001.

6. Seyed Hossein Mousavian with Shahir ShahidSaless, *Iran and the United States: An Insider's View on the Failed Past and the Road to Peace* (New York: Bloomsbury, 2014), pp. 156–157.

7. Mousavian, *Iran and the United States*, p. 167.

8. Ibid., pp. 166–167.

9. For Crocker's comments, see Dexter Filkins, "The Shadow Commander," *The New Yorker*, September 30, 2013.

10. Ibid.

11. Mousavian, *Iran and the United States*, pp. 168–169,

12. Filkins, "Shadow Commander." For consistency, the spelling of Soleimani's name in the quotes attributed to Ryan Crocker was changed from the original rendering.

13. Mousavian, *Iran and the United States*, p. 169.

14. See the National Intelligence Council's January 2003 report "Regional Consequences of Regime Change in Iraq," included in the Select Committee on Intelligence's report "Prewar Intelligence Assessments about Postwar Iraq Together with Additional Views," May 25, 2007, http://www.intelligence.senate.gov/11076.pdf.

15. "Iranian Supreme Leader Says US President 'Thirsty for Human Blood,'" *Vision of the Islamic Republic of Iran Network 1* (Tehran) in Persian, January 31, 2002, *BBCWM*, February 1, 2002.

16. "Daily Accuses Reformers of Helping the Enemies," *Kayhan* (website) in Persian, February 5, 2002, *BBCMME*, February 6, 2002.

17. On the constraints on Khatami's presidency, see Ali Ansari, *Iran, Islam and Democracy: The Politics of Managing Change* (London: Chatham House, 2006), pp. 218–239; also see Ehteshami and Zweiri, *Neoconservatives*, pp. 1–29.

18. For John Simpson's account of the incident, see "Khatami Election Soured by Vigilantes," *BBC*, June 10, 2001, http://news.bbc.co.uk/2/hi/middle_east/1381859.stm.

19. On these murders, see Kasra Naji, *Ahmadinejad: The Secret History of Iran's Radical Leader* (Berkeley and Los Angeles: The University of California Press, 2008), pp. 102–106.

20. On the trials, see *Gooya*, December 20, 2004, http://news.gooya.com/politics/archives/020687.php; and Massoud Behnoud, *BBC Persian*, November 19, 2004, http://www.bbc.co.uk/persian/iran/story/2004/11/041119_mf_mb_kerman.shtml.

21. The MKO is often credited with discovering Iran's nuclear facilities through its own intelligence network; however, others have argued that the intelligence was given to the MKO to disclose by Israel's Mossad. See Fayazmanesh, *United States and Iran*, pp. 120–161.

22. On Iran's nuclear program, see Shahram Chubin, *Iran's Nuclear Ambitions* (Washington, DC: Carnegie Endowment for International Peace, 2006).

23. The November 2007 National Intelligence Estimate claims that Iran's nuclear weapons program was "halted" in fall 2003 due to international pressure. See "Iran: Nuclear Intentions and Capabilities," http://www.dni.gov/files/documents/Newsroom/Reports%20and%20Pubs/20071203_release.pdf; Also see David Sanger, *The Inheritance: The World Obama Confronts and the Challenges to American Power* (New York: Harmony Books, 2009), pp. 1–26.

24. For details on this letter and the Bush administration's response to it, see Sanger, *Inheritance*, pp. 47–50.

25. Citing unnamed sources investigative journalist Nicholas Kristof claims that both Khatami and Khamenei approved the proposal. See "Iran's Proposal for a 'Grand Bargain,'" http://kristof.blogs.nytimes.com/2007/04/28/irans-proposal-for-a-grand-bargain/.

26. For a facsimile of the purported proposal, see http://www.mideastweb.org/iranian_letter_of_2003.htm (Accessed April 2009).

27. Glenn Kessler, "In 2003, U.S. Spurned Iran's Offer of Dialogue," *Washington Post*, June 18, 2006. Also see the interview with John Bolton in the PBS *Frontline* episode "Showdown with Iran," http://www.pbs.org/wgbh/pages/frontline/showdown/themes/grandbargain.html#bolton.

28. Sanger, *Inheritance*, pp. 47–51.

29. Chubin, *Nuclear*, pp. 63–80.

30. Interview with Mohsen Rezai, *ISNA*, November 24, 2008, http://isna.ir/ISNA/NewsView.aspx?ID=News-460160 (Accessed April 2009).

31. *Fars News Agency*, November 25, 2004, http://www.farsnews.net/newstext.php? nn=8309050056.
32. *ILNA* Tehran (in Persian), November 19, 2004, *BBCMME*, November 19, 2004.
33. On the conservatives return to electoral power, see Eheteshami and Zweiri, *Neoconservatives*, pp. 33–45.
34. For a detailed analytical narrative of the 2005 presidential elections, see Naji, *Ahmadinejad*, pp. 57–90; also see Ehteshami and Zweiri, *Neoconservatives*, pp. 41–45.
35. Naji, *Ahmadinejad*, p. 75.
36. "Tehran University's Basij Students Favor Tehran Mayor in Pre-Election Poll," *IRNA, World News Connection*, June 13, 2005.
37. *Sobh-e Sadeq*, June 13, 2005, p. 1.
38. "Guardian Council Spokesman Denies Military Involvement in Election," *Tehran Sharq*, June 2, 2005, *World News Connection*, 2005.
39. "Daily Cites Interior Minister on Military Forces' Presence in Election," *Aftab-e Yazd*, June 1, 2005, *World News Connection*, June 1, 2005.
40. *ISNA*, June 6, 2005, http://isna.ir/ISNA/NewsView.aspx?ID=News-537385 (Accessed January 2009).
41. *Baztab*, June 14, 2005, http://web.archive.org/web/20050617025712/http://www.baztab.com/news/25322.php (Accessed January 2009).
42. *Fars News Agency*, June 13, 2005, http://www.farsnews.net/newstext.php?nn=8403230300.
43. See *Baztab*, June 14, 2005.
44. Naji, *Ahmadinejad*, p. 72.
45. *Baztab*, June 19, 2005, http://www.baztab.com/news/25542.php (Accessed January 2009).
46. *Fars News Agency*, June 22, 2005, http://www.farsnews.com/newstext.php?nn=8404010269.
47. Naji, *Ahmadinejad*, pp. 73–74.
48. For an analysis on the questionable math of the second round election results, see Bill Samii, "Iran: A New Paradigm and New Math," *Radio Free Europe / Radio Liberty*, June 26, 2005, http://www.rferl.org/Content/Article/1059502.html.
49. *ISNA*, June 25, 2006, http://isna.ir/Isna/NewsView.aspx?ID=News-546231(Accessed January 2009).
50. See for instance, *Fars News Agency*, July 2, 2005, http://www.farsnews.com/newstext.php?nn=8404110095.
51. On the so-called plot to elect Ahmadinejad, see Naji, *Ahmadinejad*, pp. 75–90.
52. See for instance the IRGC Public Relations Office's statement on the organization's efforts to maximize voter participation. *Fars News Agency*, June 25, 2005, http://www.farsnews.com/newstext.php?nn=8404040320.
53. "Iranian Guards Corps Says New President Must Remain 'Loyal' to Campaign Promises," *ILNA*, June 25, 2005, *World News Connection*, June 25, 2005.
54. On Ahmadinejad's first cabinet, see Ehteshami and Zweiri, *Neoconservatives*, pp. 67–69.
55. "Venezuelan Investment Authority Ranks USA, Iran Top Investors in 2006," *El Nacional* (Caracas), January 18, 2007, *BBCWM*, January 26, 2007.
56. *Mehr News*, January 16, 2006, http://web.archive.org/web/20060117065456/http://www.mehrnews.com/en/NewsDetail.aspx?NewsID=278772.
57. For instance, Mohsen Rezai's news organ *Tabnak* confirmed that four IRGC officers were killed on May 3, 2009 in a helicopter crash along the Venezuelan-Columbian border. *Tabnak*, May 24, 2009, http://www.tabnak.ir/fa/pages/?cid=49107.
58. On Hariri's assassination and its impact on Lebanon, see Nicholas Blanford, *Killing Mr. Lebanon: The assassination of Rafik Hariri and Its Impact on the Middle East* (London: I. B. Tauris, 2006).
59. Jefferson Morley, "The Branding of Lebanon's 'Revolution,'" *The Washington Post*, March 3, 2005, http://www.washingtonpost.com/wp-dyn/articles/A1911-2005Mar2.html; also, "Allies Resisting as U.S. Pushes for Hezbollah," *The New York Times*, February 17, 2005, http://www.nytimes.com/2005/02/17/world/middleeast/allies-resisting-as-us-pushes-terror-label-for-hezbollah.html.
60. On Hezbollah's postwar push for power, see Augustus Norton, "The Role of Hezbollah in Domestic Politics," *The International Spectator* 42, no. 4 (December 2007): pp. 475–491. Also see the chapter on Lebanon in Juan R. Cole, *Engaging the Muslim World* (New York: Palgrave MacMillan, 2009).

61. Robert F. Worth, "Deal for Lebanese Factions Leaves Hezbollah Stronger," *The New York Times*, May 22, 2008, http://www.nytimes.com/2008/05/22/world/middleeast/22lebanon.html?_r=1.

62. For the Hamas election victory and reaction inside the Bush administration, see Zaki Chehab, *Inside Hamas: The Untold Story of Militants, Martyrs and Spies* (London: I. B. Tauris, 2007), pp. 1–14.

63. Ibid., pp. 134–172.

64. "Hardline Daily Condemns MPs for Criticizing IRGC Deputy Commander," *Kayhan* (website) in Persian, February 16, 2002, *BBCMME*, February 17, 2002.

65. On SICI and Badr, see Juan R. Cole, "Shia Militias in Iraqi Politics," in *Iraq: Preventing a New Generation of Conflict*, eds. M. E. Bouillon et al. (Boulder and London: Lynne Rienner Publishers, 2007), pp. 109–123; Juan R. Cole, "The United States and Shi'ite Religious Factions in Post-Ba'thist Iraq," *Middle East Journal* 57, no. 4 (Autumn 2003), pp. 543–566; and International Crisis Group, "Shiite Politics in Iraq: The Role of the Supreme Council," November 15, 2007.

66. On an early assessment of Iran's involvement in Iraq, see International Crisis Group, "Iran in Iraq: How Much Influence?," March 21, 2005; also see Joseph Felter and Brian Fishman, "Iranian Influence in Iraq: Politics and 'Other Means,'" Occasional Paper Series, West Point: Combating Terrorism Center, October 1, 2008.

67. *CNN*, March 7, 2006, http://www.cnn.com/2006/WORLD/meast/03/07/rumsfeld.iraq/index.html.

68. Dafna Linzer, "Troops Authorized to Kill Iranian Operatives in Iraq," *The Washington Post*, January 26, 2007, http://www.washingtonpost.com/wp-dyn/content/article/2007/01/25/AR2007012502199.html.

69. The five Iranian detainees were ultimately released by the Obama administration in July 2009. See Liz Sly and Ned Parker, "U.S releases five Iranians in Iraq," *Los Angeles Times*, July 10, 2009, http://articles.latimes.com/2009/jul/10/world/fg-iranians-freed10.

70. *FarsNewsAgency*, January 12, 2007, http://www.farsnews.com/newstext.php?nn=8510220162.

71. "Military Admits G.I.s Kidnapped and Killed," *Daily News* (New York), January 27, 2007.

72. John F. Burns and Michael R. Gordon, "U.S. Says Iran Helped Iraqis Kill 5 G.I.s," *The New York Times*, July 3, 2007, http://www.nytimes.com/2007/07/03/world/middleeast/03iraq.html.

73. On Iranian involvement in hostage-taking during the Lebanese civil war, see Magnus Ranstorp, *Hizb'allah in Lebanon: The Politics of the Western Hostage Crisis* (New York, St. Martins Press, 1997).

74. *Sobh-e Sadeq*, February 12, 2007, p. 2.

75. On the sanctions, see Fayazmanesh, *United States and Iran*, pp. 202–228.

76. On the kidnapping of Robert Levinson, see Scott Peterson, "Exclusive: Iran nabbed CIA Asset Levinson, Says Witness." *Christian Science Monitor*, December 16, 2013, http://www.csmonitor.com/World/Middle-East/2013/1216/Exclusive-Iran-nabbed-CIA-asset-Levinson-says-witness-video.

77. Marisa Choncrane, "The Fragmentation of the Sadrist Movement," Iraq Report no. 12, Institute for the Study of War, 2009.

78. Michael R. Gordon, "U.S. Ties Iran to Deadly Iraq Attack," *The New York Times*, July 2, 2007, http://www.nytimes.com/2007/07/02/world/middleeast/02cnd-iran.html.

79. See the US charge sheet against Daqduq, "Continuation Sheet—MC Form 458 Jan 07, Block II Charges and Specifications in the case of United States of America v. Ali Musa Daqduq Al Musawi." January 2007. A copy of the charge sheet can be found here: http://www.documentcloud.org/documents/302052-daqduq-tribunal-chargesheet.html.

80. Felter and Fishman, "Iranian Influence in Iraq."

81. See Reidar Visser, "Basra, the Reluctant Seat of Shiastan," *Middle East Reports*, http://www.merip.org/mer/mer242/basra-reluctant-seat-shiastan; also, Michael Gordon, "The Last Battle," *New York Times*, August 3, 2008, http://www.nytimes.com/2008/08/03/magazine/03IRAQ-t.html.

82. Leila Fadel, "Iranian General Played Key Role in Iraq Cease-Fire," *McClatchy*, March 30, 2008, http://www.mcclatchydc.com/news/nation-world/world/middle-east/article24479815.html.

83. *Al-Zaman*, April 1, 2008, http://www.azzaman.com/index.asp?fname=2008\04\04–01\999.htm&storytitle= (Accessed June 2009).

84. Scott Peterson and Howard LaFranchi, "Iran's Role Rises as Iraq Peace Broker," *Christian Science Monitor*, May 14, 2008.

85. *Mehr News Agency*, September 23, 2007, http://www.mehrnews.com/fa/newsdetail. aspx?pr=a&NewsID=556030 (Accessed April 2009).

86. See Interview with IRGC commander-in-chief Mohammad Ali Jafari, *Jam-e Jam*, June 28, 2008, http://www.jamejamonline.ir/archnewstext.aspx?year=1387&month=4&day=8&n ewsnum=100942312993.

87. David Sanger argues that the intelligence officials who produced the 2007 NIE report intentionally sought to mitigate the Iranian threat so that if a war with Iran was to occur it could not be blamed on faulty intelligence as had been the case with Iraq. See Sanger, *The Inheritance*, pp. 16–26.

88. For instance, see Ali M. Ansari, *Confronting Iran: the Failure of American Foreign Policy and the Next Great Crisis in the Middle East* (New York: Basic Books, 2006); Scott Ritter, *Target Iran: The Truth about the White House's Plans for Regime Change* (New York: Nation Books, 2006); and David Barsamian, with Noam Chomsky, Ervand Abrahamian, and Nahid Mozaffari, *Targeting Iran* (San Francisco: Open Lights Books, 2007).

89. Seymour Hersh's chief articles on Iran during this period were "The Coming Wars: What the Pentagon Can Now Do in Secret," *The New Yorker*, January 24, 2005; "The Iran Plans: Would President Bush Go to War to Stop Tehran from Getting the Bomb?," *The New Yorker*, April 17, 2006; "Last Stand: The Military's Dissent on Iran Policy," *The New Yorker*, July 10, 2006; "The Redirection: Is the Administration's New Policy Benefitting Our Enemies in the War on Terrorism?," *The New Yorker*, March 5, 2007; "Shifting Targets: The Administration's Plan for Iran," *The New Yorker*, October 8, 2007; "Preparing the Battlefield: The Bush Administration Steps Up Its Secret Moves against Iran," *The New Yorker*, July 7, 2008.

90. The text of Senate Amendment 3017 can be found at: https://www.congress.gov/amend-ment/110th-congress/senate-amendment/3017/text.

91. On the establishment and use of Executive Order 13224, see Yonah Alexander and Michael Kraft, *Evolution of U.S. Counterterrorism Policy* (Praeger and Greenwood Publishing Group, 2008), pp. 992–994; also see Thomas J. Biersteke et al., *Countering the Financing of Terrorism* (New York: Taylor and Francis, 2007), pp. 214–216.

92. David M. Herszenhorn, "Senate Urges Bush to Declare Iran Guard a Terrorist Group," *The New York Times*, September 27, 2007, http://www.nytimes.com/2007/09/27/washing-ton/27cong.html (Accessed 12 May 2009).

93. A facsimile of the handwritten final revisions to amendment 3017 can be found at: http://thinkprogress.org/wp-content/uploads/2007/09/kyl-lieberman.pdf (Accessed 14 April 2009).

94. See for instance the Friday sermon delivered in Tehran by conservative cleric Ayatollah Ahmad Khatami before the amendment passed, *Voice of the Islamic Republic of Iran Tehran* (in Persian), August 10, 2007, *BBCMME*, August 17, 2007.

95. Iranian forces regularly clash with the Kurdish separatist Pjak organization along the border with Iraq and Azeri criminal networks along its northern border. For instance, see "Kurdish Rebels Said to Have Killed 15 Iranian Revolution Guards," Sbay Media (in Sorani Kurdish), May 29, 2008, *BBCMME*, May 29, 2008.

96. Jondollah claimed responsibility for these attacks and discussed its reasons behind them on its now-defunct website: "Jonbesh-e Moqavemat-e Mardomi-e Iran" (http://junbish. blogspot.com).

97. "Sunni Group Claims Bombing of Iran Mosque," *Reuters*, June 18, 2008, http://uk.reuters. com/article/worldNews/idUKL1840003220080618.

98. Indeed, despite the claims by a Balochi terrorist group, Iranian officials tried to place blame of the April Shiraz bombing on "Israeli agents" from within the local Baha'i religious minor-ity community—an erroneous claim that lacked both credibility and supporting evidence. See for instance, *Qods*, June 18, 2008, https://web.archive.org/web/20080601044353/ http://www.qodsdaily.com/news/politics/990.html .

99. For instance, see *Fars News Agency*, May 25, 2008, http://www.farsnews.com/newstext. php?nn=8703050116.

100. Seymour Hersh, "Preparing the Battlefield: the Bush Administration Steps Up Its Secret Moves against Iran," *The New Yorker*, June 2008, http://www.newyorker.com/reporting/2008/07/07/080707fa_fact_hersh?currentPage=all.
101. *Fars News Agency*, October 24, 2005, http://www.farsnews.com/newstext.php?nn=8408020316.
102. For a biography of Jafari, see *BBC Persian*, September 1, 2007, http://www.bbc.co.uk/persian/iran/story/2007/09/070901_mv-sepah-jafari.shtml.
103. This conclusion was also suggested by some IRGC officials. See for instance *E'temad-e Melli*'s interview with retired IRGC commander Mohammad Nabi-Rudaki, "Former Commander Speaks on Paramilitary Reforms," *E'temad-e Melli* (in Persian), July 7, 2008, *World News Connection*, July 9, 2008. However, alternative theories regarding the dismissal of Safavi and the promotion of Jafari have suggested a more political angle in the Supreme Leader's decision. See for instance Naji, *Ahmadinejad*, p. 271.
104. Babak Rahimi has argued that Jafari's expansion of the IRGC and Basij has also given these organizations a greater political role, see: "IRGC Reshuffling Aimed at Boosting Political Role," *Payvand News*, July 28, 2008, http://www.payvand.com/news/08/jul/1264.html. Also see Ali Alfoneh, "What Do Structural Changes in the Revolutionary Guards Mean?," *AEI Outlook Series*, no. 7, September 2008, http://www.aei.org/publication/what-do-structural-changes-in-the-revolutionary-guards-mean/.
105. *Fars News Agency*, July 8, 2008, http://www.farsnews.com/newstext.php?nn=8704180833.
106. *Aftab-e Yazd*, September 29, 2008, https://web.archive.org/web/20080930020703/http://www.aftab-yazd.com/textdetalis.asp?at=9/29/2008&aftab=8&TextID=62701 .
107. *Mehr News*, August 12, 2008, http://www.mehrnews.com/error.htm?aspxerrorpath=/fa/NewsDetail.aspx(Accessed August 2008).
108. Interview with Mohammad Ali Jafari, *Jam-e Jam*, June 28, 2008, http://www.jamejamonline.ir/archnewstext.aspx?year=1387&month=4&day=8&newsnum=100942312993.
109. *Aftab-e Yazd*, September 29. 2008.
110. *Fars News Agency*, July 2, 2008, http://www.farsnews.com/newstext.php?nn=8704120626.
111. Interview with retired IRGC commander Mohammad Nabi-Rudaki, "Former Commander Speaks on Paramility Reforms," *E'temad-e Melli* (in Persian), July 7, 2008, *World News Connection*, July 9, 2008.
112. *Fars News Agency*, July 13, 2008, http://www.farsnews.com/newstext.php?nn=8704230228.
113. See interview with Reza Saraj, president of the Basij Student Organization, *Fars News Agency*, July 20, 2008, http://www.farsnews.net/newstext.php?nn=8704301045.

## Chapter 10

1. Address to students at Shahid Beheshti University, May 28, 2003. Cited in Sadjadpour, *Reading Khamenei*.
2. "Videotaped Remarks by the President in Celebration of Nowruz." Office of the Press Secretary, March 20, 2009, http://www.whitehouse.gov/the_press_office/VIDEOTAPED-REMARKS-BY-THE-PRESIDENT-IN-CELEBRATION-OF-NOWRUZ.
3. "Rezaei Rejects Dull Debate with Ahmadinejad," *Press TV* (Tehran), June 8, 2009, http://edition.presstv.ir/detail/97403.html.
4. Nazila Fathi, "Chief Cleric of Iran Defends President," *The New York Times*, August 24, 2008, http://www.nytimes.com/2008/08/25/world/middleeast/25iran.html.
5. Ali M. Ansari, *Crisis of Authority: Iran's 2009 Presidential Election* (London: Chatham House, 2010), p. 27.
6. "Vakonesh-e nemayandeh-ye vali-ye faqih dar sepah beh yek shaye'eh." *Siyasat-e Ruz*, May 23, 2009, http://www.siasatrooz.ir/vdcc1eqs.2bqem8laa2.html.
7. Ibid.
8. *Sobh-e Sadeq*, June 13, 2005, p. 1.
9. For example, see *Sobh-e Sadeq*, nos. 399 and 400. Also, "Pasdaran Guard Publications Attacks Reformists," *Rooz Online*, 27 May 2009, http://www.roozonline.com/persian/news/newsitem/article/passdaran-guard-publications-attack-reformers.html.

10. Muhammad Sahimi, "Open Letter: Fatwa Issued for Changing the Vote in Favor of Ahmadinejad," *Tehran Bureau*, June 7, 2009, http://www.pbs.org/wgbh/pages/frontline/tehranbureau/2009/06/open-letter-fatwa-issued-for-changing-the-vote-in-favor-of-ahmadinejad.html. For the Persian text of the letter, see: http://tehranbureaublog.blogspot.com/2009/06/open-letter-fatwa-issued-for-changing_07.html.

11. Ali M. Ansari, *Crisis of Authority: Iran's 2009 Presidential Election* (London: Chatham House, 2010), pp. 46 and 48.

12. Ansari, *Crisis*, p. 50.

13. Ali M. Ansari, Daniel Berman, and Thomas Rintoul, "A Preliminary Analysis of the Voting Figures in Iran's 2009 Presidential Election." Chatham House, June 21, 2009, p. 50.

14. Scott Peterson, *Let the Swords Encircle Me: Iran—A Journey behind the Headlines* (New York: Simon & Schuster, 2010), p. 503.

15. Ansari, *Crisis*, p. 51.

16. Much of the violence recorded during this time is still accessible through videos on YouTube and in the reporting that came during the time. However, an excellent single source narrative of the violence of the early post-election unrest can be found in chapter eight of Peterson's *Let the Swords Encircle Me*.

17. Peterson, *Let the Swords*, pp. 518–519; also, Maziar Bahari, "Eyewitness Report from Bloody Iran Protest," *Newsweek*, June 14, 2009, http://www.newsweek.com/eyewitness-report-bloody-iran-protest-80901

18. The story of Neda Agha-Soltani's life and the circumstances of her death are best told in the documentary *A Death in Tehran*, Frontline-BBC, PBS, November 17, 2009.

19. Peterson, *Let the Swords*, p. 538.

20. Lindsey Hilsum, "Iran Militia Man: 'I Hope God Forgives Me.'" December 16, 2009, http://www.channel4.com/news/iran-militia-man-i-hope-god-forgives-me.

21. Robert F. Worth and Nazila Fathi, "Iranian Acknowledges Torture of Some Protesters," *The New York Times*, August 8, 2009, http://www.nytimes.com/2009/08/09/world/middleeast/09iran.html.

22. Simon Tisdall, "Iran Admits Election Demonstrators Were Tortured," *The Guardian*, August 9, 2009, http://www.theguardian.com/world/2009/aug/09/iran-protesters-torture-election.

23. Excerpts of Ahmad Khatami's sermon can be found in *Fars News Agency*, August 14, 2009, http://farsnews.com/newstext.php?nn=8805230493.

24. *Fars News Agency*, June 12, 2009, http://www.farsnews.com/newstext.php?nn=8803220007.

25. "Defa' az enqelab haqq-e sepah ast va sepah har-ja lazem bashad, vared mi-shavad." *E'temad*, January 14, 2014.

26. Ibid.

27. Arash Karami, "Leaked Video Renews Accusations of 2009 Election Fraud," *Al-Monitor*, June 2, 2014, http://www.al-monitor.com/pulse/originals/2014/06/leaked-video-accuses-2009-election-fraud.html.

28. *Jahan News*, June 17, 2009, http://jahannews.com/vdcc1xqp.2bqpx8laa2.html.

29. *Sobh-e Sadeq*, no. 411, August 10, 2009, p. 8.

30. "Iran Commander Accuses 'Foreigners' for Post-Election 'Plots,'" *Mehr News Agency*, August 22, 2009, *BBCMME*, August 22, 2009.

31. Maziar Bahari with Aimee Molloy, *Then They Came for Me: A Family's Story of Love, Captivity, and Survival* (New York: Random House, 2011), pp. 114–115.

32. Bahari, *Then They Came*, pp. 135–136.

33. "Guards Corps Commander Emphasizes "Obedience" to Iran Leader," *Qods* (Mashhad), May 8, 2011, *BBCMME*, May 11, 2011.

34. Naqdi was appointed Basij commander in October 2009, replacing Hojjat al-Islam Mehdi Taeb.

35. Interview with Commander Mohammad Reza Naqdi, *Iran*, November 24, 2009, p. 5.

36. That the Basij actively tried to improve its image after the 2009 unrest was confirmed by other officials, such as Brigadier General Ezzatollah Zarghami, the head of Iran's state-run radio and television network (*Sad o Sima*) who told an audience during the launch of a Basij center at the network on January 2, 2011: "since the sedition of 2009 one of the policies of the Basij has

been to improve the image of the Basij in [Iranian] society." Quoted in "Bazsazi-ye chehreh-ye basij dar jame'eh," *Rooz*, January 3, 2011, http://www.roozonline.com/english/news3/news-item/archive/2011/january/03/article/-d8fefcd55f.html.

37. Interview with Commander Mohammad Reza Naqdi, *Fars News Agency*, November 25, 2009, http://www.farsnews.com/newstext.php?nn=8809041854.
38. Interview with Commander Mohammad Reza Naqdi, *Fars News Agency*, November 25, 2009, http://www.farsnews.com/newstext.php?nn=8809041854.
39. *Fars News Agency*, July 24, 2010, http://www.farsnews.com/newstext.php?nn=8905020568.
40. Ibid.
41. Golkar, *Captive Society*.
42. Afshon Ostovar, "Iran's Basij: Membership in a Militant Islamic Organization," *Middle East Journal* 67, no. 3 (Summer 2013), pp. 345–361.
43. *Fars News Agency*, July 24, 2010, http://www.farsnews.com/newstext.php?nn=8905020568.
44. Ostovar, "Iran's Basij."
45. *Sobh-e Sadeq*, no. 399, May 18, 2009, p. 4.
46. Interview with Commander Mohammad Reza Naqdi, *Iran*, November 24, 2009, p. 5.
47. See "*Tavafoq-e basij beh niru-ye darya'i-ye sepah*," *Hamshahri Online*, November 19, 2008, http://hamshahrionline.ir/details/68807. Also, "Sardar Hamdani: Khalebanan va Yegan-haye Darya'i-ye Basij Vared-e Sazman-e Razm Khwahand Shod," *Kayhan*, September 28, 2008, available at: http://www.magiran.com/npview.asp?ID=1709058.
48. *Fars News Agency*, July 24, 2010, http://www.farsnews.com/newstext.php?nn=8905020568.
49. Golkar, "Ideological and Political Training."
50. Ostovar, "Iran's Basij."
51. Mohammad Javad Akhavan, '*Obur az Fetneh: Bazkhwani-ye Parvandeh-ye Yeksal-e Nabard-e Narm*. Jeld-e aval. Tehran: Markaz-e Motala'at va Pazhuheshha-ye Sazman-e Basij-e Daneshjuyi, Spring 2010, pp. 49–54.
52. Ibid., pp. 61–64.
53. Ibid., pp. 65–76.
54. Ibid., pp. 41–42.
55. Ibid., p. 15.
56. Ostovar, "Iran's Basij."
57. "Moqabeleh-ye kanandegan ba fetneh 88 gardan-haye imam-e 'ali (a.) ra tashkil dadand." *Jam-e Jam*, August 30, 2014, http://www.jamejamonline.ir/newspreview/1626061285877029851. Also see Galen Wright, "The Imam Ali Security Battalion," *The Arkenstone* (blog), October 11, 2014, http://thearkenstone.blogspot.com/2014/10/basij-organization-imam-ali-security.html.
58. "Sardar jafari: 100 gardan-e amniyati va 400 gardan-e nezami dar basij tashkil shodeh ast," *Iranian Students News Agency*, September 28, 2012, http://isna.ir/fa/news/91070704488/
59. *Sobh-e Sadeq*, no. 486, February 7, 2011, p. 2.
60. "IRGC Commander: US Unable to Control Political Hurricane in Region," *Fars News Agency*, February 19, 2011, http://english2.farsnews.com/newstext.php?nn=8911300865.
61. Ibid.
62. Marc Fisher, "In Tunisia, Act of One Fruit Vendor Sparks Wave of Revolution through Arab World," *The Washington Post*, March 26, 2011, http://www.washingtonpost.com/world/in-tunisia-act-of-one-fruit-vendor-sparks-wave-of-revolution-through-arab-world/2011/03/16/AFjfsueB_story.html.
63. *Fars News Agency*, February 13, 2011, http://www.farsnews.com/newstext.php?nn=8911240058.
64. Frederick Wehrey, "The Unforgotten Uprising in Eastern Saudi Arabia," Washington, DC: Carnegie Endowment for International Peace, June 2013, pp. 10–12.
65. Emile Hokayem, *Syria's Uprising and the Fracturing of the Levant* (London: Routledge, 2013).
66. Afshon Ostovar and Will McCants, *The Rebel Alliance: Why Syria's Armed Opposition Has Failed to Unify* (Alexandria, VA: CNA, 2013).
67. Jason Ukman and Liz Sly, "Obama: Syrian President Assad Must Step Down," *The Washington Post*, August 18, 2011, http://www.washingtonpost.com/blogs/checkpoint-washington/post/obama-syrian-president-assad-must-step-down/2011/08/18/gIQAM75UNJ_blog.html.

68. Iran's leaders walked a fine line between condemning foreign intervention in Libya while morally supporting the protestors. See for instance, Semira N. Nikou, "Iran Backs Libyan Rebels, Chastises West over Oil, Bahrain," *Tehran Bureau*, April 6, 2011, http://www.pbs.org/wgbh/pages/frontline/tehranbureau/2011/04/iran-backs-libyan-rebels-chastises-west-over-oil-bahrain.html.

69. On the Bahrain uprising, see Toby Matthiesen, *Sectarian Gulf: Bahrain, Saudi Arabia, and the Arab Spring That Wasn't* (Stanford: Stanford University Press, 2013).

70. Wehrey, "The Forgotten Uprising," pp. 12–16.

71. *Fars News Agency*, March 16, 2011, http://www.farsnews.com/newstext.php?nn=8912251009.

72. *Fars News Agency*, March 16, 2011, http://www.farsnews.com/printable.php?nn=8912250900.

73. *Fars News Agency*, March 16, 2011, http://www.farsnews.com/newstext.php?nn=8912251033.

74. *Fars News Agency*, March 16, 2011, http://www.farsnews.com/newstext.php?nn=8912251030.

75. *Javan*, March 17, 2011, http://javanonline.ir/fa/news/443704/.

76. *Fars News Agency*, April 26, 2011, http://www.farsnews.com/newstext.php?nn=9002031362.

77. David Ignatius, "Intelligence Links Iran to Saudi Diplomat's Murder," *The Washington Post*, October 13, 2011, http://www.washingtonpost.com/blogs/post-partisan/post/intelligence-links-iran-to-saudi-diplomats-murder/2011/10/13/gIQAFzCPiL_blog.html.

78. Charlie Savage and Scott Shane, "Iranians Accused of a Plot to Kill Saudis' U.S. Envoy," *The New York Times*, October 11, 2011, http://www.nytimes.com/2011/10/12/us/us-accuses-iranians-of-plotting-to-kill-saudi-envoy.html.

79. See the US District Court of Southern New York's indictment of Arbabsiar and Shakuri, "United States of America v. Mannsor Arbabsiar (a/k/a "Mansour Arbabsiar") and Gholam Shakuri (a/k/a "Ali Gholam Shakuri"), Defendants," 2011.

80. "2 charged in Saudi plot; Iran rejects allegations," *CBS News*, October 20, 2011, http://www.cbsnews.com/news/2-charged-in-saudi-plot-iran-rejects-allegations.

81. I was among the skeptics. See, Afshon Ostovar, "Worst. Plot. Ever.," *Foreign Policy*, October 13, 2011, http://www.foreignpolicy.com/articles/2011/10/13/worst_plot_ever.

82. See Clinton's interview with the Associated Press. Matthew Lee, "AP Interview: Plot to Kill Envoy Will Hurt Iran," October 11, 2011, "http://www.boston.com/news/nation/washington/articles/2011/10/11/ap_interview_plot_to_kill_envoy_will_hurt_iran/.

83. Vytenis Didziulis, "Behind Manssor Arbabsiar's Plot to Kill the Saudi U.S. Ambassador," *ABC News*, October 22, 2011, http://abcnews.go.com/ABC_Univision/mansour-arbabsiars-twisted-plot-kill-saudi-us-ambassador/story?id=17533527.

84. David Ignatius, "Intelligence Links Iran to Saudi Diplomat's Murder," *The Washington Post*, October 13, 2011, http://www.washingtonpost.com/blogs/post-partisan/post/intelligence-links-iran-to-saudi-diplomats-murder/2011/10/13/gIQAFzCPiL_blog.html; also, Crist, *Twilight War*, p. 562.

85. Crist, *Twilight War*, pp. 564–566.

86. "Manssor Arbabsiar Sentenced in New York City Federal Court to 25 Years in Prison for Conspiring with Iranian Military Officials to Assassinate the Saudi Arabian Ambassador to the United States," US Department of Justice Office of Public Affairs, May 30, 2013, http://www.justice.gov/opa/pr/manssor-arbabsiar-sentenced-new-york-city-federal-court-25-years-prison-conspiring-iranian.

87. http://www.justice.gov/opa/pr/manssor-arbabsiar-sentenced-new-york-city-federal-court-25-years-prison-conspiring-iranian.

88. Crist, *Twilight War*, p. 566.

89. Vytenis Didziulis, "Behind Manssor Arbabsiar's Plot to Kill the Saudi U.S. Ambassador," *ABC News*, October 22, 2011, http://abcnews.go.com/ABC_Univision/mansour-arbabsiars-twisted-plot-kill-saudi-us-ambassador/story?id=17533527.

90. "Man Sentenced in Plot to Kill Saudi Ambassador," *The New York Times*, May 30, 2013, http://www.nytimes.com/2013/05/31/nyregion/mansour-arbabsiar-sentenced-for-plot-to-kill-saudi-ambassador.html.

91. I explored an earlier version of this thesis in Afshon Ostovar et al., *On Shifting Sands: Iranian Strategy in a Changing Middle East* (Alexandria, VA: CNA, 2013).

92. See the International Monetary Fund's World Economic Outlook, April 2013, http://www.imf.org/external/pubs/ft/weo/2013/01/pdf/text.pdf.

93. US Department of State, "Treasury Targets Iran's Islamic Revolutionary Guard Corps," February 10, 2010, http://www.state.gov/r/pa/prs/ps/2010/02/136595.htm.

94. US Department of Treasury, "Treasury Sanctions Major Iranian Commercial Entities," June 23, 2011, http://www.treasury.gov/press-center/press-releases/Pages/tg1217.aspx.

95. US Department of Treasury, "Treasury Sanctions Two Iranian Officials for Serious Human Rights Abuses," December 13, 2011, http://www.treasury.gov/press-center/press-releases/Pages/tg1383.aspx.

96. UNSC Resolution 1929 (2010), June 9, 2010, http://www.iaea.org/newscenter/focus/iaeairan/unsc_res1929-2010.pdf.

97. US Department of State, "Treasury Targets Iran's Islamic Revolutionary Guard Corps," February 10, 2010, http://www.state.gov/r/pa/prs/ps/2010/02/136595.htm.

98. Ibid. These included: Ali Akbar Ahmadian (former IRGC joint staff chief), Mohammad Hejazi (deputy chief of staff of Iran's armed forces, former Basij commander), Hosayn Salimi (IRGC Air Force commander), and Morteza Rezai (IRGC deputy commander).

99. See David Albright, Paul Brannan, and Christina Walrond, *Did Stuxnet Take Out 1,000 Centrifuges at the Natanz Enrichment Plant?* ISIS Report, Institute for Science and International Security, December 22, 2010.

100. On these attacks, see David Crist, *The Twilight War: The Secret History of America's Thirty-Year Conflict with Iran* (New York: Penguin Press, 2012), p. 552.

101. *Fars News Agency*, July 23, 2011, http://www.farsnews.com/newstext.php?nn=9005011495; also, *Press TV*, July 24, 2011, http://edition.presstv.ir/detail.fa/190606.html.

102. "Iran Car Explosion Kills Nuclear Scientist in Tehran," *BBC News*, January 11, 2012, http://www.bbc.co.uk/news/world-middle-east-16501566.

103. *Press TV*, July 23, 2011, http://edition.presstv.ir/detail.fa/190414.html.

104. *Asr-e Iran*, July 31, 2012, http://www.asriran.com/fa/news/224185/.

105. *Fars News Agency*, July 22, 2012, http://english2.farsnews.com/newstext.php?nn=9104251006.

106. Crist, *Twilight Wars*, pp. 550–552.

107. David E. Sanger, "Obama Order Sped Up Wave of Cyberattacks against Iran," *New York Times*, June 1, 2012, http://www.nytimes.com/2012/06/01/world/middleeast/obama-ordered-wave-of-cyberattacks-against-iran.

108. Dan Raviv and Yossi Melman, *Spies against Armageddon: Inside Israel's Secret Wars* (Sea Cliff, NY: Levant Books, 2012), pp. 10–14.

109. *Fars News Agency*, November 13, 2011, http://www.farsnews.com/newstext.php?nn=13900822000290 ; For further details on the incident and Tehrani Moghadam, see Mohammad Reza Yazdanpanha, "Explosion at Shahab Missile Depot," *Rooz*, November 14, 2011, http://www.roozonline.com/english/news3/newsitem/article/explosion-at-shahab-missile-depot.html; and "The Mysterious Death of Brigadier General Hassan Tehrani-Moghadam," *IranPolitik*, November 16, 2011, http://www.iranpolitik.com/2011/11/16/news/mysterious-death-brigadier-general-hassan-tehrani-moghadam/.

110. Ibid., 14.

111. An example here is the arrest of two Iranian nationals in Nairobi, Kenya, in June 2012. The two had stored over thirty pounds of RDX explosives at a safe house—explosives Kenyan authorities later determined were to be used in terrorist attacks against Israeli officials. The Iranian nationals, who had purported links to Quds Force, were sentenced by a Kenyan court to life in prison on terrorism charges in May 2013. Iran denied involvement. See "Iranians Jailed for Life in Kenya over Terror Charges," *BBC News*, May 6, 2013, http://www.bbc.com/news/world-africa-22425366.

112. Jason Burke, "How Iran's Revenge Bomb Plot over Nuclear Programme Took Shape," *The Guardian*, June 18, 2012, http://www.theguardian.com/world/2012/jun/17/iran-nuclear-revenge-bomb-plot.

113. "Car Bombs 'Target Israel Envoys' in India and Georgia," *BBC News*, February 13, 2012, http://www.bbc.com/news/world-asia-india-17013987.

114. Thomas Fuller and Rick Gladstone, "Blasts in Bangkok Add to Suspicions about Iran," *The New York Times*, February 14, 2014, http://www.nytimes.com/2012/02/15/world/asia/explosions-in-bangkok-injures-suspected-iranian-national.html; also, Levitt, *Hezbollah*, pp. 366–367.

115. "ThaiCourtHandsIranianLifeSentenceoverBotchedBombing,"*Reuters*,August22,2013,http://www.reuters.com/article/2013/08/22/us-thailand-iran-bomb-idUSBRE97L06Z20130822.

116. Jason Burke, "How Iran's Revenge Bomb Plot over Nuclear Programme Took Shape," *The Guardian*, June 18, 2012, http://www.theguardian.com/world/2012/jun/17/iran-nuclear-revenge-bomb-plot.

117. The family of the suspected accomplice, Syed Mohammed Kazmi, a local Indian journalist, has vigorously maintained his innocence. See for example, Naziya Alvi, "Israel Embassy Car Attack: Kazmi 'Honest', but Few Vouch for His Innocence," *The Times of India*, March 10, 2012, http://timesofindia.indiatimes.com/city/delhi/Israel-embassy-car-attack-Kazmi-honest-but-few-vouch-for-his-innocence/articleshow/12204231.cms.

118. Neeraj Chauhan, "Cops Name Iran Military Arm for Attack on Israeli Diplomat," *The Times of India*, July 30, 2012, http://timesofindia.indiatimes.com/city/delhi/Cops-name-Iran-military-arm-for-attack-on-Israeli-diplomat/articleshow/15263013.cms. Also, Jason Burke, "Iran Was behind Bomb Plot against Israeli Diplomats, Investigators Find," *The Guardian*, June 17, 2008, http://www.theguardian.com/world/2012/jun/17/iran-bomb-plot-israel-nuclear-talks.

119. Kate Hodal, "Iranians Convicted over Bangkok Bomb Plot," *The Guardian*, August 22, 2013, http://www.theguardian.com/world/2013/aug/22/thai-court-convicts-iranians-bomb-plot.

120. Jason Burke, "Iran Was behind Bomb Plot against Israeli Diplomats, Investigators Find," *The Guardian*, June 17, 2008, http://www.theguardian.com/world/2012/jun/17/iran-bomb-plot-israel-nuclear-talks.

121. Levitt, *Hezbollah*, pp. 361–365.

## *Chapter 11*

1. Speech to the residents of Qom, January 8, 2007. Cited in Sadjadpour, *Reading Khamenei*, p. 25.

2. Vali Nasr, *The Shia Revival*, p. 20.

3. Excerpts from Soleimani's May 22, 2011 Qom speech are included here: *Mashreq*, November 7, 2011, http://www.mashreghnews.ir/fa/news/77605/.

4. "In His Own Words, an Iranian Fighter Explains Tehran's War in Syria," *Medium*, December 8, 2014, https://medium.com/war-is-boring/in-his-own-words-an-iranian-fighter-explains-tehrans-war-in-syria-f2fd509c7885 (some spellings changed for consistency); also see the original, *Mashreq News*, Dec 1, 2014, http://www.mashreghnews.ir/fa/print/367190.

5. Taeb's comments were controversial and subsequently censored. This statement can still be found here: *BBC News* (Persian Service), February 14, 2013, http://www.bbc.co.uk/persian/iran/2013/02/130214_nm_tayeb_syria_basij.shtml.

6. *Fars News Agency*, September 14, 2013, http://www.farsnews.com/newstext.php?nn=13920623001002.

7. On the contours of the rebellion, see Emile Hokayem, *Syria's Uprising and the Fracturing of the Levant* (New York: Routledge, 2013).

8. Afshon Ostovar and William McCants, *The Rebel Alliance: Why Syria's Armed Opposition Has Failed to Unify*, Alexandria, VA: CNA, March 2013.

9. See for instance, Jonathan Saul, "Exclusive: Russia Steps Up Military Lifeline to Syria's Assad—Sources," *Reuters*, January 17, 2014, http://www.reuters.com/article/2014/01/17/us-syria-russia-arms-idUSBREA0G0MN20140117; and Michael Peel, "Iran, Russia and China Prop Up Assad Economy," *The Financial Times*, June 27, 2013, http://www.ft.com/intl/cms/s/0/79eca81c-df48-11e2-a9f4-00144feab7de.html#axzz3Igyo7hbo.

10. In March 2011 Turkish authorities detained an Iranian Yas Air flight destined for Syria. The plane carried crates of weapons and ammunition in its cargo hold. See http://www.securitycouncilreport.org/atf/cf/%7B65BFCF9B-6D27-4E9C-8CD3-CF6E4FF96FF9%7D/s_2012_395.pdf.

11. "Administration Takes Additional Steps to Hold the Government of Syria Accountable for Violent Repression Against the Syrian People," US Department of the Treasury, May 18, 2011, http://www.treasury.gov/press-center/press-releases/Pages/tg1181.aspx.

12. "Treasury Sanctions Syrian, Iranian Security Forces for Involvement in Syrian Crackdown," US Department of the Treasury, June 29, 2011, http://www.treasury.gov/press-center/press-releases/Pages/tg1224.aspx.

13. "Treasury Designates Iranian Commercial Airline Linked to Iran's Support for Terrorism," US Department of the Treasury, October 12, 2011, http://www.treasury.gov/press-center/press-releases/Pages/tg1322.aspx.

14. "Treasury Targets Iranian Arms Shipments," US Department of the Treasury, March 27, 2012, http://www.treasury.gov/press-center/press-releases/Pages/tg1506.aspx.

15. "Treasury Designates Syrian Entity, Others Involved in Arms and Communications Procurement Networks and Identifies Blocked Iranian Aircraft," US Department of the Treasury, September 19, 2012, http://www.treasury.gov/press-center/press-releases/Pages/tg1714.aspx.

16. Louis Charbonneau, "Exclusive: Western Report—Iran Ships Arms, Personnel to Syria via Iraq," *Reuters*, September 19, 2012, http://www.reuters.com/article/2012/09/19/us-syria-crisis-iran-iraq-idUSBRE88I17B20120919.

17. Will Fulton, Joseph Holliday, and Sam Wyer, "Iranian Strategy in Syria." AEI and The Institute for the Study of War, May 2013, p. 17.

18. *Quds Online*, May 27, 2012, http://qudsonline.ir/detail/News/50685.

19. Mehdi Taeb interview, *Asr-e Iran*, February 14, 2013, http://www.asriran.com/fa/print/257730.

20. *Iranian Students News Agency*, September 16, 2012, http://isna.ir/fa/news/0000178343/.

21. Mehdi Taeb interview, *Asr-e Iran*, February 14, 2013.

22. See comments by IRGC commander Hosayn Hamedani here: *Parsine*, May 7, 2014, http://www.parsine.com/fa/news/188383.

23. "Treasury Sanctions Al-Nusrah Front Leadership in Syria and Militias Supporting the Asad Regime," US Department of the Treasury, December 11, 2012, http://www.treasury.gov/press-center/press-releases/pages/tg1797.aspx.

24. "Insight: Syrian Government Guerilla Fighters Being Sent to Iran for Training," *Reuters*, April 4, 2013, http://www.reuters.com/article/2013/04/04/us-syria-iran-training-insight-idUSBRE9330DW20130404.

25. Ostovar, et al. "Iranian Strategy in Syria," p. 20.

26. Mehdi Taeb interview, *Asr-e Iran*, February 14, 2013.

27. *Fars News Agency*, September 23, 2013, http://www.farsnews.com/newstext.php?nn=13920701001324.

28. Caleb Weiss, "Iranian Basij General Killed in Aleppo," *The Long War Journal*, October 16, 2014, http://www.longwarjournal.org/threat-matrix/archives/2014/10/iranian_basij_general_killed_i.php.

29. *Etemad*, September 9, 2014.

30. Ewen MacAskill, "Iraq Rejects US Request to Maintain Bases after Troop Withdrawal," *The Guardian*, October 21, 2011, http://www.theguardian.com/world/2011/oct/21/iraq-rejects-us-plea-bases.

31. Jassem Al Salami, "In His Own Words, an Iranian Fighter Explains Tehran's War in Syria," https://medium.com/war-is-boring/in-his-own-words-an-iranian-fighter-explains-tehrans-war-in-syria-f2fd509c7885 (some spellings changed for consistency); also see the original, http://www.mashreghnews.ir/fa/print/367190.

32. The article containing these comments was originally published by *Fars News Agency* on May 5, 2014, and removed from the site shortly thereafter. However, the article was re-posted by the *Parsine* website on May 7, 2014 and is available here: http://www.parsine.com/fa/news/188383. Also see Arash Karami, "Former IRGC Commander's Syria Comments Censored," *Al Monitor*, May 5, 2014, http://www.al-monitor.com/pulse/originals/2014/05/former-irgc-commander-syria-comments-censored.html.

33. *Iranian Labor News Agency (ILNA)*, October 2, 2014, http://www.ilna.ir/news/news.cfm?id=210406.

34. Jonathan Saul and Parisa Hafezi, "Iran Boosts Military Support in Syria to Bolster Assad," *Reuters*, February 21, 2014, http://www.reuters.com/article/2014/02/21/us-syria-crisis-iran-idUSBREA1K09U20140221.

35. See "Update to the Iranian Financial Sanctions Regulations; Sanctions Designations; Non-proliferation Sanctions Designations; Anti-terrorism Designations; Non-proliferation Sanctions Designations Updates; Anti-terrorism Sanctions Designations Updates," US Department of the Treasury, November 8, 2012, http://www.treasury.gov/resource-center/sanctions/OFAC-Enforcement/Pages/20121108.aspx.

36. Farnaz Fassihi, "Tensions Rise over Iranian Hostages," *The Wall Street Journal*, August 8, 2012, http://online.wsj.com/articles/SB10000872396390443792604577575221903873222.

37. Babak Dehghanpisheh, "Syria Releases 2,130 Captives to Rebels in Exchange for 48 Iranian Prisoners," *The Washington Post*, January 9, 2013, http://www.washingtonpost.com/world/middle_east/syria-frees-2000-rebel-captives-in-exchange-for-48-iranian-prisoners/2013/01/09/f05bc3ba-5a5b-11e2-beee-6e38f5215402_story.html.

38. *Digarban*, January 11, 2013, http://digarban.com/node/10609.

39. All references to these videos are drawn from the version compiled and released as part of the September 2013 BBC documentary, "Iran's Secret Army." That documentary is available here: https://www.youtube.com/watch?v=ZI_88ChjQtU.

40. On the circumstances of Shateri's death, see Will Fulton, "The Assassination of Iranian Quds Force General Hassan Shateri in Syria," Iran Tracker, February 28, 2013, http://www.iran-tracker.org/analysis/fulton-assassination-iranian-quds-force-general-hassan-shateri-syria-february-28-2013.

41. Dexter Filkins, "The Shadow Commander," *The New Yorker*, September 13, 2013.

42. *Fars News Agency*, February 13, 2014, http://farsnews.com/printable.php?nn=13921124000724.

43. "Treasury Targets Hizballah for Supporting the Assad Regime" US Department of the Treasury, August 10, 2012, http://www.treasury.gov/press-center/press-releases/Pages/tg1676.aspx.

44. Marisa Sullivan, "Hezbollah in Syria," Institute for the Study of War, Middle East Security Report no. 19, April 2014.

45. Wassim Mroueh, "Drastic Rise in Hezbollah Death Toll as Party Battles for Yabroud," *Daily Star*, March 10, 2014, http://www.dailystar.com.lb/News/Lebanon-News/2014/Mar-10/249775-drastic-rise-in-hezbollah-death-toll-as-party-battles-for-yabroud.ashx.

46. Hisham Ashkar, "Hezbollah Fighters Killed in Syria," *Al-Akhbar*, March 31, 2014, http://english.al-akhbar.com/node/19226.

47. "Lebanon Says Arrest of Man behind Iran Embassy Attacks Unclear," *Press TV*, January 1, 2014, http://www.presstv.com/detail/2014/01/01/343168/alqaeda-leader-arrest-unclear-lebanon/.

48. Lina Saigol, David Gardener, and Borzou Daraghi, "Twin Explosions Leave 23 Dead Near Iran's Embassy in Beirut," *The Financial Times*, November 19, 2013, http://www.ft.com/intl/cms/s/0/ea0bfb2e-50f5-11e3-b499-00144feabdc0.html.

49. Laila Bassam and Erika Solomon, "Suicide Bombings Kill 23 Near Iran Embassy in Beirut," *Reuters*, November 19, 2013, http://www.reuters.com/article/2013/11/19/us-lebanon-blast-idUSBRE9AI08G20131119.

50. Loveday Morris and Ahmed Ramadan, "Deadly Blasts Near Iran's Embassy in Lebanon Linked to Syrian War, Sectarian Divisions," *The Washington Post*, November 19, 2013, http://www.washingtonpost.com/world/double-bombing-kills-at-least-10-near-iranian-embassy-in-beirut/2013/11/19/2cbee066-50fc-11e3-9ee6-2580086d8254_story.html.

51. "Saudis behind Blasts at Iran Embassy, Hezbollah Says," *BBC News*, December 3, 2013, http://www.bbc.com/news/world-middle-east-25210712.

52. Laila Bassam and Erika Solomon, "Suicide Bombings Kill 23 Near Iran Embassy in Beirut," *Reuters*, November 19, 2013, http://www.reuters.com/article/2013/11/19/us-lebanon-blast-idUSBRE9AI08G20131119.

53. Oliver Poole, "Fears of Retaliatory Attacks in Lebanon after al-Qaida Chief Dies in Army Hospital," *The Independent*, January 5, 2013, http://www.independent.co.uk/news/world/middle-east/fears-of-retaliatory-attacks-in-lebanon-after-alqaida-chief-dies-in-army-hospital-9039189.html.

54. Farnaz Fassihi, "Beirut Bombs Target Iranian Center," *The Wall Street Journal*, February 19, 2014, http://online.wsj.com/articles/SB10001424052702304914204579392450552660172.

55. Anne Barnard, "Sectarian Wedge Pushes Syria into Lebanon," *The New York Times*, October 27, 2014, http://www.nytimes.com/2014/10/28/world/middleeast/a-sectarian-wedge-pushes-from-syria-into-lebanon.html.

56. Qassim Abdul-Zahra, "Prominent Shiite Cleric Backs Fighting in Syria," *The Associated Press*, December 15, 2013, http://bigstory.ap.org/article/prominent-shiite-cleric-backs-fighting-syria.

57. Martin Chulov, "Controlled by Iran, the Deadly Militia Recruiting Iraq's Men to Die in Syria," *The Guardian*, March 12, 2014, http://www.theguardian.com/world/2014/mar/12/iraq-battle-dead-valley-peace-syria.

58. Ibid.

59. Christopher Anzalone, "Zaynab's Guardians: The Emergence of Shi'a Militias in Syria," *CTC Sentinel*, July 23, 2013, https://www.ctc.usma.edu/posts/zaynabs-guardians-the-emergence-of-shia-militias-in-syria.

60. This image can be found at Imageprop: http://imageprop.tumblr.com/page/2.

61. *Raja News*, May 8, 2013, http://www.rajanews.com/detail.asp?id=156851.

62. The vast majority of non-Iranian Shiite fighters in Syria come from Lebanon, Iraq, and, to a lesser extent, Afghanistan. Much smaller numbers come from other countries. On this, see Phillip Smyth, "Fighters from Exotic Locales In Syria's Shia Militias," Jihadology, July 30, 2013, http://jihadology.net/2013/07/30/hizballah-cavalcade-the-lion-of-damascus-and-afghans-and-africans-oh-my-fighters-from-exotic-locales-in-syrias-shia-militias/.

63. On Afghans fighting in Syria, see Phillip Smyth, "Iran's Afghan Shiite Fighters in Syria," The Washington Institute for Near East Policy, June 3, 2014, http://www.washingtoninstitute.org/policy-analysis/view/irans-afghan-shiite-fighters-in-syria.

64. Farnaz Fassihi, "Iran Pays Afghans to Fight for Assad," *The Wall Street Journal*, May 22, 2014, http://online.wsj.com/articles/SB10001424052702304908304579564161508613846.

65. *Fars News Agency*, December 8, 2013, http://www.farsnews.com/newstext.php?nn=13920917000459.

66. Jassem Al Salami, "Iran Is Forcing Poor Afghans to Fight and Die in Syria," *Medium*, October 21, 2014, https://medium.com/war-is-boring/iran-is-forcing-poor-afghans-to-fight-and-die-in-syria-4e58fc839be2.

67. Julia Preston, "Military Path Opened for Young Immigrants," *The New York Times*, September 26, 2014, http://www.nytimes.com/2014/09/26/us/military-path-opened-for-young-immigrants.html?_r=0. Also see Molly F. McIntosh, Seema Sayala, and David Gregory, *Non-Citizens in the Enlisted U.S. Military*, CNA Corporation, November 2011, http://www.cna.org/research/2011/non-citizens-enlisted-us-military.

68. Laura Rozen, "Inside the Secret US-Iran Diplomacy That Sealed Nuke Deal," *Al-Monitor*, August 11, 2015, http://www.al-monitor.com/pulse/originals/2015/08/iran-us-nuclear-kham enei-salehi-jcpoa-diplomacy.html.

69. Peter Baker, Mark Landler, David E. Sanger, and Anne Barnard, "Off-the-Cuff Obama Line Put U.S. in Bind on Syria," *The New York Times*, May 4, 2013, http://www.nytimes.com/2013/05/05/world/middleeast/obamas-vow-on-chemical-weapons-puts-him-in-tough-spot.html.

70. *Tabnak*, September 1, 2013, http://www.tabnak.ir/fa/news/342160/.

71. Consider the perspectives of Iraqi Sunni leaders on the abuses of the Maliki government: "In Their Own Words: Sunnis on Their Treatment in Maliki's Iraq," *Frontline* (PBS), October 28, 2014, http://www.pbs.org/wgbh/pages/frontline/iraq-war-on-terror/rise-of-isis/in-their-own-words-sunnis-on-their-treatment-in-malikis-iraq/.

72. Ned Parker, Ahmed Rasheed, and Raheem Salman, "Before Iraq Election, Shi`ite Militias Unleashed in War on Sunni Insurgents," *Reuters*, April 27, 2014, http://uk.reuters.com/article/2014/04/27/uk-iraq-strife-idUKBREA3Q0FO20140427.

73. Matt Bradley and Ali A. Nabhan, "Iraqi Officer Takes a Dark Turn to al Qaeda," *The Wall Street Jounral*, March 17, 2014, http://online.wsj.com/articles/SB100014240527023048347045794054407673594 48.

74. On the Islamic State's relationship to Al Qaeda and the broader jihadist movement see, Daniel Byman, *Al Qaeda, the Islamic State, and the Global Jihadist Movement: What Everyone Needs to Know*. (New York: Oxford University Press, 2015).

75. On the Islamic State and its leader, Abu Bakr Baghdadi, see: William McCants, *The ISIS Apocalypse: the History, Strategy, and Doomsday Vision of the Islamic State*. (New York: St. Martin's Press, 2015).

76. See this statement by Sistani, originally delivered by his representative Shaykh Abd al-Mahdi al-Karbalai as part of a Friday prayer sermon in Karbala on July 11, 2014: http://www.sistani.org/arabic/archive/24925/.

77. "Iran Congratulates Iraq on New Premier Designate," *Press TV*, August 12, 2014, http://www.presstv.com/detail/2014/08/12/375066/iran-congratulates-iraq-on-pm-pick/.

78. See for instance, "Iraq Conflict: Iran's Rouhani 'Ready to Help,' " http://www.bbc.com/news/world-middle-east-27847498; also, Hugh Tomlinson, "Iran's Special Forces Rush to Help Floundering Ally," *The Times*, June 12, 2014, http://www.thetimes.co.uk/tto/news/world/middleeast/iraq/article4116273.ece.

79. Michael R. Gordon and Eric Schmitt, "Iran Secretly Sending Drones and Supplies Into Iraq, U.S. Officials Say," *The New York Times*, June 25, 2014, http://www.nytimes.com/2014/06/26/world/middleeast/iran-iraq.html

80. "Barzani Says Turkey Sent Arms to KRG, PYD Members Treated in Turkey," *Hurriyet Daily News*, October 13, 2014, http://www.hurriyetdailynews.com/Default.aspx?pageID=238&nID=72924&NewsCatID=352.

81. Michael R. Gordon and Eric Schmitt, "Iran Sends 3 Attack Planes to Iraqi Government," *The New York Times*, July 8, 2014, http://www.nytimes.com/2014/07/09/world/middleeast/iran-sends-3-attack-planes-to-iraqi-government.html.

82. Joseph Dempsey, "Iraqi's Latest Su-25s Come from Iran," International Institute of Strategic Studies, *Military Balance* (blog), July 2, 2014, http://www.iiss.org/en/militarybalanceblog/blogsections/2014-3bea/july-8d3b/iraqis-latest-su-25s-come-from-iran-889a.

83. Golnaz Esfandiari, "Iran IRGC's First 'Martyr' Versus ISIS?," *RFE/RL*, June 16, 2014, http://www.rferl.mobi/a/iran-iraq-irgc-death-ISIS-moshajari/25424430.html.

84. Images of Murjani's funeral were posted in Iranian press. See *Fars News Agency*, July 4, 2014, http://farsnews.com/imgrep.php?nn=13930413000621.

85. *Fars News Agency*, March 29, 2014, http://www.farsnews.com/newstext.php?nn=13930108000154.

86. Arash Karami, "Khamenei Rep Blames Saudi Arabia, Qatar for Insurgents," *Al-Monitor*, June 13, 2014, http://www.al-monitor.com/pulse/originals/2014/06/khamenei-representative-blames-qatar-saudi-iraq-crisis.html.

87. "Iraq Crisis: Battle Grips Baiji Oil Refinery," *BBC News*, June 18, 2014, http://www.bbc.com/news/world-middle-east-27897648.

88. "Grand Ayatollah: Defending Iraq, Religious Duty," *IRNA*, June 23, 2014, http://irna.ir/en/News/2719082/Politic/Grand_Ayatollah__Defending_Iraq,_religious_duty.

89. Joel Wing, "Militia Mobilization Started in 2013 Due to Renewed Iraq Insurgency," *Musings on Iraq* (blog), August 19, 2014, http://musingsoniraq.blogspot.com/2014/08/militia-mobilization-in-iraq-started-in.html.

90. The Hazrat-e Zaynab Brigade alone is said to have returned four thousand of its fighters to Iraq from Syria. *ABNA*, June 15, 2014, http://www.abna.ir/persian/service/middle/archive/2014/06/15/616256/story.html.

91. *ABNA*, June 16, 2014, http://www.abna.ir/persian/service/middle/archive/2014/06/16/616517/story.html.

92. Abbas Qaidaari, "Comparing Iraq's Shiite forces to Iran's Basij," *Al-Monitor*, May 11, 2015, http://www.al-monitor.com/pulse/ru/contents/articles/originals/2015/05/iran-iraq-iraq-basij-forces.html.

93. *Nama News*, November 17, 2014, http://namanews.com/News/105938/.

94. Martin Chulov, "Iran Sends Troops into Iraq to Aid Fight against Isis Militants," *The Guardian*, June 14, 2014, http://www.theguardian.com/world/2014/jun/14/iran-iraq-isis-fight-militants-nouri-maliki.

95. *ABNA*, November 10, 2014, http://www.abna.ir/persian/service/iran/archive/2014/11/10/650472/story.html.

96. *Tasnim News*, November 6, 2014, http://www.tasnimnews.com/Home/Single/550169.

97. "Qassem: Hezbollah Inspired by Wilayat al-Faqih," *The Daily Star* (Lebanon), September 18, 2014, http://www.dailystar.com.lb/News/Lebanon-News/2014/Sep-18/271178-qassem-hezbollah-inspired-by-wilayat-al-faqih.ashx.

98. *Fars News Agency*, November 16, 2014, http://farsnews.com/newstext.php? nn=1393082400 0516.

99. Nicholas Blanford, "Why ISIS in Iraq Are reshaping Syrian Regime's War Strategy," *The Christian Science Monitor*, June 16, 2014, http://www.csmonitor.com/World/Middle-East/2014/0616/Why-ISIS-gains-in-Iraq-are-reshaping-Syrian-regime-s-war-strategy-video.

100. Babak Dehghanpisheh, "Iran Dramatically Shifts Iraq Policy to Confront Islamic State," *Reuters*, September 2, 2014, http://uk.reuters.com/article/2014/09/02/uk-iran-iraq-politics-security-idUKKBN0GX28Z20140902; also, Najmeh Bozorgmehr, "Iranian General Is New Hero in Battle against Isis," *The Financial Times*, November 7, 2014, http://www.ft.com/intl/cms/s/0/301d445a-6406-11e4-bac8-00144feabdc0.html#axzz3IUilWRyH.

101. Alex Vatanka, "Ali Shamkhani: Rouhani's Bridge-Builder to the Arab World," *The National Interest*, October 20, 2014, http://nationalinterest.org/feature/ali-shamkhani-rouhani%E2%80%99s-bridge-builder-the-arab-world-11500.

102. On the roots and proliferation of Sunni-Shia sectarianism, particularly in the Persian Gulf since the fall of Saddam, see Nasr, *Shia Revivial*; Frederic M. Wehrey, *Sectarian Politics in the Gulf: From the Iraq War to the Arab Uprisings* (New York: Columbia University Press, 2013); Matthiesen, *Sectarian Gulf*; and Fanar Haddad, *Sectarianism in Iraq: Antagonistic Visions of Unity* (London: Hurst Publishers, 2011).

103. "Iran Removes Qassem Suleimani from Iraqi Affairs," *Bas News*, August 25, 2014, http://basnews.com/en/News/Details/Iran-Removes-Qassem-Suleimani-From-Iraqi-Affairs-/31755. The original link is no longer available, but the article can still be found at https://web.archive.org/web/20141007004445/http://basnews.com/en/News/Details/Iran-Removes-Qassem-Suleimani-From-Iraqi-Affairs-/31755.

104. Dalshad Abdullah, "Iran Replaces Revolutionary Guard Commander in Iraq," *Asharq al-Awsat*, August 26, 2014, http://www.aawsat.net/2014/08/article55335874.

105. *Iran-e Hasteh'i*, August 27, 2014, http://irannuc.ir/content/2330.

106. *Jam News*, http://jamnews.ir/detail/News/410177.

107. For example, see: *Raja News*, September 5, 2014, http://www.rajanews.com/detail.asp?id=202309 ; also, *ABNA*, November 10, 2014, http://www.abna.ir/english/service/middle-east-west-asia/archive/2014/11/10/650450/story.html.

108. *Tabnak*, September 24, 2014, http://www.tabnak.ir/fa/news/436814/.

109. See for instance pictures of Soleimani and other commanders reportedly taken after the victories of Jalawla and Saadia, *Diyar Mirza News Agency*, November 25, 2014, http://diyarmirza.ir/1393/09/.

110. Ahmed Rasheed and Isabel Coles, "Jubilant Iraqi Forces Break Two-Month Siege of Amerli—Officials," *Reuters*, August 31, 2014, http://uk.reuters.com/article/2014/08/31/uk-iraq-security-idUKKBN0GU0OT20140831.

111. Said Hameed, "Iraqi Forces Say Retake Two Towns from Islamic State," *Reuters*, November 23, 2014, http://www.reuters.com/article/2014/11/23/us-mideast-crisis-iraq-towns-idUSKCN0J70AX20141123; also, Nuwar Faqie, "Qasim Sulaimani Commands Jalawla and Saadia Clashes," *Bas News*, November 23, 2014, http://basnews.com/en/news/2014/11/23/qasim-sulaimani-commands-jalawla-and-saadia-clashes/.

112. Dion Nissenbaum, Benoit Faucon, and Matt Bradley, "Iran Attacked Islamic State Forces in Iraq," *The Wall Street Journal*, December 3, 2014, http://www.wsj.com/articles/pentagon-officials-believe-iran-attacked-islamic-state-forces-in-iraq-1417623790.

113. Ghaith Abdul-Ahad, "Iraq: On the Frontline with the Shia Fighters Taking the War to Isis," *The Guardian*, August 24, 2014, http://www.theguardian.com/world/2014/aug/24/iraq-frontline-shia-fighters-war-isis. Some spellings changed for consistency.

## Chapter 12

1. Eric Schmitt and Michael R. Gordon, "Russian Moves in Syria Widen Role in Mideast," *The New York Times*, September 14, 2015, http://www.nytimes.com/2015/09/15/world/middleeast/russian-moves-in-syria-widen-role-in-mideast.html.

2. Michael R. Gordon, "Russia Surprised U.S. with Accord on Battling ISIS," *The New York Times*, September 27, 2015, http://www.nytimes.com/2015/09/28/world/middleeast/iraq-agrees-to-share-intelligence-on-isis-with-russia-syria-and-iran.html.

3. "President Rouhani Rejects Iran-Russia Joint Cooperation in Syria War," *Al-Alam*, September 26, 2015, http://en.alalam.ir/news/1742647.

4. *Fars News Agency*, April 8, 2015, http://www.farsnews.com/newstext.php?nn=13940119000085; also, Rohollah Faghihi, "Iran's Rezaei Returns to His Military Roots," *Al-Monitor*, May 13, 2015, http://www.al-monitor.com/pulse/originals/2015/05/iran-mohsen-rezaei-irgc-return.html.

5. "Iran's Rezaei Says Russia's Anti-ISIL Attacks in Syria Effective," *Tasnim News Agency*, October 11, 2015, http://www.tasnimnews.com/en/news/2015/10/11/885399/iran-s-rezaei-says-russia-s-anti-isil-attacks-in-syria-effective.

6. "Rezaei Urges Islamic Countries to Join anti-Daesh Coalition," *IRNA*, October 15, 2015, http://www3.irna.ir/en/News/81800142/.

7. See comments by Iran's Ministry of Foreign Affairs spokesperson Marzieh Afkham, *Tasnim News Agency*, October 1, 2015, http://www.tasnimnews.com/fa/news/1394/07/09/876220/.

8. "Iran Quds Chief Visited Russia Despite U.N. Travel Ban: Iran Official," *Reuters*, August 7, 2015, http://www.reuters.com/article/2015/08/07/us-russia-iran-soleimani-idUSKCN0QC1KM20150807.

9. Ian Black, "Wake-Up Call on Syrian Army Weakness Prompted Russian Intervention," *The Guardian*, October 1, 2015, http://www.theguardian.com/world/2015/oct/01/syrian-military-weakness-russian-intervention.

10. Missy Ryan and Greg Jaffe, "With Fight Against the Islamic State in Iraq Stalled, U.S. Looks to Syria for Gains," *The Washington Post*, September 21, 2015, https://www.washingtonpost.com/world/national-security/with-fight-against-the-islamic-state-in-iraq-stalled-us-looks-to-syria-for-gains/2015/09/21/0c473098-607e-11e5-9757-e49273f05f65_story.html.

11. Black, "Wake-Up Call on Syrian Army Weakness Prompted Russian Intervention."

12. Louisa Loveluck and Nabih Bulos, "Hundreds of Iranian Troops 'Arrive in Syria' for Aleppo Offensive," *The Telegraph*, October 27, 2015, http://www.telegraph.co.uk/news/worldnews/middleeast/syria/11930415/Thousands-of-Iranian-troops-arrive-in-Syria-for-Aleppo-offensive.html.

13. Ian Black, "Iran Sending More Advisers to Syria to Defeat 'Terrorism,' Says Deputy Minister," *The Guardian*, October 21, 2015, http://www.theguardian.com/world/2015/oct/21/iran-advisers-syria-terrorism-deputy-minister.

14. Yeganeh Torbati, Phil Stewart, and David Alexander, "Iran Has Over 1,000 Troops in Iraq, Less Than 2,000 in Syria: U.S. General," *Reuters*, October 27, 2015, http://www.reuters.com/article/2015/10/27/us-mideast-crisis-dunford-iranians-idUSKCN0SL23E20151027.

15. See Supreme National Security Council secretary Ali Shamkhani's statement on Hamedani's death, *Farau*, October 10, 2015, http://fararu.com/fa/news/249199/.

16. On Hasunizadeh's death, see *Tabnak*, October 13, 2015, https://www.tabnak.ir/fa/news/539086/. On Mokhtarband's death, see *IRNA*, October 14, 2015, http://www.irna.ir/fa/News/81799442/.

17. On Baqeri's death, see *Defa Press*, October 28, 2015, http://www.defapress.ir/Fa/News/56022.

18. This estimate is based on the number of deaths reported in the Iranian press. See Ali Alfoneh, "The IRGC Transforms into an Expeditionary Force," FDD Policy Brief, October 29, 2015, http://www.defenddemocracy.org/media-hit/ali-alfoneh-the-irgc-transforms-into-an-expeditionary-force/.

19. *Tasnim News Agency*, October 25, 2015, http://www.tasnimnews.com/fa/news/1394/08/03/897366/.

20. See interview with Brigadier General Hosayn Salami, *Sepah News*, October 28, 2015, http://sepahnews.com/shownews.Aspx?ID=4352426a-e21c-4c9b-a154-736f84b6e27b.

21. *Sepah News*, October 28, 2015, http://sepahnews.com/shownews.Aspx?ID=4352426a-e21c-4c9b-a154-736f84b6e27b.

22. *Alef*, October 6, 2015, http://alef.ir/vdcepo8wwjh8ooi.b9bj.html?29txt.

23. William MacLean, "Weapons Bound for Yemen Seized on Iranian Boat: Coalition," *Reuters*, September 30, 2015, http://www.reuters.com/article/2015/09/30/us-yemen-security-idUSKCN0RU0R220150930.

24. Mohammad Al Qalisi, "Saudi-led Coalition Sinks Boats Carrying Arms to Yemen Houthis," *The National*, October 28, 2015, http://www.thenational.ae/world/middle-east/saudi-led-coalition-sinks-boats-carrying--arms-to-yemen-houthis. The aerial surveillance video was released by *Reuters* and posted to its official YouTube channel. See "Saudi Air Strike at Sea Caught on Camera," October 27, 2015, https://www.youtube.com/watch?v=-yTXS8bQhUw.

25. "Ayatollah Khamenei Calls for Saudis' Apology over Mina Trajedy," The Office of the Supreme Leader Sayyid Ali Khamenei, September 27, 2015, http://www.leader.ir/langs/en/index.php?p=contentShow&id=13683.

26. "IRGC Ready for Rapid, Tough Response to Al Saud: Commander," *Tasnim News Agency*, October 3, 2015, http://www.tasnimnews.com/en/news/2015/10/03/878057/irgc-ready-for-rapid-tough-response-to-al-saud-commander.

27. Thomas Erdbrink, "Iran Accuses Saudi Arabia of Kidnapping Officials in Chaos of Hajj Stampede," *The New York Times*, October 29, 2015, http://www.nytimes.com/2015/10/30/world/middleeast/iran-saudi-arabia-hajj-stampede.html.

28. "Deputy-Minister Raises Kidnapping Concerns about Roknabadi," *Mehr News Agency*, September 30, 2015, http://en.mehrnews.com/news/110599/Deputy-minister-raises-kidnapping-concerns-about-Roknabadi.

## *Chapter 13*

1. See for instance, Shounaz Meky, "Inside Iran: Militias and Expanding the Persian Empire," *Al Arabiya*, May 18, 2015, http://english.alarabiya.net/en/perspective/features/2015/05/18/Inside-Iran-militias-and-expanding-the-Persian-Empire-.html.

# BIBLIOGRAPHY

## Persian Books and Articles

*Amr beh ma'ruf va nahy az monkar.* [Tehran?]: Setad-e Ehya-ye Amr beh Ma'ruf va Nahy az Monkar.

*Jang va jehad dar Qur'an.* Tehran: Vahed-e Amuzesh: Setad-e Markazi-e Sepah-e Pasdaran-e Enqelab-e Eslami, 1981.

*Jang va tajavoz: jebhe-ye impirialisti 'alayh-e enqelab-e eslami.* Tehran: Daftar-e Siyasi-e Sepah-e Pasdaran-e Enqelab-e Eslami, 1981.

*Jangha-ye Payambar.* Tehran: Vahed-e Amuzeshi-e 'Aqidati-e Siyasi-e Sepah-e Pasdaran-e Enqilab-e Eslami, 1984.

*Qanun-e moqarrarat-e estekhadami-ye Sepah-e Pasdaran-e Enqelab-e Eslami.* [Tehran?]: Edareh-ye Koll-e Qavanin va Moqarrarat-e Keshvar, 1995/1996.

*Amr beh ma'ruf va nahy az monkar.* [Tehran?]: Namayandegi-e Vali-e Faqih dar Sepah, 1997.

*Amr beh ma'ruf va nahy az monkar az didgah-ye Imam Khomeini.* [Tehran?]: Mo'asseseh-ye Tanzim va Nashr-e Asar-e Imam Khomeini, 1998.

*Sepah dar gozar-e enqelab: majmu'eh-ye ettela'iyeh, bayaniyeh, akhbar va. . . sepah.* Jeld-e avval. Tehran: Mo'avenat-e ravabet-e 'omumi va entesharat-e sepah, 2011.

*Shahid Hojjat al-Islam Mohammad Montazeri.* Tehran: Markaz-e Barresi-e Esnad-e Tarikhi-e Vezarat-e Ettela'at, 2006/2007.

*Ansar-e hezbollah dar yek negah.* http://ansarehezbollah.org/UI/View/AboutUs.aspx. (Accessed March 10, 2009).

Akhavan, Mohammad Javad. *'Obur az Fetneh: Bazkhwani-ye Parvandeh-ye Yeksal-e Nabard-e Narm.* Jeld-e aval. Tehran: Markaz-e Motala'at va Pazhuheshha-ye Sazman-e Basij-e Daneshjuyi, Spring 2010.

A'li, Abulfazl, ed. *Honar-e grafik dar enqelab-e eslami.* [Tehran?]: Vahed-e Entesharat-e Hawzah-ye Hunari-e Sazman-e Tablighat-e Eslami. 1985.

Amini, Davud. *Jam'iyat-e Fada'iyan-i Eslam va naqsh-e an dar tahavvulat-e siyasi-e ejtema'i-e Iran.* Tehran: Entesharat-e Markaz-e Esnad-e Enqelab-e Eslami-e Iran, 2002.

Ansari Mehdi, et al. *Khorramshahr dar jang-e tulani* [*Khorramshahr during the Long War*]. Vol. 3, Tehran: Markaz-e Asnad-e Dafa'-e Moqaddas (Sepah-e Pasdaran-e Enqelab-e Eslami), 2008.

Chamran, Mostafa. *Lobnan.* [Tehran?]: Bonyad-e Shahid-e Chamran. 1983.

Ebrahimi, Amir Farshad. "Matn-e e'terafat-e Amir Farshad Ebrahimi." *Mihan* (59), January 2003.

Jamshidi, Mohammad Hosayn. "Tahajom-e farhangi." *Basij: majallah-ye 'elmi-e pazhuheshi*, no. 7/8 (Summer/Fall 1995).

Keshtgar, Ali. Ali Khamenei, "Ansar-e Hezbollah, va eteqad beh r'ab." *Mihan* (57), October 2002.

Mahfoozi, Alireza. In an interview recorded by Zia Sedghi, April 7, 1984. Paris, France. Iranian Oral History Collection, Harvard University, 19.

Mas'udi, Mohammad Eshaq. *Pazhuheshi dar amr beh ma'ruf va nahy az monkar: az didgah-ye qor'an va ravayat.* Tehran: Sazman-e Tablighat-e Eslami, 1999/2000.

Mohtashami, Sayyed Ali Akbar. *Khaterat-e siyasi-e Sayyed Ali Akbar Mohtashami.* Vol. 2. Tehran: Khaneh-ye Andisheh-ye Javan, 2000.

Monfared, Ali Danesh. *Khaterat-e Ali Danesh Monfared.* Edited by R. Bastami. Tehran: Markaz-e Esnad-e Enqelab-e Eslami, 2005.

Montazeri, Hosayn-Ali. *Khaterat-e Ayatollah Hosayn-Ali Montazeri.* Los Angeles: Ketab Corp, 2001.

Motahhari, Ayatollah Morteza. *Rahbari-e nasl-e javan.* [Tehran?]: Kanun-e khedamat-e farhangi-e alast, 1982.

Rafiqdust, Mohsen. *Khaterat-e Mohsen Rafiqdust.* Edited by D. Qasempur. Vol. 1. Tehran: Markaz-e Esnad-e Enqelab-e Eslami, 2004.

Rezai, Mohsen. *Zendegi-e doktor-e Mohsen Reza'i dar yek negah:* www.rezaee.ir (Accessed February 12, 2008).

Safavi, Yahya Rahim. *Az jonub-e lobnan ta jonub-e iran: khaterat-e Sardar-e Sayyed Rahim Safavi.* Edited by M. Najafpour. Tehran: Markaz-e Esnad-e Enqelab-e Eslami, 2006.

Saidi, Mehdi. *Sazman-e mojahedin-e enqelab-e eslami: az tasis ta enhelal.* Vol. 1. Tehran: Markaz-e Esnad-e Enqelab-e Eslami, 2007.

Salek, Davud. *Sevvomin parchamdar: zendaginnameh-ye shahid Sayyed Mojtaba Navvab Safavi.* Tehran: Hawzah-e Honari, 1999.

Sazegara, Mohsen. "Sepah va seh enheraf." http://www.sazegara.net/persian/archives/2006/07/060723_154435.html. (Accessed October 27, 2008).

### English Books and Articles

Abisaab, Riba. *Converting Persia: Religion and Power in the Safavid Empire.* London: I. B. Tauris, 2004.

Abrahamian, Ervand. *Iran between Two Revolutions.* Princeton: Princeton UP, 1982.

———. *Radical Islam: The Iranian Mojahedin.* London: I. B. Tauris, 1989.

———. *Khomeinism: Essays on the Islamic Republic.* Berkeley: University of California Press, 1993.

———. *Tortured Confessions: Prisons and Public Recantations in Modern Iran.* Berkeley: University of California Press, 1999.

Afary, Janet. *The Iranian Constitutional Revolution, 1906–1911.* New York: Columbia UP, 1996.

Aghaie, Kamran Scott. *The Martyrs of Karbala: Shi'i Symbols and Rituals in Modern Iran.* Seattle and London: University of Washington Press, 2004.

Ajami, Fouad. *The Vanished Imam: Musa Al-Sadr and the Shia of Lebanon.* Ithaca: Cornell University Press, 1986.

Alagha, Joseph. *The Shifts in Hizbullah's Ideology: Religious Ideology, Political Ideology, and Political Program.* Amsterdam: Amsterdam University Press, 2006.

Albright, David, et al. *Did Stuxnet Take Out 1,000 Centrifuges at the Natanz Enrichment Plant?* ISIS Report, Institute for Science and International Security, December 22, 2010.

Alexander, Yonah, and Michael Kraft. *Evolution of U.S. Counterterrorism Policy.* Westport, CT: Praeger and Greenwood Publishing Group, 2008.

Alfoneh, Ali. *Iran Unveiled: How the Revolutionary Guards Is Turning Theocracy into Military Dictatorship.* Washington, DC: American Enterprise Institute, 2013.

———. "What Do Structural Changes in the Revolutionary Guards Mean?" *AEI Outlook Series,* no. 7. September 2008.

Algar, Hamid. "Shi'ism and Iran in the Eighteenth Century." In *Studies in Eighteenth Century Islamic History,* edited by Thomas Naff and Roger Owen. Carbondale, IL: Southern Illinois University Press, 1977.

———. *Religion and State in Iran, 1785–1906: The Role of the Ulama in the Qajar Period.* Berkeley: University of California Press,1980.

Amanat, Abbas. *Resurrection and Renewal: The Making of the Babi Movement in Iran, 1844–1850.* Ithaca: Cornell University Press, 1989.

Amirahmadi, Hooshang, and Manoucher Parvin, ed. *Post-Revolutionary Iran.* Boulder: Westview Press, 1988.

Ansari, Ali M., Daniel Berman, and Thomas Rintoul, "A Preliminary Analysis of the Voting Figures in Iran's 2009 Presidential Election." London: Chatham House, June 21, 2009.

Ansari, Ali M. *Iran, Islam and Democracy: The Politics of Managing Change.* London: Chatham House, 2006.

———. *Confronting Iran: The Failure of American Foreign Policy and the Next Great Crisis in the Middle East.* New York: Basic Books, 2006.

———. *Crisis of Authority: Iran's 2009 Presidential Election.* London: Chatham House, 2010.

Anzalone, Christopher. "Zaynab's Guardians: The Emergence of Shi'a Militias in Syria." *CTC Sentinel,* July 23, 2013: https://www.ctc.usma.edu/posts/zaynabs-guardians-the-emergence-of-shia-militias-in-syria.

Arjomand, Said Amir. "Religion, Political Action and Legitimate Domination in Shi'ite Iran: Fourteenth to Eighteenth Centuries A.D." *Archives Européennes de Sociologie* 20, no. 1 (1979): 59–109.

———. *The Shadow of the Hidden Imam: Religion, Political Order, and Societal Change in Shi'ite Iran from the Beginning to 1890.* Chicago: The University of Chicago Press, 1984.

———, ed. *From Nationalism to Revolutionary Islam.* Albany: State University of New York Press, 1984.

———. *Traditionalism in Twentieth-Century Iran.* In *From Nationalism to Revolutionary Islam,* edited by S. A. Arjomand. Albany: State University of New York Press, 1984, pp. 195–232.

———. "Revolution in Shi'ism." In *Islam and the Political Economy of Meaning: Comparative Studies of Muslim Discourse,* edited by William R. Roff. Berkeley: University of California Press, 1987, pp. 111–131.

———. *The Turban for the Crown: The Islamic Revolution in Iran.* New York and Oxford: Oxford University Press, 1988.

———. "Imam Absconditus and the Beginnings of a Theology of Occultation: Imami Shi'ism Circa 280–90 A. H./900 A. D." *Journal of the American Oriental Society* 117, no. 1 (January–March 1997): 1–12.

———. "The Crisis of the Imamate and the Institution of Occultation in Twelver Shiism: A Sociohistorical Perspective." *International Journal of Middle East Studies* 28, no. 4 (November 1996): 491–515.

———. "The Consolation of Theology: Absence of the Imam and Transition from Chiliasm to Law in Shi'ism." *The Journal of Religion* 76, no. 4 (October 1996): 548–571.

As-Sadr, Muhammad Baqir. *Lessons in Islamic Jurisprudence.* Translated by Roy Mottahedeh. Oxford: Oneworld, 2005.

Axeworthy, Michael. *Revolutionary Iran: A History of the Islamic Republic.* New York: Oxford University Press, 2013.

Ayoub, Mahmoud. *Redemptive Suffering in Islam: A Study of the Devotional Aspects of 'Ashura' in Twelver Shi'ism.* The Hague: Mouton, 1978.

Babaie, Sussan, Kathryn Babayan, Ina Baghdiantz-McCabe, and Massumeh Farhad. *Slaves of the Shah: New Elites of Safavid Iran.* London: I. B. Tauris, 2004.

Babayan, Kathryn. *Mystics, Monarchs, and Messiahs: Cultural Landscapes in Early Modern Iran.* Cambridge, MA.: Center of Middle Eastern Studies of Harvard University, 2002.

Baer, Robert. *See No Evil: The True Story of a Ground Soldier in the CIA's War on Terrorism.* New York: Three Rivers Press, 2002.

Bahari, Maziar, with Aimee Molloy. *Then They Came for Me: A Family's Story of Love, Captivity, and Survival.* New York: Random House, 2011.

Bakhash, Shaul. *The Reign of the Ayatollahs: Iran and the Islamic Revolution.* New York: Basic Books, 1984.

Baktiari, Bahman. *Parliamentary Politics in Revolutionary Iran: The Institutionalization of Factional Politics.* Gainesville: University Press of Florida, 1996.

Balaghi, Shiva, and Lynn Gumpert, eds. *Picturing Iran: Art, Society, and Revolution*. New York: I. B. Tauris, 2002.

Bani-Sadr, Abol Hassan. *My Turn to Speak: Iran, the Revolution, and Secret Deals with the U.S.* New York: Brassey's, 1991

Barsamian, David, et al. *Targeting Iran*. San Francisco: Open Lights Books, 2007.

Barthes, Roland. *The Responsibility of Forms: Critical Essays on Music, Art, and Representation*. Translated by Richard Howard. New York: Hill and Wang, 1985.

Basmenji, Kaveh. *Tehran Blues: Youth Culture in Iran*. London: Saqi, 2005.

Bayat, Mangol. *Iran's First Revolution: Shi'ism and the Constitutional Revolution of 1905–1909*. Oxford: Oxford University Press, 1991.

Beckwith, Christopher I. *Empires of the Silk Road: A History of Central Eurasia from the Bronze Age to the Present*. Princeton University Press, 2009.

Behrooz, Maziar. "The Islamic State and the Crisis of Marja'iyat in Iran." *Comparative Studies of South Asia, Africa and the Middle East* 16, no. 2 (1996): 93–100.

Berger, Mark T. "After the Third World? History, Destiny and the Fate of Third Worldism." *Third World Quarterly* 25, no. 1 (2004).

Biersteke, Thomas J., et al. *Countering the Financing of Terrorism*. New York: Taylor and Francis, 2007.

Blanford, Nicholas. *Killing Mr. Lebanon: The Assassination of Rafik Hariri and Its Impact on the Middle East*. London: I. B. Tauris, 2006.

Bonnell, Victoria E. *Iconography of Power: Soviet Political Posters under Lenin and Stalin*. Berkeley: University of California Press, 1997.

Brown, Ian. *Khomeini's Forgotten Sons: The Story of Iran's Boy Soldiers, Child Victims of Saddam's Iraq*. London: Grey Seal Books, 1990.

Brumberg, Daniel. *Reinventing Khomeini: The Struggle for Reform in Iran*. Chicago: University of Chicago Press, 2001.

Byman, Daniel. *A High Price: The Triumphs and Failures of Israeli Counterterrorism*. New York: Oxford University Press, 2011.

Bytwerk, Randall L. *Bending Spines: The Propagandas of Nazi Germany and the German Democratic Republic*. East Lansing: Michigan State University Press, 2004.

Chehab, Zaki. *Inside Hamas: The Untold Story of Militants, Martyrs and Spies*. London: I. B. Tauris, 2007.

Chehabi, H. E., ed. *Distant Relations: Iran and Lebanon in the Last 500 Years*. New York: St. Martin's Press, 2006.

Chelkowski, Peter J., ed. *Ta'ziyah: Ritual and Drama in Iran*. Washington Square: New York University Press, 1979.

Chelkowski, Peter and Hamid Dabashi. *Staging a Revolution: The Art of Persuasion in the Islamic Republic of Iran*. New York: New York University Press, 1999.

Choncrane, Marisa. "The Fragmentation of the Sadrist Movement." Iraq Report no. 12, Institute for the Study of War, 2009.

Chubin, Shahram. *Iran's Nuclear Ambitions*. Washington, DC: Carnegie Endowment for International Peace, 2006.

Chubin, Shahram, and Charles Tripp. *Iran and Iraq at War*. London: I. B. Tauris, 1988.

Cole, Juan R. *Modernity and the Millennium: The Genesis of the Baha'i Faith in the Nineteenth-Century Middle East*. New York: Columbia University Press, 1998.

———. "Millennialism in Modern Iranian History." In *Imagining the End: Visions of Apocalypse from the Ancient Middle East to Modern America*, edited by Abbas Amanat and Magnus Bernhardsson, 282–311. London: I. B. Tauris, 2002.

———. *The Ayatollahs and Democracy in Contemporary Iraq*. Amsterdam: Amsterdam University Press, 2006.

———. "Shia Militias in Iraqi Politics." In *Iraq: Preventing a New Generation of Conflict*, edited by M. E. Bouillon et al. Boulder and London: Lynne Rienner Publishers, 2007.

———. *Engaging the Muslim World*. New York: Palgrave MacMillan, 2009.

——. "The United States and Shi'ite Religious Factions in Post-Ba'thist Iraq." *The Middle East Journal* 57, no. 4 (Autumn 2003): 543–566.

Cole, Juan R., and Nikkie R. Keddie, eds. *Shi'ism and Social Protest*. New Haven: Yale University Press, 1986.

Cole, Juan R., and Moojan Momen."Mafia, Mob, and Shiism in Iraq: The Rebellion of Ottoman Karbala, 1824–43." *Past and Present*, no. 112 (August 1986), pp. 112–143.

Cook, Michael. *Commanding Right and Forbidding Wrong in Islamic Thought*. Cambridge: Cambridge University Press, 2000.

——. *Forbidding Wrong in Islam*. Cambridge: Cambridge University Press, 2003.

Cooper, Tom, and Farzad Bishop. *Iran-Iraq War in the Air, 1980–88*. Atglen, PA: Schiffer Military History, 2000.

Cooper, Tom, and Farzad Bishop. *Iranian F-14 Tomcat Units in Combat*. Oxford: Osprey Publishing, 2004.

Cordesman, Anthony H., and Ahmed S. Hashim. *Iran: Dilemmas of Dual Containment*. Boulder: Westview Press, 1997.

Cordesman, Anthony H. *Iran's Military in Transition: Conventional Threats and Weapons of Mass Destruction*. Westport, CT: Praeger, 1999.

Cordesman, Anthony H., and Abraham R. Wagner. *The Lessons of Modern War, Volume II: The Iran-Iraq War*. Boulder, CO: Westview Press, 1990.

Crist, David. *The Twilight War: the Secret History of America's Thirty-Year Conflict with Iran*. New York: Penguin Press, 2012.

Cronin, Stephanie, ed. *The Making of Modern Iran: State and Society under Riza Shah 1921–1941*. London: Routledge Curzon, 2003.

——, ed. *Reformers and Revolutionaries in Modern Iran: New Perspectives on the Iranian Left*. London: Routledge, 2004.

Dabashi, Hamid. *Theology of Discontent: The Ideological Foundation of the Islamic Revolution in Iran*. Piscataway, NJ: Transaction Publishers, 1993.

——. *Close Up: Iranian Cinema, Past, Present and Future*. London and New York: Verso, 2001.

Daftary, Farhad. *The Assassin Legends: Myth of the Isma'ilis*. London: I. B. Tauris, 1994.

Davis, Diane E., and Anthony W. Pereira, eds. *Irregular Armed Forces and Their Role in Politics and State Formation*. Cambridge: Cambridge University Press, 2003.

Dekmejian, R. Hrair. *Islam in Revolution: Fundamentalism in the Arab World*. Syracuse: Syracuse University Press, 1995.

Eagleton, Terry. *Holy Terror*. Oxford: Oxford University Press, 2005.

Edwards, David B. *Before Taliban: Genealogies of the Afghan Jihad*. Berkeley: University of California Press, 2002.

Ehteshami, Anoushiravan, and Gerd Nonneman. *War and Peace in the Gulf*. Reading, PA: Ithaca Press, 1991.

Ehteshami, Anoushirvan, and Mahjoob Zweiri. *Iran and the Rise of Its Neoconservatives: The Politics of Tehran's Silent Revolution*. London and New York: I. B. Tauris, 2007.

Eisenstadt, Michael. *Iranian Military Power: Capabilities and Intentions*. Washington, DC: Washington Institute of Near East Policy, 1996.

Esposito, John L., and R. K. Ramazani, eds. *Iran at the Crossroads*. New York: Palgrave, 2001.

Fanon, Frantz. *Wretched of the Earth*. Translated by Constance Farrington. New York: Grove Press, 1968.

Farhi, Farideh. "The Antinomies of Iran's War Generation." In *Iran, Iraq, and the Legacies of War*, edited by Lawrence G. Potter and Gary Sick. New York: Palgrave Macmillan, 2004, pp. 101–120.

Fayazmanesh, Sasan. *The United States and Iran: Sanctions, Wars, and the Policy of Dual Containment*. New York: Routledge, 2008.

Felter, Joseph, and Brian Fishman. "Iranian Influence in Iraq: Politics and 'Other Means.'" West Point: Combating Terrorism Center, October 1, 2008.

Ferdows, Adele K. "Religion in Iranian Nationalism: The Study of the Fadayan-i Islam." PhD diss., Indiana University, 1967.

Ferdowsi, Abol-Qasem. *Shahnameh: The Persian Book of Kings.* Translated by Dick Davis. Forward by Azar Nafisi. New York: Viking, 2006.

Filkins, Dexter. "The Shadow Commander." *The New Yorker*, September 30, 2013.

Fischer, Michael M. J. *Iran, from Religious Dispute to Revolution.* Cambridge, MA: Harvard University Press, 1980.

Fischer, Michael M. J., and Mehdi Abedi. *Debating Muslims: Cultural Dialogues in Postmodernity and Tradition.* Madison: The University of Wisconsin Press, 1990.

Fulton, Will, et al. "Iranian Strategy in Syria." AEI and The Institute for the Study of War, May 2013.

Gasiorowski, Mark J. "The 1953 Coup D'etat in Iran." *International Journal of Middle East Studies* 19, no. 3 (August 1987): pp. 261–286.

Ghaffarzadegan, Davud. *Fortune Told in Blood.* Translated by M. R. Ghanoonparvar. Austin: The Center for Middle Eastern Studies and the University of Texas at Austin, 2008.

Ghani, Cyrus. *Iran and the Rise of Reza Shah: From Qajar Collapse to Pahlavi Rule.* London: I. B. Tauris, 1998.

*Glance at Two Years of War.* Translated by Setad-e Tablighat-e Jang-e Sepah. [Tehran?]: Political Office: Islamic Revolution's Guards Corps, 1982.

Goldstone, Jack. "States Making Wars Making States Making Wars . . ." *Contemporary Sociology* 20, no. 2 (March 1991): pp. 176–178.

Golkar, Saeid. *Captive Society: The Basij Militia and Social Control in Iran.* New York: Columbia University Press, 2015.

———. "Paramilitarization of the Economy: The Case of Iran's Basij Militia." *Armed Forces & Society* 38, no. 4 (2012): 625–648.

Gumpert, Lynn, and Shiva Balaghi, eds. *Picturing Iran: Art, Society and Revolution.* London: I. B. Tauris, 2002.

Haeri, Shahla. *Law of Desire: Temporary Marriage in Shi'i Iran.* Syracuse: Syracuse University Press, 1989.

Hall, John A., and Ralph Schroeder, eds. *An Anatomy of Power: The Social Theory of Michael Mann.* Cambridge: Cambridge University Press, 2006.

Halliday, Fred. "Three Concepts of Internationalism." *International Affairs* 64, no. 2 (Spring 1988): pp. 187–198.

Halm, Heinz. *Shi'a Islam: From Religion to Revolution.* Princeton, NJ: Markus Wiener Publishers, 1997.

———. *Shi'ism.* Translated by Janet Watson and Marian Hill. 2nd ed. New York: Columbia University Press, 2004.

Hamzeh, Ahmad Nizar. *In the Path of Hizbullah.* Syracuse: Syracuse University Press, 2004.

Hanaway, William. "The Symbolism of the Persian Revolutionary Posters." In *Iran since the Revolution: Internal Dynamics, Regional Conflicts, and the Superpowers*, edited by Barry Rosen. New York: Columbia University Press, 1985, pp. 31–50.

Harik, Judith Palmer. *Hezbollah: The Changing Face of Terrorism.* London and New York: I. B. Tauris, 2004.

Hersh, Seymour. "The Redirection: Is the Administration's New Policy Benefitting Our Enemies in the War on Terrorism?" *The New Yorker*, March 5, 2007.

Hiltermann, Joost R. *A Poisonous Affair: America, Iraq, and the Gassing of Halabja.* New York: Cambridge University Press, 2007.

Hiro, Dilip. *The Longest War: The Iran-Iraq Military Conflict.* New York: Routledge, 1991.

Hodgson, Marshall G. S. "How Did the Early Shi'a Become Sectarian?" *Journal of the American Oriental Society* 75, no. 1 (1955): pp. 1–13.

Hokayem, Emile. *Syria's Uprising and the Fracturing of the Levant.* London: Routledge, 2013.

Huntington, Samuel. *The Soldier and the State: The Theory and Politics of Civil-Military Relations.* Cambridge: Harvard University Press, 1959.

Hyder, Syed Akbar. *Reliving Karbala: Martyrdom in South Asian Memory*. Oxford: Oxford University Press, 2006.

Ibrahimi, Nimatullah. "The Failure of a Clerical Proto-State: Hazarajat, 1979–1984." Working Paper Series Number 2, Crisis States Research Center, London: Destin LSE (2006).

International Crisis Group. "Shiite Politics in Iraq: The Role of the Supreme Council," November 15, 2007.

Jabar, Faleh A. *The Shi'ite Movement in Iraq*. London: Saqi, 2003.

Jaber, Hala. *Hezbollah: Born with a Vengeance*. Columbia University Press: New York, 1997.

Jafri, S. Husain M. *The Origins and Early Development of Shi'a Islam*. Oxford: Oxford University Press, 2002.

Katouzian, Homa. *Musaddiq and the Struggle for Power in Iran*. London: I. B. Tauris, 1990.

———. *State and Society in Iran: The Eclipse of the Qajars and the Emergence of the Pahlavis*. London: I. B. Tauris, 2000.

Katzman, Kenneth. *The Warriors of Islam: Iran's Revolutionary Guard*. Boulder: Westview Press, 1993.

———. "The Pasdaran: Institutionalization of Revolutionary Armed Force." *Iranian Studies* 26, no. 3–4 (1993): pp. 389–402.

———. "The People's Mojahedin Organization of Iran." In *Iran: Outlaw, Outcast, or Normal Country?*, edited by Albert V. Benliot. Huntington: Nova Science Publishers, 2001, pp. 97–110.

Kazemi, Farhad. *Poverty and Revolution in Iran: The Migrant Poor, Urban Marginality and Politics*. New York: New York University Press, 1980.

Keddie, Nikki R. *Modern Iran: Roots and Results of Revolution*. New Haven: Yale University Press, 2003.

———. *Religion and Rebellion in Iran: The Tobacco Protest of 1891–1892*. London: Cass, 1966.

———. *Sayyid Jamal Al-Din Afghani*. Berkeley: University of California Press, 1972.

Keddie, Nikki R., and Mark J. Gasiorowski, eds. *Neither East nor West: Iran, the Soviet Union, and the United States*. New Haven: Yale University Press, 1990.

Kepel, Gilles. *Jihad: The Trail of Political Islam*. Cambridge, MA: The Belknap Press, 2003.

———. *The War for Muslim Minds: Islam and the West*. Translated by Pascale Ghazaleh. Cambridge, M: The Belknap Press, 2004.

Keshavarzian, Arang. *Bazaar and State in Iran: The Politics of the Tehran Marketplace*. Cambridge and New York: Cambridge University Press, 2007.

Khadduri, Majid. *The Gulf War: The Origins and Implications of the Iraq-Iran Conflict*. New York and Oxford: Oxford University Press, 1988.

Khomeini, Ruhullah. *Islam and Revolution: Writings and Declarations of Imam Khomeini (1941–1980)*. Translated by Hamid Algar. North Haledon: Mizan Press, 1981.

Kinzer, Stephen. *All the Shah's Men: An American Coup and the Roots of Middle East Terror*. Hoboken: John Wiley and Sons, 2003.

Kohlberg, Etan. *Belief and Law in Imami Shi'ism*. Aldershot, Hampshire, Great Britain and Brookfield, VT, USA: Variorum; Gower, 1991.

Kramer, Martin, ed. *Shi'ism, Resistance, and Revolution*. Boulder: Westview Press, 1987.

Kriger, Norma. *Guerilla Veterans in Post-War Zimbabwe: Symbolic and Violent Politics, 1980–1987*. Cambridge and New York: Cambridge University Press, 2003.

Lassner, Jacob. *Islamic Revolution and Historical Memory: An Inquiry into the Art of 'Abbasid Apologetics*. New Haven: American Oriental Society, 1986.

Lawrence, Bruce. *Defenders of God: The Fundamentalist Revolt against the Modern Age*. New York: Harper & Row, 1989.

Levitt, Matthew. *Hezbollah: The Global Footprint of Lebanon's Party of God*. Washington, DC: Georgetown University Press, 2015.

Lia, Brynjar. *The Society of the Muslim Brothers in Egypt: The Rise of an Islamic Mass Movement 1928–1942*. Reading, PA: Ithaca Press, 1998.

Lister, Charles. "Profiling the Islamic State." Brookings Doha Analysis Paper, no. 13, November 2014.

Litvak, Meir. *Shi'i Scholars of Nineteenth-Century Iraq: The 'Ulama' of Najaf and Karbala.* Cambridge: Cambridge University Press, 1998.

Lowe, Robert, and Claire Spencer, eds. *Iran, Its Neighbours and the Regional Crises.* London: Chatham House, 2006.

Maasri, Zeina. *Off the Wall: Political Posters of the Lebanese Civil War.* New York: I. B. Tauris, 2009.

Mackenzie, S. P. *Revolutionary Armies in the Modern Era: A Revisionist Approach.* London: Routledge, 1997

Madelung, Wilferd. *Religious Schools and Sects in Medieval Islam.* London: Variorum Reprints, 1985.

———. *Religious and Ethnic Movements in Medieval Islam,* vol. CS364. Aldershot, Hampshire and Brookfield, VT: Variorum, 1992.

———. *The Succession to Muhammad: A Study of the Early Caliphate.* Cambridge and New York: Cambridge University Press, 1997.

Mahdjoub, Mohammad-Dja'far. "The Evolution of Popular Eulogy of the Imams among the Shi'a." In *Authority and Political Culture in Shi'ism,* edited by S. A. Arjomand. Albany: State University of New York Press, 1988, pp. 54–79.

Majd, Mohammad G. *Resistance to the Shah: Landowners and Ulama in Iran.* Gainesville: University Press of Florida, 2005.

Mallat, Chibli. *The Renewal of Islamic Law: Muhammad Baqer as-Sadr, Najaf, and the Shi'i International.* New York: Cambridge University Press, 1993.

Malkasian, Carter. *War Comes to Garmser: Thirty Years of Conflict on the Afghan Frontier.* New York: Oxford University Press, 2013.

Maloney, Suzanne. "Islamism in Iran's Postrevolutionary Economy: The Case of the Bonyads." In *Gods, Guns, and Globalization: Religious Radicalism and International Political Economy,* International Political Economy Yearbook vol. 13, edited by Mary Ann Tétrault and Robert A. Denemark, Boulder: Lynne Rienner Publishers, 2004.

Mann, Michael. *The Sources of Social Power, volume I: A History of Power from the Beginning to A.D. 1760.* Cambridge: Cambridge University Press, 1986.

———. *States, War, and Capitalism.* Oxford: Blackwell, 1988.

———. *The Sources of Social Power, volume II: The Rise of Classes and Nation States, 1760–1914.* Cambridge: Cambridge University Press, 1993.

Manning, John. *The Emblem.* London: Reaktion Books, 2004.

Martin, Vanessa. *Creating an Islamic State: Khomeini and the Making of a New Iran.* London: I. B. Tauris, 2003.

Matthiesen, Toby. *Sectarian Gulf: Bahrain, Saudi Arabia, and the Arab Spring that Wasn't.* Stanford: Stanford University Press, 2013.

McAlister, Melani. *Epic Encounters: Culture, Media, & U.S. Interests in the Middle East since 1945.* Berkeley: University of California Press, 2005.

McEoin, Denis. "Aspects of Militancy and Quietism in Imami Shi'ism." *Bulliten (British Society for Middle Eastern Studies)* 11, no. 1 (1984): pp. 18–27.

Menashri, David. *Iran: A Decade of War and Revolution.* New York and London: Holmes & Meier, 1990.

———. *Post-Revolutionary Politics in Iran: Religion, Society, and Power.* London and Portland: Frank Cass, 2001.

Milani, Abbas. *The Shah.* New York: Palgrave MacMillan, 2011.

Mirsepassi, Ali. *Intellectual Discourse and the Politics of Modernization.* Cambridge: Cambridge University Press, 2000.

Mitchell, Richard P. *The Society of Muslim Brothers.* New York: Oxford University Press, 1993.

Modarressi, Hossein. *Crisis and Consolidation in the Formative Period of Shi'ite Islam: Abu Ja'far Ibn Qiba Al-Razi and His Contribution to Imamite Shi'ite Thought.* Princeton: Darwin Press, 1993.

Moghaddam, Adib. *Iran and Global Politics.* New York: Columbia University Press, 2008.

Moin, Baqer. *Khomeini: Life of the Ayatollah.* London: I. B. Tauris, 1999.

Momen, Moojan. *An Introduction to Shi'i Islam: The History and Doctrines of Twelver Shi'ism.* Oxford: George Ronald, 1985.

Moslem, Mehdi. *Factional Politics in Post-Khomeini Iran.* Syracuse: Syracuse University Press, 2002.

Mottahedeh, Roy. *Mantle of the Prophet: Religion and Politics in Iran.* New York: Simon & Schuster, 1985.

Mousavian, Seyed Hossein, with Shahir ShahidSaless. *Iran and the United States: An Insider's View on the Failed Past and the Road to Peace.* New York: Bloomsbury, 2014.

Mutahhari, Ayatullah Murtaza. *Fundamentals of Islamic Thought: God, Man and the Universe.* Translated by R. Campbell. Berkeley: Mizan Press, 1985.

Naji, Kasra. *Ahmadinejad: The Secret History of Iran's Radical Leader.* Berkeley and Los Angeles: The University of California Press, 2008.

Nakash, Yitzhak. "An Attempt to Trace the Origin of the Rituals of 'Ashura'." *Die Welt des Islams* 33 (1993): pp. 161–181.

———. *The Shi'is of Iraq.* Princeton: Princeton University Press, 2003.

Nasr, Seyyed Vali Reza. *The Vanguard of the Islamic Revolution: The Jama'at-i Islami of Pakistan.* Berkeley: University of California Press, 1994.

———. *The Shia Revival: How Conflicts within Islam Will Shape the Future.* New York and London: W.W. Norton, 2006.

National Intelligence Estimate. "Iran: Nuclear Intentions and Capabilities", November 2007.

Newman, Andrew J. "The Myth of the Clerical Migration to Safawid Iran: Arab Shiite Opposition to 'Ali Al-Karaki and Safawid Shiism." *Die Welt des Islams* 33 (1993): pp. 66–112.

———. *The Formative Period of Twelver Shi'ism.* Richmond: Curzon Press, 2000.

Nissman, David B. *The Soviet Union and Iranian Azerbaijan: The Use of Nationalism for Political Penetration.* Boulder: Westview Press, 1987.

Norton, Augustus. *Hezbollah: A Short History.* Princeton: Princeton University Press, 2007.

———. "The Role of Hezbollah in Domestic Politics." *The International Spectator* 42, no. 4 (December 2007): pp. 475–491.

O'Ballance, Edgar. *The Gulf War.* London: Brassey's, 1988.

Ostovar, Afshon. "Iran's Basij: Membership in a Militant Islamist Organization." *The Middle East Journal,* 67, no. 3 (Summer 2013): 345–361.

———. "Worst. Plot. Ever." *Foreign Policy,* October 13, 2011. http://www.foreignpolicy.com/articles/2011/10/13/worst_plot_ever.

Ostovar, Afshon, et al. *On Shifting Sands: Iranian Strategy in a Changing Middle East.* Alexandria, VA. CNA, October 2013.

Ostovar, Afshon, and Will McCants. *The Rebel Alliance: Why Syria's Armed Opposition Has Failed to Unify.* Alexandria, VA: CNA, March 2013.

Parsi, Trita. *Treacherous Alliance: The Secret Dealings of Israel, Iran, and the U.S.* New Haven and London: Yale University Press, 2007.

Pelly, Col. Sir Lewis, ed. *The Miracle Play of Hasan and Husain: Collected from Oral Tradition by Col. Sir Lewis Pelly,* vol. 1. London: W. H. Allen and Co., 1879.

Perlmutter, Amos. *Politics and Military Rulers.* New York: Routledge, 2013.

Peterson, Scott. *Let the Swords Encircle Me: Iran—A Journey behind the Headlines.* New York: Simon & Schuster, 2010.

Pinault, David. *The Shiites: Ritual and Popular Piety in a Muslim Community.* New York: St. Martin's Press, 1992.

Piscatori, James. *Islamic Fundamentalisms and the Gulf Crisis.* Chicago: The American Academy of Arts and Sciences, 1991.

Potter, Lawrence G., and Gary G. Sick, eds. *Iran, Iraq, and the Legacies of War.* New York: Palgrave, 2004.

Quinn, Sholeh. *Historical Writing during the Reign of Shah Abbas: Ideology, Imitation, and Legitimacy in Safavid Chronicles.* Salt Lake City: University of Utah Press, 2000.

Rahnema, Saeed, and Sohrab Behdad, eds. *Iran after the Revolution: Crisis of an Islamic State.* London and New York: I. B. Tauris, 1995.

Rahnema, Ali. *An Islamic Utopian : A Political Biography of Ali Shariati.* London: I. B. Tauris, 2000.

Rajaee, Farhang. *Islamism and Modernism: The Changing Discourse in Iran.* Austin: University of Texas Press, 2007.

Ram, Haggay. *Myth and Mobilization in Revolutionary Iran.* Washington, DC: The American University Press, 1994.

Ranstorp, Magnus. *Hizb'allah in Lebanon: The Politics of the Western Hostage Crisis.* London: MacMillan Press, 1997.

Rashid, Ahmed. *Taliban: Militant Islam, Oil & Fundamentalism in Central Asia.* New Haven & London: Yale Nota Bene, 2001.

Raviv, Dan, and Yossi Melman. *Spies against Armageddon: Inside Israel's Secret Wars.* Sea Cliff, NY: Levant Books, 2012.

Remmer, Karen. *Military Rule in Latin America.* Boston: Unwin Hyman, 1989.

Rezun, Miron. *Soviet Policy in Iran from the Beginnings of the Pahlavi Dynasty until the Soviet Invasion in 1941.* Alphen aan den Rijn: Sijthoff & Noordhoff International, 1981.

Ritter, Scott. *Target Iran: The Truth about the White House's Plans for Regime Change.* New York: Nation Books, 2006.

Roemer, H.R. "Jalayirids, Muzaffarids, and Sarbadars." In *The Cambridge History of Iran,* vol. 6. Cambridge: University of Cambridge Press, 1986, pp. 1–97.

Rouquie, Alain. *The Military and the State in Latin America.* Translated by Paul E. Sigmund. Berkeley: University of California Press, 1987.

Roy, Olivier. *Globalized Islam: The Search for a New Ummah.* New York: Columbia University Press, 2004.

Rubin, Barnett, ed. *Armed Forces in the Middle East Politics and Strategy.* London: Routledge, 2002.

Saad-Ghorayeb, Amal. *Hizbu'Llah : Politics and Religion.* London: Pluto Press, 2002.

Sachedina, Abdulaziz A. *Islamic Messianism: The Idea of the Mahdi in Twelver Shi'ism.* Albany: State University of New York Press, 1981.

Sachedina, Abdulaziz. "The Rule of the Religious Jurist in Iran." In *Iran at the Crossroads,* edited by John Esposito and R. K. Ramazani, pp. 123–148. New York: Palgrave, 2001.

Sadjadpour, Karim. *Reading Khamenei: The World View of Iran's Most Powerful Leader.* Washington, DC: Carnegie Endowment for International Peace, 2009.

Safshekan, Roozbeh, and Farzan Sabet. "The Ayatollah's Praetorians: The Islamic Revolutionary Guard Corps and the 2009 Election Crisis." *The Middle East Journal* 64, no. 4 (2010).

Sanger, David. *The Inheritance: The World Obama Confronts and the Challenges to American Power.* New York: Harmony Books, 2009.

Schahgaldian, Nikola B., and Gina Barkhordarian. *The Iranian Military under the Islamic Republic.* Santa Monica, CA: RAND, 1987.

Schnapp, Jeffrey T. *Revolutionary Tides: The Art of the Political Poster 1914–1989.* Milan: Skira, 2005.

Shaery-Eisenlohr, Roschanack. *Shi'ite Lebanon: Transnational Religion and the Making of National Identities.* New York: Columbia University Press, 2008.

Shaffer, Brenda, ed. *The Limits of Culture: Islam and Foreign Policy.* Cambridge: The MIT Press, 2006.

Shariati, Ali. *Red Shi'ism.* Translated by Habib Shirazi. Houston: Free Islamic Literatures, 1980.

Shemirani, S. Taheri. "The War of the Cities." In *The Iran-Iraq War: The Politics of Aggression.* Edited by Farhang Rajaee. Gainesville: University Press of Florida, 1993.

Sick, Gary. "Iran's Quest for Super Power Status." *Foreign Affairs,* Spring 1987.

———. *October Surprise: America's Hostages in Iran and the Election of Ronald Reagan.* New York: Times Books, 1991.

Sicker, Martin. *The Bear and the Lion: Soviet Imperialism and Iran.* New York: Praeger, 1988.

Sidahmen, Abdel Salam, and Anoushiravan Ehteshami, eds. *Islamic Fundamentalism.* Boulder: Westview Press, 1996.

Sivan, Immanuel. "Sunni Radicalism in the Middle East and the Iranian Revolution." *International Journal of Middle East Studies* 21 (1989): pp. 1–30.

———. *Radical Islam: Medieval Theology and Modern Politics.* New Haven: Yale University Press, 1990.

Smith, John Masson Jr. *The History of the Sarbadar Dynasty: 1336–1381 A.D. and Its Sources.* Paris: Mouton, 1970.

Smyth, Phillip. "Iran's Afghan Shiite Fighters in Syria." *The Washington Institute for Near East Policy,* June 3, 2014.

Sobhani, Ayatollah Jafar. *Doctrines of Shi'i Islam: A Compendium of Imami Beliefs and Practices.* Translated by Reza Shah Kazemi. London: I. B. Tauris, 2001.

Sontag, Susan. *On Photography.* New York: Picador USA; Farrar, Straus and Giroux, 2001.

Sreberny-Mohammadi, Annabelle, and Ali Mohammadi. *Small Media, Big Revolution: Communication, Culture, and the Iranian Revolution.* Minneapolis: University of Minnesota Press, 1994.

Stewart, Devin J. *Islamic Legal Orthodoxy : Twelver Shiite Responses to the Sunni Legal System.* Salt Lake City: University of Utah Press, 1998.

Sullivan, Denis J., and Sana Abed-Kotob. *Islam in Contemporary Egypt: Civil Society vs. the State.* Boulder: Lynne Rienner Publishers, 1999.

Takeyh, Ray. *Guardians of the Revolution: Iran and the World in the Age of the Ayatollahs.* New York: Oxford University Press, 2009.

———. *Hidden Iran: Paradox and Power in the Islamic Republic.* New York: Times Books, 2006.

Tarock, Adam. "The Muzzling of the Liberal Press in Iran." *Third World Quarterly* 22, no. 4 (August 2001): pp. 585–602.

Thurfjell, David. *Living Shi'ism: Instances of Ritualisation among Islamist Men in Contemporary Iran.* Leiden and Boston: Brill, 2006.

Tibi, Bassam. *Conflict and War in the Middle East.* New York: St. Martin's Press, 1993.

———. *The Challenge of Fundamentalism : Political Islam and the New World Disorder.* Berkeley: University of California Press, 1998.

Tilly, Charles. "War Making and State Making as Organized Crime." In *Bringing the State Back In,* edited by Peter B. Evans et al., pp. 169–191. Cambridge: Cambridge University Press, 1985.

———. *Coercion, Capital, and European States, AD 990–1990.* Cambridge, MA: Blackwell, 1990.

Timmers, Margaret. *The Power of the Poster.* London: V&A Publications, 1998.

US Senate Select Committee on Intelligence. "Prewar Intelligence Assessments About Postwar Iraq Together with Additional Views," May 25, 2007.

Vagts, Alfred. *A History of Militarism.* New York: Free Press, 1973.

Vatanka, Alex. "Ali Shamkhani: Rouhani's Bridge-Builder to the Arab World." *The National Interest,* October 20, 2014, http://nationalinterest.org/feature/ali-shamkhani-rouhani%E2%80%99s-bridge-builder-the-arab-world-11500.

Vazeri, Haleh. "Iran's Involvement in Lebanon: Polarization and Radicalization of Militant Islamic Movements." *Journal of South Asian and Middle Eastern Studies* 16, no. 2 (Winter 1992): 1–16.

Walbridge, Linda S., ed. *The Most Learned of the Shi'a: The Institution of the Marja' Taqlid.* Oxford: Oxford University Press, 2001.

Ward, Steven M. *Immortal: A Military History of Iran and Its Armed Forces.* Washington, DC: Georgetown University Press, 2009.

Wege, Carl Anthony. "Iranian Intelligence Organizations." *International Journal of Intelligence and Counterintelligence* 10, no. 3 (1997): pp. 287–298.

Wehrey, Frederic, et al. *Dangerous but Not Omnipotent: Exploring the Reach and Limitations of Iranian Power in the Middle East.* Santa Monica: RAND, 2009.

———. *Rise of the Pasdaran: Assessing the Domestic Roles of Iran's Islamic Revolutionary Guards Corps.* Santa Monica: RAND, 2009.

———. *Sectarian Politics in the Gulf: From the Iraq War to the Arab Uprisings.* New York: Columbia University Press, 2013.

———. "The Unforgotten Uprising in Eastern Saudi Arabia." Washington, DC: Carnegie Endowment for International Peace, June 2013.

Wells, Matthew C. "Thermidor in the Islamic Republic of Iran: The Rise of Muhammad Khatami." *British Journal of Middle Eastern Studies* 26, no. 1 (May 1999): 27–39.

Wiktorowicz, Quintan. *The Management of Islamic Activism: Salafis, the Muslim Brotherhood, and State Power in Jordan.* Albany: SUNY, 2001.

Woods, Kevin M., et al. *Saddam's Generals: Perspectives of the Iran-Iraq War.* Alexandria, VA: Institute for Defense Analyses, 2011.

Zabih, Sepehr. *The Iranian Military in Revolution and War.* London and New York: Routledge, 1988.

Zatarain, Lee Allen. *Tanker War: America's First Conflict with Iran, 1987–1988.* Philadelphia and Newbury, England: Casemate, 2008.

# INDEX

CPSIA information can be obtained
at www.ICGtesting.com
Printed in the USA
BVHW03s2032230218
508836BV00003B/15/P